Śrīmad-Bhāgavatam

Fourth Canto
"The Creation of the Fourth Order"

(Part Three—Chapters 20-24)

With the Original Sanskrit Text,
Its Roman Transliteration, Synonyms,
Translation and Elaborate Purports by

His Divine Grace
A.C. Bhaktivedanta Swami Prabhupāda
Founder-Ācārya of the International Society for Krishna Consciousness

THE BHAKTIVEDANTA BOOK TRUST
New York · Los Angeles · London · Bombay

Readers interested in the subject matter of this book
are invited by the International Society for Krishna Consciousness
to correspond with its Secretary.

International Society for Krishna Consciousness
3959 Landmark Street
Culver City, California 90230

Library of Congress Catalogue Card Number: 75-189067
International Standard Book Number: 0-912776-48-X

Printed by Dai Nippon Printing Co., Ltd., Tokyo, Japan

TABLE OF CONTENTS

CHAPTER TWENTY

Lord Viṣṇu's Appearance in the Sacrificial Arena of Mahārāja Pṛthu

TEXT 1

मैत्रेय उवाच
भगवानपि वैकुण्ठः साकं मघवता विभुः ।
यज्ञैर्यज्ञपतिस्तुष्टो यज्ञभुक् तमभाषत ॥ १ ॥

maitreya uvāca
bhagavān api vaikuṇṭhaḥ
sākaṁ maghavatā vibhuḥ
yajñair yajña-patis tuṣṭo
yajña-bhuk tam abhāṣata

maitreyaḥ uvāca—the great sage Maitreya continued to speak; *bhagavān*—the Supreme Personality of Godhead, Viṣṇu; *api*—also; *vaikuṇṭhaḥ*—the Lord of Vaikuṇṭha; *sākam*—along with; *maghavatā*—King Indra; *vibhuḥ*—the Lord; *yajñaiḥ*—by the sacrifices; *yajña-patiḥ*—the Lord of all *yajñas; tuṣṭaḥ*—satisfied; *yajña-bhuk*—the enjoyer of the *yajña; tam*—unto King Pṛthu; *abhāṣata*—said.

TRANSLATION

The great sage Maitreya continued: My dear Vidura, being very much satisfied by the performance of ninety-nine horse sacrifices, the Supreme Personality of Godhead, Lord Viṣṇu, appeared on the scene. Accompanying Him was King Indra. Lord Viṣṇu then began to speak.

TEXT 2

श्रीभगवानुवाच
एष तेऽकार्षीद्भङ्गं हयमेधशतस्य ह ।
क्षमापयत आत्मानममुष्य क्षन्तुमर्हसि ॥ २ ॥

śrī bhagavān uvāca
eṣa te 'kārṣīd bhaṅgaṁ
haya-medha-śatasya ha
kṣamāpayata ātmānam
amuṣya kṣantum arhasi

śrī bhagavān uvāca—the Supreme Personality of Godhead, Lord Viṣṇu, spoke; *eṣaḥ*—this Lord Indra; *te*—your; *akārṣīt*—performed; *bhaṅgam*—disturbance; *haya*—horse; *medha*—sacrifice; *śatasya*—of the one-hundredth; *ha*—indeed; *kṣamāpayataḥ*—who is asking pardon; *ātmānam*—unto yourself; *amuṣya*—him; *kṣantum*—to forgive; *arhasi*—you ought.

TRANSLATION

Lord Viṣṇu, the Supreme Personality of Godhead, said: My dear King Pṛthu, Indra, the King of heaven, has disturbed your execution of one hundred sacrifices. Now he has come with Me to be forgiven by you. Therefore excuse him.

PURPORT

In this verse the word *ātmānam* is very significant. It is a custom among *yogīs* and *jñānīs* to address one another (even an ordinary man) as one's self, for a transcendentalist never accepts a living being to be the body. Since the individual self is part and parcel of the Supreme Personality of Godhead, the self and the Superself are qualitatively nondifferent. As the next verse will explain, the body is only a superficial covering, and consequently an advanced transcendentalist will not make a distinction between one self and another.

TEXT 3

सुधियः साधवो लोके नरदेव नरोत्तमाः ।
नाभिद्रुह्यन्ति भूतेभ्यो यर्हि नात्मा कलेवरम् ॥ ३ ॥

sudhiyaḥ sādhavo loke
naradeva narottamāḥ
nābhidruhyanti bhūtebhyo
yarhi nātmā kalevaram

su-dhiyaḥ—the most intelligent persons; *sādhavaḥ*—who are inclined to perform welfare activities; *loke*—in this world; *nara-deva*—O King; *nara-uttamāḥ*—the best of human beings; *na abhidruhyanti*—never become malicious; *bhūtebhyaḥ*—toward other living beings; *yarhi*—because; *na*—never; *ātmā*—the self or soul; *kalevaram*—this body.

TRANSLATION

O King, one who is advanced in intelligence and eager to perform welfare activities for others is considered best amongst human beings. An advanced human being is never malicious to others. Those with advanced intelligence are always conscious that this material body is different from the soul.

PURPORT

In daily life we find that when a madman commits murder, he is excused even by a high-court judge. The idea is that a living entity is always pure because he is part and parcel of the Supreme Personality of Godhead. When he falls into the clutches of material energy, he becomes a victim of the three modes of material nature. Indeed, whatever he does, he does under the influence of material nature. As stated in *Bhagavad-gītā:*

na kartṛtvaṁ na karmāṇi
lokasya sṛjati prabhuḥ
na karma-phala-saṁyogaṁ
svabhāvas tu pravartate

"The embodied spirit, master of the city of his body, does not create activities, nor does he induce people to act, nor does he create the fruits of action. All this is enacted by the modes of material nature." (Bg. 5.14)

Actually the living entity or soul does not do anything; everything is done under the influence of the modes of material nature. When a man is diseased, the symptoms of the disease become a source of all kinds of pain. Those who are advanced in transcendental consciousness or Kṛṣṇa consciousness are never envious, neither of the soul nor of the activities of the soul under the influence of material nature. Advanced transcendentalists are called *sudhiyaḥ*. *Sudhī* means intelligence, *sudhī* means highly advanced, and *sudhī* means devotee. One who is both devoted and highly advanced in intelligence does not take action against the soul or the body. If there is any discrepancy, he forgives. It is said that forgiveness is a quality of those who are advancing in spiritual knowledge.

TEXT 4

पुरुषा यदि मुह्यन्ति त्वादृशा देवमायया ।
श्रम एव परं जातो दीर्घया वृद्धसेवया ॥ ४ ॥

puruṣā yadi muhyanti
tvādṛśā deva-māyayā
śrama eva paraṁ jāto
dīrghayā vṛddha-sevayā

puruṣāḥ—persons; *yadi*—if; *muhyanti*—become bewildered; *tvā-dṛśāḥ*—like you; *deva*—of the Supreme Lord; *māyayā*—by the energy; *śramaḥ*—exertion; *eva*—certainly; *param*—only; *jātaḥ*—produced; *dīrghayā*—for a long time; *vṛddha-sevayā*—by serving the superiors.

TRANSLATION

If a personality like you, who are so much advanced because of executing the instructions of the previous ācāryas, is carried away by the influence of My material energy, then all your advancement may be considered simply a waste of time.

PURPORT

In this verse the word *vṛddha-sevayā* is very significant. *Vṛddha* means "old." *Sevayā* means "by service." Perfect knowledge is acquired from the *ācāryas* or liberated souls. No one can be perfect in knowledge without being trained by the *paramparā* system. Pṛthu Mahārāja was completely trained in that line; therefore he did not deserve to be considered an ordinary man. An ordinary man, who has only a conception of bodily existence, is always bewildered by the modes of material nature.

TEXT 5

अतः कायमिमं विद्वानविद्याकामकर्मभिः ।
आरब्ध इति नैवास्मिन् प्रतिबुद्धोऽनुषज्जते ॥ ५ ॥

ataḥ kāyam imaṁ vidvān
avidyā-kāma-karmabhiḥ
ārabdha iti naivāsmin
pratibuddho 'nuṣajjate

ataḥ—therefore; *kāyam*—body; *imam*—this; *vidvān*—he who has knowledge; *avidyā*—by nescience; *kāma*—desires; *karmabhiḥ*—and by activities; *ārabdhaḥ*—created; *iti*—thus; *na*—never; *eva*—certainly; *asmin*—to this body; *pratibuddhaḥ*—one who knows; *anuṣajjate*—becomes addicted.

TRANSLATION

Those who are in full knowledge of the bodily conception of life, who know that this body is composed of nescience, desires and activities resulting from illusion, do not become addicted to the body.

PURPORT

As stated in a previous verse, those with good intellect (*sudhiyaḥ*) do not accept themselves to be the body. Being a creation of nescience, the body has two types of activities. In the bodily conception, when we think that sense gratification will help us, we are in illusion. Another kind of illusion is to think that one will become happy by trying to satisfy the desires that arise from the illusory body, or by attaining elevation to the higher planetary systems, or by performing various types of Vedic rituals. This is all illusion. Similarly, material activities performed for political emancipation and social and humanitarian activities performed with an idea that people of the world will be happy are also illusory because the basic principle is the bodily conception, which is illusory. Whatever we desire or perform under the bodily conception is all illusion. In other words, Lord Viṣṇu informed Pṛthu Mahārāja that although the sacrificial performances set an example for ordinary people, there was no need for such sacrificial performances as far as his personal self was concerned. As confirmed in *Bhagavad-gītā:*

traiguṇya-viṣayā vedā
nistraiguṇyo bhavārjuna
nirdvandvo nitya-sattva-stho
niryoga-kṣema ātmavān

"The *Vedas* mainly deal with the subject of the three modes of material nature. Rise above these modes, O Arjuna. Be transcendental to all of them. Be free from all dualities and from all anxieties for gain and safety, and be established in the self." (Bg. 2.45)

The ritualistic performances recommended in the *Vedas* mainly depend on the three modes of material nature. Consequently Arjuna was advised to transcend the Vedic activities. The activities Arjuna was advised to perform were the transcendental activities of devotional service.

TEXT 6

असंसक्तः शरीरेऽस्मिन्नमुनोत्पादिते गृहे ।
अपत्ये द्रविणे वापि कः कुर्यान्ममतां बुधः ॥ ६ ॥

asaṁsaktaḥ śarīre 'sminn
amunotpādite gṛhe
apatye draviṇe vāpi
kaḥ kuryān mamatāṁ budhaḥ

asaṁsaktaḥ—being unattached; *śarīre*—to the body; *asmin*—this; *amunā*—by such a bodily conception; *utpādite*—produced; *gṛhe*—house; *apatye*—children; *draviṇe*—wealth; *vā*—or; *api*—also; *kaḥ*—who; *kuryāt*—would do; *mamatām*—affinity; *budhaḥ*—learned person.

TRANSLATION

How can a highly learned person who has absolutely no affinity for the bodily conception of life be affected by the bodily conception in regard to house, children, wealth and similar other bodily productions?

PURPORT

The Vedic ritualistic ceremonies are certainly meant to please the Supreme Personality of Godhead, Lord Viṣṇu. However, by such activities one does not factually satisfy the Lord. Rather, with the sanction of the Lord, one tries to satisfy his own senses. In other words, materialists who are especially interested in sense gratification are given permission or license to enjoy sense gratification by executing the Vedic ritualistic ceremonies. That is called *traiguṇya-viṣayā vedāḥ*. The Vedic performances are based on the three modes of material nature. Those who are elevated above the material condition are not at all interested in such Vedic performances. Rather, they are interested in the higher duties of transcendental loving service to the Supreme Personality of Godhead. Such devotional service is called *nistraiguṇya*. Devotional service to the Lord has nothing to do with the material conception of bodily comfort.

TEXT 7

एकः शुद्धः स्वयंज्योतिर्निर्गुणोऽसौ गुणाश्रयः ।
सर्वगोऽनावृतः साक्षी निरात्माऽऽत्माऽऽत्मनः परः ७

ekaḥ śuddhaḥ svayaṁ-jyotir
nirguṇo 'sau guṇāśrayaḥ
sarva-go 'nāvṛtaḥ sākṣī
nirātmātmātmanaḥ paraḥ

ekaḥ—one; *śuddhaḥ*—pure; *svayam*—self; *jyotiḥ*—effulgent; *nirguṇaḥ*—without material qualifications; *asau*—that; *guṇa-āśrayaḥ*—the reservoir of good qualities; *sarva-gaḥ*—able to go everywhere; *anāvṛtaḥ*—without being covered by matter; *sākṣī*—witness; *nirātmā*—without another self; *ātma-ātmanaḥ*—to the body and mind; *paraḥ*—transcendental.

TRANSLATION

The individual soul is one, pure, nonmaterial and self-effulgent. He is the reservoir of all good qualities, and He is all-pervading. He is without material covering, and He is the witness of all activities. He is completely distinguished from other living entities, and He is transcendental to all embodied souls.

PURPORT

In the previous verse two significant words are used: *asaṁsaktaḥ,* meaning "without attachment," and *budhaḥ,* meaning "fully cognizant of everything." By full cognizance it is meant that one should know about his own constitutional position as well as the position of the Supreme Personality of Godhead. According to Śrī Viśvanātha Cakravartī Ṭhākura, in this verse Lord Viṣṇu is describing Himself or the Paramātmā. The Paramātmā is always distinguished from the embodied soul as well as the material world. Therefore He has been described as *para.* That *para,* or Supreme Personality of Godhead, is *eka,* meaning one. The Lord is one, whereas the conditioned souls embodied within the material world exist in many varieties of form. There are demigods, human beings, animals, trees, birds, bees, and so forth. Thus the living entities are not *eka* but many. As confirmed in the *Vedas: nityo nityānāṁ cetanaś cetanānām.* The living entities, who are many and who are entangled in this material world, are not pure. However, the Supreme Personality of Godhead is pure and detached. Due to being covered by the material body, the living entities are not self-effulgent, but the Supreme Personality of Godhead, Paramātmā, is self-effulgent. The living entities, being contaminated by the modes of material nature, are called *saguṇa,* whereas Paramātmā, the Supreme Personality of Godhead, is *nirguṇa,* not being under the influence of the material modes. The living entities, being encaged in material qualities, are *guṇāśrita,* whereas the Supreme Personality of Godhead is *guṇāśraya.* The conditioned soul's vision is covered by material contamination; therefore he cannot see the cause of his resultant action and he cannot see his past lives. The Supreme Personality of Godhead, not being covered by a material body, is the witness of all the activities of the living entity. But both of them, the living entity and the Paramātmā, the Supreme Personality of Godhead, are *ātmā*, or spirit. They are one in quality, yet they are different in so many ways, especially in regard to the six opulences the Supreme Personality of Godhead has in full. Full knowledge means that the *jīva-ātmā*, the living entity, must know both his position and the Supreme's position. That is full knowledge.

TEXT 8

य एवं सन्तमात्मानमात्मस्थं वेद पूरुषः ।
नाज्यते प्रकृतिस्थोऽपि तद्गुणैः स मयि स्थितः ॥८॥

ya evaṁ santam ātmānam
ātma-sthaṁ veda pūruṣaḥ
nājyate prakṛti-stho 'pi
tad-guṇaiḥ sa mayi sthitaḥ

yaḥ—anyone who; *evam*—thus; *santam*—existing; *ātmānam*—the individual *ātmā* and the Supreme Personality of Godhead, Paramātmā; *ātma-stham*—situated within his body; *veda*—knows; *pūruṣaḥ*—person; *na*—never; *ajyate*—is affected; *prakṛti*—in material nature; *sthaḥ*—situated; *api*—although; *tat-guṇaiḥ*—by the material modes of nature; *saḥ*—such a person; *mayi*—in Me; *sthitaḥ*—situated.

TRANSLATION

Although within the material nature, one who is thus situated in full knowledge of the Paramātmā and ātmā is never affected by the modes of material nature, for he is always situated in My transcendental loving service.

PURPORT

When the Supreme Personality of Godhead appears in this material world, He is not affected by the modes of material nature. Similarly, those who are always connected with the Supreme Personality of Godhead, even though they be within the material body or the material world, are not affected by the material qualities. That is explained very nicely in *Bhagavad-gītā:*

māṁ ca yo 'vyabhicāreṇa
bhakti-yogena sevate
sa guṇān samatītyaitān
brahma-bhūyāya kalpate

"One who engages in full devotional service, who does not fall down in any circumstance, at once transcends the modes of material nature and thus comes to the level of Brahman." (Bg. 14.26)

Thus one who is unflinchingly engaged in the devotional service of the Lord surpasses the material qualities and attains Brahman realization. In this connection Śrīla Rūpa Gosvāmī says that if a person is always engaged in the service of the Lord with his body, words and mind, he is to be considered liberated, although living in the material world.

TEXT 9

यः स्वधर्मेण मां नित्यं निराशीः श्रद्धयान्वितः ।
भजते शनकैस्तस्य मनो राजन् प्रसीदति ॥ ९ ॥

yaḥ sva-dharmeṇa māṁ nityaṁ
nirāśīḥ śraddhayānvitaḥ
bhajate śanakais tasya
mano rājan prasīdati

yaḥ—anyone who; *sva-dharmeṇa*—by his occupational duties; *mām*—Me; *nityam*—regularly; *nirāśīḥ*—without any motive; *śraddhayā*—with faith and devotion; *anvitaḥ*—endowed; *bhajate*—worships; *śanakaiḥ*—gradually; *tasya*—his; *manaḥ*—mind; *rājan*—O King Pṛthu; *prasīdati*—becomes fully satisfied.

TRANSLATION

The Supreme Personality of Godhead, Lord Viṣṇu, continued: My dear King Pṛthu, when one situated in his occupational duty engages in My loving service without motive for material gain, he gradually becomes very satisfied within.

PURPORT

This verse is also confirmed by the *Viṣṇu Purāṇa.* Occupational duties are known as *varṇāśrama-dharma* and apply to the four divisions of material and spiritual life—namely, *brāhmaṇa, kṣatriya, vaiśya* and *śūdra,* and *brahmacarya, gṛhastha, vānaprastha* and *sannyāsa.* If one works according to the *varṇāśrama-dharma* system and does not desire fruitive results, he gets satisfaction gradually. Discharging one's occupational duty as a means of rendering devotional service unto the Supreme Personality of Godhead is the ultimate goal of life. *Bhagavad-gītā* confirms this as the process of *karma-yoga.* In other words, we should act only for the satisfaction and service of the Lord. Otherwise we will be entangled by the resultant actions.

Everyone is situated in his occupational duty, but the purpose of material occupations should not be for material gain. Rather, everyone should offer the results of his occupational activities. A *brāhmaṇa* especially should execute his occupational duties not for material gain but to please the Supreme Personality of Godhead. The *kṣatriya, vaiśya* and *śūdra* should work in a similar way. In this material world everyone is engaged in various professional and occupational duties, but the purpose of such activities should be to please the Supreme Personality of Godhead. Devotional service is very simple, and anyone can adopt it. Let one remain what he is; he need only install the Deity of the Supreme Lord in his house. The Deity may be Rādhā-Kṛṣṇa or Lakṣmī-Nārāyaṇa (there are many other forms of the Lord). In this way a *brāhmaṇa, kṣatriya, vaiśya* or *śūdra* can worship the Deity with the results of his honest labor. Regardless of one's occupational duty, one should adopt the devotional means of hearing, chanting, remembering, worshiping, offering everything to the Lord, and engaging in His service. In this way one can very easily engage himself in the service of the Lord. When the Lord is pleased with one's service, one's mission in life is fulfilled.

TEXT 10

परित्यक्तगुणः सम्यग्दर्शनो विशदाशयः ।
शान्तिं मे समवस्थानं ब्रह्म कैवल्यमश्नुते ॥१०॥

parityakta-guṇaḥ samyag
darśano viśadāśayaḥ
śāntiṁ me samavasthānaṁ
brahma kaivalyam aśnute

parityakta-guṇaḥ—one who is disassociated from the material modes of nature; *samyak*—equal; *darśanaḥ*—whose vision; *viśada*—uncontaminated; *āśayaḥ*—whose mind or heart; *śāntim*—peace; *me*—My; *samavasthānam*—equal situation; *brahma*—spirit; *kaivalyam*—freedom from material contamination; *aśnute*—achieves.

TRANSLATION

When the heart is cleansed of all material contamination, the devotee's mind becomes broader and transparent, and he can see things equally. At that stage of life there is peace, and one is situated equally with Me as sac-cid-ānanda-vigraha.

PURPORT

The Māyāvāda conception of *kaivalya* and that of the Vaiṣṇava community is different. The Māyāvādī thinks that as soon as one is free from all material contamination, he is merged into the existence of the Supreme. The Vaiṣṇava philosopher's conception of *kaivalya* is different. He understands both his position and the position of the Supreme Personality of Godhead. In the uncontaminated condition, the living entity understands that he is the eternal servitor of the Supreme, and that is called Brahman realization, the spiritual perfection of the living entity. This rapport is very easily achieved. As stated in *Bhagavad-gītā,* when one is engaged in the transcendental loving service of the Lord, he is immediately situated on the transcendental platform of *kaivalya* or Brahman.

TEXT 11

उदासीनमिवाध्यक्षं द्रव्यज्ञानक्रियात्मनाम् ।
कूटस्थमिममात्मानं यो वेदाप्नोति शोभनम् ॥११॥

udāsīnam ivādhyakṣaṁ
dravya-jñāna-kriyātmanām
kūṭastham imam ātmānaṁ
yo vedāpnoti śobhanam

udāsīnam—indifferent; *iva*—simply; *adhyakṣam*—the superintendent; *dravya*—of the physical elements; *jñāna*—knowledge-acquiring senses; *kriyā*—working senses; *ātmanām*—and of the mind; *kūṭa-stham*—fixed; *imam*—this; *ātmānam*—soul; *yaḥ*—anyone who; *veda*—knows; *āpnoti*—gets; *śobhanam*—all good fortune.

TRANSLATION

Anyone who knows that this material body made of the five gross elements, the sense organs, the working senses and the mind is simply supervised by the fixed soul is eligible to be liberated from material bondage.

PURPORT

This verse describes how one can become liberated from material bondage. The first point is that one must know that the soul is different from his body. The soul is called *dehī,* or one who possesses the body, and the material body is called *deha,* or the embodiment of the soul. The body is changing at every moment, but the soul is fixed; therefore the soul is called *kūṭastham.* The change of body is enacted by the reactions of the three modes of nature. One who has understood the fixed position of the soul should not be disturbed by the incoming and outgoing interactions of the modes of material nature in the form of happiness and distress. In *Bhagavad-gītā* also Lord Kṛṣṇa recommends that since happiness and distress come and go due to the interaction of the modes of nature on the body, one should not be disturbed by such external movements. Even though one is sometimes absorbed in such external movements, he has to learn to tolerate them. The living entity should be always indifferent to the action and reaction of the external body.

Lord Kṛṣṇa says in *Bhagavad-gītā* that the body made of the gross physical elements (earth, water, fire, air and sky) and the subtle elements (mind, intelligence and ego) is completely different from the soul proper. One should therefore not be disturbed by the action and reaction of these eight gross and subtle material elements. The practical process to attain this stage of indifference is to execute devotional service. Only one who constantly engages in devotional service twenty-four hours a day can be indifferent to the action and reaction of the external body. When a man is absorbed in a particular thought, he does not hear or see any external activities, even though they are enacted in his presence. Similarly, those who are fully absorbed in devotional service do not care what is going on with the external body. That status is called *samādhi.* One who is actually situated in *samādhi* is understood to be a first-class *yogī.*

TEXT 12

भिन्नस्य लिङ्गस्य गुणप्रवाहो
द्रव्यक्रियाकारकचेतनात्मनः ।
दृष्टासु सम्पत्सु विपत्सु सूरयो
न विक्रियन्ते मयि बद्धसौहृदाः ॥१२॥

bhinnasya liṅgasya guṇa-pravāho
dravya-kriyā-kāraka-cetanātmanaḥ
dṛṣṭāsu sampatsu vipatsu sūrayo
na vikriyante mayi baddha-sauhṛdāḥ

bhinnasya—different; *liṅgasya*—of the body; *guṇa*—of the three modes of material nature; *pravāhaḥ*—the constant change; *dravya*—physical elements; *kriyā*—activities of the senses; *kāraka*—demigods; *cetanā*—and the mind; *ātmanaḥ*—consisting of; *dṛṣṭāsu*—when experienced; *sampatsu*—happiness; *vipatsu*—distress; *sūrayaḥ*—those who are advanced in knowledge; *na*—never; *vikriyante*—become disturbed; *mayi*—unto Me; *baddha-sauhṛdāḥ*—bound in friendship.

TRANSLATION

Lord Viṣṇu told King Pṛthu: My dear King, the constant change of this material world is due to the interaction of the three modes of material nature. The five elements, the senses, the demigods who control the senses, as well as the mind, which is agitated by spirit soul—all these taken together comprise the body. Since the spirit soul is completely different from this combination of gross and subtle material elements, My devotee who is connected with Me in intense friendship and affection, being completely in knowledge, is never agitated by material happiness and distress.

PURPORT

The question may be raised that if the living entity has to act as the superintendent of the activities of the bodily combination, then how can he be indifferent to the activities of the body? The answer is given here: these activities are completely different from the activities of the spirit soul of the living entity. A crude example can be given in this connection. A businessman riding in a motorcar sits in the car, supervises its running, and advises the driver. He knows how much gasoline is used up, and he knows everything about the car, but still he is apart from the car and is more concerned with his business. Even while riding in the car, he thinks of his business and his office. He has no connection with the car, although he is sitting there. As the businessman is always absorbed in thoughts of his business, so the living entity can be absorbed in thoughts of rendering loving service to the Lord. Then it will be possible to remain separate from the activities of the material body. This position of neutrality can only be possible for a devotee.

The word *baddha-sauhṛdāḥ*—"bound in friendship"—is particularly used here. *Karmīs*, *jñānīs* and *yogīs* cannot be bound in devotional service. *Karmīs* fully engage in the activities of the body. Their aim of life is to give comfort to the body only. *Jñānīs* try to get out of entanglement by philosophical speculation, but they have no standing in the liberated position. Because they do not take shelter under the lotus feet of the Lord, they fall down from the exalted position of Brahman realization. *Yogīs* also have a bodily concept of life—they think that they can achieve something spiritual by exercising the body through *dhāraṇā, āsana, prāṇāyāma,* etc. A devotee's position is always transcendental because of his intimate relationship with the Supreme Personality of Godhead. Therefore, to remain always aloof from the actions and reactions of the body and engage in one's real occupation, namely, rendering service to the Lord, can only be possible for devotees.

TEXT 13

समः समानोत्तममध्यमाधमः
सुखे च दुःखे च जितेन्द्रियाशयः ।
मयोपक्लृप्ताखिललोकसंयुतो
विधत्स्व वीराखिललोकरक्षणम् ॥१३॥

samaḥ samānottama-madhyamādhamaḥ
sukhe ca duḥkhe ca jitendriyāśayaḥ
mayopaklptākhila-loka-saṁyuto
vidhatsva vīrākhila-loka-rakṣaṇam

samaḥ—equipoised; *samāna*—all equal; *uttama*—one who is greater; *madhyama*—one who is in an intermediate position; *adhamaḥ*—one who is in a lower standard of life; *sukhe*—in happiness; *ca*—and; *duḥkhe*—in distress; *ca*—also; *jita-indriya*—having controlled the senses; *āśayaḥ*—and mind; *mayā*—by Me; *upakḷpta*—arranged; *akhila*—all; *loka*—by people; *saṁyutaḥ*—being accompanied; *vidhatsva*—give; *vīra*—O hero; *akhila*—all; *loka*—to the citizens; *rakṣaṇam*—protection.

TRANSLATION

My dear heroic King, please keep yourself always equipoised and treat people equally, whether they are greater than you, in the intermediate stage or lower than you. Do not be disturbed by temporary distress or happiness. Fully control your mind and senses. In this transcendental position, try to execute your duty as king in whatever condition of life

you may be posted by My arrangement, for your only duty here is to give protection to the citizens of your kingdom.

PURPORT

Here is an example of receiving direct instruction from the Supreme Personality of Godhead, Lord Viṣṇu. One has to execute the order of Lord Viṣṇu, whether receiving it directly from Him or from His bona fide representative, the spiritual master. Arjuna fought the Battle of Kurukṣetra under the direct order of the Supreme Personality of Godhead, Kṛṣṇa. Similarly, here Pṛthu Mahārāja is also being given orders by Lord Viṣṇu regarding the execution of his duty. We have to stick to the principles stated in the *Bhagavad-gītā. Vyavasāyātmikā buddhiḥ:* every man's duty is to receive orders from Lord Kṛṣṇa or from His bona fide representative and take these orders as his life and soul, without personal considerations. Śrīla Viśvanātha Cakravartī Ṭhākura states that one should not care very much whether he is going to be liberated or not, but he should simply execute the direct order received from the spiritual master. If one sticks to the principle of abiding by the order of the spiritual master, he will always remain in a liberated position. A common man must execute the rules and regulations of *varṇāśrama-dharma* by working in his prescribed duty according to the caste system *(brāhmaṇa, kṣatriya, vaiśya* and *śūdra)* and the spiritual order system *(brahmacarya, gṛhastha, vānaprastha* and *sannyāsa).* If one simply executes regularly and strictly the injunctions given for the different divisions of life, then one satisfies Lord Viṣṇu.

As a king, Pṛthu Mahārāja was ordered by Lord Viṣṇu to keep himself always aloof from the activities of the bodily situation and to engage always in the service of the Lord and thus keep himself in the liberated stage. The word *baddha-sauhṛdāḥ* in the previous verse is explained herewith. One can fully remain in intimate connection with the Supreme Lord directly or receive orders from His bona fide representative the spiritual master and execute the orders sincerely when one keeps aloof from the activities of the body. The Lord helps us by giving us directions how to act in devotional service and thus advance on the path back home, back to Godhead. He instructs us outwardly in the form of the spiritual master. Therefore, one should not accept the spiritual master as an ordinary human being. The Lord says, *ācāryaṁ māṁ vijānīyān nāvamanyeta karhicit:* one should not treat the spiritual master as an ordinary human being because he is the substitute for the Supreme Personality of Godhead. (*Bhāg.* 11.17.27) One should treat the spiritual master as the Supreme Personality of Godhead and never be envious of him or consider him to be an ordinary human being. If we follow the instruction of the spiritual master and execute devotional service to the Lord, we will remain always free from the contamination of bodily or material activities, and our life will be successful.

TEXT 14

श्रेयः प्रजापालनमेव राज्ञो
यत्साम्पराये सुकृतात् षष्ठमंशम् ।
हर्तान्यथा हृतपुण्यः प्रजाना-
मरक्षिता करहारोऽघमत्ति ॥१४॥

śreyaḥ prajā-pālanam eva rājño
yat sāmparāye sukṛtāt ṣaṣṭham aṁśam
hartānyathā hṛta-puṇyaḥ prajānām
arakṣitā karahāro 'gham atti

śreyaḥ—auspicious; *prajā-pālanam*—ruling over the general mass of people; *eva*—certainly; *rājñaḥ*—for the king; *yat*—because; *sāmparāye*—in the next birth; *su-kṛtāt*—from the pious activities; *ṣaṣṭham aṁśam*—one-sixth part; *hartā*—collector; *anyathā*—otherwise; *hṛta-puṇyaḥ*—being bereft of the results of pious activities; *prajānām*—of the citizens; *arakṣitā*—one who does not protect; *kara-hāraḥ*—tax collector; *agham*—sin; *atti*—receives or suffers.

TRANSLATION

To give protection to the general mass of people who are citizens of the state is the prescribed occupational duty for a king. By acting in that way, the king in his next life shares one sixth of the result of the pious activities of the citizens. But a king or executive head of state who simply collects taxes from the citizens but does not give them proper protection as human beings has the results of his own pious activities taken away by the citizens, and in exchange for his not giving protection he becomes liable to punishment for the impious activities of his subjects.

PURPORT

The question may be raised here that if everyone engaged in spiritual activities to attain salvation and became indifferent to the activities of the material world, then how could things as they are go on? And if things are to go on as they ought to, how can a head of state be indifferent to such activities? In answer to this question the word *śreyaḥ*, "auspicious," is used here. The division of activities in society as arranged by the Supreme Personality of Godhead was not blindly or accidently created, as foolish people say. The *brāhmaṇa* must do his duty properly, and the *kṣatriya*, the *vaiśya* and even the *śūdra* must do the same. And every one of them can achieve the highest perfection of life–liberation from this material bondage. This is confirmed in *Bhagavad-gītā*. *Sve sve karmaṇy abhirataḥ saṁsiddhiṁ labhate naraḥ:* "By executing one's prescribed duties, one can attain the highest perfection." (Bg. 18.45)

Lord Viṣṇu advised Mahārāja Pṛthu that a king is not enjoined to give up his kingdom and the responsibility of protecting the *prajās* or citizens to instead go away to the Himalayas for liberation. He can attain liberation while executing his royal duties. The royal duty or the duty of the head of state is to see that the *prajās* or the general mass of people are doing their respective duties for spiritual salvation. A secular state does not necessitate a king or head of state who is indifferent to the activities of the *prajās*. In the modern state the government has many rules and regulations for conducting the duties of the *prajās*, but the government neglects to see that the citizens advance in spiritual knowledge. If the government is careless in this matter, the citizens will act whimsically, without any sense of God realization or spiritual life, and thus become entangled in sinful activities.

An executive head should not be callous to the welfare of the general mass of people while he simply goes on collecting taxes. The king's real duty is to see that the citizens gradually become fully Kṛṣṇa conscious. Kṛṣṇa conscious means completely free from all sinful activities. As soon as there is complete eradication of sinful activities in the state, then there will be no more war, pestilence, famine or natural disturbances. This was actually prevailing during the reign of Mahārāja Yudhiṣṭhira. If a king or head of the government is able to induce the citizens to become Kṛṣṇa conscious, then he is worthy to rule over the mass of people; otherwise, he has no right to levy taxes. If the king looks after the spiritual interests of the citizens, he can levy taxes without difficulties. In this way both the subjects and the king will be happy during this life, and in the next life the king will be able to share one sixth of the pious activities of the citizens. Otherwise, by levying taxes on the sinful citizens he will have to share the reactions of their sinful activities.

This same principle can be applied to parents and the spiritual masters as well. If parents simply give birth to children like cats and dogs but cannot save their children from imminent death, they become responsible for the activities of their animalistic children. Lately, such children are turning into hippies. Similarly, if a spiritual master cannot direct his disciples to become free of sinful activities, he becomes responsible for their sinful acts. These subtle laws of nature are unknown to the present leaders of society. Since the leaders of society have a poor fund of knowledge and the citizens in general are rogues and thieves, there cannot be an auspicious situation for human society. At the present moment the whole world is full of such an incompatible combination of state and citizens, and therefore there is constant tension, war and anxiety as an inevitable result of such social conditions.

TEXT 15

एवं द्विजाग्र्यानुमतानुवृत्त-
धर्मप्रधानोऽन्यतमोऽवितास्याः ।
ह्रस्वेन कालेन गृहोपयातान्
द्रष्टासि सिद्धाननुरक्तलोकः ॥१५॥

evaṁ dvijāgryānumatānuvṛtta-
dharma-pradhāno 'nyatamo 'vitāsyāḥ
hrasvena kālena gṛhopayātān
draṣṭāsi siddhān anurakta-lokaḥ

evam—thus; *dvija*—of the *brāhmaṇas; agrya*—by the foremost; *anumata*—approved; *anuvṛtta*—received by disciplic succession; *dharma*—religious principles; *pradhānaḥ*—he whose chief interest is; *anyatamaḥ*—unattached; *avitā*—the protector; *asyāḥ*—of the earth; *hrasvena*—short; *kālena*—in time; *gṛha*—to your home; *upayātān*—having come personally; *draṣṭāsi*—you will see; *siddhān*—perfected personalities; *anurakta-lokaḥ*—being loved by the citizens.

TRANSLATION

Lord Viṣṇu continued: My dear King Pṛthu, if you continue to protect the citizens according to the instructions of the learned brāhmaṇa authorities, as they are received by the disciplic succession—by hearing—from master to disciple, and if you follow the religious principles laid down by them, without attachment to ideas manufactured by mental concoction, then every one of your citizens will be happy and will love you, and very soon you will be able to see such already liberated personalities as the four Kumāras [Sanaka, Sanātana, Sananda and Sanat-kumāra].

PURPORT

Lord Viṣṇu advised King Pṛthu that everyone should follow the principles of *varṇāśrama-dharma;* then, in whatever capacity one remains within this material world, his salvation is guaranteed after death. In this age, however, since the system of *varṇāśrama-dharma* is topsy-turvy, it is very difficult to strictly follow all the principles. The only method for becoming perfect in life is to develop Kṛṣṇa consciousness. As *varṇāśrama-dharma* is executed from different positions by different men, so the Kṛṣṇa consciousness principles can be followed by everyone in every part of the world.

There is a specific purpose in mentioning herein that one should follow the *dvijāgryas,* the most prominent *brāhmaṇas* like Parāśara and Manu. These great sages have already given us instructions how to live according to the principles of *varṇāśrama-dharma.* Similarly, Sanātana Gosvāmī and Rūpa Gosvāmī have given us rules and regulations for becoming pure devotees of the Lord. It is essential, therefore, to follow the instructions of the *ācāryas* in the *paramparā* system who have received the knowledge as passed down from spiritual master to disciple. In this way, although living in our material condition of life, we can get out of the entanglement of material contamination without leaving our positions. Lord Caitanya Mahāprabhu advises, therefore, that one does not have to change his position. One simply has to hear from the perfect source (this is called *paramparā*) and follow the principles for practical application in life; thus one can attain the highest perfection of life, liberation, and go back home, back to Godhead. In other words, the change required is a change in consciousness, not in the body. Unfortunately, in this fallen age, people are concerned with the body, not with the soul. They have invented so many "isms" pertaining to the body only, not to the soul.

In the modern age of democracy there are so many government representatives voting for legislation. Every day they bring out a new law. But because these laws are only mental concoctions manufactured by inexperienced conditioned souls, they cannot give relief to human society. Formerly, although the kings were autocrats, they strictly followed the principles laid down by great sages and saintly persons. There were no mistakes in ruling over the country, and everything went perfectly. The citizens were completely pious, the king levied taxes legitimately, and therefore the situation was very happy. At the present moment the so-called executive heads are more or less selected from materially ambitious persons who simply look after their own personal interests; they have no knowledge of the *śāstras.* In other words, the executive heads are fools and rascals in the strict sense of the terms, and the people in general are *śūdras.* This combination of fools and rascals and *śūdras* cannot bring about peace and prosperity in this world. Therefore we find periodic upheavals in society in the forms of battles, communal riots and fratricidal quarrels. Under these circumstances, not only are the leaders unable to lead the people towards liberation, but they cannot even give them peace of mind. In *Bhagavad-gītā* it is stated that anyone who lives on concocted ideas, without reference to the *śāstras,* never becomes successful and does not attain happiness or liberation after death.

TEXT 16

वरं च मत् कञ्चन मानवेन्द्र
वृणीष्व तेऽहं गुणशीलयन्त्रितः ।
नाहं मखैर्वै सुलभस्तपोभि-
र्योगेन वा यत्समचित्तवर्ती ॥१६॥

varaṁ ca mat kañcana mānavendra
vṛṇīṣva te 'haṁ guṇa-śīla-yantritaḥ
nāhaṁ makhair vai sulabhas tapobhir
yogena vā yat sama-citta-vartī

varam—benediction; *ca*—also; *mat*—from Me; *kañcana*—whatever you like; *mānava-indra*—O chief of human beings; *vṛṇīṣva*—please request; *te*—your; *aham*—I; *guṇa-śīla*—by elevated qualities and excellent behavior; *yantritaḥ*—being captivated; *na*—not; *aham*—I; *makhaiḥ*—by sacrifices; *vai*—certainly; *su-labhaḥ*—easily obtained; *tapobhiḥ*—by austerities; *yogena*—by practice of mystic *yoga; vā*—or; *yat*—because of which; *sama-citta*—in one who is equipoised; *vartī*—being situated.

TRANSLATION

My dear King, I am very captivated by your elevated qualities and excellent behavior, and thus I am very favorably inclined towards you. You may therefore ask from Me any benediction you like. One who does not possess elevated qualities and behavior cannot possibly achieve My favor simply by performance of sacrifices, severe austerities, or mystic yoga. I always remain equipoised in the heart of one who is also equipoised in all circumstances.

PURPORT

Lord Viṣṇu was very pleased with Mahārāja Pṛthu's good character and behavior and offered him a benediction. The Lord openly says that performing great sacrifices or undergoing the austerities of mystic *yoga* practice cannot satisfy Him. He is only pleased by elevated character and behavior. But these cannot develop unless one becomes a pure devotee of the Lord. Anyone who has developed unalloyed, unflinching devotional service unto the Lord develops his original good qualities as spirit soul. The spirit soul, as part and parcel of the Supreme Personality of Godhead, has all the good qualities of the Lord. When the spirit soul is contaminated by the material modes of nature, one is considered good or bad with reference to the material qualities. But when one is transcendental to all material qualities, all the good qualities come out. These qualities of a devotee, twenty-six in number, are listed as follows: (1) kind to everyone, (2) does not quarrel with anyone, (3) fixed in the Absolute Truth, (4) equal to everyone, (5) faultless, (6) charitable, (7) mild, (8) clean, (9) simple, (10) benevolent, (11) peaceful, (12) completely attached to Kṛṣṇa, (13) has no material hankering, (14) meek, (15) steady, (16) self-controlled, (17) does not eat more than required, (18) sane, (19) respectful, (20) humble, (21) grave, (22) compassionate, (23) friendly, (24) poetic, (25) expert, (26) silent. The Lord is satisfied by development of the transcendental qualities of the living entity and not by artificial performance of sacrifices and mystic *yoga*. In other words, unless one is fully qualified to become a pure devotee of the Lord one cannot expect to be liberated from material entanglement.

TEXT 17

मैत्रेय उवाच

स इत्थं लोकगुरुणा विष्वक्सेनेन विश्वजित् ।
अनुशासित आदेशं शिरसा जगृहे हरेः ॥१७॥

maitreya uvāca
sa ittharh loka-guruṇā
viṣvaksenena viśva-jit
anuśāsita ādeśam
śirasā jagṛhe hareḥ

maitreyaḥ uvāca—Maitreya said; *saḥ*—he; *ittham*—thus; *loka-guruṇā*—by the supreme master of all people; *viśvak-senena*—by the Personality of Godhead; *viśva-jit*—the conqueror of the world (Mahārāja Pṛthu); *anuśāsitaḥ*—being ordered; *ādeśam*—instructions; *śirasā*—on the head; *jagṛhe*—accepted; *hareḥ*—of the Personality of Godhead.

TRANSLATION

The great saint Maitreya continued: My dear Vidura, in this way Mahārāja Pṛthu, the conqueror of the entire world, accepted the instructions of the Supreme Personality of Godhead on his head.

PURPORT

One should accept the instructions of the Supreme Personality of Godhead by bowing down at the lotus feet of the Lord. This means that anything spoken by the Personality of Godhead should be taken as it is, with great care and attention and with great respect. It is not our business to amend the words of the Supreme Personality of Godhead or make additions or alterations, as it has become a custom for many so-called scholars and *svāmīs* who comment on the words of *Bhagavad-gītā.* Here the practical example of how to accept the instruction of the Supreme Personality of Godhead is shown by Pṛthu Mahārāja.This is the way to receive knowledge through the *paramparā* system.

TEXT 18

स्पृशन्तं पादयोः प्रेम्णा व्रीडितं स्वेन कर्मणा ।
शतक्रतुं परिष्वज्य विद्वेषं विससर्ज ह ॥१८॥

spṛśantaṁ pādayoḥ premṇā
vrīḍitaṁ svena karmaṇā
śata-kratuṁ pariṣvajya
vidveṣaṁ visasarja ha

spṛśantam—touching; *pādayoḥ*—the feet; *premṇā*—in ecstasy; *vrīḍitam*—ashamed; *svena*—his own; *karmaṇā*—by activities; *śata-kratum*—King Indra; *pariṣvajya*—embracing; *vidveṣam*—envy; *visasarja*—gave up; *ha*—of course.

TRANSLATION

As King Indra was standing by, he became ashamed of his own activities and fell down before King Pṛthu to touch his lotus feet. But Pṛthu Mahārāja immediately embraced him in great ecstasy and gave up all his envy against him because of his stealing the horse meant for the sacrifice.

PURPORT

There are many cases in which a person becomes an offender to the lotus feet of a Vaiṣṇava and later becomes repentant. Here also we find that although the King of heaven, Indra, is so powerful that he accompanied Lord Viṣṇu, he felt himself a great offender for stealing Pṛthu Mahārāja's horse that was meant for sacrifice. An offender at the lotus feet of a Vaiṣṇava is never excused by the Supreme Personality of Godhead. There are many instances illustrating this fact. Ambarīṣa Mahārāja was offended by Durvāsā Muni, a great sage and mystic *yogī,* and Durvāsā also had to fall down at the lotus feet of Ambarīṣa Mahārāja.

Indra decided to fall down at the lotus feet of King Pṛthu, but the King was so magnanimous a Vaiṣṇava that he did not want Mahārāja Indra to fall down at his feet. He immediately picked him up and embraced him, and both of them forgot all the past incidents. Both King Indra and Mahārāja Pṛthu were envious and angry with each other, but since both of them were Vaiṣṇavas, or servants of Lord Viṣṇu, it was their duty to adjust the cause of their envy. This is also a first-class example of cooperative behavior between Vaiṣṇavas. In the present days, however, because people are not Vaiṣṇavas, they fight perpetually among one another and are vanquished without finishing the mission of human life. There is a great need to propagate the Kṛṣṇa consciousness movement in the world so that even though sometimes people become angry and malicious towards one another, because of their being Kṛṣṇa conscious such rivalry, competition and envy could be adjusted without difficulty.

TEXT 19

भगवानथ विश्वात्मा पृथुनोपहृतार्हणः ।
सम्मुज्जिहानया भक्त्या गृहीतचरणाम्बुजः ॥१९॥

bhagavān atha viśvātmā
pṛthunopahṛtārhaṇaḥ

samujjihānayā bhaktyā
gṛhīta-caraṇāmbujaḥ

bhagavān—the Supreme Personality of Godhead; *atha*—thereupon; *viśva-ātmā*—the Supersoul; *pṛthunā*—by King Pṛthu; *upahṛta*—being offered; *arhaṇaḥ*—all the paraphernalia for worship; *samujjihānayā*—gradually increased; *bhaktyā*—whose devotional service; *gṛhīta*—taken; *caraṇa-ambujaḥ*—His lotus feet.

TRANSLATION

King Pṛthu abundantly worshiped the lotus feet of the Supreme Personality of Godhead, who was so merciful to him. While worshiping the lotus feet of the Lord, Pṛthu Mahārāja gradually increased his ecstasy in devotional service.

PURPORT

When various ecstasies appear in the body of a devotee, it is to be understood that his devotional service has become perfect. There are many types of transcendental ecstasies in the forms of crying, laughing, perspiring, falling down, and crying like a madman. All these symptoms are sometimes visible on the body of a devotee. They are called *aṣṭa-sāttvika-vikāra*, which means eight kinds of transcendental transformations. They are never to be imitated, but when a devotee actually becomes perfect, these symptoms are visible on his body. The Lord is *bhakta-vatsala*, which means that He is inclined towards His pure devotee (*bhakta*). Therefore the transcendental ecstatic transaction between the Supreme Lord and His devotee is never like the activities of this material world.

TEXT 20

प्रस्थानाभिमुखोऽप्येनमनुग्रहविलम्बितः ।
पश्यन् पद्मपलाशाक्षो न प्रतस्थे सुहृत्सताम् ॥२०॥

prasthānābhimukho 'py enam
anugraha-vilambitaḥ
paśyan padma-palāśākṣo
na pratasthe suhṛt satām

prasthāna—to leave; *abhimukhaḥ*—ready; *api*—although; *enam*—him (Pṛthu); *anugraha*—by kindness; *vilambitaḥ*—detained; *paśyan*—seeing;

padma-palāśa-akṣaḥ—the Lord, whose eyes are like the petals of a lotus flower; *na*—not; *pratasthe*—departed; *suhṛt*—the well-wisher; *satām*—of the devotees.

TRANSLATION

The Lord was just about to leave, but because He was so greatly inclined towards the behavior of King Pṛthu, He did not depart. Seeing the behavior of Mahārāja Pṛthu with His lotus eyes, He was detained because He is always the well-wisher of His devotees.

PURPORT

Here the words *suhṛt satām* are very significant. The Supreme Personality of Godhead is always very inclined towards His devotee and is always thinking of his well-being. This is not partiality. As stated in *Bhagavad-gītā*, the Lord is equal to everyone (*samo 'haṁ sarva-bhūteṣu*), but to one who particularly engages in His service, He is very much inclined. In another place, the Lord says that a devotee always exists in His heart, and He also exists always in the heart of the devotee.

The special inclination of the Supreme Personality of Godhead for His pure devotee is not unnatural, nor is it partiality. For example, sometimes a father has several children, but he has special affection for one child who is very much inclined towards him. This is explained in *Bhagavad-gītā* (10.10):

teṣāṁ satata-yuktānāṁ
bhajatāṁ prīti-pūrvakam
dadāmi buddhi-yogaṁ taṁ
yena mām upayānti te

Those who constantly engage in the devotional service of the Lord in love and affection are directly in contact with the Supreme Personality of Godhead sitting as the Supersoul in everyone's heart. The Lord is not far away from the devotee. He is always in everyone's heart, but only the devotee can realize the Lord's presence, and thus he is directly connected, and he takes instruction from the Lord at every moment. Therefore, there is no chance of a devotee's being in error, nor is there any partiality on the part of the Lord for His pure devotees.

TEXT 21

स आदिराजो रचिताञ्जलिर्हरिं
विलोकितुं नाशकदश्रुलोचनः ।

न किञ्चनोवाच स बाष्पविक्लवो
हृदोपगुह्यामुमधादवस्थितः ॥२१॥

sa ādi-rājo racitāñjalir hariṁ
vilokituṁ nāśakad aśru-locanaḥ
na kiñcanovāca sa bāṣpa-viklavo
hṛdopaguhyāmum adhād avasthitaḥ

saḥ—he; *ādi-rājaḥ*—the original King; *racita-añjaliḥ*—with folded hands; *harim*—the Supreme Personality of Godhead; *vilokitum*—to look upon; *na*—not; *aśakat*—was able; *aśru-locanaḥ*—his eyes full of tears; *na*—nor; *kiñcana*—anything; *uvāca*—spoke; *saḥ*—he; *bāṣpa-viklavaḥ*—his voice being choked up; *hṛdā*—with his heart; *upaguhya*—embracing; *amum*—the Lord; *adhāt*—he remained; *avasthitaḥ*—standing.

TRANSLATION

The original King, Mahārāja Pṛthu, his eyes full of tears and his voice faltering and choked up, could neither see the Lord very distinctly nor speak to address the Lord in any way. He simply embraced the Lord within his heart and remained standing in that way with folded hands.

PURPORT

Just as Kṛṣṇa is addressed in the *Brahma-saṁhitā* as *ādi-puruṣa,* the original personality, so King Pṛthu, being an empowered incarnation of the Lord, is referred to in this verse as *ādi-rājaḥ,* the original or ideal King. He was a great devotee and at the same time a great hero who conquered over all undesirable elements in his kingdom. He was so powerful that he was equal to fighting with Indra, the King of heaven. He gave protection to his citizens, keeping them engaged in pious activities and devotion to the Lord. He did not collect a single cent of taxes from the citizens without being able to give them protection from all calamities. The greatest calamity in life is to become godless and therefore sinful. If the state head or king allows the citizens to become sinful by indulging in illicit sex life, intoxication, meat-eating and gambling, then the king is responsible, and he has to suffer the resultant sequence of reactions for the sinful lives of the citizens because he levies taxes on them unnecessarily. These are the principles for a ruling power, and because Mahārāja Pṛthu observed all the principles for a ruling chief, he is referred to here as *ādi-rājaḥ.*

Even a responsible king like Mahārāja Pṛthu can become a pure devotee of the first order. We can distinctly see from his behavior how he became ecstatic, both externally and internally, in pure devotional service.

Just today we have seen in the newspapers of Bombay that the government is going to repeal its prohibition laws. Ever since Gandhi's noncooperation movement, Bombay has been kept dry and has not allowed its citizens to drink. But unfortunately the citizens are so clever that they have increased illicit distillation of liquor, and although not being sold publicly in shops, liquor is being sold in public lavatories and similar abnormal places. Unable to check such illicit smuggling, the government has decided to manufacture the liquor at cheaper prices so that people can have their supply of intoxication directly from the government instead of purchasing it in public lavatories. The government failed to change the hearts of the citizens from indulging in sinful life, so instead of losing the taxes they collect to inflate the treasury, they have decided to manufacture liquor to supply to the citizens who hanker after it.

This kind of government cannot check the resultant actions of sinful life, namely, war, pestilence, famine, earthquakes and similar other disturbances. Nature's law is that as soon as there are discrepancies in the laws of God (which are described in *Bhagavad-gītā* as *dharmasya glāniḥ,* or disobedience to the laws of nature of God), at once there will be heavy punishment in the form of sudden outbreak of war. We have recently experienced a war between India and Pakistan. Within fourteen days there have been immense losses of men and money, and there have been disturbances to the entire world. These are the reactions of sinful life. The Kṛṣṇa consciousness movement is meant to make people pure and perfect. If we become even partially pure, as described in the *Bhāgavatam* (*naṣṭa-prāyeṣv abhadreṣu*), by development of Kṛṣṇa consciousness, then lust and greed, the material diseases of the citizens, will be reduced. This can be made possible simply by broadcasting the pure message of *Śrīmad-Bhāgavatam* or Kṛṣṇa consciousness. Big commercial and industrial firms have contributed many thousands of rupees to a Defense Fund that burns the money in the form of gunpowder, but unfortunately if they are asked to contribute liberally to advance the Kṛṣṇa consciousness movement, they are reluctant. Under the circumstances, the world will periodically suffer from such upsurges and outbreaks of war, which are the consequences of not being Kṛṣṇa conscious.

TEXT 22

अथावमृज्याश्रुकला विलोकयन्-
नतृप्तदृग्गोचरमाह पूरुषम् ।

पदा स्पृशन्तं क्षितिमंस उन्नते
विन्यस्तहस्ताग्रमुरङ्गविद्विषः ॥२२॥

athāvamṛjyāśru-kalā vilokayann
atṛpta-dṛg-gocaram āha pūruṣam
padā spṛśantaṁ kṣitim aṁsa unnate
vinyasta-hastāgram uraṅga-vidviṣaḥ

atha—thereupon; *avamṛjya*—wiping; *aśru-kalāḥ*—the tears in his eyes; *vilokayan*—observing; *atṛpta*—not satisfied; *dṛk-gocaram*—visible to his naked eyes; *āha*—he said; *pūruṣam*—unto the Supreme Personality of Godhead; *padā*—with His lotus feet; *spṛśantam*—just touching; *kṣitim*—the ground; *aṁse*—on the shoulder; *unnate*—raised; *vinyasta*—rested; *hasta*—of this hand; *agram*—the front part; *uraṅga-vidviṣaḥ*—of Garuḍa, the enemy of the snakes.

TRANSLATION

The Supreme Personality of Godhead stood with His lotus feet almost touching the ground while He rested the front of His hand on the raised shoulder of Garuḍa, the enemy of the snakes. Mahārāja Pṛthu, wiping the tears from his eyes, tried to look upon the Lord, but it appeared that he was not fully satisfied by looking at Him. Thus he offered the following prayers.

PURPORT

The significant point in this verse is that the Lord was standing above the ground, almost touching it. The residents of the upper planetary systems, beginning from Brahmaloka (the planet where Lord Brahmā lives) down to Svargaloka (the heavenly planet of Indra), are so advanced in spiritual life that when they come to visit this or similar other lower planetary systems, they keep their weightlessness. This means that they can stand without touching the ground. Lord Viṣṇu is the Supreme Personality of Godhead, but because He lives in one of the planetary systems within this universe, He sometimes plays as if one of the demigods of this universe. When He first appeared before Pṛthu Mahārāja, He was not touching the ground of this earth, but when He was fully satisfied with the behavior and character of Mahārāja Pṛthu, He immediately acted as the Supreme Personality of Godhead Nārāyaṇa from Vaikuṇṭha. Out of affection for Pṛthu Mahārāja, He touched the earth, but He rested the front of His hand on the raised shoulder of Garuḍa, His carrier, as if to prevent Himself from falling down, since the Lord is not accustomed to stand on earthly ground.

These are all symptoms of His great affection for Pṛthu Mahārāja. Perceiving his fortunate position, Pṛthu Mahārāja could not fully look upon the Lord due to ecstasy, but still, in a faltering voice, he began to offer prayers.

TEXT 23

पृथुरुवाच
वरान् विभो त्वद्वरदेश्वराद् बुधः
कथं वृणीते गुणविक्रियात्मनाम् ।
ये नारकाणामपि सन्ति देहिनां
तानीश कैवल्यपते वृणे न च ॥२३॥

pṛthur uvāca
varān vibho tvad varadeśvarād budhaḥ
kathaṁ vṛṇīte guṇa-vikriyātmanām
ye nārakāṇām api santi dehināṁ
tān īśa kaivalya-pate vṛṇe na ca

pṛthuḥ uvāca—Pṛthu Mahārāja said; *varān*—benedictions; *vibho*—my dear Supreme Lord; *tvat*—from You; *vara-da-īśvarāt*—from the Supreme Personality of Godhead, the highest of the bestowers of benediction; *budhaḥ*—a learned person; *katham*—how; *vṛṇīte*—could ask for; *guṇa-vikriyā*—bewildered by the modes of material nature; *ātmanām*—of the living entities; *ye*—which; *nārakāṇām*—of the living entities living in hell; *api*—also; *santi*—exist; *dehinām*—of the embodied; *tān*—all those; *īśa*—O Supreme Lord; *kaivalya-pate*—O bestower of merging in the existence of the Lord; *vṛṇe*—I ask for; *na*—not; *ca*—also.

TRANSLATION

My dear Lord, You are the best of the demigods who can offer benedictions. Why therefore should any learned person ask You for benedictions that are meant for living entities who are bewildered by the modes of nature? Such benedictions are available automatically, even in the lives of living entities who are suffering in hellish conditions. My dear Lord, You can certainly bestow merging into Your existence, but I do not wish to have such a benediction.

PURPORT

There are different kinds of benedictions according to a person's demands. For *karmīs* the best benediction is promotion to the higher planetary systems where the duration of life is very long and the standard of living and happiness is very high. There are others, namely *jñānīs* and *yogīs,* who want the benediction of merging into the existence of the Lord. This is called *kaivalya.* The Lord is therefore addressed as *kaivalya-pati,* the master or Lord of the benediction known as *kaivalya.* But devotees receive a different type of benediction from the Lord. Devotees are anxious neither for the heavenly planets nor for merging into the existence of the Lord. According to devotees, *kaivalya,* or merging into the existence of the Lord, is considered as good as hell. The word *nāraka* means hell. Similarly, everyone who exists in this material world is called *nāraka* because this material existence itself is known as a hellish condition of life. Pṛthu Mahārāja, however, expressed that he was interested neither in the benediction desired by the *karmīs* nor that desired by the *jñānīs* and *yogīs.* Śrīla Prabodhānanda Sarasvatī Prabhu, a great devotee of Lord Caitanya, described that *kaivalya* is no better than a hellish condition of life, and as for the delights of the heavenly planets, they are factually will-o'-the-wisps or phantasmagoria. They are not wanted by devotees. Devotees do not even care for the positions held by Lord Brahmā or Lord Śiva, nor does a devotee desire to become equal with Lord Viṣṇu. As a pure devotee of the Lord, Pṛthu Mahārāja made his position very clear.

TEXT 24

न कामये नाथ तदप्यहं क्वचिन्-
न यत्र युष्मच्चरणाम्बुजासवः ।
महत्तमान्तर्हृदयान्मुखच्युतो
विधत्स्व कर्णायुतमेष मे वरः ॥२४॥

na kāmaye nātha tad apy ahaṁ kvacin
na yatra yuṣmac-caraṇāmbujāsavaḥ
mahattamāntar-hṛdayān mukha-cyuto
vidhatsva karṇāyutam eṣa me varaḥ

na—not; *kāmaye*—do I desire; *nātha*—O master; *tat*—that; *api*—even; *aham*—I; *kvacit*—at any time; *na*—not; *yatra*—where; *yuṣmat*—Your; *caraṇa-ambuja*—of the lotus feet; *āsavaḥ*—the nectarean beverage; *mahattama*—of the great devotees; *antaḥ-hṛdayāt*—from the core of the heart; *mukha*—from the mouths; *cyutaḥ*—being delivered; *vidhatsva*—give; *karṇa*—ears; *ayutam*—one million; *eṣaḥ*—this; *me*—my; *varaḥ*—benediction.

TRANSLATION

My dear Lord, I therefore do not wish to have the benediction of merging into Your existence because in that position there is no existence of the nectarean beverage of Your lotus feet. I want the benediction of at least one million ears, for thus I may be able to hear about the glories of Your lotus feet from the mouths of Your pure devotees.

PURPORT

In the previous verse Mahārāja Pṛthu addressed the Lord as *kaivalya-pati,* the master of the liberation of merging into His existence. This does not mean that he was anxious for *kaivalya* liberation. That is made clear in this verse: "My dear Lord, I do not want such a benediction." Mahārāja Pṛthu wanted to have a million ears to hear the glories of the lotus feet of the Lord. He specifically mentioned that the glories of the Lord should emanate from the mouths of pure devotees who speak from the cores of their hearts. It is stated in the beginning of *Śrīmad-Bhāgavatam, śuka-mukhād amṛta-drava-saṁyutam:* the nectar of *Śrīmad-Bhāgavatam* became more relishable because it emanated from the mouth of Śrīla Śukadeva Gosvāmī (*Bhāg.* 1.1.3). One might think that these glories of the Lord can be heard from anywhere, from the mouths of either devotees or nondevotees, but here it is specifically mentioned that the glories of the Lord must emanate from the mouths of pure devotees. Śrī Sanātana Gosvāmī has strictly prohibited hearing from the mouth of a nondevotee. There are many professional reciters of *Śrīmad-Bhāgavatam* who speak the narrations very ornamentally, but a pure devotee does not like to hear from them because such glorification of the Lord is simply a vibration of material sound. When it is heard from the mouth of a pure devotee, glorification of the Lord is immediately effective.

The words *satāṁ prasaṅgān mama vīrya-saṁvidaḥ* mean that glorification of the Lord is potent when uttered from the mouth of a pure devotee. The Lord has innumerable devotees all over the universe, and they have been glorifying the Lord since time immemorial and for an unlimited time. But still they cannot completely finish enumerating the glories of the Lord. Pṛthu Mahārāja therefore wanted innumerable ears, as Rūpa Gosvāmī also desired to have millions of ears and millions of tongues to chant and hear the glorification of the Lord. In other words, if our ears are always engaged in hearing the glorification of the Lord, there will be no scope for hearing the Māyāvāda philosophy, which is doom to spiritual progress. Śrī Caitanya Mahāprabhu said that if anyone hears from a Māyāvādī philosopher preaching about the activities of the Lord, even if it is a description from the Vedic literature, he is ultimately doomed. By hearing such Māyāvāda philosophy one cannot come to the destination of spiritual perfection of life.

TEXT 25

स उत्तमश्लोक महन्मुखच्युतो
भवत्पदाम्भोजसुधाकणानिलः ।
स्मृतिं पुनर्विस्मृततत्त्ववर्त्मनां
कुयोगिनां नो वितरत्यलं वरैः ॥२५॥

sa uttamaśloka mahan-mukha-cyuto
bhavat-padāmbhoja-sudhā-kaṇānilaḥ
smṛtiṁ punar vismṛta-tattva-vartmanām
kuyoginām no vitaraty alaṁ varaiḥ

saḥ—that; *uttama-śloka*—O Lord, who is praised by selected verses; *mahat*—of great devotees; *mukha-cyutaḥ*—delivered from the mouths; *bhavat*—Your; *pada-ambhoja*—from the lotus feet; *sudhā*—of nectar; *kaṇā*—particles; *anilaḥ*—soothing breeze; *smṛtim*—remembrance; *punaḥ*—again; *vismṛta*—forgotten; *tattva*—to the truth; *vartmanām*—of persons whose path; *ku-yoginām*—of persons not in the line of devotional service; *naḥ*—of us; *vitarati*—restores; *alam*—unnecessary; *varaiḥ*—other benedictions.

TRANSLATION

My dear Lord, You are glorified by the selected verses uttered by great personalities. Such glorification of Your lotus feet is just like saffron particles. When the transcendental vibration from the mouths of great devotees carries the aroma of the saffron dust of Your lotus feet, the forgetful living entity gradually remembers his eternal relationship with You. Devotees thus gradually come to the right conclusion about the value of life. My dear Lord, I therefore do not need any other benediction but the opportunity to hear from the mouth of Your pure devotee.

PURPORT

It is explained in the previous verse that one has to hear glorification of the Lord from the mouth of a pure devotee. This is further explained here. The transcendental vibration from the mouth of a pure devotee is so powerful that it can revive the living entity's memory of his eternal relationship with the Supreme Personality of Godhead. In our material existence, under the influence of illusory *māyā,* we have almost forgotten our eternal relationship with the Lord, exactly like a man sleeping very deeply who forgets his duties. In the *Vedas* it is said that every one of us is sleeping under the influence of *māyā.* We must get up from this slumber and engage in the right service, for thus we can properly utilize the facility of this human form of life. As expressed in a song by Ṭhākura Bhaktivinoda, Lord Caitanya says, "*jīva jāgo, jīva jāgo.*" The Lord asks every sleeping living entity to get up and engage in devotional service so that his mission in this human form of life may be fulfilled. This awakening voice comes through the mouth of a pure devotee.

A pure devotee always engages in the service of the Lord, taking shelter of His lotus feet, and therefore he has direct connection with the saffron mercy particles that are strewn over the lotus feet of the Lord. Although when a pure devotee speaks the articulation of his voice may resemble the sound of this material sky, because the voice touches the particles of saffron dust on the lotus feet of the Lord, the voice is spiritually very powerful. As soon as a sleeping living entity hears the powerful voice emanating from the mouth of a pure devotee, he immediately remembers his eternal relationship with the Lord, although up until that moment he had forgotten everything.

For a conditioned soul, therefore, it is very important to hear from the mouth of a pure devotee who is fully surrendered to the lotus feet of the Lord without any material desire, speculative knowledge or contamination of the modes of material nature. Every one of us is *kuyogī* because we have engaged in the service of this material world, forgetting our eternal relationship with the Lord as His eternal loving servants. It is our duty to rise from the *kuyoga* platform to become *suyogīs,* perfect mystics. The process of hearing from a pure devotee is recommended in all Vedic scriptures, especially by Lord Caitanya Mahāprabhu. One may stay in his position of life—it doesn't matter what it is—but if one hears from the mouth of a pure devotee, he gradually comes to the understanding of his relationship with the Lord and thus engages in His loving service, and his life becomes completely perfect. Therefore, this process of hearing from the mouth of a pure devotee is very important for making progress in the line of spiritual understanding.

TEXT 26

यशः शिवं सुश्रव आर्यसङ्गमे
यदृच्छया चोपशृणोति ते सकृत ।

कथं गुणज्ञो विरमेद्विना पशुं
श्रीर्यत्प्रववे गुणसंग्रहेच्छया ॥२६॥

yaśaḥ śivaṁ suśrava ārya-saṅgame
yadṛcchayā copaśṛṇoti te sakṛt
kathaṁ guṇa-jño viramed vinā paśuṁ
śrīr yat pravavre guṇa-saṅgrahecchayā

yaśaḥ—glorification; *śivam*—all-auspicious; *su-śravaḥ*—O highly glorified Lord; *ārya-saṅgame*—in the association of advanced devotees; *yadṛcchayā*—somehow or other; *ca*—also; *upaśṛṇoti*—hears; *te*—Your; *sakṛt*—even once; *katham*—how; *guṇa-jñaḥ*—one who appreciates good qualities; *viramet*—can cease; *vinā*—unless; *paśum*—an animal; *śrīḥ*—the goddess of fortune; *yat*—which; *pravavre*—accepted; *guṇa*—Your qualities; *saṅgraha*—to receive; *icchayā*—with a desire.

TRANSLATION

My dear highly glorified Lord, if one, in the association of pure devotees, hears even once the glories of Your activities, he does not, unless he is nothing but an animal, give up the association of devotees, for no intelligent person would be so careless as to leave their association. The perfection of chanting and hearing about Your glories was even accepted by the goddess of fortune, who desired to hear of Your unlimited activities and transcendental glories.

PURPORT

The association of devotees *(ārya-saṅgama)* is the most important factor in this world. The word *ārya* refers to those who are advancing spiritually. In the history of the human race, the Āryan family is considered to be the most elevated community in the world because it adopts the Vedic civilization. The Āryan family is distributed all over the world and is known as Indo-Āryan. In prehistoric days all of the members of the Āryan family followed the Vedic principles, and therefore they became spiritually advanced. The kings, known as *rājarṣis,* were so perfectly educated as *kṣatriyas,* or protectors of the citizens, and so greatly advanced in spiritual life, that there was not a bit of trouble for the citizens.

The glorification of the Supreme Lord can be very much appreciated by the Āryan family. Although there is no bar for others, the members of the Āryan family very quickly catch the essence of spiritual life. How is it we are finding it very easy to spread Kṛṣṇa consciousness amongst the Europeans and Americans? History reports that the Americans and Europeans proved their capability when they were anxious to expand colonization, but at the present time, being contaminated by the advancement of material science, their sons and grandsons are turning into reprobates. This is due to their having lost their original spiritual culture, which is Vedic civilization. Presently these descendants of the Āryan family are taking this Kṛṣṇa consciousness movement very seriously. Others also who are associating with them and hearing the chanting of the Hare Kṛṣṇa *mahā-mantra* from the lips of pure devotees are also becoming captivated by the transcendental vibration. Transcendental vibrations are very much effective when chanted amongst Āryans, but even though one does not belong to the Āryan family, he will become a Vaiṣṇava simply by hearing the *mantra* because the vibration has great influence over everyone.

Mahārāja Pṛthu points out that even the goddess of fortune, who is the constant companion of Lord Nārāyaṇa, specifically wanted to hear about the Lord's glories, and for the association of the *gopīs,* who are pure devotees, the goddess of fortune, Lakṣmī, underwent severe austerities. The impersonalist may ask why one should bother chanting the Hare Kṛṣṇa *mahā-mantra* continually for so many years instead of stopping and trying for *kaivalya,* liberation, or merging into the existence of the Lord. In answer, Mahārāja Pṛthu maintains that the attraction of this chanting is so great that one cannot give up the process unless he is an animal. This is the case even if one comes in contact with this transcendental vibration by chance. Pṛthu Mahārāja is very emphatic in this connection—only an animal can give up the practice of chanting Hare Kṛṣṇa. Those who are not animals, who are actually intelligent, advanced, human, civilized men, cannot give up this practice of continually chanting Hare Kṛṣṇa, Hare Kṛṣṇa, Kṛṣṇa Kṛṣṇa, Hare Hare / Hare Rāma, Hare Rāma, Rāma Rāma, Hare Hare.

TEXT 27

अथाभजे त्वाखिलपूरुषोत्तमं
गुणालयं पद्मकरेव लालसः ।
अप्यावयोरेकपतिस्पृधोः कलि-
र्न स्यात्कृतत्वच्चरणैकतानयोः ॥२७॥

athābhaje tvākhila-pūruṣottamaṁ
guṇālayaṁ padma-kareva lālasaḥ

apy āvayor eka-pati-spṛdhoḥ kalir
na syāt kṛta-tvac-caraṇaika-tānayoḥ

atha—therefore; *ābhaje*—I shall engage in devotional service; *tvā*—unto You; *akhila*—all-inclusive; *pūruṣa-uttamam*—the Supreme Personality of Godhead; *guṇa-ālayam*—the reservoir of all transcendental qualities; *padma-karā*—the goddess of fortune, who carries a lotus flower in her hand; *iva*—like; *lālasaḥ*—being desirous; *api*—indeed; *āvayoḥ*—of Lakṣmī and me; *eka-pati*—one master; *spṛdhoḥ*—competing; *kaliḥ*—quarrel; *na*—not; *syāt*—may take place; *kṛta*—having done; *tvat-caraṇa*—unto Your lotus feet; *eka-tānayoḥ*—one attention.

TRANSLATION

Now I wish to engage in the service of the lotus feet of the Supreme Personality of Godhead and to serve just as the goddess of fortune who carries a lotus flower in her hand because His Lordship, the Supreme Personality of Godhead, is the reservoir of all transcendental qualities. I am afraid that the goddess of fortune and I will quarrel because both of us would be attentively engaged in the same service.

PURPORT

The Lord is here addressed as *akhila-pūruṣottama,* the Supreme Personality of Godhead who is Lord of the entire creation. *Puruṣa* means the enjoyer, and *uttama* means the best. There are different kinds of *puruṣas* or enjoyers within the universe. Generally they can be divided into three classes—those who are conditioned, those who are liberated, and those who are eternal. In the *Vedas* the Supreme Lord is called the supreme eternal of all eternals *(nityo nityānām).* Both the Supreme Personality of Godhead and the living entities are eternal. The supreme eternals are the *viṣṇu-tattva* or Lord Viṣṇu and His expansions. So *nitya* refers to the Personality of Godhead beginning from Kṛṣṇa up to Mahā-Viṣṇu, Nārāyaṇa and other expansions of Lord Kṛṣṇa. As stated in the *Brahma-saṁhitā (rāmādi-mūrtiṣu)* there are millions and trillions of expansions of Lord Viṣṇu as Rāma, Nṛsiṁha, Varāha and other incarnations. All of them are called eternals.

The word *mukta* refers to the living entities who never come within this material world. The *baddhas* are those living entities who are almost eternally living within this material world. The *baddhas* are struggling very hard within this material world to become free from the threefold miseries of material nature and to enjoy life, whereas the *muktas* are already liberated. They never come into this material world. Lord Viṣṇu is the master of this material world, and there is no question of His being controlled by material nature. Consequently, Lord Viṣṇu is addressed here as *pūruṣottama,* the best of all living entities—namely *viṣṇu-tattvas* and *jīva-tattvas.* It is a great offense, therefore, to compare Lord Viṣṇu and the *jīva-tattva* or consider them on an equal level. The Māyāvādī philosophers equalize the *jīvas* and the Supreme Lord and consider them to be one, but that is the greatest offense to the lotus feet of Lord Viṣṇu.

Here in the material world we have practical experience that a superior person is worshiped by an inferior one. Similarly, *pūruṣottama,* the greatest, the Supreme Personality of Godhead Kṛṣṇa or Lord Viṣṇu, is always worshiped by others. Pṛthu Mahārāja therefore decided to engage in the service of the lotus feet of Lord Viṣṇu. Pṛthu Mahārāja is considered to be an incarnation of Lord Viṣṇu, but he is called a *śaktyāveśa* incarnation. Another significant word in this verse is *guṇālayam,* which refers to Viṣṇu as the reservoir of all transcendental qualities. The Māyāvādī philosophers take the Absolute Truth to be *nirguṇa* (without qualities), in accordance with the impersonalistic view, but actually the Lord is the reservoir of all good qualities. One of the most important qualities of the Lord is His inclination to His devotees, called *bhakta-vatsala.* The devotees are always very much inclined to render service to the lotus feet of the Lord, and the Lord is also very much inclined to accept loving service from His devotees. In that exchange of service there are so many transcendental transactions which are called transcendental qualitative activities. Some of the transcendental qualities of the Lord are that He is omniscient, omnipresent, all-pervasive, all-powerful, the cause of all causes, the Absolute Truth, the reservoir of all pleasures, the reservoir of all knowledge, the all-auspicious and so on.

Pṛthu Mahārāja desired to serve the Lord with the goddess of fortune, but this desire does not mean that he was situated on the platform of *mādhurya-rasa.* The goddess of fortune is engaged in the service of the Lord in the *mādhurya-rasa* of conjugal love. Although her position is on the chest of the Lord, the goddess of fortune, in her position as a devotee, takes pleasure in serving the lotus feet of the Lord. Pṛthu Mahārāja was thinking only of the lotus feet of the Lord because he is on the platform of *dāsya-rasa* or servitorship of the Lord. From the next verse we learn that Pṛthu Mahārāja was thinking of the goddess of fortune as the universal mother, *jagan-mātā.* Consequently there was no question of his competing with her on the platform of *mādhurya-rasa.* Nonetheless he feared that she might take offense at his engaging in the service of the Lord. This suggests that in the absolute world there is sometimes competition between servitors in the service of the Lord, but such competition is without malice. In the Vaikuṇṭha worlds if a devotee excels in the service of the Lord, others do not become envious of his excellent service but rather aspire to come to the platform of that service.

TEXT 28

जगज्जनन्यां जगदीश वैशसं
स्यादेव यत्कर्मणि नः समीहितम् ।
करोषि फल्ग्वप्युरु दीनवत्सलः
स्व एव धिष्ण्येऽभिरतस्य किं तया ॥२८॥

jagaj-jananyāṁ jagad-īśa vaiśasaṁ
syād eva yat-karmaṇi naḥ samīhitam
karoṣi phalgv apy uru dīna-vatsalaḥ
sva eva dhiṣṇye 'bhiratasya kiṁ tayā

jagat-jananyām—in the mother of the universe (Lakṣmī); *jagat-īśa*—O Lord of the universe; *vaiśasam*—anger; *syāt*—may arise; *eva*—certainly; *yat-karmaṇi*—in whose activity; *naḥ*—my; *samīhitam*—desire; *karoṣi*—You consider; *phalgu*—insignificant service; *api*—even; *uru*—very great; *dīna-vatsalaḥ*—favorably inclined to the poor; *sve*—own; *eva*—certainly; *dhiṣṇye*—in Your opulence; *abhiratasya*—of one who is fully satisfied; *kim*—what need is there; *tayā*—with her.

TRANSLATION

My dear Lord of the universe, the goddess of fortune Lakṣmī is the mother of the universe, and yet I think that she may be angry with me because of my intruding on her service and my acting on that very platform to which she is so much attached. Yet I am hopeful that, even though there is some misunderstanding, You will take my part because You are very much inclined to the poor, and You always magnify even insignificant service unto You. Therefore even though she becomes angry, I think that there is no harm for You, because You are so self-sufficient that You can do without her.

PURPORT

Mother Lakṣmījī, the goddess of fortune, is well known for always massaging the lotus feet of Lord Nārāyaṇa. She is an ideal wife because she takes care of Lord Nārāyaṇa in every detail. She not only takes care of His lotus feet but of the household affairs of the Lord as well. She cooks nice foods for Him, fans Him while He eats, smoothes sandalwood pulp on His face, and sets His bed and sitting places in the right order. In this way she is always engaged in the service of the Lord, and there is hardly any opportunity for any other devotee to intrude upon His daily activities. Pṛthu Mahārāja is therefore almost certain that his intrusion into the service of the goddess of fortune would irritate her and cause her to become angry with him. But why should mother Lakṣmī, the mother of the universe, be angry with an insignificant devotee like Pṛthu Mahārāja? All this is not very likely. Yet Pṛthu Mahārāja, just for his personal protection, appealed to the Lord to take his part. Pṛthu Mahārāja was engaged in performing the ordinary Vedic rituals and in performing sacrifices according to *karma-kāṇḍa,* or fruitive activities, but the Lord, being so kind and magnanimous, was ready to award Pṛthu Mahārāja the highest perfectional stage of life, namely devotional service.

When a person performs Vedic rituals and sacrifices, he does so to elevate himself to the heavenly planets. No one can become qualified to go back home, back to Godhead, by means of such sacrifices. But the Lord is so kind that He accepts a little insignificant service, and therefore it is stated in the *Viṣṇu Purāṇa* that by following the principles of *varṇāśrama-dharma* one can satisfy the Supreme Lord. When the Lord is satisfied, the performer of sacrifices is elevated to the platform of devotional service. Pṛthu Mahārāja therefore expected that his insignificant service to the Lord would be accepted by Him as being greater than that of Lakṣmījī. The goddess of fortune is called *cañcalā* (restless) because she is very restless and is always coming and going. So Pṛthu Mahārāja indicates that even though she might go away out of anger, there would be no harm for Lord Viṣṇu, because He is self-sufficient and can do anything and everything without the help of Lakṣmījī. For example, when Garbhodakaśāyī Viṣṇu begot Lord Brahmā from His navel, He didn't take any help from Lakṣmī, who was just sitting by Him and massaging His lotus feet. Generally if a son is to be begotten, the husband impregnates the wife, and in due course of time the son is born. But in the case of Lord Brahmā's birth, Garbhodakaśāyī Viṣṇu did not impregnate Lakṣmījī. Being self-sufficient, the Lord begot Brahmā from His own navel. Therefore, Pṛthu Mahārāja is confident that even if the goddess of fortune became angry with him there would be no harm, neither to the Lord nor to himself.

TEXT 29

भजन्त्यथ त्वामत एव साधवो
व्युदस्तमायागुणविभ्रमोदयम् ।

भवत्पदानुस्मरणादृते सतां
निमित्तमन्यद्भगवन्न विद्महे ॥२९॥

bhajanty atha tvām ata eva sādhavo
vyudasta-māyā-guṇa-vibhramodayam
bhavat-padānusmaraṇād ṛte satām
nimittam anyad bhagavan na vidmahe

bhajanti—they worship; *atha*—therefore; *tvām*—You; *ata eva*—therefore; *sādhavaḥ*—all saintly persons; *vyudasta*—who dispel; *māyā-guṇa*—the modes of material nature; *vibhrama*—misconceptions; *udayam*—produced; *bhavat*—Your; *pada*—lotus feet; *anusmaraṇāt*—constantly remembering; *ṛte*—except; *satām*—of great saintly persons; *nimittam*—reason; *anyat*—other; *bhagavan*—O Supreme Personality of Godhead; *na*—not; *vidmahe*—I can understand.

TRANSLATION

Great saintly persons who are always liberated take to Your devotional service because only by devotional service can one be relieved from the illusions of material existence. O my Lord, there is no other reason for the liberated souls to take shelter at Your lotus feet except for the fact that they are constantly thinking of them.

PURPORT

The *karmīs* are generally engaged in fruitive activities for material bodily comforts. The *jñānīs,* however, are disgusted with searching after material comforts. They understand that they have nothing to do with this material world, being spirit souls. After self-realization, the *jñānīs* who are actually matured in their knowledge must surrender unto the lotus feet of the Lord, as is stated in *Bhagavad-gītā (bahūnāṁ janmanām ante).* Self-realization is not complete unless one comes to the devotional platform. Therefore it is stated in the *Śrīmad-Bhāgavatam* that those who are *ātmārāma,* self-satisfied, are freed from all contaminations of the material modes of nature. As long as one is affected by the modes of material nature, especially by *rajaḥ* and *tamaḥ,* he will be very greedy and lusty and will therefore engage in hard tasks, laboring all day and night. Such false egoism carries one from one species of life into another perpetually, and there is no rest in any species of life. The *jñānī* understands this fact and therefore ceases to work and takes to *karma-sannyāsa.*

Yet this is not actually the platform of satisfaction. After self-realization, the material wisdom of the *jñānī* leads him to the shelter of the lotus feet of the Lord. Then he is only satisfied in contemplating the lotus feet of the Lord constantly. Pṛthu Mahārāja therefore concludes that liberated persons taking to the devotional path have acquired the ultimate goal of life. If liberation were the end in itself, there would be no question of a liberated person's taking to devotional service. In other words, the transcendental bliss derived from self-realization, known as *ātmānanda,* is very insignificant in the presence of the bliss derived from devotional service to the lotus feet of the Lord. Pṛthu Mahārāja therefore concluded that he would simply hear of the glories of the Lord constantly and thus engage his mind upon the lotus feet of the Lord. That is the highest perfection of life.

TEXT 30

मन्ये गिरं ते जगतां विमोहिनीं
वरं वृणीष्वेति भजन्तमात्थ यत् ।
वाचा नु तन्त्या यदि ते जनोऽसितः
कथं पुनः कर्म करोति मोहितः ॥३०॥

manye giraṁ te jagatāṁ vimohinīṁ
varaṁ vṛṇīṣveti bhajantam āttha yat
vācā nu tantyā yadi te jano 'sitaḥ
kathaṁ punaḥ karma karoti mohitaḥ

manye—I consider; *giram*—words; *te*—Your; *jagatām*—to the material world; *vimohinīm*—bewildering; *varam*—benediction; *vṛṇīṣva*—just accept; *iti*—in this way; *bhajantam*—unto Your devotee; *āttha*—You spoke; *yat*—because; *vācā*—by the statements of the *Vedas; nu*—certainly; *tantyā*—by the ropes; *yadi*—if; *te*—Your; *janaḥ*—the people in general; *asitaḥ*—not bound; *katham*—how; *punaḥ*—again and again; *karma*—fruitive activities; *karoti*—perform; *mohitaḥ*—being enamored.

TRANSLATION

My dear Lord, what You have said to Your unalloyed devotee is certainly very much bewildering. The allurements which You offer in the Vedas are certainly not suitable for pure devotees. People in general are bound

by the sweet words of the Vedas, and they engage themselves again and again in fruitive activities, enamored by the results of their actions.

PURPORT

Śrīla Narottama dāsa Ṭhākura, a great *ācārya* of the Gauḍīya-sampradāya, has said that persons who are very much attached to the fruitive activities of the *Vedas,* namely *karma-kāṇḍa* and *jñāna-kāṇḍa,* are certainly doomed. In the *Vedas* there are three categories of activities known as *karma-kāṇḍa,* fruitive activities, *jñāna-kāṇḍa,* philosophical research, and *upāsana-kāṇḍa,* worship of different demigods for receiving material benefits. Those who are engaged in *karma-kāṇḍa* and *jñāna-kāṇḍa* are doomed in the sense that everyone is doomed who is entrapped by this material body, whether it is a body of a demigod, a king, a lower animal or whatever. The sufferings of the threefold miseries of material nature are the same for all. Cultivation of knowledge to understand one's spiritual position is also, to a certain extent, a waste of time. Because he is an eternal part and parcel of the Supreme Lord, the immediate business of the living entity is to engage himself in devotional service. Pṛthu Mahārāja therefore says that the allurement of material benedictions is another trap to entangle one in this material world. He therefore frankly tells the Lord that the Lord's offerings of benedictions in the form of material facilities are certainly causes for bewilderment. A pure devotee is not at all interested in *bhukti* or *mukti.*

The Lord sometimes offers benedictions to the neophyte devotees who have not yet understood that material facilities will not make them happy. In the *Caitanya-caritāmṛta* the Lord therefore says that a sincere devotee who is not very intelligent may ask some material benefit from the Lord, but the Lord, being omniscient, does not generally give material rewards but, on the contrary, takes away whatever material facilities are being enjoyed by His devotee so that ultimately the devotee will completely surrender unto Him. In other words, the offering of benedictions in the form of material profit is never auspicious for the devotee. The statements of the *Vedas* which offer elevation to heavenly planets in exchange for great sacrifices are simply bewildering. Therefore in *Bhagavad-gītā* the Lord says: *yām imāṁ puṣpitāṁ vācaṁ pravadanty avipaścitaḥ* (Bg. 2.42). The less intelligent class of men *(avipaścitaḥ)* are attracted by the flowery language of the *Vedas* and therefore engage in fruitive activities to become materially benefited. Thus they continue life after life, in different bodily forms, to search very, very hard.

TEXT 31

त्वन्माययाद्धा जन ईश खण्डितो
यदन्यदाशास्त ऋतात्मनोऽबुधः ।
यथा चरेद्बालहितं पिता स्वयं
तथा त्वमेवार्हसि नः समीहितुम् ॥३१॥

tvan-māyayāddhā jana īśa khaṇḍito
yad anyad āśāsta ṛtātmano 'budhaḥ
yathā cared bāla-hitaṁ pitā svayaṁ
tathā tvam evārhasi naḥ samīhitum

tvat—Your; *māyayā*—by illusory energy; *addhā*—certainly; *janaḥ*—the people in general; *īśa*—O my Lord; *khaṇḍitaḥ*—separated; *yat*—because; *anyat*—other; *āśāste*—they desire; *ṛta*—real; *ātmanaḥ*—from the self; *abudhaḥ*—without proper understanding; *yathā*—as; *caret*—would engage in; *bāla-hitam*—the welfare of one's child; *pitā*—the father; *svayam*—personally; *tathā*—similarly; *tvam*—Your Lordship *eva*—certainly; *arhasi naḥ samīhitum*—please act on my behalf.

TRANSLATION

My Lord, due to Your illusory energy, all living beings in this material world have forgotten their real constitutional position, and out of ignorance they are always desirous of material happiness in the form of society, friendship and love. Therefore, please do not ask me to take some material benefits from You, but as the father, not waiting for the son's demand, does everything for the benefit of the son, please bestow upon me whatever You think best for me.

PURPORT

It is the duty of the son to depend upon his father without asking anything from him. The good son has faith that the father knows best how to benefit him. Similarly, a pure devotee does not ask anything from the Lord for material benefit. Nor does he ask anything for spiritual benefit. The pure devotee is fully surrendered unto the lotus feet of the Lord, and the Lord takes charge of him, as stated in *Bhagavad-gītā: ahaṁ tvāṁ sarva-pāpebhyo mokṣayiṣyāmi* (Bg. 18.66). The father knows the necessities of the son and supplies them, and the Supreme Lord knows the necessities of the living entities and supplies them sumptuously. Therefore the *Īśopaniṣad* states that everything in this material world is complete (*pūrṇam idam*). The difficulty is that due to forgetfulness the living entities create unnecessary demands and entangle themselves in material activities. The result is that there is no end to material activities life after life.

Before us there are varieties of living entities, and everyone is entangled in transmigrations and activities. Our duty is simply to surrender unto the Supreme Personality of Godhead and let Him take charge, for He knows what is good for us.

Pṛthu Mahārāja therefore tells the Lord that as the Supreme Father He may elect to bestow whatever He considers beneficial for Pṛthu Mahārāja. That is the perfect position of the living entity. Therefore Śrī Caitanya Mahāprabhu teaches us in His *Śikṣāṣṭaka:*

na dhanaṁ na janaṁ na sundarīṁ kavitāṁ vā jagad-īśa kāmaye
mama janmani janmanīśvare bhavatād bhaktir ahaitukī tvayi

"O Almighty Lord! I have no desire to accumulate wealth, nor have I any desire to enjoy beautiful women, nor do I want any number of followers. I only want Your causeless devotional service in my life, birth after birth."

The conclusion is that the pure devotee should not aspire after any material benefit from devotional service, nor should he be enamored by fruitive activities or philosophical speculation. He should always be engaged favorably in the service of the Lord. That is the highest perfection of life.

TEXT 32

मैत्रेय उवाच
इत्यादिराजेन नुतः स विश्वदृक्
तमाह राजन् मयि भक्तिरस्तु ते ।
दिष्ट्येदृशी धीर्मयि ते कृता यया
मायां मदीयां तरति स्म दुस्त्यजाम् ॥३२॥

maitreya uvāca
ity ādi-rājena nutaḥ sa viśva-dṛk
tam āha rājan mayi bhaktir astu te
diṣṭyedṛśī dhīr mayi te kṛtā yayā
māyāṁ madīyāṁ tarati sma dustyajām

maitreyaḥ—Maitreya, the great sage; *uvāca*—spoke; *iti*—thus; *ādi-rājena*—by the original King (Pṛthu); *nutaḥ*—being worshiped; *saḥ*—He (the Supreme Personality of Godhead); *viśva-dṛk*—the seer of the whole universe; *tam*—unto him; *āha*—said; *rājan*—my dear King; *mayi*—unto Me; *bhaktiḥ*—devotional service; *astu*—let it be; *te*—your; *diṣṭyā*—by good fortune; *īdṛśī*—like this; *dhīḥ*—intelligence; *mayi*—unto Me; *te*—by you; *kṛtā*—having been performed; *yayā*—by which; *māyām*—illusory energy; *madīyām*—My; *tarati*—crosses over; *sma*—certainly; *dustyajām*—very difficult to give up.

TRANSLATION

The great sage Maitreya continued to speak: The Lord, the seer of the universe, after hearing Pṛthu Mahārāja's prayer, addressed the King: My dear King, may you always be blessed by engaging in My devotional service. Only by such purity of purpose, as you yourself very intelligently express, can one cross over the insurmountable illusory energy of māyā.

PURPORT

This is also confirmed in *Bhagavad-gītā* wherein the Lord also claims that the illusory energy is insurmountable. No one can transcend the illusory energy of *māyā* by fruitive activity, speculative philosophy or mystic *yoga*. The only means for transcending illusory energy is devotional service, as the Lord Himself states.

mām eva ye prapadyante
māyām etāṁ taranti te (Bg. 7.14)

If one wants to cross over the ocean of material existence, there is no alternative than to take to devotional service. A devotee, therefore, should not care for any material position, whether in heaven or in hell. A pure devotee should always engage in the service of the Lord, for that is his real occupation. Simply by sticking to that position one can overcome the stringent laws of material nature.

TEXT 33

तत्त्वं कुरु मयाऽऽदिष्टमप्रमत्तः प्रजापते ।
मदादेशकरो लोकः सर्वत्राप्नोति शोभनम् ॥३३॥

tat tvaṁ kuru mayādiṣṭam
apramattaḥ prajāpate

mad-ādeśa-karo lokaḥ
sarvatrāpnoti śobhanam

tat—therefore; *tvam*—you; *kuru*—do; *mayā*—by Me; *ādiṣṭam*—what is ordered; *apramattaḥ*—without being misguided; *prajā-pate*—O master of the citizens; *mat*—of Me; *ādeśa-karaḥ*—who executes the order; *lokaḥ*—any person; *sarvatra*—everywhere; *āpnoti*—achieves; *śobhanam*—all good fortune.

TRANSLATION

My dear King, O protector of the citizens, henceforward be very careful to execute My orders and not be misled by anything. Anyone who lives in that way, simply carrying out My orders faithfully, will always find good fortune all over the world.

PURPORT

The sum and substance of religious life is to execute the orders of the Supreme Personality of Godhead, and one who does so is perfectly religious. In *Bhagavad-gītā* the Supreme Lord Kṛṣṇa says, *man-manā bhava mad-bhaktaḥ:* "Just think of Me always and become My devotee." (Bg. 18.65) Furthermore, the Lord says, *sarva-dharmān parityajya māṁ ekaṁ śaraṇaṁ vraja:* "Give up all kinds of material engagement and simply surrender unto Me." (Bg. 18.66) This is the primary principle of religion. Anyone who directly executes such an order from the Personality of Godhead is actually a religious person. Others are described as pretenders, for there are many activities going on throughout the world in the name of religion which are not actually religious. For one who executes the order of the Supreme Personality of Godhead, however, there is only good fortune throughout the world.

TEXT 34

मैत्रेय उवाच

इति वैन्यस्य राजर्षेः प्रतिनन्द्यार्थवद्वचः ।
पूजितोऽनुगृहीत्वैनं गन्तुं चक्रेऽच्युतो मतिम् ॥३४॥

maitreya uvāca
iti vainyasya rājarṣeḥ
pratinandyārthavad vacaḥ

pūjito 'nugṛhītvainaṁ
gantuṁ cakre 'cyuto matim

maitreyaḥ uvāca—the great sage Maitreya continued to speak; *iti*—thus; *vainyasya*—of the son of King Vena (Pṛthu Mahārāja); *rāja-ṛṣeḥ*—of the saintly King; *pratinandya*—appreciating; *artha-vat vacaḥ*—the prayers, which were full of meaning; *pūjitaḥ*—being worshiped; *anugṛhītvā*—sufficiently benedicting; *enam*—King Pṛthu; *gantum*—to go from that place; *cakre*—made up; *acyutaḥ*—the infallible Lord; *matim*—His mind.

TRANSLATION

The great saint Maitreya told Vidura: The Supreme Personality of Godhead amply appreciated the meaningful prayers of Mahārāja Pṛthu. Thus, after being properly worshiped by the King, the Lord benedicted him and decided to depart.

PURPORT

Most important in this verse are the words *pratinandyārthavad vacaḥ,* which indicate that the Lord appreciated the very meaningful prayers of the King. When a devotee prays to the Lord, it is not to ask for material benefits but to ask the Lord for His favor; he prays that he may be engaged in the service of the Lord's lotus feet birth after birth. Lord Caitanya therefore uses the words *mama janmani janmani,* which mean "birth after birth," because a devotee is not even interested in stopping the repetition of birth. The Lord and the devotee appear in this material world birth after birth, but such births are transcendental. In the Fourth Chapter of *Bhagavad-gītā* the Lord informed Arjuna that both He and Arjuna had undergone many, many births previously, but the Lord remembered everything about them whereas Arjuna had forgotten. The Lord and His confidential devotees appear many times to fulfill the Lord's mission, but since such births are transcendental, they are not accompanied by the miserable conditions of material birth, and they are therefore called *divya,* transcendental.

One must understand the transcendental birth of the Lord and the devotee. The purpose of the Lord's taking birth is to establish devotional service, which is the perfect system of religion, and the purpose of the birth of a devotee is to broadcast the same system of religion, or the *bhakti* cult, all over the world. Pṛthu Mahārāja was an incarnation of the power of the Lord to spread the *bhakti* cult, and the Lord blessed him to remain fixed in his position. Thus when the King refused to accept any material benediction, the Lord appreciated that refusal very much. Another significant word in this verse is *acyuta,* which means "infallible." Although the Lord appears in this material world, He is never to be considered one of the conditioned souls, who are all fallible. When the Lord appears, He remains in His spiritual position, uncontaminated by the modes of material nature, and therefore in *Bhagavad-gītā* the Lord expresses the quality of His appearance as *ātma-māyayā,* "performed by internal potency." The Lord, being infallible, is not forced by material nature to take birth in this material world. He appears in order to reestablish the perfect order of religious principles and to vanquish the demoniac influence in human society.

TEXTS 35-36

देवर्षिपितृगन्धर्वसिद्धचारणपन्नगाः ।
किन्नराप्सरसो मर्त्याः खगा भूतान्यनेकशः ॥३५॥
यज्ञेश्वरधिया राज्ञा वाग्वित्ताञ्जलिभक्तितः ।
सभाजिता ययुः सर्वे वैकुण्ठानुगतास्ततः ॥३६॥

devarṣi-pitṛ-gandharva-
siddha-cāraṇa-pannagāḥ
kinnarāpsaraso martyāḥ
khagā bhūtāny anekaśaḥ

yajñeśvara-dhiyā rājñā
vāg-vittāñjali-bhaktitaḥ
sabhājitā yayuḥ sarve
vaikuṇṭhānugatās tataḥ

deva—the demigods; *ṛṣi*—the great sages; *pitṛ*—inhabitants of Pitṛloka; *gandharva*—inhabitants of Gandharvaloka; *siddha*—inhabitants of Siddhaloka; *cāraṇa*—inhabitants of the Cāraṇaloka; *pannagāḥ*—inhabitants of the planets where serpents live; *kinnara*—inhabitants of the Kinnara planets; *apsarasaḥ*—inhabitants of the Apsaroloka; *martyāḥ*—inhabitants of the earthly planets; *khagāḥ*—birds; *bhūtāni*—other living entities; *anekaśaḥ*—many; *yajña-īśvara-dhiyā*—with perfect intelligence of thinking as part and parcel of the Supreme Lord; *rājñā*—by the King; *vāk*—with sweet words; *vitta*—wealth; *añjali*—with folded hands; *bhaktitaḥ*—in a spirit of devotional service; *sabhājitāḥ*—being properly worshiped; *yayuḥ*—went; *sarve*—all; *vaikuṇṭha*—of the Supreme Personality of Godhead, Viṣṇu; *anugatāḥ*—followers; *tataḥ*—from that place.

TRANSLATION

King Pṛthu worshiped the demigods, the great sages, the inhabitants of Pitṛloka, the inhabitants of Gandharvaloka, and those of Siddhaloka, Cāraṇaloka, Pannagaloka, Kinnaraloka, Apsaroloka, the earthly planets and the planets of the birds. He also worshiped many other living entities who presented themselves in the sacrificial arena. With folded hands he worshiped all these, as well as the Supreme Personality of Godhead and the personal associates of the Lord, by offering sweet words and as much wealth as possible. After this function, they all went back to their respective abodes, following in the footsteps of Lord Viṣṇu.

PURPORT

In modern so-called scientific society the idea is very prevalent that there is no life on other planets but that only on this earth do living entities with intelligence and scientific knowledge exist. The Vedic literatures, however, do not accept this foolish theory. The followers of Vedic wisdom are fully aware of various planets inhabited by varieties of living entities such as the demigods, the sages, the Pitās, the Gandharvas, the Pannagas, the Kinnaras, the Cāraṇas, the Siddhas and the Apsarās. The *Vedas* give information that in all planets—not only within this material sky but also in the spiritual sky—there are varieties of living entities. Although all these living entities are of one spiritual nature, in quality the same as the Supreme Personality of Godhead, they have varieties of bodies due to the embodiment of the spirit soul by the eight material elements, namely, earth, water, fire, air, sky, mind, intelligence and false ego. In the spiritual world, however, there is no such distinction between the body and the embodied. In the material world, distinctive features are manifested in different types of bodies in the various planets. We have full information from the Vedic literature that in each and every planet, both material and spiritual, there are living entities of varied intelligence. The earth is one of the planets of the Bhūrloka planetary system. There are six planetary systems above Bhūrloka and seven planetary systems below it. Therefore the entire universe is known as *caturdaśa-bhuvana,* indicating that it has fourteen different planetary systems. Beyond the planetary systems in the material sky, there is another sky, which is known as *paravyoma,* or the spiritual sky, where there are spiritual planets. The inhabitants of those planets engage in varieties of loving service unto the Supreme Personality of Godhead, which include different *rasas* or relationships known as *dāsya-rasa, sakhya-rasa, vātsalya-rasa, mādhurya-rasa* and, above all, *parakīya-rasa.* This *parakīya-rasa,* or paramour love, is prevalent in Kṛṣṇaloka, where Lord Kṛṣṇa lives. This planet is also called Goloka Vṛndāvana, and although Lord Kṛṣṇa lives there perpetually, He also expands Himself in millions and trillions of forms. In one of such forms He appears on this material planet in a particular place known as Vṛndāvana-dhāma, where He displays His original pastimes of Goloka Vṛndāvana-dhāma in the spiritual sky in order to attract the conditioned souls back home, back to Godhead.

TEXT 37

भगवानपि राजर्षेः सोपाध्यायस्य चाच्युतः ।
हरन्निव मनोऽमुष्य स्वधाम प्रत्यपद्यत ॥३७॥

bhagavān api rājarṣeḥ
sopādhyāyasya cācyutaḥ
harann iva mano 'muṣya
sva-dhāma pratyapadyata

bhagavān—the Supreme Personality of Godhead; *api*—also; *rāja-ṛṣeḥ*—of the saintly King; *sa-upādhyāyasya*—along with all the priests; *ca*—also; *acyutaḥ*—the infallible Lord; *haran*—captivating; *iva*—indeed; *manaḥ*—the mind; *amuṣya*—of him; *sva-dhāma*—to His abode; *pratyapadyata*—returned.

TRANSLATION

The infallible Supreme Personality of Godhead, having captivated the minds of the King and the priests who were present, returned to His abode in the spiritual sky.

PURPORT

Because the Supreme Personality of Godhead is all-spiritual, He can descend from the spiritual sky without changing His body, and thus He is known as *acyuta,* or infallible. When a living entity falls down to the material world, however, he has to accept a material body, and therefore, in his material embodiment, he cannot be called *acyuta.* Because he falls down from his real engagement in the service of the Lord, the living entity gets a material body to suffer or try to enjoy in the miserable material conditions of life. Therefore the fallen living entity is *cyuta,* whereas the Lord is called *acyuta.* The Lord was attractive for everyone—not only the King but also the priestly order, who were very much addicted to the performance of Vedic rituals. Because the Lord is all-attractive, He is called Kṛṣṇa, or "one who attracts everyone." As will be explained in the next verse, the Lord appeared in the sacrificial arena of Mahārāja Pṛthu as Kṣīrodakaśāyī Viṣṇu, who is a plenary expansion of Lord Kṛṣṇa. He is the second incarnation from Kāraṇodakaśāyī Viṣṇu, who is the origin of material creation and who expands as Garbhodakaśāyī Viṣṇu, who then enters into each and every universe. Kṣīrodakaśāyī Viṣṇu is one of the *puruṣas* who control the material modes of nature.

TEXT 38

अदृष्टाय नमस्कृत्य नृपः सन्दर्शितात्मने ।
अव्यक्ताय च देवानां देवाय स्वपुरं ययौ ॥३८॥

adṛṣṭāya namas-kṛtya
nṛpaḥ sandarśitātmane
avyaktāya ca devānāṁ
devāya sva-puraṁ yayau

adṛṣṭāya—unto one who is beyond the purview of material vision; *namaḥ-kṛtya*—offering obeisances; *nṛpaḥ*—the King; *sandarśita*—revealed; *ātmane*—unto the Supreme Soul; *avyaktāya*—who is beyond the manifestation of the material world; *ca*—also; *devānām*—of the demigods; *devāya*—unto the Supreme Lord; *sva-puram*—to his own house; *yayau*—returned.

TRANSLATION

King Pṛthu then offered his respectful obeisances unto the Supreme Personality of Godhead, who is the Supreme Lord of all demigods. Although not an object of material vision, the Lord revealed Himself to the sight of Mahārāja Pṛthu. After offering obeisances to the Lord, the King returned to his home.

PURPORT

The Supreme Lord is not visible to material eyes, but when the material senses are inclined to the transcendental loving service of the Lord and are thus purified, the Lord reveals Himself to the vision of the devotee. *Avyakta* means "unmanifested." Although the material world is the creation of the Supreme Personality of Godhead, He is unmanifested to material eyes. Mahārāja Pṛthu, however, developed spiritual eyes by his pure devotional service. Here, therefore, the Lord is described as *sandarśitātmā,* for He reveals Himself to the vision of the devotee, although He is not visible to ordinary eyes.

Thus end the Bhaktivedanta purports of the Fourth Canto, Twentieth Chapter, of the Śrīmad-Bhāgavatam, *entitled "Lord Viṣṇu's Appearance in the Sacrificial Arena of Mahārāja Pṛthu."*

CHAPTER TWENTY-ONE

Instructions by Mahārāja Pṛthu

TEXT 1

मैत्रेय उवाच

मौक्तिकैः कुसुमस्रग्भिर्दुकूलैः स्वर्णतोरणैः ।
महासुरभिभिर्धूपैर्मण्डितं तत्र तत्र वै ॥ १ ॥

maitreya uvāca
mauktikaiḥ kusuma-sragbhir
dukūlaiḥ svarṇa-toraṇaiḥ
mahā-surabhibhir dhūpair
maṇḍitaṁ tatra tatra vai

maitreyaḥ uvāca—the great sage Maitreya continued to speak; *mauktikaiḥ*—with pearls; *kusuma*—of flowers; *sragbhiḥ*—with garlands; *dukūlaiḥ*—cloth; *svarṇa*—golden; *toraṇaiḥ*—by gates; *mahā-surabhibhiḥ*—highly perfumed; *dhūpaiḥ*—by incense; *maṇḍitam*—decorated; *tatra tatra*—here and there; *vai*—certainly.

TRANSLATION

The great sage Maitreya told Vidura: When the King entered his city, it was very beautifully decorated to receive him with pearls, flower garlands, beautiful cloth and golden gates, and the entire city was perfumed with highly fragrant incense.

PURPORT

Real opulence is supplied by natural gifts such as gold, silver, pearls, valuable stones, fresh flowers, trees and silken cloth. Thus the Vedic civilization recommends opulence and decoration with these natural gifts of the Supreme Personality of Godhead. Such opulence immediately changes the condition of the mind, and the entire atmosphere becomes spiritualized. King Pṛthu's capital was decorated with such highly opulent decorations.

TEXT 2

चन्दनागुरुतोयार्द्ररथ्याचत्वरमार्गवत् ।
पुष्पाक्षतफलैस्तोक्मैर्लाजैरर्चिर्भिरर्चितम् ॥ २ ॥

candanāguru-toyārdra-
rathyā-catvara-mārgavat
puṣpākṣata-phalais tokmair
lājair arcirbhir arcitam

candana—sandalwood; *aguru*—a kind of fragrant herb; *toya*—the water of; *ārdra*—sprinkled with; *rathyā*—a path for driving a chariot; *catvara*—small parks; *mārgavat*—lanes; *puṣpa*—flowers; *akṣata*—unbroken; *phalaiḥ*—by the fruits; *tokmaiḥ*—minerals; *lājaiḥ*—wetted grains; *arcirbhiḥ*—by lamps; *arcitam*—decorated.

TRANSLATION

Fragrant water distilled from sandalwood and aguru herb was sprinkled everywhere on the lanes, roads and small parks throughout the city, and everywhere were decorations of unbroken fruits, flowers, wetted grains, varied minerals, and lamps, all presented as auspicious paraphernalia.

TEXT 3

सवृन्दैः कदलीस्तम्भैः पूगपोतैः परिष्कृतम् ।
तरुपल्लवमालाभिः सर्वतः समलंकृतम् ॥ ३ ॥

savṛndaiḥ kadalī-stambhaiḥ
pūga-potaiḥ pariṣkṛtam
taru-pallava-mālābhiḥ
sarvataḥ samalaṅkṛtam

sa-vṛndaiḥ—along with fruits and flowers; *kadalī-stambhaiḥ*—by the pillars of banana trees; *pūga-potaiḥ*—by collections of young animals and by processions of elephants; *pariṣkṛtam*—very nicely cleansed; *taru*—young plants; *pallava*—new leaves of mango trees; *mālābhiḥ*—by garlands; *sarvataḥ*—everywhere; *samalaṅkṛtam*—nicely decorated.

TRANSLATION

At the street crossings there were bunches of fruits and flowers, as well as pillars of banana trees and betel nut branches. All these combined decorations everywhere looked very attractive.

TEXT 4

प्रजास्तं दीपबलिभिः सम्भृताशेषमङ्गलैः ।
अभीयुर्मृष्टकन्याश्च मृष्टकुण्डलमण्डिताः ॥ ४ ॥

prajās taṁ dīpa-balibhiḥ
sambhṛtāśeṣa-maṅgalaiḥ
abhīyur mṛṣṭa-kanyāś ca
mṛṣṭa-kuṇḍala-maṇḍitāḥ

prajāḥ—citizens; *tam*—to him; *dīpa-balibhiḥ*—with lamps; *sambhṛta*—equipped with; *aśeṣa*—unlimited; *maṅgalaiḥ*—auspicious articles; *abhīyuḥ*—came forward to welcome; *mṛṣṭa*—with beautiful bodily luster; *kanyāḥ ca*—and unmarried girls; *mṛṣṭa*—colliding with; *kuṇḍala*—earrings; *maṇḍitāḥ*—being bedecked with.

TRANSLATION

As the King entered the gate of the city, all the citizens received him with many auspicious articles like lamps, flowers and yogurt. The King was also received by many beautiful unmarried girls whose bodies were bedecked with various ornaments, especially with earrings which collided with one another.

PURPORT

Offerings of natural products such as betel nuts, bananas, newly grown wheat, paddy, yogurt and vermillion, carried by the citizens and scattered throughout the city, are all auspicious paraphernalia, according to Vedic civilization, for receiving a prominent guest like a bridegroom, king or spiritual master. Similarly, a welcome offered by unmarried girls who are internally and externally clean and are dressed in nice garments and ornaments is also auspicious. *Kumārī,* or unmarried girls untouched by the hand of any member of the opposite sex, are auspicious members of society. Even today in Hindu society the most conservative families do not allow unmarried girls to go out freely or mix with boys. They are very carefully protected by their parents while unmarried; after marriage they are protected by their young husbands, and when elderly they are protected by their children. When thus protected, women as a class remain an always auspicious source of energy to man.

TEXT 5

शङ्खदुन्दुभिघोषेण ब्रह्मघोषेण चर्त्विजाम् ।
विवेश भवनं वीरः स्तूयमानो गतस्मयः ॥ ५ ॥

śaṅkha-dundubhi-ghoṣeṇa
brahma-ghoṣeṇa cartvijām
viveśa bhavanaṁ vīraḥ
stūyamāno gatasmayaḥ

śaṅkha—conchshells; *dundubhi*—kettledrums; *ghoṣeṇa*—by the sound of; *brahma*—Vedic; *ghoṣeṇa*—chanting; *ca*—also; *ṛtvijām*—of the priests; *viveśa*—entered; *bhavanam*—the palace; *vīraḥ*—the King; *stūyamānaḥ*—being worshiped; *gata-smayaḥ*—without pride.

TRANSLATION

When the King entered the palace, conchshells and kettledrums were sounded, priests chanted Vedic mantras, and professional reciters offered different prayers. But in spite of all this ceremony to welcome him, the King was not the least bit affected.

PURPORT

The reception given to the King was full of opulence, yet he did not become proud. It is said, therefore, that great personalities of power and opulence never become proud, and the example is given that a tree which is full of fruits and flowers does not stand erect in pride but instead bends downwards to show submissiveness. This is a sign of the wonderful character of great personalities.

TEXT 6

पूजितः पूजयामास तत्र तत्र महायशाः ।
पौराञ्जानपदांस्तांस्तान् प्रीतः प्रियवरप्रदः ॥ ६ ॥

pūjitaḥ pūjayāmāsa
tatra tatra mahā-yaśāḥ
paurāñ jānapadāṁs tāṁs tān
prītaḥ priyavara-pradaḥ

pūjitaḥ—being worshiped; *pūjayāmāsa*—offered worship; *tatra tatra*—here and there; *mahā-yaśāḥ*—with a background of great activities; *paurān*—the noble men of the city; *jāna-padān*—common citizens; *tān tān*—in that way; *prītaḥ*—being satisfied; *priya-vara-pradaḥ*—was ready to offer them all benediction.

TRANSLATION

Both the important citizens and the common citizens welcomed the King very heartily, and he also benedicted them with their desired blessings.

PURPORT

A responsible king was always approachable by his citizens. Generally the citizens, great and common, all had an aspiration to see the king and take benediction from him. The king knew this, and therefore whenever he met the citizens he immediately fulfilled their desires or mitigated their grievances. In such dealings, a responsible monarchy is better than a so-called democratic government in which no one is responsible to mitigate the grievances of the citizens, who are unable to personally meet the supreme executive head. In a responsible monarchy the citizens had no grievances against the government, and even if they did, they could approach the king directly for immediate satisfaction.

TEXT 7

स एवमादीन्यनवद्यचेष्टितः
कर्माणि भूयांसि महान्महत्तमः ।
कुर्वन् शशासावनिमण्डलं यशः
स्फीतं निधायारुरुहे परं पदम् ॥ ७ ॥

sa evam ādīny anavadya-ceṣṭitaḥ
karmāṇi bhūyāṁsi mahān mahattamaḥ
kurvan śaśāsāvani-maṇḍalaṁ yaśaḥ
sphītaṁ nidhāyāruruhe paraṁ padam

saḥ—King Pṛthu; *evam*—thus; *ādīni*—from the very beginning; *anavadya*—magnanimous; *ceṣṭitaḥ*—performing various works; *karmāṇi*—work; *bhūyāṁsi*—repeatedly; *mahān*—great; *mahattamaḥ*—greater than the greatest; *kurvan*—performing; *śaśāsa*—ruled; *avani-maṇḍalam*—the surface of the earth; *yaśaḥ*—reputation; *sphītam*—widespread; *nidhāya*—achieving; *āruruhe*—was elevated; *param padam*—to the lotus feet of the Supreme Lord.

TRANSLATION

King Pṛthu was greater than the greatest soul and was therefore worshipable by everyone. He performed many glorious activities in ruling over the surface of the world and was always magnanimous. After achieving such great success and a reputation which spread throughout the universe, he at last obtained the lotus feet of the Supreme Personality of Godhead.

PURPORT

A responsible king or chief executive has many responsible duties to attend to in ruling over the citizens. The most important duty of the monarch or the government is to perform various sacrifices as enjoined in the Vedic literatures. The next duty of the king is to see that every citizen executes the prescribed duties for his particular community. It is the king's duty to see that everyone perfectly executes the duties prescribed for the *varṇa* and *āśrama* divisions of society. Besides that, as exemplified by King Pṛthu, he must develop the earth for the greatest possible production of food grains.

There are different types of great personalities—some are positive great personalities, some comparative and some superlative—but King Pṛthu exceeded all of them. He is therefore described here as *mahattamaḥ,* "greater than the greatest." Mahārāja Pṛthu was a *kṣatriya,* and he discharged his *kṣatriya* duties perfectly. Similarly, *brāhmaṇas, vaiśyas* and *śūdras* can discharge their respective duties perfectly and thus at the ultimate end of life be promoted to the transcendental world, which is called *paraṁ padam. Paraṁ padam,* or the Vaikuṇṭha planets, can be achieved only by devotional service. The impersonal Brahman region is also called *paraṁ padam,* but unless one is attached to the Personality of Godhead one must again fall down to the material world from the impersonal *paraṁ padam* situation. It is said, therefore, *āruhya kṛcchreṇa paraṁ padaṁ tataḥ:* the impersonalists endeavor very strenuously to achieve the *paraṁ padam* or impersonal *brahmajyoti,* but unfortunately, being bereft of a relationship with the Supreme Personality of Godhead, they come down again to the material world. If one flies in outer space, he can go very high up, but unless he reaches a planet he must come down again to earth. Similarly, because the impersonalists who reach the *paraṁ padam* of the impersonal *brahmajyoti* do not enter into the Vaikuṇṭha planets, they come down again to this material world and are given shelter in one of the material planets. Although they may attain Brahmaloka or Satyaloka, all such planets are situated in the material world.

TEXT 8

सूत उवाच
तदादिराजस्य यशो विजृम्भितं
गुणैरशेषैर्गुणवत्सभाजितम् ।
क्षत्ता महाभागवतः सदस्पते
कौषारविं प्राह गृणन्तमर्चयन् ॥ ८ ॥

sūta uvāca
tad ādi-rājasya yaśo vijṛmbhitaṁ
guṇair aśeṣair guṇavat-sabhājitam
kṣattā mahābhāgavataḥ sadaspate
kauṣāraviṁ prāha gṛṇantam arcayan

sūtaḥ uvāca—Sūta Gosvāmī said; *tat*—that; *ādi-rājasya*—of the original king; *yaśaḥ*—reputation; *vijṛmbhitam*—highly qualified; *guṇaiḥ*—by qualities; *aśeṣaiḥ*—unlimited; *guṇavat*—fittingly; *sabhājitam*—being praised; *kṣattā*—Vidura; *mahā-bhāgavataḥ*—the great saintly devotee; *sadaspate*—leader of the great sages; *kauṣāravim*—unto Maitreya; *prāha*—said; *gṛṇantam*—while talking; *arcayan*—offering all respectful obeisances.

TRANSLATION

Sūta Gosvāmī continued: O Śaunaka, leader of the great sages, after hearing Maitreya speak about the various activities of King Pṛthu, the original King, who was fully qualified, glorified and widely praised all over the world, Vidura, the great devotee, very submissively worshiped Maitreya Ṛṣi and asked him the following question.

TEXT 9

विदुर उवाच
सोऽभिषिक्तः पृथुर्विप्रैर्लब्धाशेषसुरार्हणः ।
बिभ्रत् स वैष्णवं तेजो बाह्वोर्याभ्यां दुदोह गाम् ॥९॥

vidura uvāca
so 'bhiṣiktaḥ pṛthur viprair
labdhāśeṣa-surārhaṇaḥ
bibhrat sa vaiṣṇavaṁ tejo
bāhvor yābhyāṁ dudoha gām

viduraḥ uvāca—Vidura said; *saḥ*—he (King Pṛthu); *abhiṣiktaḥ*—when enthroned; *pṛthuḥ*—King Pṛthu; *vipraiḥ*—by the great sages and *brāhmaṇas; labdha*—achieved; *aśeṣa*—innumerable; *sura-arhaṇaḥ*—presentations by the demigods; *bibhrat*—expanding; *saḥ*—he; *vaiṣṇavam*—who has received through Lord Viṣṇu; *tejaḥ*—strength; *bāhvoḥ*—arms; *yābhyām*—by which; *dudoha*—exploited; *gām*—the earth.

TRANSLATION

Vidura said: My dear brāhmaṇa Maitreya, it is very enlightening to understand that King Pṛthu was enthroned by the great sages and brāhmaṇas. All the demigods presented him with innumerable gifts, and he also expanded his influence upon personally receiving strength from Lord Viṣṇu. Thus he greatly developed the earth.

PURPORT

Because Pṛthu Mahārāja was an empowered incarnation of Lord Viṣṇu and was naturally a great Vaiṣṇava devotee of the Lord, all the demigods were pleased with him and presented different gifts to help him in exercising his royal power, and the great sages and saintly persons also joined in his coronation. Thus blessed by them, he ruled over the earth and exploited its resources for the greatest satisfaction of the people in general. This has already been explained in the previous chapters regarding the activities of King Pṛthu. As will be apparent from the next verse, every executive head of state should follow in the footsteps of Mahārāja Pṛthu in ruling over his kingdom. Regardless of whether the chief executive is a king or president, or whether the government is monarchical or democratic, this process is so perfect that if it is followed, everyone will become happy, and thus it will be very easy for all to execute devotional service to the Supreme Personality of Godhead.

TEXT 10

को न्वस्य कीर्तिं न शृणोत्यभिज्ञो
यद्विक्रमोच्छिष्टमशेषभूपाः ।
लोकाः सपाला उपजीवन्ति काम-
मद्यापि तन्मे वद कर्म शुद्धम् ॥१०॥

ko nv asya kīrtiṁ na śṛṇoty abhijño
yad-vikramocchiṣṭam aśeṣabhūpāḥ

lokāḥ sapālā upajīvanti kāmam
adyāpi tan me vada karma śuddham

kaḥ—who; *nu*—but; *asya*—King Pṛthu; *kīrtim*—glorious activities; *na śṛṇoti*—does not hear; *abhijñaḥ*—intelligent; *yat*—his; *vikrama*—chivalry; *ucchiṣṭam*—remnants; *aśeṣa*—innumerable; *bhūpāḥ*—kings; *lokāḥ*—planets; *sa-pālāḥ*—with their demigods; *upajīvanti*—execute livelihood; *kāmam*—desired objects; *adyāpi*—up to that; *tat*—that; *me*—unto me; *vada*—please speak; *karma*—activities; *śuddham*—auspicious.

TRANSLATION

Pṛthu Mahārāja was so great in his activities and magnanimous in his method of ruling that all the kings and demigods on the various planets still follow in his footsteps. Who is there who will not try to hear about his glorious activities? I wish to hear more and more about Pṛthu Mahārāja because his activities are so pious and auspicious.

PURPORT

Saint Vidura's purpose in hearing about Pṛthu Mahārāja over and over again was to set an example for ordinary kings and executive heads, who should all be inclined to hear repeatedly about Pṛthu Mahārāja's activities in order to also be able to rule over their kingdoms or states very faithfully for the peace and prosperity of the people in general. Unfortunately, at the present moment no one cares to hear about Pṛthu Mahārāja or to follow in his footsteps; therefore no nation in the world is either happy or progressive in spiritual understanding, although that is the sole aim and objective of human life.

TEXT 11

मैत्रेय उवाच
गङ्गायमुनयोर्नद्योरन्तरा क्षेत्रमावसन् ।
आरब्धानेव बुभुजे भोगान् पुण्यजिहासया ॥११॥

maitreya uvāca
gaṅgā-yamunayor nadyor
antarā kṣetram āvasan
ārabdhān eva bubhuje
bhogān puṇya-jihāsayā

maitreyaḥ uvāca—the great saint Maitreya said; *gaṅgā*—the River Ganges; *yamunayoḥ*—of the River Yamunā; *nadyoḥ*—of the two rivers; *antarā*—between; *kṣetram*—the land; *āvasan*—living there; *ārabdhān*—destined; *eva*—like; *bubhuje*—enjoyed; *bhogān*—fortunes; *puṇya*—pious activities; *jihāsayā*—for the purpose of diminishing.

TRANSLATION

The great saintly sage Maitreya told Vidura: My dear Vidura, King Pṛthu lived in the tract of land between the two great rivers Ganges and Yamunā. Because he was very opulent, it appeared that he was enjoying his destined fortune in order to diminish the results of his past pious activities.

PURPORT

The terms "pious" and "impious" are applicable only in reference to the activities of an ordinary living being. But Mahārāja Pṛthu was a directly empowered incarnation of Lord Viṣṇu; therefore he was not subject to the reactions of pious or impious activities. As we have already explained previously, when a living being is specifically empowered by the Supreme Lord to act for a particular purpose, he is called a *śaktyāveśa-avatāra.* Pṛthu Mahārāja was not only a *śaktyāveśa-avatāra* but also a great devotee. A devotee is not subjected to the reactions resulting from past deeds. In the *Brahma-saṁhitā* it is said, *karmāṇi nirdahati kintu ca bhakti-bhājām:* for devotees the results of past pious and impious activities are nullified by the Supreme Personality of Godhead. The words *ārabdhān eva* mean "as if achieved by past deeds," but in the case of Pṛthu Mahārāja there was no question of reaction to past deeds, and thus the word *eva* is used here to indicate comparison to ordinary persons. In *Bhagavad-gītā* the Lord says, *avajānanti māṁ mūḍhāḥ.* This means that sometimes people misunderstand an incarnation of the Supreme Personality of Godhead to be an ordinary man. The Supreme Godhead, His incarnations or His devotees may pose themselves as ordinary men, but they are never to be considered as such. Nor should an ordinary man not supported by authorized statements of the *śāstras* and *ācāryas* be accepted as an incarnation or devotee. By the evidence of *śāstra,* Sanātana Gosvāmī detected Lord Caitanya Mahāprabhu to be a direct incarnation of Kṛṣṇa, the Supreme Personality of Godhead, although Lord Caitanya never disclosed the fact. It is therefore generally recommended that the *ācārya* or *guru* should not be accepted as an ordinary man.

TEXT 12

सर्वत्रास्खलितादेशः सप्तद्वीपैकदण्डधृक् ।
अन्यत्र ब्राह्मणकुलादन्यत्राच्युतगोत्रतः ॥१२॥

sarvatrāskhalitādeśaḥ
sapta-dvīpaika-daṇḍadhṛk
anyatra brāhmaṇa-kulād
anyatrācyuta-gotrataḥ

sarvatra—everywhere; *askhalita*—irrevocable; *ādeśaḥ*—order; *sapta-dvīpa*—seven islands; *eka*—one; *daṇḍa-dhṛk*—the ruler who holds the scepter; *anyatra*—except; *brāhmaṇa-kulāt*—*brāhmaṇas* and saintly persons; *anyatra*—except; *acyuta-gotrataḥ*—descendants of the Supreme Personality of Godhead (Vaiṣṇavas).

TRANSLATION

Mahārāja Pṛthu was an unrivalled king and possessed the scepter for ruling all the seven islands on the surface of the globe. No one could disobey his irrevocable orders but the saintly persons, the brāhmaṇas and the descendants of the Supreme Personality of Godhead [the Vaiṣṇavas].

PURPORT

Sapta-dvīpa refers to the seven great islands or continents on the surface of the globe: (1) Asia, (2) Europe, (3) Africa, (4) North America,(5) South America, (6) Australia, and (7) Oceania. In the modern age people are under the impression that during the Vedic period or the prehistoric ages America and many other parts of the world had not been discovered, but that is not a fact. Pṛthu Mahārāja ruled over the world many thousands of years before the so-called prehistoric age, and it is clearly mentioned here that in those days not only were all the different parts of the world known, but they were ruled by one king, Mahārāja Pṛthu. The country where Pṛthu Mahārāja resided must have been India because it is stated in the eleventh verse of this chapter that he lived in the tract of land called Brahmāvarta, which consists of what is known in the modern age as portions of Punjab and northern India. It is clear that the kings of India once ruled all the world and that their culture was Vedic.

The word *askhalita* indicates that orders by the king could not be disobeyed by anyone in the entire world. Such orders, however, were never issued to control saintly persons or the descendants of the Supreme Personality of Godhead, Viṣṇu. The Supreme Lord is known as *acyuta,* and Lord Kṛṣṇa is addressed as such by Arjuna in *Bhagavad-gītā (senayor ubhayor madhye rathaṁ sthāpaya me 'cyuta). Acyuta* refers to one who does not fall because He is never influenced by the modes of material nature. When a living entity falls down to the material world from his original position, he becomes *cyuta,* which means that he forgets his relationship with *acyuta.* Actually every living entity is a part and parcel or a son of the Supreme Personality of Godhead. When influenced by the modes of material nature, a living entity forgets this relationship and thinks in terms of different species of life; but when he again comes to his original consciousness, he does not observe such bodily designations. This is indicated in *Bhagavad-gītā* by the words *paṇḍitāḥ sama-darśinaḥ* (Bg. 5.18).

Material designations create differentiation in terms of caste, color, creed, nationality, etc. Different *gotras* or family designations are distinctions in terms of the material body, but when one comes to Kṛṣṇa consciousness he immediately becomes transcendental to all considerations of caste, creed, color and nationality.

Pṛthu Mahārāja had no control over the *brāhmaṇa-kula,* which refers to the learned scholars in Vedic knowledge, nor over the Vaiṣṇavas, who are above the considerations of Vedic knowledge. It is therefore said:

arcye viṣṇau śilādhīr guruṣu nara-matir vaiṣṇave jāti-buddhir
viṣṇor vā vaiṣṇavānāṁ kali-mala-mathane pāda-tīrthe 'mbu-buddhiḥ
śrī-viṣṇor nāmni mantre sakala-kaluṣa-he śabda-sāmānya-buddhir
viṣṇau sarveśvareśe tad-itara-sama-dhīr yasya vā nārakī saḥ

"One who thinks the Deity in the temple to be made of wood or stone, who thinks of the spiritual master in the disciplic succession as an ordinary man, who thinks the Vaiṣṇava in the *acyuta-gotra* to belong to a certain caste or creed, or who thinks of *caraṇāmṛta* or Ganges water as ordinary water, is taken to be a resident of hell." *(Padma Purāṇa)*

From the facts presented in this verse, it appears that people in general should be controlled by a king until they come to the platform of Vaiṣṇavas and *brāhmaṇas,* who are not under the control of anyone. *Brāhmaṇa* refers to one who knows Brahman, or the impersonal feature of the Absolute Truth, and a Vaiṣṇava is one who serves the Supreme Personality of Godhead.

TEXT 13

एकदाऽऽसीन्महासत्रदीक्षा तत्र दिवौकसाम् ।
समाजो ब्रह्मर्षीणां च राजर्षीणां च सत्तम ॥१३॥

ekadāsīn mahāsatra-
dīkṣā tatra divaukasām
samājo brahmarṣīṇāṁ ca
rājarṣīṇāṁ ca sattama

ekadā—once upon a time; *āsīt*—took a vow; *mahā-satra*—great sacrifice; *dīkṣā*—initiation; *tatra*—in that function; *divaukasām*—of the demigods; *samājaḥ*—assembly; *brahmarṣīṇām*—of great saintly *brāhmaṇas; ca*—also; *rājarṣīṇām*—of great saintly kings; *ca*—also; *sattama*—the greatest of devotees.

TRANSLATION

Once upon a time King Pṛthu Mahārāja initiated the performance of a very great sacrifice in which great saintly sages, brāhmaṇas, demigods from higher planetary systems and great saintly kings known as rājarṣis all assembled together.

PURPORT

In this verse the most significant point is that although King Pṛthu's residential quarters were in India, between the rivers Ganges and Yamunā, the demigods also participated in the great sacrifice he performed. This indicates that formerly the demigods used to come to this planet. Similarly, great personalities like Arjuna, Yudhiṣṭhira and many others used to visit higher planetary systems. Thus there was interplanetary communication via suitable airplanes and space vehicles.

TEXT 14

तस्मिन्नर्हत्सु सर्वेषु स्वर्चितेषु यथार्हतः ।
उत्थितः सदसो मध्ये ताराणामुडुराडिव ॥१४॥

tasminn arhatsu sarveṣu
sv-arciteṣu yathārhataḥ
utthitaḥ sadaso madhye
tārāṇām uḍurāḍ iva

tasmin—in that great meeting; *arhatsu*—of all those who are worshipable; *sarveṣu*—all of them; *su-arciteṣu*—being worshiped according to their respective positions; *yathārhataḥ*—as they deserved; *utthitaḥ*—stood up; *sadasaḥ*—amongst the assembly members; *madhye*—within the midst; *tārāṇām*—of the stars; *uḍu-rāṭ*—the moon; *iva*—like.

TRANSLATION

In that great assembly, Mahārāja Pṛthu first of all worshiped all the respectable visitors according to their respective positions. After this, he stood up in the midst of the assembly, and it appeared that the full moon had arisen amongst the stars.

PURPORT

According to the Vedic system, the reception of great, exalted personalities, as arranged by Pṛthu Mahārāja in that great sacrificial arena, is very important. The first procedure in receiving guests is to wash their feet, and it is learned from Vedic literature that one time when Mahārāja Yudhiṣṭhira performed a *rājasūya-yajña*, Kṛṣṇa took charge of washing the feet of the visitors. Similarly, Mahārāja Pṛthu also arranged for the proper reception of the demigods, the saintly sages, the *brāhmaṇas* and the great kings.

TEXT 15

प्रांशुः पीनायतभुजो गौरः कञ्जारुणेक्षणः ।
सुनासः सुमुखः सौम्यः पीनांसः सुद्विजस्मितः ॥१५॥

prāṁśuḥ pīnāyata-bhujo
gauraḥ kañjāruṇekṣaṇaḥ
sunāsaḥ sumukhaḥ saumyaḥ
pīnāṁsaḥ su-dvija-smitaḥ

prāṁśuḥ—very tall; *pīnāyata*—full and broad; *bhujaḥ*—arms; *gauraḥ*—fair complexioned; *kañja*—lotuslike; *aruṇa-īkṣaṇaḥ*—with bright eyes like a morning sunrise; *su-nāsaḥ*—straight nose; *su-mukhaḥ*—with a beautiful face; *saumyaḥ*—of a grave bodily stature; *pīna-aṁsaḥ*—shoulders raised; *su*—beautiful; *dvija*—teeth; *smitaḥ*—smiling.

TRANSLATION

King Pṛthu's body was tall and sturdy, and his complexion was fair. His arms were full and broad and his eyes as bright as the rising sun. His nose

was straight, his face very beautiful and his personality grave. His teeth were set beautifully in his smiling face.

PURPORT

Amongst the four social orders *(brāhmaṇas, kṣatriyas, vaiśyas* and *śūdras),* the *kṣatriyas,* both men and women, are generally very beautiful. As will be apparent from the following verses, it is to be concluded that not only were Mahārāja Pṛthu's bodily features attractive, as described here, but he had specific all-auspicious signs in his bodily construction.

As it is said, "The face is the index of the mind." One's mental constitution is exhibited by his facial features. The bodily features of a particular person are exhibited in accordance with his past deeds, for according to one's past deeds, his next bodily features—whether in human society, animal society or demigod society—are determined. This is proof of the transmigration of the soul through different types of bodies.

TEXT 16

व्यूढवक्षा बृहच्छ्रोणिर्वलिवल्गुदलोदरः ।
आवर्तनाभिरोजस्वी काञ्चनोरुरुदग्रपात् ॥१६॥

vyūḍha-vakṣā bṛhac-chroṇir
vali-valgu-dalodaraḥ
āvarta-nābhir ojasvī
kāñcanorur udagra-pāt

vyūḍha—broad; *vakṣāḥ*—chest; *bṛhat-śroṇiḥ*—thick waist; *vali*—wrinkles; *valgu*—very beautiful; *dala*—like a leaf of a banyan tree; *udaraḥ*—abdomen; *āvarta*—coiled; *nābhiḥ*—navel; *ojasvī*—lustrous; *kāñcana*—golden; *uruḥ*—thighs; *udagra-pāt*—arched instep.

TRANSLATION

The chest of Mahārāja Pṛthu was very broad, his waist was very thick, and his abdomen, wrinkled by lines of skin, resembled in construction a banyan tree. His navel was coiled and deep, his thighs were of a golden hue, and his instep was arched.

TEXT 17

सूक्ष्मवक्रासितस्निग्धमूर्धजः कम्बुकन्धरः ।
महाधने दुकूलाग्र्ये परिधायोपवीय च ॥१७॥

sūkṣma-vakrāsita-snigdha-
mūrdhajaḥ kambu-kandharaḥ
mahā-dhane dukūlāgrye
paridhāyopavīya ca

sūkṣma—very fine; *vakra*—curly; *asita*—black; *snigdha*—greasy; *mūrdhajaḥ*—hairs on the head; *kambu*—like a conch; *kandharaḥ*—neck; *mahā-dhane*—very valuable; *dukūla-agrye*—dressed with a dhoti; *paridhāya*—on the upper portion of the body; *upavīya*—placed like a sacred thread; *ca*—also.

TRANSLATION

The black, slick hair on his head was very fine and curly, and his neck, like a conchshell, was decorated with auspicious lines. He wore a very valuable dhoti, and there was a nice wrapper on the upper part of his body.

TEXT 18

व्यञ्जिताशेषगात्रश्रीर्नियमे न्यस्तभूषणः ।
कृष्णाजिनधरः श्रीमान् कुशपाणिः कृतोचितः ॥१८॥

vyañjitāśeṣa-gātra-śrīr
niyame nyasta-bhūṣaṇaḥ
kṛṣṇājina-dharaḥ śrīmān
kuśa-pāṇiḥ kṛtocitaḥ

vyañjita—indicating; *aśeṣa*—innumerable; *gātra*—bodily; *śrīḥ*—beauty; *niyame*—regulated; *nyasta*—given up; *bhūṣaṇaḥ*—garments; *kṛṣṇa*—black; *ajina*—skin; *dharaḥ*—putting on; *śrīmān*—beautiful; *kuśa-pāṇiḥ*—having *kuśa* grass on the fingers; *kṛta*—performed; *ucitaḥ*—as it is required.

TRANSLATION

As Mahārāja Pṛthu was being initiated to perform the sacrifice, he had to leave aside his valuable dress, and therefore his natural bodily beauty was visible. It was very pleasing to see him put on a black deerskin and wear a ring of kuśa grass on his finger, for this increased the natural beauty of his body. It appears that Mahārāja Pṛthu observed all the regulative principles before he performed the sacrifice.

TEXT 19

शिशिरस्निग्धताराक्षः समैक्षत समन्ततः ।
ऊचिवानिदमुर्वीशः सदः संहर्षयन्निव ॥१९॥

śiśira-snigdha-tārākṣaḥ
samaikṣata samantataḥ
ūcivān idam urvīśaḥ
sadaḥ saṁharṣayann iva

śiśira—dew; *snigdha*—wet; *tārā*—stars; *akṣaḥ*—eyes; *samaikṣata*—glanced over; *samantataḥ*—all around; *ūcivān*—began to speak; *idam*—this; *urvīśaḥ*—highly elevated; *sadaḥ*—amongst the members of the assembly; *saṁharṣayan*—enhancing their pleasure; *iva*—like.

TRANSLATION

Just to encourage the members of the assembly and to enhance their pleasure, King Pṛthu glanced over them with eyes that seemed like stars in a sky wet with dew. He then spoke to them in a great voice.

TEXT 20

चारु चित्रपदं श्लक्ष्णं मृष्टं गूढमविक्लवम् ।
सर्वेषामुपकारार्थं तदा अनुवदन्निव ॥२०॥

cāru citra-padaṁ ślakṣṇaṁ
mṛṣṭaṁ gūḍham aviklavam
sarveṣām upakārārthaṁ
tadā anuvadann iva

cāru—beautiful; *citra-padam*—flowery; *ślakṣṇam*—very clear; *mṛṣṭam*—very great; *gūḍham*—meaningful; *aviklavam*—without any doubt; *sarveṣām*—for all; *upakāra-artham*—just to benefit them; *tadā*—at that time; *anuvadan*—began to repeat; *iva*—like.

TRANSLATION

Mahārāja Pṛthu's speech was very beautiful, full of metaphorical language, clearly understandable and very pleasing to hear. His words were all grave and certain. It appears that when he spoke, he expressed his personal realization of the Absolute Truth in order to benefit all who were present.

PURPORT

Mahārāja Pṛthu was beautiful in his external bodily features, and his speech was also very glorious in all respects. His words, which were nicely composed in highly metaphorical ornamental language, were pleasing to hear and were not only mellow but also very clearly understandable and without doubt or ambiguity.

TEXT 21

राजोवाच
सभ्याः शृणुत भद्रं वः साधवो य इहागताः ।
सत्सु जिज्ञासुभिर्धर्ममावेद्यं स्वमनीषितम् ॥२१॥

rājovāca
sabhyāḥ śṛṇuta bhadraṁ vaḥ
sādhavo ya ihāgatāḥ
satsu jijñāsubhir dharmam
āvedyaṁ sva-manīṣitam

rājā uvāca—the King began to speak; *sabhyāḥ*—addressing the ladies and gentlemen; *śṛṇuta*—kindly hear; *bhadram*—good fortune; *vaḥ*—your; *sādhavaḥ*—all great souls; *ye*—who; *iha*—here; *āgatāḥ*—present; *satsu*—unto the noble men; *jijñāsubhiḥ*—one who is inquisitive; *dharmam*—religious principles; *āvedyam*—must be presented; *sva-manīṣitam*—concluded by someone.

TRANSLATION

King Pṛthu said: O gentle members of the assembly, may all good fortune be upon you! May all of you great souls who have come to attend this meeting kindly hear my prayer attentively. A person who is actually inquisitive must present his decision before an assembly of noble souls.

PURPORT

In this verse the word *sādhavaḥ* ("all great souls") is very significant. When a person is very great and famous, many unscrupulous persons become his enemies, for envy is the nature of materialists. In any meeting there are different classes of men, and it is to be supposed, therefore, that because Pṛthu Mahārāja was very great, he must have had several enemies present in the assembly, although they could not express themselves. Mahārāja Pṛthu, however, was concerned with persons who were gentle, and therefore he first addressed all the honest persons, not caring for the envious. He did not, however, present himself as a royal authority empowered to command everyone because he wanted to present his statement in humble submission before the assembly of great sages and saintly persons. As a great king of the entire world, he could have given them orders, but he was so humble, meek and honest that he presented his statement for approval in order to clarify his mature decision. Everyone within this material world is conditioned by the modes of material nature and therefore has four defects. But although Pṛthu Mahārāja was above all these, still, like an ordinary conditioned soul, he presented his statements to the great souls, sages and saintly persons present there.

TEXT 22

अहं दण्डधरो राजा प्रजानामिह योजितः ।
रक्षिता वृत्तिदः स्वेषु सेतुषु स्थापिता पृथक् ॥२२॥

ahaṁ daṇḍa-dharo rājā
prajānām iha yojitaḥ
rakṣitā vṛtti-daḥ sveṣu
setuṣu sthāpitā pṛthak

aham—I; *daṇḍa-dharaḥ*—carrier of the scepter; *rājā*—king; *prajānām*—of the citizens; *iha*—in this world; *yojitāḥ*—engaged; *rakṣitā*—protector; *vṛtti-daḥ*—employer; *sveṣu*—in their own; *setuṣu*—respective social orders; *sthāpitā*—established; *pṛthak*—differently.

TRANSLATION

King Pṛthu continued: By the grace of the Supreme Lord I have been appointed the King of this planet, and I carry the scepter to rule the citizens, protect them from all danger and give them employment according to their respective positions in the social order established by Vedic injunction.

PURPORT

A king is supposed to be appointed by the Supreme Personality of Godhead to look after the interests of his particular planet. On every planet there is a predominating person, just as we now see that in every country there is a president. If one is president or king, it should be understood that this opportunity has been given to him by the Supreme Lord. According to the Vedic system, the king is considered a representative of Godhead and is offered respects by the citizens as God in the human form of life. Actually, according to Vedic information, the Supreme Lord maintains all living entities, and especially human beings, to elevate them to the highest perfection. After many, many births in lower species, when a living entity evolves to the human form of life and in particular to the civilized human form of life, his society must be divided into four gradations, as ordered by the Supreme Personality of Godhead in *Bhagavad-gītā (cātur-varṇyaṁ mayā sṛṣṭam,* etc.). The four social orders—the *brāhmaṇas, kṣatriyas, vaiśyas* and *śūdras*—are natural divisions of human society, and, as declared by Pṛthu Mahārāja, every man in his respective social order must have proper employment for his livelihood. It is the duty of the king or the government to insure that the people observe the social order and that they are also employed in their respective occupational duties. In modern times, since the protection of the government or the king has been withdrawn, social order has practically collapsed. No one knows who is a *brāhmaṇa,* who is a *kṣatriya,* who is a *vaiśya* or who is a *śūdra,* and people claim to belong to a particular social order by birthright only. It is the duty of the government to reestablish social order in terms of occupational duties and the modes of material nature, for that will make the entire world population actually civilized. If it does not observe the institutional functions of the four social orders, human society is no better than animal society in which there is never tranquility, peace and prosperity but only chaos and confusion. Mahārāja Pṛthu, as an ideal king, strictly observed the maintenance of the Vedic social order.

Prajāyate iti prajā. The word *prajā* refers to one who takes birth. Therefore Pṛthu Mahārāja guaranteed protection for *prajānām*—all living entities who took birth in his kingdom. *Prajā* refers not only to human beings but also to animals, trees and every other living entity. It is the duty of the king to give all living entities protection and food. The fools and rascals of modern society have no knowledge of the extent of the responsibility of the government. Animals are also citizens of the land in which they happen to be born, and they also have the right to continue their existence at the cost of the Supreme Lord. The disturbance of the animal population by wholesale slaughter produces a catastrophic future reaction for the butcher, his land and his government.

TEXT 23

तस्य मे तदनुष्ठानाद्यानाहुर्ब्रह्मवादिनः ।
लोकाः स्युः कामसन्दोहा यस्य तुष्यति दिष्टदृक् ॥२३॥

tasya me tad-anuṣṭhānād
yān āhur brahma-vādinaḥ
lokāḥ syuḥ kāma-sandohā
yasya tuṣyati diṣṭa-dṛk

tasya—his; *me*—mine; *tat*—that; *anuṣṭhānāt*—by executing; *yān*—that which; *āhuḥ*—is spoken; *brahma-vādinaḥ*—by the experts in Vedic knowledge; *lokāḥ*—planets; *syuḥ*—become; *kāma-sandohāḥ*—fulfilling one's desirable objectives; *yasya*—whose; *tuṣyati*—becomes satisfied; *diṣṭa-dṛk*—the seer of all destiny.

TRANSLATION

Mahārāja Pṛthu said: I think that upon the execution of my duties as king, I shall be able to achieve the desirable objectives described by experts in Vedic knowledge. This destination is certainly achieved by the pleasure of the Supreme Personality of Godhead, who is the seer of all destiny.

PURPORT

Mahārāja Pṛthu gives special stress to the word *brahma-vādinaḥ* ("by the experts in the Vedic knowledge"). *Brahma* refers to the *Vedas,* which are also known as *śabda-brahma,* or transcendental sound. Transcendental sound is not ordinary language, although it appears to be written in ordinary language. Evidence from the Vedic literature should be accepted as final authority. In the Vedic literature there is much information, and of course there is information about the execution of a king's duty. A responsible king who executes his appointed duty by giving proper protection to all living entities on his planet is promoted to the heavenly planetary system. This is also dependent upon the pleasure of the Supreme Lord. It is not that if one executes his duty properly he is automatically promoted, for promotion depends upon the satisfaction of the Supreme Personality of Godhead. It must ultimately be concluded that one can achieve the desired result of his activities upon satisfying the Supreme Lord. This is also confirmed in the Second Chapter, First Canto, of *Śrīmad-Bhāgavatam:*

ataḥ pumbhir dvija-śreṣṭhā
varṇāśrama-vibhāgaśaḥ
svanuṣṭhitasya dharmasya
saṁsiddhir hari-toṣaṇam.

The perfection of one's execution of his appointed duties is the ultimate satisfaction of the Supreme Lord. The word *kāma-sandohāḥ* means "achievement of the desired result." Everyone desires to achieve the ultimate goal of life, but in modern civilization the great scientists think that man's life has no plan. This gross ignorance is very dangerous and makes civilization very risky. People do not know the laws of nature, which are the rulings of the Supreme Personality of Godhead. Because they are atheists of the first order, they have no faith in the existence of God and His rulings and therefore do not know how nature is working. This gross ignorance of the mass of people, including even the so-called scientists and philosophers, makes life a risky situation in which human beings do not know whether they are making progress in life. According to *Śrīmad-Bhāgavatam,* they are simply progressing to the darkest region of material existence. *Adānta-gobhir viśatāṁ tamisram* (*Bhāg.* 7.5.30). The Kṛṣṇa consciousness movement has therefore been started to give philosophers, scientists and people in general the proper knowledge about the destiny of life. Everyone should take advantage of this movement and learn the real goal of life.

TEXT 24

य उद्धरेत्करं राजा प्रजा धर्मेष्वशिक्षयन् ।
प्रजानां शमलं भुङ्क्ते भगं च स्वं जहाति सः ॥२४॥

ya uddharet karaṁ rājā
prajā dharmeṣv aśikṣayan
prajānāṁ śamalaṁ bhuṅkte
bhagaṁ ca svaṁ jahāti saḥ

yaḥ—anyone (king or governor); *uddharet*—exact; *karam*—taxes; *rājā*—king; *prajāḥ*—the citizens; *dharmeṣu*—in executing their respective duties; *aśikṣayan*—without teaching them how to execute their respective duties; *prajānām*—of the citizens; *śamalam*—impious; *bhuṅkte*—enjoys; *bhagam*—fortune; *ca*—also; *svam*—own; *jahāti*—gives up; *saḥ*—that king.

TRANSLATION

Any king who does not teach his citizens about their respective duties in terms of varṇa and āśrama but who simply exacts tolls and taxes from them is liable to suffer for the impious activities which have been performed by the citizens. In addition to such degradation, the king also loses his own fortune.

PURPORT

A king, governor or president should not take the opportunity to occupy his post without also discharging his duty. He must teach the people within the state how to observe the divisions of *varṇa* and *āśrama.* If a king neglects to give such instructions and is simply satisfied with levying taxes, then those who share in the collection—namely, all the government servants and the head of the state—are liable to share in the impious activities of the general masses. The laws of nature are very subtle. For example, if one eats in a place which is very sinful, he shares in the resultant reaction of the sinful activities performed there. (It is a Vedic system, therefore, for a householder to call *brāhmaṇas* and Vaiṣṇavas to eat at ceremonial performances in his house because the *brāhmaṇas* and Vaiṣṇavas can immunize him from sinful activities. But it is not the duty of rigid *brāhmaṇas* and Vaiṣṇavas to accept invitations everywhere. There is, of course, no objection to taking part in feasts in which *prasāda* is distributed.) There are many subtle laws which are practically unknown to people in general, but the Kṛṣṇa consciousness movement is very scientifically distributing all this Vedic knowledge for the benefit of the people of the world.

TEXT 25

तत् प्रजा भर्तृपिण्डार्थं स्वार्थमेवानसूयवः ।
कुरुताधोक्षजधियस्तर्हि मेऽनुग्रहः कृतः ॥२५॥

tat prajā bhartṛ-piṇḍārthaṁ
svārtham evānasūyavaḥ
kurutādhokṣaja-dhiyas
tarhi me 'nugrahaḥ kṛtaḥ

tat—therefore; *prajāḥ*—my dear citizens; *bhartṛ*—of the master; *piṇḍa-artham*—welfare after death; *sva-artham*—own interest; *eva*—certainly; *anasūyavaḥ*—without being envious; *kuruta*—just execute; *adhokṣaja*—the Supreme Personality of Godhead; *dhiyaḥ*—thinking of Him; *tarhi*—therefore; *me*—unto me; *anugrahaḥ*—mercy; *kṛtaḥ*—being done.

TRANSLATION

Pṛthu Mahārāja continued: Therefore, my dear citizens, for the welfare of your king after his death, you should execute your duties properly in terms of your positions of varṇa and āśrama and should always think of the Supreme Personality of Godhead within your hearts. By doing so, your interests will be protected, and you will bestow mercy upon your king for his welfare after death.

PURPORT

The words *adhokṣaja-dhiyaḥ*, meaning "Kṛṣṇa consciousness," are very important in this verse. The king and citizens should both be Kṛṣṇa conscious, otherwise both of them will be doomed to lower species of life after death. A responsible government must teach Kṛṣṇa consciousness very vigorously for the benefit of all. Without Kṛṣṇa consciousness, neither the state nor the citizens of the state can be responsible. Pṛthu Mahārāja therefore specifically requested the citizens to act in Kṛṣṇa consciousness, and he was also very anxious to teach them how to become Kṛṣṇa conscious. A summary of Kṛṣṇa consciousness is given in *Bhagavad-gītā:*

yat karoṣi yad aśnāsi
yaj juhoṣi dadāsi yat
yat tapasyasi kaunteya
tat kuruṣva mad-arpaṇam

"Whatever you do, whatever you eat, whatever you give in charity and whatever penances you undergo should be done in Kṛṣṇa consciousness or for the satisfaction of the Supreme Personality of Godhead." (Bg. 9.27) If all the people of the state, including the government servants, are taught the techniques of spiritual life, then although everyone is liable to be punished in different ways by the stringent laws of material nature, they will not be implicated.

TEXT 26

यूयं तदनुमोदध्वं पितृदेवर्षयोऽमलाः ।
कर्तुः शास्तुरनुज्ञातुस्तुल्यं यत्प्रेत्य तत्फलम् ॥२६॥

yūyaṁ tad anumodadhvaṁ
pitṛ-devarṣayo 'malāḥ
kartuḥ śāstur anujñātus
tulyaṁ yat pretya tat-phalam

yūyam—all you respectable persons who are present here; *tat*—that; *anumodadhvam*—kindly approve of my proposal; *pitṛ*—persons coming from Pitṛloka; *deva*—persons coming from the heavenly planets; *ṛṣayaḥ*—great sages and saintly persons; *amalāḥ*—those who are cleansed of all sinful activities; *kartuḥ*—the performer; *śāstuḥ*—the order-giver; *anujñātuḥ*—of the supporter; *tulyam*—equal; *yat*—which; *pretya*—after death; *tat*—that; *phalam*—result.

TRANSLATION

I request all the pure-hearted demigods, forefathers and saintly persons to support my proposal because after death the result of an action is equally shared by its doer, its director and its supporter.

PURPORT

The government of Pṛthu Mahārāja was perfect because it was administered exactly according to the orders of the Vedic injunctions. Pṛthu

Mahārāja has already explained that the chief duty of the government is to see that everyone executes his respective duty and is elevated to the platform of Kṛṣṇa consciousness. The government should be so conducted that automatically one is elevated to Kṛṣṇa consciousness. King Pṛthu therefore wanted his citizens to cooperate fully with him, for if they assented, they would enjoy the same profit as him after death. If Pṛthu Mahārāja, as a perfect king, were elevated to the heavenly planets, the citizens who cooperated by approving of his methods would also be elevated with him. Since the Kṛṣṇa consciousness movement which is going on at the present moment is genuine, perfect and authorized and is following in the footsteps of Pṛthu Mahārāja, anyone who cooperates with this movement or accepts its principles will get the same result as the workers who are actively propagating Kṛṣṇa consciousness.

TEXT 27

अस्ति यज्ञपतिर्नाम केषाञ्चिदर्हसत्तमाः ।
इहामुत्र च लक्ष्यन्ते ज्योत्स्नावत्यः क्वचिद्भुवः ॥२७॥

asti yajñapatir nāma
keṣāñcid arha-sattamāḥ
ihāmutra ca lakṣyante
jyotsnāvatyaḥ kvacid bhuvaḥ

asti—there must be; *yajña-patiḥ*—the enjoyer of all sacrifices; *nāma*—of the name; *keṣāñcit*—in the opinion of some; *arha-sattamāḥ*—O most respectable; *iha*—in this material world; *amutra*—after death; *ca*—also; *lakṣyante*—it is visible; *jyotsnāvatyaḥ*—powerful, beautiful; *kvacit*—somewhere; *bhuvaḥ*—bodies.

TRANSLATION

My dear respectable ladies and gentlemen, according to the authoritative statements of śāstra, there must be a supreme authority who is able to award the respective benefits of our present activities. Otherwise, why should there be persons who are unusually beautiful and powerful both in this life and in the life after death?

PURPORT

Pṛthu Mahārāja's sole aim in ruling his kingdom was to raise the citizens to the standard of God consciousness. Since there was a great assembly in the arena of sacrifice, there were different types of men present, but he was especially interested in speaking to those who were not atheists. It has already been explained in the previous verses that Pṛthu Mahārāja advised the citizens to become *adhokṣaja-dhiyaḥ,* which means God conscious or Kṛṣṇa conscious, and in this verse he specifically presents the authority of *śāstra,* even though his father was a number one atheist who did not abide by the injunctions mentioned in the Vedic *śāstras*, who practically stopped all sacrificial performances, and who so disgusted the *brāhmaṇas* that they not only dethroned him but cursed and killed him. Atheistic men do not believe in the existence of God, and thus they understand everything which is happening in our daily affairs to be due to physical arrangement and chance. Atheists believe in the atheistic Sāṅkhya philosophy of the combination of *prakṛti* and *puruṣa.* They believe only in matter and hold that matter under certain conditions of amalgamation gives rise to the living force, which then appears as *puruṣa,* the enjoyer; then, by a combination of matter and the living force, the many varieties of material manifestation come into existence. Nor do atheists believe in the injunctions of the *Vedas.* According to them, all the Vedic injunctions are simply theories that have no practical application in life. Taking all this into consideration, Pṛthu Mahārāja suggested that theistic men will solidly reject the views of the atheists on the grounds that there cannot be many varieties of existence without the plan of a superior intelligence. Atheists very vaguely explain that these varieties of existence occur simply by chance, but the theists who believe in the injunctions of the *Vedas* must reach all their conclusions under the direction of the *Vedas.*

In the *Viṣṇu Purāṇa* it is said that the entire *varṇāśrama* institution is meant to satisfy the Supreme Personality of Godhead. The rules and regulations set up for the execution of the duties of *brāhmaṇas, kṣatriyas, vaiśyas* and *śūdras* or *brahmacārīs, gṛhasthas, vānaprasthas* and *sannyāsīs* are all meant to satisfy the Supreme Lord. At the present moment, although the so-called *brāhmaṇas, kṣatriyas, vaiśyas* and *śūdras* have lost their original culture, they claim to be *brāhmaṇas, kṣatriyas, vaiśyas* and *śūdras* by birthright. Yet they have rejected the proposition that such social and spiritual orders are especially meant for worship of Lord Viṣṇu. The dangerous Māyāvāda theory set forth by Śaṅkarācārya—that God is impersonal—does not tally with the injunctions of the *Vedas.* Śrī Caitanya Mahāprabhu therefore described the Māyāvādī philosophers as the greatest offenders against the Personality of Godhead. According to the Vedic system, one who does not abide by the orders of the *Vedas* is called a *nāstika,* or atheist. When Lord Buddha preached his theory of nonviolence, he was obliged to deny the authority of the *Vedas,* and for this reason he was considered by the followers of the *Vedas* to be a *nāstika.* But although

Śrī Caitanya Mahāprabhu very clearly enunciated that the followers of Lord Buddha's philosophy are *nāstikas* or atheists because of their denial of the authority of the *Vedas*, He considered the Śaṅkarites, who wanted to establish Vedic authority by trickery and who actually followed the Māyāvāda philosophy of Buddha's school, to be more dangerous than the Buddhists themselves. The Śaṅkarite philosophers' theory that we have to imagine a shape of God is more dangerous than denial of the existence of God. Notwithstanding all the philosophical theorizing by atheists or Māyāvādīs, the followers of Kṛṣṇa consciousness rigidly live according to the injunctions given in *Bhagavad-gītā*, which is accepted as the essence of all Vedic scripture. In *Bhagavad-gītā* it is said:

yataḥ pravṛttir bhūtānāṁ yena sarvam idaṁ tatam
sva-karmaṇā tam abhyarcya siddhiṁ vindati mānavaḥ. (Bg.18.46)

This means that the Supreme Personality of Godhead is the original source of everything, as described in the *Vedānta-sūtra (janmādy asya yataḥ)*. The Lord Himself also confirms in *Bhagavad-gītā*, *ahaṁ sarvasya prabhavo:* "I am the origin of everything." The Supreme Personality of Godhead is the original source of all emanations, and at the same time, as Paramātmā, He is spread all over existence. The Absolute Truth is therefore the Supreme Personality of Godhead, and every living being is meant to satisfy the Supreme Godhead by performing his respective duty (*sva-karmaṇā tam abhyarcya*). Mahārāja Pṛthu wanted to introduce this formula amongst his citizens.

The most important point in human civilization is that while one engages in different occupational duties, he must try to satisfy the Supreme Lord by the execution of such duties. That is the highest perfection of life. *Svanuṣṭhitasya dharmasya saṁsiddhir hari-toṣaṇam:* by discharging one's prescribed duty, one can become very successful in life if he simply satisfies the Supreme Personality of Godhead. The vivid example is Arjuna. He was a *kṣatriya*, his duty was to fight, and by executing his prescribed duty he satisfied the Supreme Lord and therefore became perfect. Everyone should follow this principle. The atheists who do not are condemned in *Bhagavad-gītā*, in the Sixteenth Chapter, by the following statement: *tān ahaṁ dviṣataḥ krūrān saṁsāreṣu narādhamān* (Bg. 16.19). In this verse it is clearly said that persons who are envious of the Supreme Personality of Godhead are the lowest of mankind and are very mischievous. Under the regulative principles of the Supreme, such mischievous persons are thrown into the darkest region of material existence and are born of *asuras* or atheists. Birth after birth, such *asuras* go still farther down, finally to animal forms like those of tigers or similar ferocious beasts. Thus for millions of years they have to remain in darkness without knowledge of Kṛṣṇa.

The Supreme Personality of Godhead is known as Puruṣottama, or the best of all living entities. He is a person like all other living entities, but He is the leader or the best of all living beings. That is stated in the *Vedas* also. *Nityo nityānāṁ cetanaś cetanānām.* He is the chief of all eternals, the chief of all living entities, and He is complete and full. He has no need to derive benefit by interfering with the affairs of other living entities, but because He is the maintainer of all, He has the right to bring them to the proper standard so that all living entities may become happy. As a father wants all of his children to become happy under his direction, similarly, God, or Kṛṣṇa, the Supreme Personality of Godhead, has the right to see that all living entities are happy. There is no possibility of becoming happy within this material world. The father and the sons are eternal, but if a living entity does not come to the platform of his eternal life of bliss and knowledge, there is no question of happiness. Although Puruṣottama, the best of all living entities, has no benefit to derive from the common living entities, He does have the right to discriminate between their right and wrong ways. The right way is the path of activities meant to satisfy the Supreme Personality of Godhead, as we have already discussed *(svanuṣṭhitasya dharmasya saṁsiddhir hari-toṣaṇam).* A living entity may engage in any occupational duty, but if he wants to have perfection in his duties, he must satisfy the Supreme Lord. As such, one who pleases Him gets better facilities for living, but one who displeases Him gets involved in undesirable situations.

It is therefore concluded that there are two kinds of duties—mundane duty and duty performed for the sake of *yajña* or sacrifice (*yajñārthāt karma*). Any *karma* or activity one performs which is not for the purpose of *yajña* is a cause of bondage. *Yajñārthāt karmaṇo 'nyatra loko 'yaṁ karma-bandhanaḥ:* "Work done as a sacrifice for Viṣṇu has to be performed, otherwise work binds one to this material world." (Bg. 3.9) *Karma-bandhanaḥ,* or the bondage of *karma,* is administered under the regulations of the stringent laws of material nature. Material existence is a struggle to conquer the impediments put forth by material nature. The *asuras* are always fighting to overcome these impediments, and by the illusory power of material nature the foolish living entities work very hard within this material world and take this to be happiness. This is called *māyā.* In that hard struggle for existence, they deny the existence of the supreme authority, Puruṣottama, the Supreme Personality of Godhead.

In order to regulate the activities of the living entities, God has given us codes, just as a king gives codes of law in a state, and whoever breaks the law is punished. Similarly, the Lord has given the infallible knowledge of the *Vedas,* which are not contaminated by the four defects of human life—namely, the tendency to commit mistakes, to be illusioned, to cheat and to have imperfect senses. If we do not take direction from the *Vedas* but act whimsically according to our own choice, we are sure to be punished by the laws of the Lord, who offers different types of bodies in the 8,400,000 species of forms. Material existence, or the sense gratification process, is conducted according to the type of body we are given by *prakṛti,* or material nature. As such, there must be divisions of pious and impious activities *(puṇya* and *pāpa).* In *Bhagavad-gītā* it is clearly stated:

yeṣāṁ tv anta-gataṁ pāpaṁ janānāṁ puṇya-karmaṇām
te dvandva-moha-nirmuktā bhajante māṁ dṛḍha-vratāḥ

"One who has completely surpassed the resultant activities of the impious path of life (this is possible only when one engages exclusively in pious activities) can understand his eternal relationship with the Supreme Personality of Godhead. Thus he engages in His transcendental loving service." (Bg. 7.28) This life of engaging always in the loving service of the Lord is called *adhokṣaja-dhiyaḥ,* or a life of Kṛṣṇa consciousness, which King Pṛthu meant his citizens to follow.

The different varieties of life and of material existence do not come about by chance and necessity; they are different arrangements made by the Supreme Lord in terms of the pious and impious activities of the living entities. By performing pious activities one can take birth in a good family in a good nation, one can get a beautiful body or can become very well-educated or very rich. We see, therefore, that in different places and in different planets there are different standards of life, bodily features and educational statuses, all awarded by the Supreme Personality of Godhead according to pious or impious activities. Varieties of life, therefore, do not develop by chance but by prearrangement. There is a plan, which is already outlined in the Vedic knowledge. One has to take advantage of this knowledge and mold his life in such a way that at the end, especially in the human form of life, he may go back home, back to Godhead, by practicing Kṛṣṇa consciousness.

The theory of chance can best be explained in the Vedic literature by the words *ajñāta-sukṛti,* which refer to pious activities performed without the actor's knowledge. But these are also planned. For example, Kṛṣṇa comes like an ordinary human being, He comes as a devotee like Lord Caitanya, or He sends His representative, the spiritual master or pure devotee. This is also the planned activity of the Supreme Personality of Godhead. They come to canvass and educate, and thus a person in the illusory energy of the Supreme Lord gets a chance to mix with them, talk with them, and take lessons from them, and somehow or other if a conditioned soul surrenders to such personalities and by intimate association with them chances to become Kṛṣṇa conscious, he is saved from the material conditions of life. Kṛṣṇa therefore instructs:

sarva-dharmān parityajya māṁ ekaṁ śaraṇaṁ vraja
ahaṁ tvāṁ sarva-pāpebhyo mokṣayiṣyāmi mā śucaḥ

"Abandon all varieties of religion and just surrender unto Me. I shall deliver you from all sinful reaction. Do not fear." (Bg. 18.66) The word *sarva-pāpebhyaḥ* means "from all sinful activities." A person who surrenders unto Him by utilizing the chance to associate with the pure devotee, spiritual master or other authorized incarnations of Godhead like Pṛthu Mahārāja, is saved by Kṛṣṇa. Then his life becomes successful.

TEXTS 28-29

मनोरुत्तानपादस्य ध्रुवस्यापि महीपतेः ।
प्रियव्रतस्य राजर्षेरङ्गस्यास्मत्पितुः पितुः ॥२८॥
ईदृशानामथान्येषामजस्य च भवस्य च ।
प्रह्लादस्य बलेश्चापि कृत्यमस्ति गदाभृता ॥२९॥

manor uttānapādasya
dhruvasyāpi mahīpateḥ
priyavratasya rājarṣer
aṅgasyāsmat-pituḥ pituḥ

īdṛśānām athānyeṣām
ajasya ca bhavasya ca
prahlādasya baleś cāpi
kṛtyam asti gadā-bhṛtā

manoḥ—of Manu (Svāyambhuva Manu); *uttānapādasya*—of Uttānapāda, the father of Dhruva Mahārāja; *dhruvasya*—of Dhruva Mahārāja; *api*—certainly; *mahīpateḥ*—of the great king; *priyavratasya*—of Priyavrata, in the family of Mahārāja Dhruva; *rājarṣeḥ*—of great saintly kings; *aṅgasya*—of the name Aṅga; *asmat*—my; *pituḥ*—of my father; *pituḥ*—of the father; *īdṛśānām*—of such personalities; *atha*—also; *anyeṣām*—of others; *ajasya*—of the supreme immortal; *ca*—also; *bhavasya*—of the living entities; *ca*—also; *prahlādasya*—of Mahārāja Prahlāda; *baleḥ*—of Mahārāja Bali; *ca*—also; *api*—certainly; *kṛtyam*—acknowledged by them; *asti*—there is; *gadā-bhṛtā*—the Supreme Personality of Godhead who carries a club.

TRANSLATION

This is confirmed not only by the evidence of the Vedas but also by the personal behavior of the great personalities like Manu, Uttānapāda, Dhruva, Priyavrata and my grandfather Aṅga, as well as by many other great personalities and ordinary living entities, exemplified by Mahārāja Prahlāda and Bali, all of whom are theists who believe in the existence of the Supreme Personality of Godhead who carries a club.

PURPORT

Narottama dāsa Ṭhākura states that one has to ascertain the right path for his activities by following in the footsteps of great saintly persons and books of knowledge under the guidance of a spiritual master *(sādhu-śāstra-guru-vākya).* A saintly person is one who follows the Vedic injunctions, which are the orders of the Supreme Personality of Godhead. The word *guru* refers to one who gives proper direction under the authority of the Vedic injunctions and according to the examples of the lives of great personalities. The best way to mold one's life is to follow in the footsteps of the authorized personalities like those mentioned herein by Pṛthu Mahārāja, beginning with Svāyambhuva Manu. The safest path in life is to follow such great personalities, especially those mentioned in the *Śrīmad-Bhāgavatam.* The *mahājanas* or great personalities are Brahmā, Lord Śiva, Nārada Muni, Manu, the Kumāras, Prahlāda Mahārāja, Bali Mahārāja, Yamarāja, Bhīṣma, Janaka, Śukadeva Gosvāmī and Kapila Muni.

TEXT 30

दौहित्रादीनृते मृत्योः शोच्यान् धर्मविमोहितान् ।
वर्गस्वर्गापवर्गाणां प्रायेणैकात्म्यहेतुना ॥३०॥

dauhitrādīn ṛte mṛtyoḥ
śocyān dharma-vimohitān
varga-svargāpavargāṇāṁ
prāyeṇaikātmya-hetunā

dauhitra-ādīn—grandsons like my father, Vena; *ṛte*—except; *mṛtyoḥ*—of personified death; *śocyān*—abominable; *dharma-vimohitān*—bewildered on the path of religiosity; *varga*—religion, economic development, sense gratification and liberation; *svarga*—elevation to the heavenly planets; *apavargāṇām*—being freed from material contamination; *prāyeṇa*—almost always; *eka*—one; *ātmya*—the Supreme Personality of Godhead; *hetunā*—on account of.

TRANSLATION

Although abominable persons like my father, Vena, the grandson of death personified, are bewildered on the path of religion, all the great personalities like those mentioned agree that in this world the only bestower of the benedictions of religion, economic development, sense gratification, liberation or elevation to the heavenly planets is the Supreme Personality of Godhead.

PURPORT

King Vena, the father of Pṛthu Mahārāja, was condemned by the *brāhmaṇas* and saintly persons due to his denying the existence of the Supreme Personality of Godhead and rejecting the method of satisfying Him by performance of Vedic sacrifice. In other words, he was an atheist who did not believe in the existence of God and who consequently stopped all Vedic ritualistic ceremonies in his kingdom. Pṛthu Mahārāja considered his character abominable because he was foolish regarding the execution of religious performances. Atheists are of the opinion that there is no need to accept the authority of the Supreme Personality of Godhead to be successful in religion, economic development, sense gratification or liberation. According to them, *dharma,* or religious principles, are meant to establish an imaginary God to encourage one to become moral, honest and just so that the social orders may be maintained in peace and tranquility. Furthermore, they say that actually there is no need to accept God for this purpose, for if one follows the principles of morality and honesty, that is sufficient. Similarly, if one makes nice plans and works very hard for economic development, automatically the result of economic development will come. Similarly, sense gratification also does not depend on the mercy of the Supreme Personality of Godhead, for if one earns enough money by any process, he will have sufficient opportunity for sense gratification. Insofar as liberation is concerned, they say that there is no need to talk of liberation because after death everything is finished. Pṛthu Mahārāja, however, does not accept the authority of such atheists, headed by his father, who was the grandson of death personified. Generally, a daughter inherits the qualities of her father, and a son gets the qualities of his mother. Thus Mṛtyu's daughter, Sunīthā, got all the qualities of her father, and Vena inherited the qualities of his mother. A person who is always subjected to the rules and regulations of repeated birth and death cannot accommodate anything beyond materialistic ideas. Since King Vena was such a man, he did not believe in the existence of God. Modern civilization agrees with the principles of King Vena, but factually if we scrutinizingly study all the conditions of religion, economic development, sense gratification and liberation, we must accept the principles of the authority of the Supreme Personality of Godhead. According to Vedic literature, religion consists only of the codes of law given by God.

If one does not accept the authority of the Supreme Godhead in matters of religion and morality, one must explain why two persons of the same moral standard achieve different results. It is generally found that even if two men have the same moral standards of ethics, honesty and morality, their positions are still not the same. Similarly, in economic development it is seen that if two men work very hard day and night, still the results are not the same. One person may enjoy great opulence without even working, whereas another person, although working very hard, does not even get two sufficient meals a day. Similarly, in the matter of sense gratification, sometimes one who has sufficient food is still not happy in his family affairs or sometimes is not even married, whereas another person, even though not economically well off, has the greatest opportunity for sense gratification. Even an animal like a hog or a dog may have greater opportunities for sense gratification than a human being. Aside from liberation, even if we consider only the preliminary necessities of life—*dharma, artha* and *kāma* (religion, economic development and sense gratification)—we will see that they are not the same for everyone. Therefore it must be accepted that there is someone who determines the different standards. In conclusion, not only for liberation must one depend on the Lord, but even for ordinary necessities in this material world. Pṛthu Mahārāja therefore indicated that in spite of having rich parents, children are sometimes not happy. Similarly, in spite of valuable medicine administered by a competent physician, sometimes a patient dies; or in spite of having a big safe boat, sometimes a man drowns. We may thus struggle to counteract impediments offered by material nature, but our attempts cannot be successful unless we are favored by the Supreme Personality of Godhead.

TEXT 31

यत्पादसेवाभिरुचिस्तपस्विना-
मशेषजन्मोपचितं मलं धियः ।
सद्यः क्षिणोत्यन्वहमेधती सती
यथा पदाङ्गुष्ठविनिःसृता सरित् ॥३१॥

yat-pāda-sevābhirucis tapasvinām
aśeṣa-janmopacitaṁ malaṁ dhiyaḥ
sadyaḥ kṣiṇoty anvaham edhatī satī
yathā padāṅguṣṭha-viniḥsṛtā sarit

yat-pāda—whose lotus feet; *sevā*—service; *abhiruciḥ*—inclination; *tapasvinām*—persons undergoing severe penances; *aśeṣa*—innumerable; *janma*—birth; *upacitam*—acquire; *malam*—dirtiness; *dhiyaḥ*—mind; *sadyaḥ*—immediately; *kṣiṇoti*—destroys; *anvaham*—day after day; *edhatī*—increasing; *satī*—being; *yathā*—as; *padāṅguṣṭha*—the toes of His lotus feet; *viniḥsṛtā*—emanating from; *sarit*—water.

TRANSLATION

By the inclination to serve the lotus feet of the Supreme Personality of Godhead, suffering humanity can immediately cleanse the dirt which has accumulated in their minds during innumerable births. Like the Ganges water which emanates from the toes of the lotus feet of the Lord, such a process immediately cleanses the mind, and thus spiritual or Kṛṣṇa consciousness gradually increases.

PURPORT

In India, one can actually see that a person who takes a bath in the Ganges waters daily is almost free from all kinds of diseases. A very respectable *brāhmaṇa* in Calcutta never took a doctor's medicine. Even though he sometimes felt sick, he would not accept medicine from the physician but would simply drink Ganges water, and he was always cured within a very short time. The glories of Ganges water are known to Indians and to ourselves also. The River Ganges flows by Calcutta. Sometimes within the water there are many stools and other dirty things which are washed away from neighboring mills and factories, but still thousands of men take baths in the Ganges water, and they are very healthy as well as spiritually inclined. That is the effect of Ganges water. The Ganges is glorified because it emanates from the toes of the lotus feet of the Lord.

Similarly, if one takes to the service of the lotus feet of the Lord or takes to Kṛṣṇa consciousness, he is immediately cleansed of the many dirty things which have accumulated in his innumerable births. We have seen that in spite of the very black record of their past lives, persons who take to Kṛṣṇa consciousness very swiftly become perfectly cleansed of all dirty things and make spiritual progress. Therefore Pṛthu Mahārāja advises that without the benediction of the Supreme Lord, one cannot make advancement—either in so-called morality, economic development or sense gratification. One should therefore take to the service of the Lord, or Kṛṣṇa consciousness, and thus very soon become a perfect man, as confirmed in *Bhagavad-gītā (kṣipraṁ bhavati dharmātmā śaśvac-chāntiṁ nigacchati).* Being a responsible king, Pṛthu Mahārāja recommends that everyone take shelter of the Supreme Personality of Godhead and thus be immediately purified. Lord Śrī Kṛṣṇa also says in *Bhagavad-gītā* that simply by surrendering unto Him one is immediately relieved of all sinful reactions. As Kṛṣṇa takes away all the sinful reactions of a person immediately upon his surrender unto Him, similarly the external manifestation of Kṛṣṇa, the representative of Kṛṣṇa who acts as the mercy of the Supreme Personality of Godhead, takes all the resultant actions of the sinful life of the disciple immediately after the disciple's initiation. Thus if the disciple follows the principles instructed by the spiritual master, he remains purified and is not contaminated by the material infection.

Śrī Caitanya Mahāprabhu therefore stated that the spiritual master who plays the part of Kṛṣṇa's representative has to consume all the sinful reactions of his disciple. Sometimes a spiritual master takes the risk of being overwhelmed by the sinful reactions of the disciples and undergoes a sort of tribulation due to their acceptance. Śrī Caitanya Mahāprabhu therefore advised that one not accept many disciples.

TEXT 32

विनिर्धुताशेषमनोमलः पुमा-
नसङ्गविज्ञानविशेषवीर्यवान् ।
यदङ्घ्रिमूले कृतकेतनः पुनर्
न संसृतिं क्लेशवहां प्रपद्यते ॥३२॥

vinirdhutāśeṣa-mano-malaḥ pumān
asaṅga-vijñāna-viśeṣa-vīryavān
yad-aṅghri-mūle kṛta-ketanaḥ punar
na saṁsṛtiṁ kleśa-vahāṁ prapadyate

vinirdhuta—being specifically cleansed; *aśeṣa*—unlimited; *manaḥ-malaḥ*—mental speculation or the dirt accumulated in the mind; *pumān*—the person; *asaṅga*—being disgusted; *vijñāna*—scientifically; *viśeṣa*—particularly; *vīryavān*—being strengthened in *bhakti-yoga; yat*—whose; *aṅghri*—lotus feet; *mūle*—at the root of; *kṛta-ketanaḥ*—taken shelter; *punaḥ*—again; *na*—never; *saṁsṛtim*—material existence; *kleśa-vahām*—full of miserable conditions; *prapadyate*—takes to.

TRANSLATION

When a devotee takes shelter at the lotus feet of the Supreme Personality of Godhead, he is completely cleansed of all misunderstanding or mental speculation, and he manifests renunciation. This is possible only when one is strengthened by practicing bhakti-yoga. Once having taken shelter at the root of the lotus feet of the Lord, a devotee never comes back to this material existence, which is full of the threefold miseries.

PURPORT

As stated by Lord Caitanya Mahāprabhu in His *Śikṣāṣṭaka* instructions, by the chanting of the holy name of the Lord—Hare Kṛṣṇa, Hare Kṛṣṇa, Kṛṣṇa Kṛṣṇa, Hare Hare/ Hare Rāma, Hare Rāma, Rāma Rāma, Hare Hare—or by the process of hearing and chanting of the glories of the Lord, one's mind is gradually cleansed of all dirt. Due to our material association since time immemorial, we have accumulated heaps of dirty things in our minds. The total effect of this takes place when a living entity identifies himself with his body and is thus entrapped by the stringent laws of material nature and put into the cycle of repeated birth and death under the false impression of bodily identification. When one is strengthened by practicing *bhakti-yoga,* his mind is cleansed of this misunderstanding, and he is no longer interested in material existence or in sense gratification.

Bhakti, or devotional service, is characterized by *vairāgya* and *jñāna. Jñāna* refers to understanding that one is not his body, and *vairāgya* means disinterest in sense gratification. These two primary principles of separation from material bondage can be realized on the strength of *bhakti-yoga.* Thus when a devotee is fixed in the loving service of the lotus feet of the Lord, he will never come back to this material existence after quitting his body, as confirmed in *Bhagavad-gītā* by the Lord (*tyaktvā dehaṁ punar janma naiti mām eti so 'rjuna*).

In this verse the word *vijñāna* is specifically important. *Jñāna,* the knowledge of spiritual identity that one attains when he does not consider himself to be the body, is explained in *Bhagavad-gītā* as *brahma-bhūta,* the revival of spiritual realization. In the conditioned state of material existence one cannot be spiritually realized because he identifies himself materially. The understanding of the distinction between material existence and spiritual existence is called *jñāna.* After coming to the platform of *jñāna,* or the *brahma-bhūta* state, one ultimately comes to devotional service, in which he completely understands his own position and the position of the Supreme Personality of Godhead. This understanding is explained here as *vijñāna-viśeṣa.* The Lord says, therefore, that knowledge of Him is *vijñāna,* science. In other words, when one is strengthened by scientific knowledge of the Supreme Personality of Godhead, his position of liberation is guaranteed. In *Bhagavad-gītā* also, the science of devotional service is described as *pratyakṣāvagamaṁ dharmyam,* direct understanding of the principles of religion by realization (Bg. 9.2).

By practicing *bhakti-yoga,* one can directly perceive his advancement in spiritual life. In other practices—like *karma-yoga, jñāna-yoga* and *dhyāna-yoga*—one may not be confident about his progress, but in *bhakti-yoga* one can become directly aware of his progress in spiritual life, just as a person who eats can understand that his hunger is satisfied. Our false appetite for enjoyment and lordship of the material world is due to a prominence of passion and ignorance. By *bhakti-yoga* these two qualities are diminished, and one becomes situated in the mode of goodness. Gradually surpassing the mode of goodness, one is situated in pure goodness, which is not contaminated by the material qualities. When thus situated, a devotee no longer has any doubts; he knows that he will not come back to this material world.

TEXT 33

तमेव यूयं भजतात्मवृत्तिभि-
र्मनोवचःकायगुणैः स्वकर्मभिः ।
अमायिनः कामदुघाङ्घ्रिपङ्कजं
यथाधिकारावसितार्थसिद्धयः ॥३३॥

tam eva yūyaṁ bhajatātma-vṛttibhir
mano-vacaḥ-kāya-guṇaiḥ sva-karmabhiḥ
amāyinaḥ kāma-dughāṅghri-paṅkajaṁ
yathādhikārāvasitārtha-siddhayaḥ

tam—unto Him; *eva*—certainly; *yūyam*—all you citizens; *bhajata*—worship; *ātma*—own; *vṛttibhiḥ*—occupational duty; *manaḥ*—mind; *vacaḥ*—

words; *kāya*—body; *guṇaiḥ*—by the particular qualities; *sva-karmabhiḥ*—by occupational duties; *amāyinaḥ*—without reservation; *kāma-dugha*—fulfilling all desires; *aṅghri-paṅkajam*—the lotus feet; *yathā*—as far as; *adhikāra*—ability; *avasita-artha*—fully convinced of one's interest; *siddhayaḥ*—satisfaction.

TRANSLATION

Pṛthu Mahārāja advised his citizens: Engaging your minds, your words, your bodies and the results of your occupational duties, and being always open-minded, you should all render devotional service to the Lord. According to your abilities and the occupations in which you are situated, you should engage your service at the lotus feet of the Supreme Personality of Godhead with full confidence and without reservation. Then surely you will be successful in achieving the final objective in your lives.

PURPORT

As stated in the Eighteenth Chapter of *Bhagavad-gītā, sva-karmaṇā tam abhyarcya:* one has to worship the Supreme Personality of Godhead by his occupational duties. This necessitates accepting the principle of four *varṇas* and four *āśramas.* Pṛthu Mahārāja therefore says, *guṇaiḥ sva-karmabhiḥ.* This phrase is explained in *Bhagavad-gītā. Cātur-varṇyaṁ mayā sṛṣṭaṁ guṇa-karma-vibhāgaśaḥ:* "The four castes (the *brāhmaṇas, kṣatriyas, vaiśyas* and *śūdras*) are created by the Supreme Personality of Godhead according to the material modes of nature and the particular duties discharged in those modes." A person who is situated in the mode of goodness is certainly more intelligent than others. Therefore he can practice the brahminical activities—namely, speaking the truth, controlling the senses, controlling the mind, remaining always clean, practicing tolerance, having full knowledge about one's self-identity, and understanding devotional service. In this way, if he engages himself in the loving service of the Lord as an actual *brāhmaṇa,* his aim to achieve the final interest of life is attained. Similarly, the *kṣatriya's* duties are to give protection to the citizens, to give all his possessions in charity, to be strictly Vedic in the management of state affairs, and to be unafraid to fight whenever there is an attack by enemies. In this way, a *kṣatriya* can satisfy the Supreme Personality of Godhead by his occupational duties. Similarly, a *vaiśya* can satisfy the Supreme Godhead by properly executing his occupational duties—engaging himself in producing foodstuffs, giving protection to cows, and trading if necessary when there is an excess of agricultural production. Similarly, because they do not have ample intelligence, *śūdras* should simply engage as workers to serve the higher statuses of social life. Everyone's aim should be to satisfy the Supreme Personality of Godhead by engaging his mind in thinking always of Kṛṣṇa, his words in always offering prayers to the Lord or preaching about the glories of the Lord, and his body in executing the service required to satisfy the Lord. As there are four divisions within our body—the head, the arms, the belly and the legs—similarly, human society, taken as a whole, is divided into four classes of men according to their material qualities and occupational duties. Thus the brahminical or intelligent men have to execute the duty of the head, the *kṣatriyas* must fulfill the duty of the arms, the *vaiśya* class must fulfill the duty of the belly, and the *śūdras* must fulfill the duty of the legs. In executing the prescribed duties of life, no one is higher or lower, for although there are such divisions as higher and lower, since there is actually a common interest—to satisfy the Supreme Personality of Godhead—there are no distinctions between them.

The question may be raised that since the Lord is supposed to be worshiped by great demigods like Lord Brahmā, Lord Śiva and others, how can an ordinary human being on this planet serve Him? This is clearly explained by Pṛthu Mahārāja by the use of the word *yathādhikāra,* "according to one's ability." If one sincerely executes his occupational duty, that will be sufficient. One does not need to become like Lord Brahmā, Lord Śiva, Indra, Lord Caitanya or Rāmānujācārya, whose capabilities are certainly far above ours. Even a *śūdra,* who is in the lowest stage of life according to the material qualities, can achieve the same success. Anyone can become successful in devotional service provided he displays no duplicity. It is explained here that one must be very frank and open-minded *(amāyinaḥ).* To be situated in a lower status of life is not a disqualification for success in devotional service. The only qualification is that whether one is a *brāhmaṇa, kṣatriya, vaiśya* or *śūdra,* he must be open, frank and free from reservations. Then, by performing his particular occupational duty under the guidance of a proper spiritual master, he can achieve the highest success in life. As confirmed by the Lord Himself, *striyo vaiśyās tathā śūdrās te 'pi yānti parāṁ gatim* (Bg. 9.32). It does not matter what one is, whether a *brāhmaṇa, kṣatriya, vaiśya, śūdra* or a degraded woman. If he engages himself seriously in devotional service, working with body, mind and intelligence, he is sure to be successful in going back home, back to Godhead. The Lord's lotus feet are described here as *kāma-dughāṅghri-paṅkajam* because they have all power to fulfill the desires of everyone. A devotee is happy even in this life because—although in material existence we have many needs—all his material needs are satisfied, and when he at last quits his body, he goes back home, back to Godhead, without a doubt.

TEXT 34

असाविहानेकगुणोऽगुणोऽध्वरः
पृथग्विधद्रव्यगुणक्रियोक्तिभिः ।
सम्पद्यतेऽर्थाशयलिङ्गनामभि-
र्विशुद्धविज्ञानघनः स्वरूपतः ॥३४॥

asāv ihāneka-guṇo 'guṇo 'dhvaraḥ
pṛthag-vidha-dravya-guṇa-kriyoktibhiḥ
sampadyate 'rthāśaya-liṅga-nāmabhir
viśuddha-vijñāna-ghanaḥ svarūpataḥ

asau—the Supreme Personality of Godhead; *iha*—in this material world; *aneka*—various; *guṇaḥ*—qualities; *aguṇaḥ*—transcendental; *adhvaraḥ*—*yajña;* *pṛthak-vidha*—varieties; *dravya*—physical elements; *guṇa*—ingredients; *kriyā*—performances; *uktibhiḥ*—by chanting different *mantras;* *sampadyate*—is worshiped; *artha*—interest; *āśaya*—purpose; *liṅga*—form; *nāmabhiḥ*—name; *viśuddha*—without contamination; *vijñāna*—science; *ghanaḥ*—concentrated; *svarūpataḥ*—in His own form.

TRANSLATION

The Supreme Personality of Godhead is transcendental and not contaminated by this material world. But although He is concentrated spirit soul without material variety, for the benefit of the conditioned soul He nevertheless accepts different types of sacrifice performed with various material elements, ritual and mantras and offered to the demigods under different names according to the interests and purposes of the performers.

PURPORT

For material prosperity there are recommendations in the *Vedas* for various types of *yajña* (sacrifice). In *Bhagavad-gītā* (3.10) it is confirmed that Lord Brahmā created all living entities, including human beings and demigods, and advised them to perform *yajña* according to their material desires *(saha-yajñāḥ prajāḥ sṛṣṭvā).* These performances are called *yajñas* because their ultimate goal is to satisfy the Supreme Personality of Godhead Viṣṇu. The purpose of performing *yajñas* is to get material benefit, but because the aim is to simultaneously satisfy the Supreme Lord, such *yajñas* have been recommended in the *Vedas*. Such performances are, of course, known as *karma-kāṇḍa* or material activities, and all material activities are certainly contaminated by the three modes of material nature. Generally the *karma-kāṇḍa* ritualistic ceremonies are performed in the mode of passion, yet the conditioned souls, both human beings and demigods, are obliged to perform these *yajñas* because without them one cannot be happy at all.

Śrīla Viśvanātha Cakravartī Ṭhākura comments that these *karma-kāṇḍa* ritualistic ceremonies, although contaminated, contain touches of devotional service because whenever there is a performance of any *yajña* Lord Viṣṇu is given a central position. This is very important because even a little endeavor to please Lord Viṣṇu is *bhakti* and is of great value. A tinge of *bhakti* purifies the material nature of the performances, which by devotional service gradually come to the transcendental position. Therefore although such *yajñas* are superficially material activities, the results are transcendental. Such *yajñas* as Sūrya-yajña, Indra-yajña, Candra-yajña, etc., are performed in the names of the demigods, but these demigods are bodily parts of the Supreme Personality of Godhead. The demigods cannot accept sacrificial offerings for themselves, but they can accept them for the Supreme Personality of Godhead, just as a departmental tax collector of a government cannot collect taxes for his personal account but can realize them for the government. Any *yajña* performed with this complete knowledge and understanding is described in *Bhagavad-gītā* as *brahmārpaṇam,* or a sacrifice offered to the Supreme Personality of Godhead. Since no one but the Supreme Lord can enjoy the results of sacrifice, the Lord says that He is the actual enjoyer of all sacrifices *(bhoktāraṁ yajña-tapasāṁ sarva-loka-maheśvaram).* Sacrifices should be performed with this view in mind. As stated in *Bhagavad-gītā:*

brahmārpaṇaṁ brahma havir
brahmāgnau brahmaṇā hutam
brahmaiva tena gantavyaṁ
brahma-karma-samādhinā

"A person who is fully absorbed in Kṛṣṇa consciousness is sure to attain the spiritual kingdom because of his full contribution to spiritual activities in which the consummation is absolute and that which is offered is of the same spiritual nature." (Bg. 4.24) The performer of sacrifices must always keep in view that the sacrifices mentioned in the *Vedas* are meant to satisfy the Supreme Personality of Godhead. *Viṣṇur ārādhyate panthā* (*Viṣṇu Purāṇa* 3.8.9). Anything material or spiritual done for the satisfaction of the Supreme Lord is understood to be an actual *yajña,* and by performing such *yajñas* one gets liberation from material bondage. The direct method of getting liberation from material bondage is devotional service, comprising the nine following methods:

śravaṇaṁ kīrtanaṁ viṣṇoḥ smaraṇaṁ pāda-sevanam
arcanaṁ vandanaṁ dāsyaṁ sakhyam ātma-nivedanam
(*Bhāg.* 7.5.23)

This ninefold process is described in this verse as *viśuddha-vijñāna-ghanaḥ*, or satisfying the Supreme Personality of Godhead directly by transcendental knowledge concentrated on the form of the Supreme Lord Viṣṇu. This is the best method for satisfying the Supreme Lord. One who cannot take to this direct process, however, should take the indirect process of performing *yajñas* for the satisfaction of Viṣṇu or Yajña. Viṣṇu is therefore called *yajña-pati. Śriyaḥ patiṁ yajña-patiṁ jagat-patim.* (*Bhāg.* 2.9.15)

The Supreme Personality of Godhead's deep scientific knowledge is concentrated to the supreme point. For example, medical science knows some things superficially, but the doctors do not know exactly how things happen in the body. Lord Kṛṣṇa, however, knows everything in detail. Therefore His knowledge is *vijñāna-ghana* because it does not have any of the defects of material science. The Supreme Personality of Godhead is *viśuddha-vijñāna-ghana,* concentrated transcendental knowledge; therefore, even though He accepts *karma-kāṇḍīya* materialistic *yajñas,* He always remains in a transcendental position. Therefore, the mention of *aneka-guṇa* refers to the Supreme Personality of Godhead's many transcendental qualities, for He is not affected by the material qualities. The different kinds of material paraphernalia or physical elements are also gradually transformed into spiritual understanding because ultimately there is no difference between material and spiritual qualities, for everything emanates from the Supreme Spirit. This is realized by a gradual process of realization and purification. One vivid example of this is Dhruva Mahārāja, who took to meditation in the forest to achieve material benefit but ultimately became spiritually advanced and did not want any benediction for material profit. He was simply satisfied with the association of the Supreme Lord. *Āśaya* means determination. Generally a conditioned soul has the determination for material profit, but when these desires for material profit are satisfied through performance of *yajña,* one gradually achieves the spiritual platform. Then his life becomes perfect. *Śrīmad-Bhāgavatam* therefore recommends:

akāmaḥ sarva-kāmo vā mokṣa-kāma udāradhīḥ
tīvreṇa bhakti-yogena yajeta puruṣaṁ param. (*Bhāg.* 2.3.10)

Everyone—whether *akāma* (a devotee), *sarva-kāma* (a *karmī*), or *mokṣa-kāma* (a *jñānī* or *yogī*)—is encouraged to worship the Supreme Personality of Godhead by the direct method of devotional service. In this way one can get both material and spiritual profit simultaneously.

TEXT 35

प्रधानकालाशयधर्मसंग्रहे
शरीर एष प्रतिपद्य चेतनाम् ।
क्रियाफलत्वेन विभुर्विभाव्यते
यथानलो दारुषु तद्गुणात्मकः ॥३५॥

pradhāna-kālāśaya-dharma-saṅgrahe
śarīra eṣa pratipadya cetanām
kriyā-phalatvena vibhur vibhāvyate
yathānalo dāruṣu tad-guṇātmakaḥ

pradhāna—material nature; *kāla*—time; *āśaya*—desire; *dharma*—occupational duties; *saṅgrahe*—aggregate; *śarīre*—body; *eṣaḥ*—this; *pratipadya*—accepting; *cetanām*—consciousness; *kriyā*—activities; *phalatvena*—by the result of; *vibhuḥ*—the Supreme Personality of Godhead; *vibhāvyate*—manifested; *yathā*—as much as; *analaḥ*—fire; *dāruṣu*—in the wood; *tat-guṇa-ātmakaḥ*—according to shape and quality.

TRANSLATION

The Supreme Personality of Godhead is all-pervading, but He is also manifested in different types of bodies which arise from a combination of material nature, time, desires and occupational duties. Thus different types of consciousness develop, just as fire, which is always basically the same, blazes in different ways according to the shape and dimension of firewood.

PURPORT

The Supreme Personality of Godhead constantly lives with the individual soul as Paramātmā. The individual soul has awareness in accord with his material body, which he attains by virtue of *prakṛti* or material nature. The material ingredients are activated by force of time, and thus the three material modes of nature are manifested. According to his association with the three modes of nature, the living entity develops a particular type of body. In animal life, the material mode of ignorance is so prominent that there is very little chance of realizing the Paramātmā, who is also present within the heart of the animal; but in the human form of life, because of developed consciousness *(cetanām)*, one can be transferred from ignorance and passion to goodness by the results of his activities *(kriyā-phalatvena)*. A human being is therefore advised to associate with spiritually advanced personalities. The *Vedas* give the direction *tad-vijñānārthaṁ sa gurum evābhigacchet:* in order to reach the perfection of life or to understand the real constitutional position of the living entity, one must approach the spiritual master. (*Muṇḍaka Up.* 1.2.12) *Gurum evābhigacchet*—one *must;* it is not optional. It is imperative that one approach the spiritual master, for by such association one proportionately develops his consciousness towards the Supreme Personality of Godhead. The highest perfection of such consciousness is called Kṛṣṇa consciousness. According to the body given by *prakṛti,* or nature, one's consciousness is present; according to the development of consciousness, one's activities are performed; and according to the purity of such activities, one realizes the Supreme Personality of Godhead, who is present in everyone's heart. The example given herein is very appropriate. Fire is always the same, but according to the size of the fuel or burning wood, the fire appears to be straight, curved, small, big, etc.

According to the development of consciousness, God realization is present. In the human form of life it is recommended, therefore, that one undergo the different types of penances and austerities described in *Bhagavad-gītā (karma-yoga, jñāna-yoga, dhyāna-yoga* and *bhakti-yoga).* Like a staircase, *yoga* has different steps for reaching the topmost floor, and according to one's position upon the staircase, he is understood to be situated in *karma-yoga, jñāna-yoga, dhyāna-yoga* or *bhakti-yoga.* Of course, *bhakti-yoga* is the topmost step on the staircase of realization of the Supreme Personality of Godhead. In other words, according to one's development in consciousness, one realizes spiritual identity, and thus when one's existential position is purified fully, he becomes situated in *brahmānanda,* which is ultimately unlimited. Therefore the *saṅkīrtana* movement contributed by the Supreme Personality of Godhead as Lord Caitanya is the direct and easiest process for coming to the purest form of consciousness—Kṛṣṇa consciousness, the platform on which the Supreme Personality is fully realized. Directions for performing different types of *yajñas* are specifically arranged for the highest realization of the Supreme Lord, as confirmed in *Bhagavad-gītā* by the Lord Himself. *Ye yathā māṁ pradadyante tāṁs tathaiva bhajāmy aham* (Bg. 4.11). The Supreme Personality of Godhead is realized according to the proportion of one's surrender. Full surrender, however, occurs when a man is perfectly in knowledge. *Bahūnāṁ janmanām ante jñānavān māṁ prapadyate* (Bg. 7.19).

TEXT 36

अहो ममामी वितरन्त्यनुग्रहं
हरिं गुरुं यज्ञभुजामधीश्वरम् ।
स्वधर्मयोगेन यजन्ति मामका
निरन्तरं क्षोणितले दृढव्रताः ॥३६॥

aho mamāmī vitaranty anugrahaṁ
hariṁ guruṁ yajña-bhujām adhīśvaram
sva-dharma-yogena yajanti māmakā
nirantaraṁ kṣoṇi-tale dṛḍha-vratāḥ

aho—O all of you; *mama*—unto me; *amī*—all of them; *vitaranti*—distributing; *anugraham*—mercy; *harim*—the Supreme Personality of Godhead; *gurum*—the supreme spiritual master; *yajña-bhujām*—all the demigods eligible to accept *yajña* offering; *adhīśvaram*—the supreme master; *sva-dharma*—occupational duties; *yogena*—by dint of; *yajanti*—worship; *māmakāḥ*—having a relationship with me; *nirantaram*—incessantly; *kṣoṇi-tale*—on the surface of the globe; *dṛḍha-vratāḥ*—with firm determination.

TRANSLATION

The Supreme Personality of Godhead is the master and enjoyer of the results of all sacrifices, and He is the supreme spiritual master as well. All of you citizens on the surface of the globe who have a relationship with me and are worshiping Him by dint of your occupational duties are bestowing your mercy upon me. Therefore, O my citizens, I thank you.

PURPORT

Mahārāja Pṛthu's advice to his citizens to take to devotional service is now concluded in two ways. He has repeatedly advised persons who are neophytes to engage themselves in devotional service according to the capacities of the different orders of social and spiritual life, but here he specifically thanks those who are already engaged in such devotional service to the Supreme Personality of Godhead, who is actually the enjoyer of all sacrificial ceremonies and who is also the supreme teacher as *antaryāmī* or Paramātmā. There is specific mention of the word *gurum,* which indicates the Supreme Personality as *citta-guru.* The Supreme Godhead in His Paramātmā feature is present in everyone's heart, and He is always trying to induce the individual soul to surrender unto Him and to engage in devotional service; therefore He is the original spiritual master. He manifests Himself as spiritual master both internally and externally to help the conditioned soul both ways. Therefore He has been mentioned herein as *gurum.* It appears, however, that in the time of Mahārāja Pṛthu all the people on the surface of the globe were his subjects. Most of them—in fact, almost all of them—were engaged in devotional service. Therefore he thanked them in a humble way for engaging in devotional service and thus bestowing their mercy upon him. In other words, in a state where the citizens and the head of state are engaged in devotional service unto the Supreme Personality of Godhead, they help one another and are mutually benefited.

TEXT 37

मा जातु तेजः प्रभवेन्महद्धिभि-
स्तितिक्षया तपसा विद्यया च ।
देदीप्यमानेऽजितदेवतानां
कुले स्वयं राजकुलाद् द्विजानाम् ॥३७॥

mā jātu tejaḥ prabhaven maharddhibhis
titikṣayā tapasā vidyayā ca
dedīpyamāne 'jita-devatānāṁ
kule svayaṁ rāja-kulād dvijānām

mā—never do it; *jātu*—at any time; *tejaḥ*—supreme power; *prabhavet*—exhibit; *mahā*—great; *ṛddhibhiḥ*—by opulence; *titikṣayā*—by tolerance; *tapasā*—penance; *vidyayā*—by education; *ca*—also; *dedīpyamāne*—upon those who are already glorified; *ajita-devatānām*—Vaiṣṇavas, or the devotees of the Supreme Personality of Godhead; *kule*—in the society; *svayam*—personally; *rāja-kulāt*—greater than the royal family; *dvijānām*—of the *brāhmaṇas.*

TRANSLATION

The brāhmanas and Vaiṣṇavas are personally glorified by their characteristic powers of tolerance, penance, knowledge and education. By dint of all these spiritual assets, Vaiṣṇavas are more powerful than royalty. It is therefore advised that the princely order not exhibit its material prowess before these two communities and should avoid offending them.

PURPORT

Pṛthu Mahārāja has explained in the previous verse the importance of devotional service for both the rulers and the citizens of the state. Now he explains how one can be steadily fixed in devotional service. Śrī

Caitanya Mahāprabhu, while instructing Śrīla Rūpa Gosvāmī, has compared the devotional service of the Lord with a creeper. A creeper has a feeble stem and requires the support of another tree to grow, and while growing, it requires sufficient protection so that it may not be lost. While describing the system of protection for the creeper of devotional service, Śrī Caitanya Mahāprabhu has especially stressed protection from offenses unto the lotus feet of Vaiṣṇavas. This is called *vaiṣṇavāparādha. Aparādha* means offense. If one commits *vaiṣṇavāparādha,* all of his progress in devotional service will be checked. Even though one is very much advanced in devotional service, if he commits offenses at the feet of a Vaiṣṇava, his advancement is all spoiled. In the *śāstras* it is found that a very great *yogī,* Durvāsā Muni, committed *vaiṣṇavāparādha,* and thus for one full year had to travel all over the universe, even to Vaikuṇṭhaloka, to defend himself from the offense. At last, even when he approached the Supreme Personality of Godhead in Vaikuṇṭha, he was refused protection. Therefore one should be very careful about committing offenses at the feet of a Vaiṣṇava. The most grievous type of *vaiṣṇavāparādha* is called *gurv-aparādha,* which refers to offenses at the lotus feet of the spiritual master. In the chanting of the holy name of the Supreme Personality of Godhead, this *gurv-aparādha* is considered the most grievous offense. *Guror avajñā śruti-śāstra-nindanam (Padma Purāṇa).* Among the ten offenses committed against the chanting of the holy name, the first offenses are disobedience of the spiritual master and blasphemy of the Vedic literature.

The simple definition of "Vaiṣṇava" is given by Śrī Caitanya Mahāprabhu: a person who immediately reminds one of the Supreme Personality of Godhead, Kṛṣṇa, is a Vaiṣṇava. In this verse, both Vaiṣṇavas and *brāhmaṇas* are mentioned. A Vaiṣṇava is a learned *brāhmaṇa* and is therefore designated as *brāhmaṇa-vaiṣṇava, brāhmaṇa-paṇḍita* or as a Vaiṣṇava and *brāhmaṇa.* In other words, a Vaiṣṇava is supposed to be a *brāhmaṇa* already, but a *brāhmaṇa* may not be a pure Vaiṣṇava. When a person understands his pure identity, *brahma jānāti,* he immediately becomes a *brāhmaṇa.* In the *brāhmaṇa* stage, one's understanding of the Absolute Truth is mainly based on the impersonal view. When a *brāhmaṇa,* however, rises to the platform of personal understanding of the Supreme Godhead, he becomes a Vaiṣṇava. A Vaiṣṇava is transcendental even to a *brāhmaṇa.* In the material conception, the position of a *brāhmaṇa* is the highest in human society, but a Vaiṣṇava is transcendental even to a *brāhmaṇa.* Both the *brāhmaṇa* and Vaiṣṇava are spiritually advanced. A *brāhmaṇa's* qualifications are mentioned in *Bhagavad-gītā* as truthfulness, mental equanimity, control of the senses, the power of tolerance, simplicity, knowledge of the Absolute Truth, firm faith in the scriptures, and practical application of the brahminical qualities in life. In addition to all these qualifications, when one fully engages in the transcendental loving service of the Lord, he becomes a Vaiṣṇava. Pṛthu Mahārāja warns his citizens who are actually engaged in the devotional service of the Lord to take care against offenses to the *brāhmaṇas* and Vaiṣṇavas. Offenses at their lotus feet are so destructive that even the descendants of Yadu who were born in the family of Lord Kṛṣṇa were destroyed due to offenses at their feet. The Supreme Personality of Godhead cannot tolerate any offense at the lotus feet of *brāhmaṇas* and Vaiṣṇavas. Sometimes, due to their powerful positions, princes or government servants neglect the positions of *brāhmaṇas* and Vaiṣṇavas, not knowing that because of their offense they will be ruined.

TEXT 38

ब्रह्मण्यदेवः पुरुषः पुरातनो
नित्यं हरिर्यच्चरणाभिवन्दनात् ।
अवाप लक्ष्मीमनपायिनीं यशो
जगत्पवित्रं च महत्तमाग्रणीः ॥३८॥

brahmaṇya-devaḥ puruṣaḥ purātano
nityaṁ harir yac-caraṇābhivandanāt
avāpa lakṣmīm anapāyinīṁ yaśo
jagat-pavitraṁ ca mahattamāgraṇīḥ

brahmaṇya-devaḥ—the Lord of the brahminical culture; *puruṣaḥ*—the Supreme Personality; *purātanaḥ*—the oldest; *nityam*—eternal; *hariḥ*—Personality of Godhead; *yat*—whose; *caraṇa*—lotus feet; *abhivandanāt*—by means of worshiping; *avāpa*—obtained; *lakṣmīm*— opulences; *anapāyinīm*—perpetually; *yaśaḥ*—reputation; *jagat*—universal; *pavitram*—purified; *ca*—also; *mahat*—great; *tama*—supreme; *agraṇīḥ*—foremost.

TRANSLATION

The Supreme Personality of Godhead, the ancient, eternal Godhead who is foremost amongst all great personalities, obtained the opulence of His staunch reputation, which purifies the entire universe, by worshiping the lotus feet of those brāhmaṇas and Vaiṣṇavas.

PURPORT

The Supreme Person is described herein as *brahmaṇya-deva. Brahmaṇya* refers to the *brāhmaṇas,* the Vaiṣṇavas or the brahminical culture, and *deva* means "worshipable Lord." Therefore unless one is on the transcendental platform of being a Vaiṣṇava, or on the highest platform of material goodness (as a *brāhmaṇa),* he cannot appreciate the Supreme Personality of Godhead. In the lower stages of ignorance and passion, it is difficult to appreciate or understand the Supreme Lord. Therefore the Lord is described herein as the worshipable Deity for persons in brahminical and Vaiṣṇava culture.

namo brahmaṇya-devāya go-brāhmaṇa-hitāya ca
jagad-dhitāya kṛṣṇāya govindāya namo namaḥ
(Viṣṇu Purāṇa 1.19.65)

Lord Kṛṣṇa, the Supreme Personality of Godhead, is the prime protector of brahminical culture and the cow. Without knowing and respecting these, one cannot realize the science of God, and without this knowledge, any welfare activities or humanitarian propaganda cannot be successful. The Lord is *puruṣa,* or the supreme enjoyer. Not only is He the enjoyer when He appears as a manifested incarnation, but He is the enjoyer since time immemorial, from the very beginning *(purātana),* and eternally *(nityam). Yac-caraṇābhivandanāt:* Pṛthu Mahārāja said that the Supreme Personality of Godhead attained this opulence of eternal fame simply by worshiping the lotus feet of the *brāhmaṇas.* In *Bhagavad-gītā* it is said that the Lord does not need to work to achieve material gain. Since He is perpetually supremely perfect, He does not need to obtain anything, but still it is said that He obtained His opulences by worshiping the lotus feet of the *brāhmaṇas.* These are His exemplary actions. When Lord Śrī Kṛṣṇa was in Dvārakā, He offered His respects by bowing down at the lotus feet of Nārada. When Sudāmā Vipra came to His house, Lord Kṛṣṇa personally washed his feet and gave him a seat on His personal bed. Although He is the Supreme Personality of Godhead, Lord Śrī Kṛṣṇa offered His respects to Mahārāja Yudhiṣṭhira and Kuntī. The Lord's exemplary behavior is to teach us. We should learn from His personal behavior how to give protection to the cow, how to cultivate brahminical qualities, and how to respect the *brāhmaṇas* and the Vaiṣṇavas. The Lord says in *Bhagavad-gītā, yad yad ācarati śreṣṭhas tat tad evetaro janaḥ:* "If the leading personalities behave in a certain manner, others follow them automatically." (Bg. 3.21) Who can be more of a leading personality than the Supreme Personality of Godhead, and whose behavior could be more exemplary? It is not that He needed to do all these things to acquire material gain, but all of these acts were performed just to teach us how to behave in this material world.

The Supreme Personality of Godhead is described herein as *mahattama-agraṇīḥ.* Within this material world, the *mahattamas* or great personalities are Lord Brahmā and Lord Śiva, but He is above them all. *Nārāyaṇaḥ paro 'vyaktāt:* the Supreme Personality of Godhead is in a transcendental position, above everything that is created within this material world. His opulence, His riches, His beauty, His wisdom, His knowledge, His renunciation and His reputation are all *jagat-pavitram,* universally purifying. The more we discuss His opulences, the more the universe becomes purer and purer. In the material world, the opulences possessed by a material person are never fixed. Today one may be a very rich man, but tomorrow he may become poor; today one is very famous, but tomorrow he may be infamous. Materially obtained opulences are never fixed, but all six opulences perpetually exist in the Supreme Personality of Godhead, not only in the spiritual world but also in this material world. Lord Kṛṣṇa's reputation is fixed, and His book of wisdom, *Bhagavad-gītā,* is still honored. Everything pertaining to the Supreme Personality of Godhead is eternally existing.

TEXT 39

यत्सेवयाशेषगुहाशयः स्वराड्
विप्रप्रियस्तुष्यति काममीश्वरः ।
तदेव तद्धर्मपरैर्विनीतैः
सर्वात्मना ब्रह्मकुलं निषेव्यताम् ॥३९॥

yat-sevayāśeṣa-guhāśayaḥ sva-rāḍ
vipra-priyas tuṣyati kāmam īśvaraḥ
tad eva tad-dharma-parair vinītaiḥ
sarvātmanā brahma-kulaṁ niṣevyatām

yat—whose; *sevayā*—by serving; *aśeṣa*—unlimited; *guha-āśayaḥ*—dwelling within the heart of everyone; *sva-rāṭ*—but still fully independent; *vipra-priyaḥ*—very dear to the *brāhmaṇas* and Vaiṣṇavas; *tuṣyati*—becomes satisfied; *kāmam*—of desires; *īśvaraḥ*—the Supreme Personality of Godhead; *tat*—that; *eva*—certainly; *tat-dharma-paraiḥ*—by following in the footsteps of the Lord; *vinītaiḥ*—by humbleness; *sarvātmanā*—in all respects; *brahma-kulam*—the descendants of *brāhmaṇas* and Vaiṣṇavas; *niṣevyatām*—always being engaged in their service.

TRANSLATION

The Supreme Personality of Godhead, who is everlastingly independent and who exists in everyone's heart, is very pleased with those who follow

in His footsteps and engage without reservation in the service of the descendants of brāhmaṇas and Vaiṣṇavas. For He is always dear to brāhmaṇas and Vaiṣṇavas, and they are always dear to Him.

PURPORT

It is said that the Lord is most pleased when He sees one engage in the service of His devotee. He does not need any service from anyone because He is complete, but it is in our own interest to offer all kinds of services to the Supreme Personality of Godhead. These services can be offered to the Supreme Person not directly but through the service of *brāhmaṇas* and Vaiṣṇavas. Śrīla Narottama dāsa Ṭhākura sings, *chāḍiyā vaiṣṇava-sevā nistāra payeche kebā,* which means that unless one serves the Vaiṣṇavas and *brāhmaṇas,* one cannot get liberation from the material clutches. Śrīla Viśvanātha Cakravartī Ṭhākura also says, *yasya prasādād bhagavat-prasādaḥ:* by satisfying the senses of the spiritual master one can satisfy the senses of the Supreme Personality of Godhead. Thus this behavior is not only mentioned in scriptures but also followed by *ācaryas.* Pṛthu Mahārāja advised his citizens to follow the exemplary behavior of the Lord Himself and thus engage in the service of *brāhmaṇas* and Vaiṣṇavas.

TEXT 40

पुमाँल्लभेतानतिवेलमात्मनः
प्रसीदतोऽत्यन्तशमं स्वतः स्वयम् ।
यन्नित्यसम्बन्धनिषेवया ततः
परं किमत्रास्ति मुखं हविर्भुजाम् ॥४०॥

pumāl̐ labhetānativelam ātmanaḥ
prasīdato 'tyanta-śamaṁ svataḥ svayam
yan-nitya-sambandha-niṣevayā tataḥ
paraṁ kim atrāsti mukhaṁ havir-bhujām

pumān—a person; *labheta*—can achieve; *anativelam*—without delay; *ātmanaḥ*—of his soul; *prasīdataḥ*—being satisfied; *atyanta*—the greatest; *śamam*—peacefulness; *svataḥ*—automatically; *svayam*—personally; *yat*—whose; *nitya*—regular; *sambandha*—relationship; *niṣevayā*—by dint of service; *tataḥ*—after that; *param*—superior; *kim*—what; *atra*—here; *asti*—there is; *mukham*—happiness; *haviḥ*—clarified butter; *bhujām*—those who drink.

TRANSLATION

By regular service to the brāhmaṇas and Vaiṣṇavas, one can clear the dirt from his heart and thus enjoy supreme peace and liberation from

material attachment and be satisfied. In this world there is no fruitive activity superior to serving the brāhmaṇa class, for this can bring pleasure to the demigods for whom the many sacrifices are recommended.

PURPORT

In *Bhagavad-gītā* it is said: *prasāde sarva-duḥkhānāṁ hānir asyopajāyate* (Bg. 2.65). Unless one is self-satisfied, he cannot be free from the miserable conditions of material existence. Therefore it is essential to render service to the *brāhmaṇas* and Vaiṣṇavas to achieve the perfection of self-satisfaction. Śrīla Narottama dāsa Ṭhākura therefore says:

tāṅdera caraṇa sevi bhakta-sane vāsa
janame janame haya, ei abhilāṣa

"Birth after birth I desire to serve the lotus feet of the *ācāryas* and live in a society of devotees." A spiritual atmosphere can be maintained only by living in a society of devotees and by serving the orders of the *ācāryas*. The spiritual master is the best *brāhmaṇa*. At present, in the age of Kali, it is very difficult to render service to the *brāhmaṇa-kula* or the *brāhmaṇa* class. The difficulty, according to the *Varāha Purāṇa*, is that demons, taking advantage of Kali-yuga, have taken birth in *brāhmaṇa* families. *Rākṣasāḥ kalim āśritya jāyante brahma-yoniṣu (Varāha Purāṇa)*. In other words, in this age there are many so-called caste *brāhmaṇas* and caste Gosvāmīs who, taking advantage of the *śāstra* and of the innocence of people in general, claim to be *brāhmaṇas* and Vaiṣṇavas by hereditary right. One will not derive any benefit by rendering service to such false *brāhmaṇa-kulas*. One must therefore take shelter of a bona fide spiritual master and his associates and should also render service to them, for such activity will greatly help the neophyte in attaining full satisfaction. This has been very clearly explained by Śrīla Viśvanātha Cakravartī Ṭhākura in his explanation of the verse *vyavasāyātmikā buddhir ekeha kuru-nandana* (Bg. 2.41). By actually following the regulated principles of *bhakti-yoga* as recommended by Śrīla Narottama dāsa Ṭhākura, one can very quickly come to the transcendental platform of liberation, as explained in this verse *(atyanta-śamam)*. The particular use of the word *anativelam* ("without delay") is very significant because simply by serving *brāhmaṇas* and Vaiṣṇavas one can get liberation. There is no need to undergo severe penances and austerities. The vivid example of this is Nārada Muni himself. In his previous birth, he was simply a maidservant's son, but he got the opportunity to serve exalted *brāhmaṇas* and Vaiṣṇavas, and thus in his next life he not only became liberated but became famous as the supreme spiritual master of the entire Vaiṣṇava disciplic succession. According to the Vedic system, therefore, it is customarily recommended that after performing a ritualistic ceremony, one should feed the *brāhmaṇas.*

TEXT 41

अश्नात्यनन्तः खलु तत्त्वकोविदैः
श्रद्धाहुतं यन्मुख इज्यनामभिः ।
न वै तथा चेतनया बहिष्कृते
हुताशने पारमहंस्यपर्यगुः ॥४१॥

aśnāty anantaḥ khalu tattva-kovidaiḥ
śraddhā-hutaṁ yan-mukha ijya-nāmabhiḥ
na vai tathā cetanayā bahiṣkṛte
hutāśane pāramahaṁsya-paryaguḥ

aśnāti—eats; *anantaḥ*—the Supreme Personality of Godhead; *khalu*—nevertheless; *tattva-kovidaiḥ*—persons who are in knowledge of the Absolute Truth; *śraddhā*—faith; *hutam*—offering fire sacrifices; *yat-mukhe*—whose mouth; *ijya-nāmabhiḥ*—by different names of demigods; *na*—never; *vai*—certainly; *tathā*—as much; *cetanayā*—by living force; *bahiṣkṛte*—being bereft of; *huta-aśane*—in the fire sacrifice; *pāramahaṁsya*—regarding devotees; *paryaguḥ*—never goes away.

TRANSLATION

Although the Supreme Personality of Godhead, Ananta, eats through the fire sacrifices offered in the names of the different demigods, He does not take as much pleasure in eating through fire as He does in accepting offerings through the mouths of learned sages and devotees, for then He does not leave the association of devotees.

PURPORT

According to Vedic injunctions, a fire sacrifice is held in order to give food to the Supreme Personality of Godhead in the names of the different demigods. While performing a fire sacrifice, one pronounces the word *svāhā* in *mantras* such as *indrāya svāhā* and *ādityāya svāhā.* These *mantras* are uttered to satisfy the Supreme Personality of Godhead through demigods such as Indra and Āditya, for the Supreme Personality of Godhead says:

nāhaṁ tiṣṭhāmi vaikuṇṭhe yogināṁ hṛdayeṣu vā
tattat tiṣṭhāmi nārada yatra gāyanti mad-bhaktāḥ

"I am not in Vaikuṇṭha nor in the hearts of the *yogīs*. I remain where My devotees engage in glorifying My activities." It is to be understood that the Supreme Personality of Godhead does not leave the company of His devotees.

Fire is certainly devoid of life, but devotees and *brāhmaṇas* are the living representatives of the Supreme Lord. Therefore to feed *brāhmaṇas* and Vaiṣṇavas is to feed the Supreme Personality of Godhead directly. It may be concluded that instead of offering fire sacrifices, one should offer foodstuffs to *brāhmaṇas* and Vaiṣṇavas, for that process is more effective than fire *yajña.* The vivid example of this principle in action was given by Advaita Prabhu. When he performed the *śrāddha* ceremony for his father, he first of all called Haridāsa Ṭhākura and offered him food. It is the practice that after finishing the *śrāddha* ceremony, one should offer food to an elevated *brāhmaṇa.* But Advaita Prabhu offered food first to Haridāsa Ṭhākura, who had taken his birth in a Mohammedan family. Therefore Haridāsa Ṭhākura asked Advaita Prabhu why he was doing something which might jeopardize his position in *brāhmaṇa* society. Advaita Prabhu replied that he was feeding millions of first-class *brāhmaṇas* by offering the food to Haridāsa Ṭhākura. He was prepared to talk with any learned *brāhmaṇa* on this point and prove definitely that by offering food to a pure devotee like Haridāsa Ṭhākura, he was equally as blessed as he would have been by offering food to thousands of learned *brāhmaṇas.* When performing sacrifices, one offers oblations to the sacrificial fire, but when such oblations are offered to Vaiṣṇavas, they are certainly more effective.

TEXT 42

यद्ब्रह्म नित्यं विरजं सनातनं
श्रद्धातपोमङ्गलमौनसंयमैः ।
समाधिना बिभ्रति हार्थदृष्टये
यत्रेदमादर्श इवावभासते ॥४२॥

yad brahma nityaṁ virajaṁ sanātanaṁ
śraddhā-tapo-maṅgala-mauna-saṁyamaiḥ
samādhinā bibhrati hārtha-dṛṣṭaye
yatredam ādarśa ivāvabhāsate

yat—that which; *brahma*—the brahminical culture; *nityam*—eternally; *virajam*—without contamination; *sanātanam*—without beginning; *śraddhā*—faith; *tapaḥ*—austerity; *maṅgala*—auspicious; *mauna*—silence; *saṁyamaiḥ*—controlling the mind and senses; *samādhinā*—with full concentration;

bibhrati—illuminates; *ha*—as he did it; *artha*—the real purpose of the *Vedas; dṛṣṭaye*—for the purpose of finding out; *yatra*—wherein; *idam*—all this; *ādarśe*—in a mirror; *iva*—like; *avabhāsate*—manifests.

TRANSLATION

In brahminical culture a brāhmaṇa's transcendental position is eternally maintained because the injunctions of the Vedas are accepted with faith, austerity, scriptural conclusions, full sense and mind control and meditation. In this way the real goal of life is illuminated, just as one's face in a clear mirror is fully reflected.

PURPORT

Since it is described in the previous verse that feeding a living *brāhmaṇa* is more effective than offering oblations in a fire sacrifice, in this verse it is now clearly described what brahminism is and who a *brāhmaṇa* is. In the age of Kali, taking advantage of the fact that by feeding a *brāhmaṇa* one obtains a more effective result than by performing sacrifices, a class of men with no brahminical qualifications claim the eating privilege known as *brāhmaṇa-bhojana* simply on the basis of their births in *brāhmaṇa* families. In order to distinguish this class of men from the real *brāhmaṇas,* Mahārāja Pṛthu is giving an exact description of a *brāhmaṇa* and brahminical culture. One should not take advantage of his position simply to live like a fire without light. A *brāhmaṇa* must be fully conversant with the Vedic conclusion, which is described in *Bhagavad-gītā. Vedaiś ca sarvair aham eva vedyaḥ.* (Bg. 15.15) The Vedic conclusion—the ultimate understanding, or *Vedānta* understanding—is knowledge of Kṛṣṇa. Actually that is a fact because simply by understanding Kṛṣṇa as He is, as described in *Bhagavad-gītā (janma karma ca me divyam evaṁ yo vetti tattvataḥ),* one becomes a perfect *brāhmaṇa.* The *brāhmaṇa* who knows Kṛṣṇa perfectly well is always in a transcendental position. This is also confirmed in *Bhagavad-gītā:*

māṁ ca yo 'vyabhicāreṇa bhakti-yogena sevate
sa guṇān samatītyaitān brahma-bhūyāya kalpate

"One who engages in full devotional service and who does not fall down in any circumstance at once transcends the modes of material nature and thus comes to the level of Brahman." (Bg. 14.26)

Therefore a devotee of Lord Kṛṣṇa is actually a perfect *brāhmaṇa.* His situation is transcendental, for he is free from the four defects of conditional life, which are the tendencies to commit mistakes, to be illusioned, to cheat and to possess imperfect senses. A perfect Vaiṣṇava or Kṛṣṇa conscious person is always in this transcendental position because he speaks according to Kṛṣṇa and His representative. Because Vaiṣṇavas speak exactly according to the tune of Kṛṣṇa, whatever they say is free from these four defects. For example, Kṛṣṇa says in *Bhagavad-gītā* that everyone should always think of Him, everyone should become His devotee, offer Him obeisances and worship Him, and ultimately everyone should surrender unto Him. These devotional activities are transcendental and free from mistakes, illusion, cheating and imperfection. Therefore anyone who is a sincere devotee of Lord Kṛṣṇa and who preaches this cult, speaking only on the basis of Kṛṣṇa's instructions, is understood to be *virajam,* or free from the defects of material contamination. A genuine *brāhmaṇa* or Vaiṣṇava therefore depends eternally on the conclusion of the *Vedas* or Vedic versions presented by the Supreme Personality of Godhead Himself. Only from Vedic knowledge can we understand the actual position of the Absolute Truth, who, as described in *Śrīmad-Bhāgavatam,* is manifested in three features—namely, impersonal Brahman, localized Paramātmā and at last the Supreme Personality of Godhead. This knowledge is perfect from time immemorial, and the brahminical or Vaiṣṇava culture depends on this principle eternally. One should therefore study the *Vedas* with faith, not only for one's personal knowledge, but for the sake of spreading this knowledge and these activities through real faith in the words of the Supreme Personality of Godhead and the *Vedas.*

The word *maṅgala* ("auspicious") in this verse is very significant. Śrīla Śrīdhara Svāmī quotes that to do what is good and to reject what is not good is called *maṅgala,* or auspicious. To do what is good means to accept everything which is favorable to the discharge of devotional service, and to reject what is not good means to reject everything not favorable for discharging devotional service. In our Kṛṣṇa consciousness movement, we accept this principle by rejecting four prohibited items—namely, illicit sex life, intoxication, gambling and flesh-eating—and accepting the daily chanting of at least sixteen rounds of the Hare Kṛṣṇa *mahā-mantra* and daily meditation three times a day by chanting the Gāyatrī *mantra.* In this way one can keep his brahminical culture and spiritual strength intact. By following these principles of devotional service strictly, chanting twenty-four hours a day the *mahā-mantra*—Hare Kṛṣṇa, Hare Kṛṣṇa, Kṛṣṇa Kṛṣṇa, Hare Hare/ Hare Rāma, Hare Rāma, Rāma Rāma, Hare Hare—one makes positive progress in spiritual life and ultimately becomes completely fit to see the Supreme Personality of Godhead face to face. Because the ultimate goal of studying or understanding the Vedic knowledge is to find Kṛṣṇa, one who follows the Vedic principles as described above can from the very beginning see all the features of Lord Kṛṣṇa, the Absolute Truth, very distinctly, as one can see his own face completely reflected in a clear mirror. The conclusion is, therefore, that a *brāhmaṇa* does not become a *brāhmaṇa* simply because he is a living entity or is born in a *brāhmaṇa* family; he must possess all the qualities mentioned in the *śāstras* and practice the brahminical principles in his life. Thus he ultimately becomes a fully Kṛṣṇa conscious person and can understand what Kṛṣṇa is. How a devotee continuously sees Kṛṣṇa face to face within his heart is described in the *Brahma-saṁhitā* as follows:

premāñjana-cchurita-bhakti-vilocanena
santaḥ sadaiva hṛdayeṣu vilokayanti
yaṁ śyāmasundaram acintya-guṇa-svarūpaṁ
govindam ādi-puruṣaṁ tam ahaṁ bhajāmi

The devotee, by development of pure love for Kṛṣṇa, constantly sees the Supreme Personality of Godhead, who is known as Śyāmasundara, within his heart. That is the perfectional stage of brahminical culture.

TEXT 43

तेषामहं पादसरोजरेणु-
मार्या वहेयाधिकिरीटमायुः ।
यं नित्यदा बिभ्रत आशु पापं
नश्यत्यमुं सर्वगुणा भजन्ति ॥४३॥

teṣām ahaṁ pāda-saroja-reṇum
āryā vaheyādhikirīṭam āyuḥ
yaṁ nityadā bibhrata āśu pāpaṁ
naśyaty amuṁ sarva-guṇā bhajanti

teṣām—of all of them; *aham*—I; *pāda*—feet; *saroja*—lotus; *reṇum*—dust; *āryāḥ*—O respectable persons; *vaheya*—shall bear; *adhi*—up to; *kirīṭam*—helmet; *āyuḥ*—up to the end of life; *yam*—which; *nityadā*—always; *bibhrataḥ*—carrying; *āśu*—very soon; *pāpam*—sinful activities; *naśyati*—are vanquished; *amum*—all those; *sarva-guṇāḥ*—fully qualified; *bhajanti*—worship.

TRANSLATION

O respectable personalities present here, I beg the blessings of all of you that I may perpetually carry on my crown the dust of the lotus feet of such

brāhmaṇas and Vaiṣṇavas until the end of my life. He who can carry such dust on his head is very soon relieved of all the reactions which arise from sinful life, and eventually he develops all good and desirable qualities.

PURPORT

It is said that one who has unflinching faith in the Supreme Personality of Godhead, which means unflinching faith in the Vaiṣṇava or the pure devotee of the Supreme Lord, develops all the good qualities of the demigods.

yasyāsti bhaktir bhagavaty akiñcanā
sarvair guṇais tatra samāsate surāḥ (*Bhāg.* 5.18.12)

Prahlāda Mahārāja also said, *naiṣāṁ matis tāvad urukramāṅghrim.* (*Bhāg.* 7.5.32) Unless one takes the dust of the lotus feet of a pure Vaiṣṇava on one's head, one cannot understand what the Supreme Personality of Godhead is, and unless one knows the Supreme Personality of Godhead, one's life remains imperfect. A great soul who has fully surrendered to the Supreme Lord after understanding Him fully and after repeatedly undergoing austerities and penances for many, many lives is very rare. The crown of a king is simply a big load if the king or head of the state does not actually bear the dust of the lotus feet of *brāhmaṇas* and Vaiṣṇavas. In other words, if a liberal king like Pṛthu Mahārāja does not follow the instructions of *brāhmaṇas* and Vaiṣṇavas or does not follow the brahminical culture, he is simply a burden on the state, for he cannot benefit the citizens. Mahārāja Pṛthu is the perfect example of an ideal chief executive.

TEXT 44

गुणायनं शीलधनं कृतज्ञं
वृद्धाश्रयं संवृणतेऽनु सम्पदः ।
प्रसीदतां ब्रह्मकुलं गवां च
जनार्दनः सानुचरश्च मह्यम् ॥४४॥

guṇāyanaṁ śīla-dhanaṁ kṛta-jñaṁ
vṛddhāśrayaṁ saṁvṛṇate 'nu sampadaḥ
prasīdatāṁ brahma-kulaṁ gavāṁ ca
janārdanaḥ sānucaraś ca mahyam

guṇa-ayanam—one who has acquired all the good qualities; *śīla-dhanam*—one whose wealth is good behavior; *kṛta-jñam*—one who is grateful; *vṛddha-āśrayam*—one who takes shelter of the learned; *saṁvṛṇate*—achieves; *anu*—

certainly; *sampadaḥ*—all opulences; *prasīdatām*—be pleased upon; *brahma-kulam*—the *brāhmaṇa* class; *gavām*—the cows; *ca*—and; *janārdanaḥ*—the Supreme Personality of Godhead; *sa*—with; *anucaraḥ*—along with His devotee; *ca*—and; *mahyam*—upon me.

TRANSLATION

Whoever acquires the brahminical qualifications—whose only wealth is good behavior, who is grateful and who takes shelter of experienced persons—gets all the opulence of the world. I therefore wish that the Supreme Personality of Godhead and His associates will be pleased with the brāhmaṇa class, with the cows and with me.

PURPORT

The Supreme Personality of Godhead is worshiped with the prayer *namo brahmaṇya-devāya go-brāhmaṇa-hitāya ca.* Thus it is clear that the Supreme Personality of Godhead respects and protects the *brāhmaṇas* and brahminical culture as well as the cows; in other words, wherever there are *brāhmaṇas* and brahminical culture, there are cows and cow protection. In a society or civilization in which there are no *brāhmaṇas* or brahminical culture, cows are treated as ordinary animals and slaughtered at the sacrifice of human civilization. The specific mention of the word *gavām* by Pṛthu Mahārāja is significant because the Lord is always associated with cows and His devotees. In pictures Lord Kṛṣṇa is always seen with cows and His associates such as the cowherd boys and the *gopīs*. Kṛṣṇa, the Supreme Personality of Godhead, cannot be alone. Therefore Pṛthu Mahārāja said, *sānucaraś ca,* indicating that the Supreme Personality of Godhead is always associated with His followers and devotees.

A devotee acquires all the good qualities of the demigods; he is *guṇāyanam,* the reservoir of all good qualities. His only asset is good behavior, and he is grateful. Gratitude for the mercy of the Supreme Personality of Godhead is one of the qualities of *brāhmaṇas* and Vaiṣṇavas. Everyone should feel grateful to the Supreme Personality of Godhead because He is maintaining all living entities and supplying all their necessities. As stated in the *Vedas, eko bahūnāṁ yo vidadhāti kāmān:* the Supreme One is supplying all necessities to the living entities (*Kaṭha Up.* 2.2.13). The living entity who is therefore grateful to the Supreme Personality of Godhead is certainly qualified with good characteristics.

The word *vṛddhāśrayam* is very significant in this verse. *Vṛddha* refers to one who is advanced in knowledge. There are two kinds of old men—he who is advanced in years and he who is experienced in knowledge. One who is advanced in knowledge is actually *vṛddha (jñāna-vṛddha);* one does not become *vṛddha* simply by advancing in age. *Vṛddhāśrayam,* a person who takes shelter of a superior person who is advanced in knowledge, can acquire all the good qualities of a *brāhmaṇa* and be trained in good behavior. When one actually attains good qualities, becomes grateful for the mercy of the Supreme Personality of Godhead and takes shelter of a bona fide spiritual master, he is endowed with all opulence. Such a person is a *brāhmaṇa* or Vaiṣṇava. Therefore Pṛthu Mahārāja invokes the blessings and mercy of the Supreme Personality of Godhead, with His associates, devotees, Vaiṣṇavas, *brāhmaṇas* and cows.

TEXT 45

मैत्रेय उवाच

इति ब्रुवाणं नृपतिं पितृदेवद्विजातयः ।
तुष्टुवुर्हृष्टमनसः साधुवादेन साधवः ॥४५॥

maitreya uvāca
iti bruvāṇaṁ nṛ-patiṁ
pitṛ-deva-dvijātayaḥ
tuṣṭuvur hṛṣṭa-manasaḥ
sādhu-vādena sādhavaḥ

maitreyaḥ uvāca—the great sage Maitreya continued to speak; *iti*—thus; *bruvāṇam*—while speaking; *nṛ-patim*—the King; *pitṛ*—the denizens of Pitṛloka; *deva*—the demigods; *dvijātayaḥ*—and the twice-born (the *brāhmaṇas* and the Vaiṣṇavas); *tuṣṭuvuḥ*—satisfied; *hṛṣṭa-manasaḥ*—greatly pacified in mind; *sādhu-vādena*—by expressing congratulations; *sādhavaḥ*—all the saintly persons present.

TRANSLATION

The great sage Maitreya said: After hearing King Pṛthu speak so nicely, all the demigods, the denizens of Pitṛloka, the brāhmaṇas and the saintly persons present at the meeting congratulated him by expressing their good will.

PURPORT

When a person speaks very nicely at a meeting, he is congratulated by the audience, who express their good will with the words *sādhu, sādhu.* This is called *sādhu-vāda.* All the saintly persons—Pitās, denizens of Pitṛloka and demigods—who were present in the meeting and heard Pṛthu Mahārāja expressed their good will with the words *sādhu, sādhu.* They all accepted the good mission of Pṛthu Mahārāja, and they were fully satisfied.

TEXT 46

पुत्रेण जयते लोकानिति सत्यवती श्रुतिः ।
ब्रह्मदण्डहतः पापो यद्वेनोऽत्यतरत्तमः ॥४६॥

putreṇa jayate lokān
iti satyavatī śrutiḥ
brahma-daṇḍa-hataḥ pāpo
yad veno 'tyatarat tamaḥ

putreṇa—by the son; *jayate*—one becomes victorious; *lokān*—all the heavenly planets; *iti*—thus; *satyavatī*—becomes true; *śrutiḥ*—the *Vedas; brahma-daṇḍa*—by the curse of *brāhmaṇas; hataḥ*—killed; *pāpaḥ*—the most sinful; *yat*—as; *venaḥ*—the father of Mahārāja Pṛthu; *ati*—great; *atarat*—become delivered; *tamaḥ*—from the darkness of hellish life.

TRANSLATION

They all declared that the Vedic conclusion that one can conquer the heavenly planets by the action of a putra, or son, was fulfilled, for the most sinful Vena, who had been killed by the curse of the brāhmaṇas, was now delivered from the darkest region of hellish life by his son, Mahārāja Pṛthu.

PURPORT

According to the Vedic version, there is a hellish planet called Put, and one who delivers a person from there is called *putra.* The purpose of marriage is, therefore, to have a *putra* or son who is able to deliver his father, even if the father falls down to the hellish condition of Put. Mahārāja Pṛthu's father, Vena, was a most sinful person and was therefore cursed to death by the *brāhmaṇas.* Now all the great saintly persons, sages and *brāhmaṇas* present in the meeting, after hearing from Mahārāja Pṛthu about his great mission in life, became convinced that the statement of the *Vedas* had been fully proved. The purpose of accepting a wife in religious marriage, as sanctioned in the *Vedas,* is to have a *putra,* a son qualified to deliver his father from the darkest region of hellish life. Marriage is not intended for sense gratification but for getting a son fully qualified to deliver his father. But if a son is raised to become an unqualified demon, how can he deliver his father from hellish life? It is therefore the duty of a father to become a Vaiṣṇava and raise his children to become Vaiṣṇavas; then even if by chance the father falls into a hellish life in his next birth, such a son can deliver him, as Mahārāja Pṛthu delivered his father.

TEXT 47

हिरण्यकशिपुश्चापि भगवन्निन्दया तमः ।
विविक्षुरत्यगात्सूनोः प्रह्लादस्यानुभावतः ॥४७॥

hiraṇyakaśipuś cāpi
bhagavan-nindayā tamaḥ
vivikṣur atyagāt sūnoḥ
prahlādasyānubhāvataḥ

hiraṇyakaśipuḥ—the father of Prahlāda Mahārāja; *ca*—also; *api*—again; *bhagavat*—of the Supreme Personality of Godhead; *nindayā*—by blaspheming; *tamaḥ*—in the darkest region of hellish life; *vivikṣuḥ*—entered; *atyagāt*—was delivered; *sūnoḥ*—of his son; *prahlādasya*—of Mahārāja Prahlāda; *anubhāvataḥ*—by the influence of.

TRANSLATION

Similarly, Hiraṇyakaśipu, who by dint of his sinful activities always defied the supremacy of the Supreme Personality of Godhead, entered into the darkest region of hellish life; but by the grace of his great son, Prahlāda Mahārāja, he also was delivered and went back home, back to Godhead.

PURPORT

When Prahlāda Mahārāja was offered benediction by Nṛsiṁhadeva, due to his great devotion and tolerance he refused to accept any benediction from the Lord, thinking that such acceptance was not befitting a sincere devotee. The rendering of service to the Supreme Personality of Godhead in expectation of a good reward is deprecated by Prahlāda Mahārāja as mercantile business. Because Prahlāda Mahārāja was a Vaiṣṇava, he did not ask benediction for his personal self but was very affectionate towards his father. Although his father tortured him and would have killed him had he himself not been killed by the Supreme Personality of Godhead, Prahlāda Mahārāja begged pardon for him from the Lord. This favor was immediately granted by the Lord, and Hiraṇyakaśipu was delivered from the darkest region of hellish life, and he returned back home, back to Godhead, by the grace of his son. Prahlāda Mahārāja is the topmost example of a Vaiṣṇava who is always compassionate toward sinful persons suffering a hellish life within this material world. Kṛṣṇa is therefore known as *para-duḥkha-duḥkhī kṛpāmbudhi,* or one who is compassionate toward others' suffering and who is an ocean of mercy. Like Prahlāda Mahārāja, all pure devotees of the Lord come to this material world with full compassion to deliver the sinful. They undergo all kinds of tribulations, suffering them with tolerance, because that is another qualification of a Vaiṣṇava, who tries to deliver all sinful persons from the hellish conditions of material existence. Vaiṣṇavas are therefore offered the following prayer:

vāñchā-kalpatarubhyaś ca kṛpā-sindhubhya eva ca
patitānāṁ pāvanebhyo vaiṣṇavebhyo namo namaḥ

The chief concern of a Vaiṣṇava is to deliver the fallen souls.

TEXT 48

वीरवर्य पितः पृथ्व्याः समाःसञ्जीव शाश्वतीः ।
यस्येदृश्यच्युते भक्तिः सर्वलोकैकभर्तरि ॥४८॥

vīra-varya pitaḥ pṛthvyāḥ
samāḥ sañjīva śāśvatīḥ
yasyedṛśy acyute bhaktiḥ
sarva-lokaika-bhartari

vīra-varya—the best of the warriors; *pitaḥ*—the father; *pṛthvyāḥ*—of the globe; *samāḥ*—equal to in years; *sañjīva*—live; *śāśvatīḥ*—forever; *yasya*—whose; *īdṛśī*—like this; *acyute*—unto the Supreme; *bhaktiḥ*—devotion; *sarva*—all; *loka*—planets; *eka*—one; *bhartari*—maintainer.

TRANSLATION

All the saintly brāhmaṇas thus addressed Pṛthu Mahārāja: O best of the warriors, O father of this globe, may you be blessed with a long life, for you have great devotion to the infallible Supreme Personality of Godhead, who is the master of all the universe.

PURPORT

Pṛthu Mahārāja was blessed by the saintly persons present at the meeting to have a long life because of his unflinching faith and his devotion to the Supreme Personality of Godhead. Although one's duration of life is limited in years, if by chance one becomes a devotee, he surpasses the duration prescribed for his life; indeed, sometimes *yogīs* die according to their wish, not according to the laws of material nature. Another feature of a devotee is that he lives forever because of his infallible devotion to the Lord. It is said, *kīrtir yasya sa jīvati:* "One who leaves a good reputation behind him lives forever." Specifically, one who is reputed as a devotee of the Lord undoubtedly lives forever. When Lord Caitanya Mahāprabhu was talking with Rāmānanda Rāya, Caitanya Mahāprabhu inquired, "What is the greatest reputation?" Rāmānanda Rāya replied that a person who is reputed as a great devotee has the greatest reputation, for a devotee not only lives forever in the Vaikuṇṭha planets, but by his reputation he also lives forever within this material world.

TEXT 49

अहो वयं ह्यद्य पवित्रकीर्ते
त्वयैव नाथेन मुकुन्दनाथाः ।
य उत्तमश्लोकतमस्य विष्णो-
र्ब्रह्मण्यदेवस्य कथां व्यनक्ति ॥४९॥

aho vayaṁ hy adya pavitra-kīrte
tvayaiva nāthena mukunda-nāthāḥ
ya uttamaślokatamasya viṣṇor
brahmaṇya-devasya kathāṁ vyanakti

aho—O goodness; *vayam*—we; *hi*—certainly; *adya*—today; *pavitra-kīrte*—O supreme purity; *tvayā*—by you; *eva*—certainly; *nāthena*—by the Lord; *mukunda*—the Supreme Personality of Godhead; *nāthāḥ*—being the subject of the Supreme; *ye*—one who; *uttamaślokatamasya*—of the Supreme Personality of Godhead, who is praised by the nicest verses; *viṣṇoḥ*—of Viṣṇu; *brahmaṇya-devasya*—of the worshipable Lord of the *brāhmaṇas; kathām*—words; *vyanakti*—expressed.

TRANSLATION

The audience continued: Dear King Pṛthu, your reputation is the purest of all, for you are preaching the glories of the most glorified of all, the Supreme Personality of Godhead, the Lord of the brāhmaṇas. Since, due to our great fortune, we have you as our master, we think that we are living directly under the agency of the Lord.

PURPORT

The citizens declared that through being under the protection of Mahārāja Pṛthu they were directly under the protection of the Supreme Personality of Godhead. This understanding is the proper situation of social steadiness within this material world. Since it is stated in the *Vedas* that the Supreme Personality of Godhead is the maintainer and leader of all living entities, the king or the executive head of the government must be a representative of the Supreme Person. Then he can claim honor exactly like the Lord's. How a king or leader of society can become the representative of the Supreme Personality of Godhead is also indicated in this verse by the statement that because Pṛthu Mahārāja was preaching the supremacy and the glories of the Supreme Personality of Godhead, Viṣṇu, he was therefore a proper representative of the Lord. To remain under the jurisdiction or administration of such a king or leader is the perfect status for human society. The primary responsibility of such a king or leader is to protect the brahminical culture and the cows in his state.

TEXT 50

नात्यद्भुतमिदं नाथ तवाजीव्यानुशासनम् ।
प्रजानुरागो महतां प्रकृतिः करुणात्मनाम् ॥५०॥

nātyadbhutam idaṁ nātha
tavājīvyānuśāsanam
prajānurāgo mahatāṁ
prakṛtiḥ karuṇātmanām

na—not; *ati*—very great; *adbhutam*—wonderful; *idam*—this; *nātha*—O lord; *tava*—your; *ājīvya*—source of income; *anuśāsanam*-ruling over the citizens; *prajā*—citizens; *anurāgaḥ*—affection; *mahatām*—of the great; *prakṛtiḥ*—nature; *karuṇa*—merciful; *ātmanām*—of the living entities.

TRANSLATION

Our dear lord, it is your occupational duty to rule over your citizens. That is not a very wonderful task for a personality like you, who are so affectionate in seeing to the interests of the citizens, because you are full of mercy. That is the greatness of your character.

PURPORT

A king's duty is to give protection to his citizens and levy taxes from them for his livelihood. Since the Vedic society is divided into four classes of men—the *brāhmaṇas, kṣatriyas, vaiśyas* and *śūdras*—their means of livelihood are also mentioned in the scriptures. The *brāhmaṇas* should live by spreading knowledge and therefore should take contributions from their disciples, whereas a king should give protection to the citizens for their development to the highest standard of life, and he can therefore levy taxes from them; businessmen or mercantile men, because they produce foodstuffs for the whole of society, can take a little profit from this, whereas the *śūdras,* who cannot work as either *brāhmaṇas, kṣatriyas* or *vaiśyas,* should give service to the higher classes of society and be provided by them with a supply of the necessities of life.

The symptom of a qualified king or political leader is mentioned herein—he must be very merciful and compassionate to the people and see to their prime interest, which is to become elevated devotees of the Supreme Personality of Godhead. Great souls are naturally inclined to do good to others, and a Vaiṣṇava especially is the most compassionate and merciful personality in society. Therefore we offer our respects to a Vaiṣṇava leader as follows:

vāñchā-kalpatarubhyaś ca kṛpā-sindhubhya eva ca
patitānāṁ pāvanebhyo vaiṣṇavebhyo namo namaḥ

Only a Vaiṣṇava leader can fulfill all the desires of the people *(vāñchā-kalpataru),* and he is compassionate because he is the contributor of the greatest benefit to human society. He is *patita-pāvana,* the deliverer of all fallen souls, because if the king or the head of the government follows in the footsteps of the *brāhmaṇas* and Vaiṣṇavas, who are naturally leaders in missionary work, similarly the *vaiśyas* will also follow in the footsteps of the Vaiṣṇavas and *brāhmaṇas,* and the *śūdras* will give them service. Thus the entire society becomes a perfect human institution for combined progress to the highest perfection of life.

TEXT 51

अद्य नस्तमसः पारस्त्वयोपासादितः प्रभो ।
भ्राम्यतां नष्टदृष्टीनां कर्मभिर्दैवसंज्ञितैः ॥५१॥

adya nas tamasaḥ pāras
tvayopāsāditaḥ prabho
bhrāmyatāṁ naṣṭa-dṛṣṭīnāṁ
karmabhir daiva-saṁjñitaiḥ

adya—today; *naḥ*—of us; *tamasaḥ*—of the darkness of material existence; *pāraḥ*—other side; *tvayā*—by you; *upāsāditaḥ*—increased; *prabho*—O lord; *bhrāmyatām*—who are wandering; *naṣṭa-dṛṣṭīnām*—who have lost their goal of life; *karmabhiḥ*—on account of past deeds; *daiva-saṁjñitaiḥ*—arranged by superior authority.

TRANSLATION

The citizens continued: Today you have opened our eyes and revealed how to cross to the other side of the ocean of darkness. By our past deeds and by the arrangement of superior authority, we are entangled in a network of fruitive activities and have lost sight of the destination of life; thus we have been wandering within the universe.

PURPORT

In this verse, the words *karmabhir daiva-saṁjñitaiḥ* are very significant. Due to the quality of our actions, we come to the association of the modes of material nature, and by superior arrangement we are given a chance to enjoy the fruitive results of such activities in different types of bodies. In this way, having lost sight of their destinations in life, all living entities are wandering in different species throughout the universe, sometimes getting birth in a lower species and sometimes existence in higher planetary systems; thus we are all wandering since time immemorial. It is by the grace of the spiritual master and the Supreme Personality of Godhead that we get the clue of devotional life, and thus progressive success in our life begins. Here this is admitted by the citizens of King Pṛthu; in full consciousness they admit the benefit they have derived from the activities of Mahārāja Pṛthu.

TEXT 52

नमो विवृद्धसत्त्वाय पुरुषाय महीयसे ।
यो ब्रह्म क्षत्रमाविश्य बिभर्तीदं स्वतेजसा ॥५२॥

namo vivṛddha-sattvāya
puruṣāya mahīyase
yo brahma kṣatram āviśya
bibhartīdaṁ sva-tejasā

namaḥ—all obeisances; *vivṛddha*—highly elevated; *sattvāya*—unto the existence; *puruṣāya*—unto the person; *mahīyase*—unto one who is so glorified; *yaḥ*—who; *brahma*—brahminical culture; *kṣatram*—administrative duty; *āviśya*—entering; *bibharti*—maintaining; *idam*—this; *sva-tejasā*—by his own prowess.

TRANSLATION

Dear lord, you are situated in your pure existential position of goodness; therefore you are the perfect representative of the Supreme Lord. You

are glorified by your own prowess, and thus you are maintaining the entire world by introducing brahminical culture and protecting everyone in your line of duty as a kṣatriya.

PURPORT

Without the spread of brahminical culture and without proper protection from the government no social standard can be maintained properly. This is admitted in this verse by the citizens of Mahārāja Pṛthu, who could maintain the wonderful situation of his government dūe to his position in pure goodness. The word *vivṛddha-sattvāya* is significant. In the material world there are three qualities—namely, goodness, passion and ignorance. One has to be raised from the platform of ignorance to the platform of goodness by devotional service. There is no other means for elevating one from the lowest stage of life to the highest stage but the execution of devotional service; as advised in the previous chapters of *Śrīmad-Bhāgavatam,* one can raise himself from the lowest position to the highest simply by associating with devotees and hearing *Śrīmad-Bhāgavatam* regularly from their mouths.

śṛṇvatāṁ sva-kathāḥ kṛṣṇaḥ puṇya-śravaṇa-kīrtanaḥ
hṛdy antaḥ-stho hy abhadrāṇi vidhunoti su-hṛt satām
(*Bhāg.* 1.2.17)

"When one engages in devotional service in the first stages of hearing and chanting, the Lord who is in everyone's heart helps the devotee in cleansing his heart." In the gradual cleansing process one is relieved of the influence of passion and ignorance and is situated on the platform of goodness. The result of association with the qualities of passion and ignorance is that one becomes lusty and greedy. But when one is elevated to the platform of goodness, he is satisfied in any condition of life and is without lust and greed. This mentality indicates one's situation on the platform of goodness. One has to transcend this goodness and raise himself to the pure goodness which is called *vivṛddha-sattva* or the advanced stage of goodness. In the advanced stage of goodness one can become Kṛṣṇa conscious. Therefore Mahārāja Pṛthu is addressed here as *vivṛddha-sattva,* or one who is situated in the transcendental position. But Mahārāja Pṛthu, although situated in the transcendental position of a pure devotee, comes down to the position of *brāhmaṇa* and *kṣatriya* for the benefit of human society and thus gives protection to the entire world by his personal prowess. Although he was a king, a *kṣatriya,* because he was a Vaiṣṇava he was also a *brāhmaṇa.* As a *brāhmaṇa* he could give proper instruction to the citizens and as a *kṣatriya* he could rightly give protection to all of them. Thus the citizens of Mahārāja Pṛthu were protected in all respects by the perfect king.

Thus end the Bhaktivedanta purports of the Fourth Canto, Twenty-first Chapter of the Śrīmad-Bhāgavatam *entitled, "Instructions by Mahārāja Pṛthu."*

CHAPTER TWENTY-TWO

Pṛthu Mahārāja's Meeting with the Four Kumaras

TEXT 1

मैत्रेय उवाच
जनेषु प्रगृणत्स्वेवं पृथुं पृथुलविक्रमम् ।
तत्रोपजग्मुर्मुनयश्चत्वारः सूर्यवर्चसः ॥ १ ॥

maitreya uvāca
janeṣu pragṛṇatsv evaṁ
pṛthuṁ pṛthula-vikramam
tatropajagmur munayaś
catvāraḥ sūrya-varcasaḥ

maitreyaḥ uvāca—the great sage Maitreya continued to speak; *janeṣu*—the citizens; *pragṛṇatsu*—while praying for; *evam*—thus; *pṛthum*—unto Mahārāja Pṛthu; *pṛthula*—highly; *vikramam*—powerful; *tatra*—there; *upajagmuḥ*—arrived; *munayaḥ*—the Kumāras; *catvāraḥ*—four; *sūrya*—as the sun; *varcasaḥ*—bright.

TRANSLATION

The great sage Maitreya said: While the citizens were thus praying to the most powerful King Pṛthu, the four Kumāras, who were as bright as the sun, arrived on the spot.

TEXT 2

तांस्तु सिद्धेश्वरान् राजा व्योम्नोऽवतरतोऽर्चिषा ।
लोकानपापान् कुर्वाणान् सानुगोऽचष्ट लक्षितान् ॥ २ ॥

tāṁs tu siddheśvarān rājā
vyomno 'vatarato 'rciṣā
lokān apāpān kurvāṇān
sānugo 'caṣṭa lakṣitān

tān—them; *tu*—but; *siddheśvarān*—masters of all mystic power; *rājā*—the King; *vyomnaḥ*—from the sky; *avatarataḥ*—while descending; *arciṣā*—by their glaring effulgence; *lokān*—all the planets; *apāpān*—sinless; *kurvāṇān*—doing so; *sa-anugaḥ*—with his associates; *acaṣṭa*—recognized; *lakṣitān*—by seeing them.

TRANSLATION

When the King and his associates saw the glowing effulgence of the four Kumāras, the masters of all mystic power, they could recognize them as they descended from the sky.

PURPORT

The four Kumāras are described herein as *siddheśvarān,* which means "masters of all mystic power." One who has attained perfection in *yoga* practice immediately becomes master of the eight mystic perfections—to become smaller than the smallest, to become lighter than the lightest, to become bigger than the biggest, to achieve anything he desires, to control everything, etc. These four Kumāras, as *siddheśvaras,* had achieved all the yogic perfectional achievements, and as such they could travel in outer space without machines. While they were coming to Mahārāja Pṛthu from other planets, they did not come by airplane, but personally. In other words, these four Kumāras were also spacemen who could travel in space without machines. The residents of the planet which is known as Siddhaloka can travel in outer space from one planet to another without vehicles. However, the special power of the Kumāras mentioned herewith is that whatever place they went to would immediately become sinless. During the reign of Mahārāja Pṛthu, everything on the surface of this globe was sinless, and therefore the Kumāras decided to see the King. Ordinarily they do not go to any planet which is sinful.

TEXT 3

तद्दर्शनोद्गतान् प्राणान् प्रत्यादित्सुरिवोत्थितः ।
ससदस्यानुगो वैन्य इन्द्रियेशो गुणानिव ॥ ३ ॥

tad-darśanodgatān prāṇān
pratyāditsur ivotthitaḥ
sa-sadasyānugo vainya
indriyeśo guṇān iva

tat—him; *darśana*—seeing; *udgatān*—being greatly desired; *prāṇān*—life; *pratyāditsuḥ*—peacefully going; *iva*—like; *utthitaḥ*—got up; *sa*—with;

sadasya—associates or followers; *anugaḥ*—officers; *vainyaḥ*—King Pṛthu; *indriya-īśaḥ*—a living entity; *guṇān iva*—as influenced by the modes of material nature.

TRANSLATION

Seeing the four Kumāras, Pṛthu Mahārāja was greatly anxious to receive them. Therefore the King, with all his officers, very hastily got up so anxiously that he is compared herewith to a conditioned soul whose senses are immediately attracted by the modes of material nature.

PURPORT

In *Bhagavad-gītā* it is said:

prakṛteḥ kriyamāṇāni guṇaiḥ karmāṇi sarvaśaḥ
ahaṅkāra-vimūḍhātmā kartāham iti manyate.
(Bg. 3.27)

Every conditioned soul is influenced by a particular mixture of the modes of material nature. As such, the conditioned soul is attracted to certain types of activity which he is forced to perform because he is completely under the influence of material nature. Here Pṛthu Mahārāja is compared to such a conditioned soul, not because he was a conditioned soul but because he was so anxious to receive the Kumāras that it was as if without them he would have lost his life. The conditioned soul is attracted by the objects of sense gratification. His eyes are attracted to see beautiful things, his ears are attracted to hear nice music, his nose is attracted to enjoy the aroma of a nice flower, and his tongue is attracted to taste nice food. Similarly, all his other senses—his hands, his legs, his belly, his genitals, his mind, etc.—are so susceptible to the attraction of the objects of enjoyment that he cannot restrain himself. Pṛthu Mahārāja, in the same way, could not restrain himself from receiving the four Kumāras, who were bright by dint of their spiritual progress, and thus not only he himself but also his officers and associates all received the four Kumāras. It is said, "Birds of a feather flock together." In this world, everyone is attracted by a person of the same category. A drunkard is attracted to persons who are also drunkards. Similarly, a saintly person is attracted by other saintly persons. Pṛthu Mahārāja was in the topmost position of spiritual advancement, and as such, he was attracted by the Kumāras, who were of the same category. It is said, therefore, that a man is known by his company.

TEXT 4

गौरवाद्यन्त्रितः सम्यः प्रश्रयानतकन्धरः ।
विधिवत्पूजयाञ्चक्रे गृहीताध्यर्हणासनान् ॥ ४ ॥

gauravād yantritaḥ sabhyaḥ
praśrayānata-kandharaḥ
vidhivat pūjayāñcakre
gṛhītādhyarhaṇāsanān

gauravāt—glories; yantritaḥ—completely; sabhyaḥ—most civilized; praś-
raya—by humbleness; ānata-kandharaḥ—bowing down his shoulder; vidhivat—according to the instructions of the śāstra; pūjayām—by worshiping;
cakre—performed; gṛhīta—accepting; adhi—including; arhaṇa—paraphernalia for reception; āsanān—sitting places.

TRANSLATION

When the great sages accepted their reception, according to the instruc-
tions of the śāstras, and finally took their seats offered by the King, the
King, influenced by the glories of the sages, immediately bowed down.
Thus he worshiped the four Kumāras.

PURPORT

The four Kumāras are the paramparā spiritual masters of the Vaiṣṇava
sampradāya. Out of the four sampradāyas, namely Brahma-sampradāya,
Śrī-sampradāya, Kumāra-sampradāya and Rudra-sampradāya, the disciplic
succession of spiritual master to disciple known as the Kumāra-sampradāya
is coming down from the four Kumāras. So Pṛthu Mahārāja was very respectful to the sampradāya-ācāryas. As it is said by Śrīla Viśvanātha
Cakravartī Ṭhākura, sākṣād-dharitvena samasta-śāstrair: a spiritual master
or the paramparā-ācārya should be respected exactly like the Supreme
Personality of Godhead. The word vidhivat is significant in this verse. This
means that Pṛthu Mahārāja also strictly followed the injunctions of the
śāstra in receiving a spiritual master or ācārya of the transcendental disciplic succession. Whenever an ācārya is seen, one should immediately bow
down before him. Pṛthu Mahārāja did this properly; therefore the words
used here are praśrayānata-kandharaḥ. Out of humility, he bowed down
before the Kumāras.

TEXT 5

तत्पादशौचसलिलैर्मार्जितालकबन्धनः ।
तत्र शीलवतां वृत्तमाचरन्मानयन्निव ॥ ५ ॥

tat-pāda-śauca-salilair
mārjitālaka-bandhanaḥ
tatra śīlavatāṁ vṛttam
ācaran mānayann iva

tat-pāda—their lotus feet; *śauca*—washed; *salilaiḥ*—water; *mārjita*—sprinkled; *alaka*—hair; *bandhanaḥ*—bunch; *tatra*—there; *śīlavatām*—of the respectable gentlemen; *vṛttam*—behavior; *ācaran*—behaving; *mānayan*—practicing; *iva*—like.

TRANSLATION

After this, the King took the water which had washed the lotus feet of the Kumāras and sprinkled it over his hair. By such respectful actions, the King, as an exemplary personality, showed how to receive a spiritually advanced personality.

PURPORT

Śrī Caitanya Mahāprabhu has said, *āpani ācari prabhu jīvere śikhāya.* It is very well known that whatever Śrī Caitanya Mahāprabhu taught in His life as *ācārya,* He Himself practiced. When He was preaching as a devotee, although He was detected by several great personalities to be the incarnation of Kṛṣṇa, He never agreed to be addressed as an incarnation. Even though one may be an incarnation of Kṛṣṇa, or especially empowered by Him, he should not advertise that he is an incarnation. People will automatically accept the real truth in due course of time. Pṛthu Mahārāja was the ideal Vaiṣṇava king; therefore he taught others by his personal behavior how to receive and respect saintly persons like the Kumāras. When a saintly person comes to one's home, it is the Vedic custom to wash his feet first with water and then sprinkle this water over the heads of oneself and his family. Pṛthu Mahārāja did this, for he was an exemplary teacher of the people in general.

TEXT 6

हाटकासन आसीनान् स्वधिष्ण्येष्विव पावकान् ।
श्रद्धासंयमसंयुक्तः प्रीतः प्राह भवाग्रजान् ॥ ६ ॥

hāṭakāsana āsīnān
sva-dhiṣṇyeṣv iva pāvakān
śraddhā-saṁyama-saṁyuktaḥ
prītaḥ prāha bhavāgrajān

hāṭaka-āsane—on the throne made of gold; *āsīnān*—when they were seated; *sva-dhiṣṇyeṣu*—on the altar; *iva*—like; *pāvakān*—the fire; *śraddhā*—

respect; *saṁyama*—restraint; *saṁyuktaḥ*—being decorated with; *prītaḥ*—pleased; *prāha*—said; *bhava*—Lord Śiva; *agrajān*—the elder brothers.

TRANSLATION

The four great sages were elder to Lord Śiva, and when they were seated on the golden throne, they appeared just like fire blazing on an altar. Mahārāja Pṛthu, out of his great gentleness and respect for them, began to speak with great restraint as follows.

PURPORT

The Kumāras are described herein as the elder brothers of Lord Śiva. When the Kumāras were born out of the body of Lord Brahmā they were requested to get married and increase the population. In the beginning of the creation there was a great need of population; therefore Lord Brahmā was creating one son after another and ordering them to increase. However, when the Kumāras were requested to do so, they declined. They wanted to remain *brahmacārī* throughout life and be engaged fully in the devotional service of the Lord. The Kumāras are called *naiṣṭhika-brahmacārī*, meaning they are never to marry. Because of their refusal to marry, Lord Brahmā became so angry that his eyes became reddish. Out of his eyes, Lord Śiva, or Rudra, appeared. The mode of anger is consequently known as *rudra.* Lord Śiva also has a *sampradāya* party known as the Rudra-sampradāya, and they are also known as Vaiṣṇavas.

TEXT 7

पृथुरुवाच
अहो आचरितं किं मे मङ्गलं मङ्गलायनाः ।
यस्य वो दर्शनं ह्यासीदुर्दर्शानां च योगिभिः ॥ ७ ॥

pṛthur uvāca
aho ācaritaṁ kiṁ me
maṅgalaṁ maṅgalāyanāḥ
yasya vo darśanaṁ hy āsīd
durdarśānāṁ ca yogibhiḥ

pṛthuḥ uvāca—King Pṛthu spoke; *aho*—O Lord; *ācaritam*—practice; *kim*—what; *me*—by me; *maṅgalam*—good fortune; *maṅgala-āyanāḥ*—O personified good fortune; *yasya*—by which; *vaḥ*—your; *darśanam*—audience; *hi*—certainly; *āsīt*—became possible; *durdarśānām*—visible with great difficulty; *ca*—also; *yogibhiḥ*—by great mystic *yogīs.*

TRANSLATION

King Pṛthu spoke: My dear great sages, auspiciousness personified, it is very difficult for even the mystic yogīs to see you. Indeed, you are very rarely seen. I do not know what kind of pious activity I performed for you to grace me by appearing before me without difficulty.

PURPORT

When something uncommon happens in one's progressive spiritual life, it should be understood to be incurred by *ajñāta-sukṛti,* or pious activities beyond one's knowledge. To see personally the Supreme Personality of Godhead or His pure devotee is not an ordinary incident. When such things happen, they should be understood to be caused by previous pious activity, as confirmed in *Bhagavad-gītā: yeṣāṁ tv anta-gataṁ pāpaṁ janānāṁ puṇya-karmaṇām* (Bg. 7.28). One who is completely freed from all the resultant actions of sinful activities and who is absorbed only in pious activities can engage in devotional service. Although Mahārāja Pṛthu's life is full of pious activities, he was wondering how his audience with the Kumāras happened. He could not imagine what kind of pious activities he had performed. This is a sign of humility on the part of King Pṛthu, whose life was so full of pious activities that even Lord Viṣṇu also came to see him and predicted that the Kumāras would also come.

TEXT 8

किं तस्य दुर्लभतरमिह लोके परत्र च ।
यस्य विप्राः प्रसीदन्ति शिवो विष्णुश्च सानुगः ॥ ८ ॥

kiṁ tasya durlabhataram
iha loke paratra ca
yasya viprāḥ prasīdanti
śivo viṣṇuś ca sānugaḥ

kim—what; *tasya*—his; *durlabhataram*—very rare to achieve; *iha*—in this world; *loke*—world; *paratra*—after death; *ca*—or; *yasya*—one whose; *viprāḥ*—the *brāhmaṇas* and Vaiṣṇavas; *prasīdanti*—become pleased; *śivaḥ*—all-auspicious; *viṣṇuḥ*—Lord Viṣṇu; *ca*—as well as; *sānugaḥ*—going along with.

TRANSLATION

Any person upon whom the brāhmaṇas and Vaiṣṇavas are pleased can achieve anything which is very rare to obtain in this world as well as after death. Not only that, but one also receives the favor of the auspicious Lord Śiva and Lord Viṣṇu, who accompany the brāhmaṇas and Vaiṣṇavas.

PURPORT

The *brāhmaṇas* and Vaiṣṇavas are the bearers of Lord Viṣṇu, the all-auspicious. As confirmed in the *Brahma-saṁhitā:*

premāñjana-cchurita-bhakti-vilocanena
santaḥ sadaiva hṛdayeṣu vilokayanti
yaṁ śyāmasundaram acintya-guṇa-svarūpaṁ
govindam ādi-puruṣaṁ tam ahaṁ bhajāmi.

The devotees, out of their extreme love for Govinda, the Supreme Personality of Godhead, always carry the Lord within their hearts. The Lord is already in the heart of everyone, but the Vaiṣṇavas and the *brāhmaṇas* actually perceive and see Him always in ecstasy. Therefore *brāhmaṇas* and Vaiṣṇavas are carriers of Viṣṇu. Wherever they go, Lord Viṣṇu, Lord Śiva or the devotees of Lord Viṣṇu are all carried. The four Kumāras are *brāhmaṇas,* and they visited the place of Mahārāja Pṛthu. Naturally Lord Viṣṇu and His devotees were also present. Under the circumstances, the conclusion is that when the *brāhmaṇas* and Vaiṣṇavas are pleased with a person, Lord Viṣṇu is also pleased. This is confirmed by Śrīla Viśvanātha Cakravartī Ṭhākura in his eight stanzas on the spiritual master: *yasya prasādād bhagavat-prasādaḥ.* By pleasing the spiritual master, who is both *brāhmaṇa* and Vaiṣṇava, one pleases the Supreme Personality of Godhead. If the Supreme Personality of Godhead is pleased, then one has nothing more to achieve either in this world or after death.

TEXT 9

नैव लक्षयते लोको लोकान् पर्यटतोऽपि यान् ।
यथा सर्वदृशं सर्व आत्मानं येऽस्य हेतवः ॥ ९ ॥

naiva lakṣayate loko
lokān paryaṭato 'pi yān
yathā sarva-dṛśaṁ sarva
ātmānaṁ ye 'sya hetavaḥ

na—not; *eva*—thus; *lakṣayate*—can see; *lokaḥ*—people; *lokān*—all planets; *paryaṭataḥ*—traveling; *api*—although; *yān*—whom; *yathā*—as much as; *sarva-dṛśam*—the Supersoul; *sarve*—in all; *ātmānam*—within everyone; *ye*—those; *asya*—of the cosmic manifestation; *hetavaḥ*—causes.

TRANSLATION

Pṛthu Mahārāja continued: Although you are traveling in all planetary systems, people cannot know you, just as they cannot know the Supersoul, although He is within everyone's heart as the witness of everything. Even Lord Brahmā and Lord Śiva cannot understand the Supersoul.

PURPORT

In the beginning of the *Śrīmad-Bhāgavatam* it is said: *muhyanti yat sūrayaḥ.* Great demigods like Lord Brahmā, Lord Śiva, Indra and Candra are sometimes bewildered trying to understand the Supreme Personality of Godhead. It so happened that when Kṛṣṇa was present on this planet, Lord Brahmā and King Indra also mistook Him. And what to speak of great *yogīs* or *jñānīs* who conclude that the Absolute Truth, the Personality of Godhead, is impersonal? In the same way, great personalities and Vaiṣṇavas like the four Kumāras are also invisible to ordinary persons, although they are traveling all over the universe in different planetary systems. When Sanātana Gosvāmī went to see Lord Śrī Caitanya Mahāprabhu, he could not be recognized by Candraśekhara Ācārya. The conclusion is that the Supreme Personality of Godhead is situated in everyone's heart, and His pure devotees, the Vaiṣṇavas, are also traveling all over the world, but those who are under the modes of material nature cannot understand the form of the Supreme Personality of Godhead, the source of this cosmic manifestation, or the Vaiṣṇavas. It is said, therefore, that one cannot see the Supreme Personality of Godhead or a Vaiṣṇava with these material eyes. One has to purify his senses and engage in the service of the Lord. Then gradually one can realize who is the Supreme Personality of Godhead and who is a Vaiṣṇava.

TEXT 10

अधना अपि ते धन्याः साधवो गृहमेधिनः ।
यद्गृहा ह्यर्हवर्याम्बुतृणभूमीश्वरावराः ॥१०॥

adhanā api te dhanyāḥ
sādhavo gṛha-medhinaḥ
yad-gṛhā hy arha-varyāmbu-
tṛṇa-bhūmīśvarāvarāḥ

adhanāḥ—not very rich; *api*—although; *te*—they; *dhanyāḥ*—glorious; *sādhavaḥ*—saintly persons; *gṛha-medhinaḥ*—persons who are attached to family life; *yat-gṛhāḥ*—whose house; *hi*—certainly; *arha-varya*—the most worshipable; *ambu*—water; *tṛṇa*—grass; *bhūmi*—land; *īśvara*—the master; *avarāḥ*—the servants.

TRANSLATION

A person who is not very rich and is attached to family life becomes highly glorified when saintly persons are present in his home. Everyone,

including master and servants who are engaged in offering the exalted visitors water, sitting place, paraphernalia for reception, and the home itself, are also glorified.

PURPORT

Materially if a man is not very rich, he is not glorious, and spiritually if a man is too attached to family life, he is also not glorious. But saintly persons are quite ready to visit the house of a poor man or a man who is attached to material family life. When this happens, the owner of the house and his servants are glorified because they offer water for washing the feet of a saintly person, sitting places and other things to receive him. The conclusion is that if a saintly person goes to the house of even an unimportant man, such a person becomes glorious by his blessings. It is therefore the Vedic system that a householder invite a saintly person in his home to receive his blessings. This system is still current in India, and therefore saintly persons, wherever they go, are hosted by the householders, who in turn get an opportunity to receive transcendental knowledge. It is the duty of a *sannyāsī,* therefore, to travel everywhere just to favor the householders who are generally ignorant of the values of spiritual life.

It may be argued that all householders are not very rich and that one cannot receive great saintly persons or preachers because they are always accompanied by their disciples. If a householder is to receive a saintly person, he has to receive his entourage also. It is said in the *śāstras* that Durvāsā Muni was always accompanied by 60,000 disciples and that if there was a little discrepancy in their reception, he would be very angry and would sometimes curse the host. The fact is that every householder, regardless of his position or economic condition, can at least receive saintly guests with great devotion and offer them drinking water, for drinking water is available always. In India the custom is that even an ordinary person is offered a glass of water if he suddenly visits and one cannot offer him foodstuff. If there is no water, then one can offer a sitting place, even if it is on straw mats. And if he has no straw mat, he can immediately cleanse the ground and ask the guest to sit there. Supposing that a householder cannot even do that, then with folded hands he can simply receive the guest, saying welcome. And if he cannot do that, then he should feel very sorry for his poor condition and shed tears and simply offer obeisances with his whole family, wife and children. In this way he can satisfy any guest, even if he is a saintly person or a king.

TEXT 11

व्यालालयद्रुमा वै तेष्वरिक्ताखिलसम्पदः ।
यद्गृहास्तीर्थपादीयपादतीर्थविवर्जिताः ॥११॥

vyālālaya-drumā vai teṣv
ariktākhila-sampadaḥ
yad-gṛhās tīrtha-pādīya-
pādatīrtha-vivarjitāḥ

vyāla—venomous serpents; *ālaya*—home; *drumāḥ*—tree; *vai*—certainly; *teṣu*—in those houses; *arikta*—abundantly; *akhila*—all; *sampadaḥ*—opulences; *yat*—that; *gṛhāḥ*—houses; *tīrtha-pādīya*—in relation with the feet of great saintly persons; *pāda-tīrtha*—the water which washed their feet; *vivarjitāḥ*—without.

TRANSLATION

On the contrary, even though full of all opulence and material prosperity, any householder's house where the devotees of the Lord are never allowed to come in, and where there is no water for washing their feet, is to be considered as a tree in which all venomous serpents live.

PURPORT

In this verse the word *tīrtha-pādīya* indicates devotees of Lord Viṣṇu, or Vaiṣṇavas. As far as *brāhmaṇas* are concerned, in the previous verse the mode of reception has been already described. Now, in this verse, special stress is being given to the Vaiṣṇavas. Generally the *sannyāsīs,* or those in the renounced order of life, take trouble to enlighten the householders. There are *ekadaṇḍī sannyāsīs* and *tridaṇḍī sannyāsīs.* The *ekadaṇḍī sannyāsīs* are generally followers of Śaṅkarācārya and are known as Māyāvādī *sannyāsīs,* whereas the *tridaṇḍī sannyāsīs* are followers of Vaiṣṇava *ācāryas*—Rāmānujācārya, Madhvācārya and so on—and they take trouble to enlighten the householders. *Ekadaṇḍī sannyāsīs* can be situated on the platform of pure Brahman because they are aware that the spirit soul is different from the body, but they are mainly impersonalists. The Vaiṣṇavas know that the Absolute Truth is the Supreme Person and that the Brahman effulgence is based on the Supreme Personality of Godhead, as confirmed in the *Bhagavad-gītā: brahmaṇo hi pratiṣṭhāham* (Bg. 14.27). The conclusion is that *tīrtha-pādīya* refers to Vaiṣṇavas. In the *Bhāgavatam* there is also another reference: *tīrthīkurvanti tīrthāni.* Wherever he goes, a Vaiṣṇava immediately makes that place a *tīrtha,* a place of pilgrimage. The Vaiṣṇava *sannyāsīs* travel all over the world to make every place a place of pilgrimage by the touch of their lotus feet. It is mentioned there that any house which does not receive a Vaiṣṇava in the manner already explained in the previous verse is to be considered the residential quarters of venomous serpents. It is said that about the sandalwood tree, which is a very valuable tree, there is a venomous serpent. Sandalwood is very cold, and venomous serpents, because of their poisonous teeth, are always very warm, and they take shelter of the sandalwood trees to become cooler. Similarly, there are many rich men who keep watchdogs or doormen and put up signs that say do not enter, trespassers not allowed, beware of the dog, etc. Sometimes in western countries a trespasser is shot, and there is no crime in such shooting. This is the position of demoniac householders, and such houses are considered to be the residential quarters of venomous snakes. The members of such families are no better than snakes because snakes are very much envious, and when that envy is directed to the saintly persons, their position becomes more dangerous. It is said by Cāṇakya Paṇḍita that there are two envious living entities, the snake and the envious man. The envious man is more dangerous than a snake because a snake can be subdued by charming *mantras* or by some herbs, but an envious person cannot be pacified by any means.

TEXT 12

स्वागतं वो द्विजश्रेष्ठा यद्व्रतानि मुमुक्षवः ।
चरन्ति श्रद्धया धीरा बाला एव बृहन्ति च ॥१२॥

svāgataṁ vo dvija-śreṣṭhā
yad-vratāni mumukṣavaḥ
caranti śraddhayā dhīrā
bālā eva bṛhanti ca

svāgatam—welcome; *vaḥ*—unto you; *dvija-śreṣṭhāḥ*—the best of the *brāhmaṇas; yat*—whose; *vratāni*—vows; *mumukṣavaḥ*—of persons desiring liberation; *caranti*—behave; *śraddhayā*—with great faith; *dhīrāḥ*—controlled; *bālāḥ*—boys; *eva*—like; *bṛhanti*—observe; *ca*—also.

TRANSLATION

Mahārāja Pṛthu offered his welcome to the four Kumāras, addressing them as the best of the brāhmaṇas. He welcomed them, saying: From the beginning of your birth you were strictly observing the vows of celibacy,

and although you are experienced in the path of liberation, you are keeping yourselves just like small children.

PURPORT

The specific importance of the Kumāras is that they were *brahmacārīs* living the life of celibacy from birth. They kept themselves as small children about four or five years old because by growing into youth one's senses sometimes become disturbed and celibacy becomes difficult. The Kumāras therefore purposefully remained children because in a child's life the senses are never disturbed by sex. This is the significance of the life of the Kumāras, and as such Mahārāja Pṛthu addressed them as the best of the *brāhmaṇas.* The Kumāras were not only born of the best *brāhmaṇa* (Lord Brahmā), but they are addressed herein as *dvija-śreṣṭhāḥ* (the best of the *brāhmaṇas*) on account of their being Vaiṣṇavas also. As we have already explained, they have their *sampradāya* (disciplic succession), and even to date the *sampradāya* is being maintained and is known as the Nimbārka-sampradāya. Out of the four *sampradāyas* of the Vaiṣṇava *ācāryas,* the Nimbārka-sampradāya is one. Mahārāja Pṛthu specifically appreciated the position of the Kumāras because they maintained the *brahmacarya* vow from the very beginning of their birth. Mahārāja Pṛthu, however, expressed his great appreciation of Vaiṣṇavism by addressing the Kumāras as *Vaiṣṇava-śreṣṭha.* In other words, everyone should offer respect to a Vaiṣṇava without considering his source of birth. *Vaiṣṇave jāti-buddhiḥ.* No one should consider a Vaiṣṇava in terms of birth. The Vaiṣṇava is always the best of the *brāhmaṇas,* and as such one should offer all respects to a Vaiṣṇava, not only as a *brāhmaṇa* but as the best of the *brāhmaṇas.*

TEXT 13

कच्चिन्नः कुशलं नाथा इन्द्रियार्थार्थवेदिनाम् ।
व्यसनावाप एतस्मिन् पतितानां स्वकर्मभिः ॥१३॥

kaccin naḥ kuśalaṁ nāthā
indriyārthārtha-vedinām
vyasanāvāpa etasmin
patitānāṁ sva-karmabhiḥ

kaccit—whether; *naḥ*—our; *kuśalam*—good fortune; *nāthāḥ*—O masters; *indriya-artha*—sense gratification as the ultimate goal of life; *artha-vedinām*—persons who understand only sense gratification; *vyasana*—illness;

āvāpe—got; *etasmin*—in this material existence; *patitānām*—those who are fallen; *sva-karmabhiḥ*—by their own ability.

TRANSLATION

Pṛthu Mahārāja inquired from the sages about persons entangled in this dangerous material existence because of their previous actions; could such persons, whose only aim is sense gratification, be blessed with any good fortune?

PURPORT

Mahārāja Pṛthu did not ask the Kumāras about their good fortune, for the Kumāras are always auspicious by dint of their life in celibacy. Since they are always engaged on the path of liberation, there was no question of ill fortune. In other words, *brāhmaṇas* and Vaiṣṇavas who are strictly following the path of spiritual advancement are always fortunate. The question was asked by Pṛthu Mahārāja for his own sake, since he was in the position of a *gṛhastha* and in charge of the royal authority. Kings are not only *gṛhasthas,* who are generally absorbed in sense gratification, but are sometimes employed to kill animals in hunting because they have to practice the killing art, otherwise it is very difficult for them to fight their enemies. Such things are not auspicious. Four kinds of sinful activities—associating with woman for illicit sex, eating meat, intoxication and gambling—are allowed for the *kṣatriyas.* For political reasons, sometimes they have to take to these sinful activities. *Kṣatriyas* do not refrain from gambling. One vivid example is the Pāṇḍavas. When the Pāṇḍavas were challenged by the opposite party, Duryodhana, to gamble and risk their kingdom, they could not refrain, and by that gambling they lost their kingdom, and their wife was insulted. Similarly, the *kṣatriyas* cannot refrain from fighting if challenged by the opposite party. Therefore Pṛthu Mahārāja, taking consideration of all these facts, inquired whether there is any auspicious path. *Gṛhastha* life is inauspicious because *gṛhastha* means consciousness for sense gratification, and as soon as there is sense gratification, one's position is always full of dangers. This material world is said to be *padaṁ padaṁ yad vipadāṁ na teṣām,* dangerous in every step (*Bhāg.* 10.14.58). Everyone in this material world is struggling hard for sense gratification. Clearing all these points, Mahārāja Pṛthu inquired from the four Kumāras about the fallen conditioned souls who are rotting in this material world due to their past bad or inauspicious activities. Is there any possibility for their auspicious spiritual life? In this verse, the word *indriyārthārtha-vedinām* is very significant. It indicates persons whose only aim is to satisfy the senses. They are also described as *patitānām,* or fallen. Only one who stops all activities for sense gratification is considered to be elevated. Another significant word is *sva-karmabhiḥ.* One becomes fallen by dint of his own past bad activities. Everyone is responsible for his fallen condition because of his own activities. When activities are changed to devotional service, one's auspicious life begins.

TEXT 14

भवत्सु कुशलप्रश्न आत्मारामेषु नेष्यते ।
कुशलाकुशला यत्र न सन्ति मतिवृत्तयः ॥१४॥

bhavatsu kuśala-praśna
ātmārāmeṣu neṣyate
kuśalākuśalā yatra
na santi mati-vṛttayaḥ

bhavatsu—unto you; *kuśala*—good fortune; *praśnaḥ*—question; *ātmārāmeṣu*—one who is always engaged in spiritual bliss; *neṣyate*—there is no need of; *kuśala*—good fortune; *akuśalāḥ*—inauspiciousness; *yatra*—where; *na*—never; *santi*—exists; *mati-vṛttayaḥ*—mental concoction.

TRANSLATION

Pṛthu Mahārāja continued: My dear sirs, there is no need to ask about your good and bad fortune because you are always absorbed in spiritual bliss. The mental concoction of the auspicious and inauspicious does not exist in you.

PURPORT

In the *Caitanya-caritāmṛta* it is said:

'dvaite' bhadrābhadra-jñāna, saba—'manodharma'
'ei bhāla, ei manda,'—ei saba 'bhrama.' (Cc. *Antya* 4.176)

In this material world the auspicious and inauspicious are simply mental concoctions because such things exist only due to association with the material world. This is called illusion or *ātma-māyā.* We think ourselves created by material nature exactly as we think ourselves experiencing so many things in a dream. The spirit soul is, however, always transcendental. There is no question of becoming materially covered. This covering is simply something like a hallucination or a dream. In *Bhagavad-gītā* it is also said, *saṅgāt sañjāyate kāmaḥ* (Bg. 2.62). Simply by association we create artificial material necessities. *Dhyāyato viṣayān puṁsaḥ saṅgas teṣūpajāyate* (Bg. 2.62). When we forget our real constitutional position and wish to enjoy the material resources, our material desires manifest, and we associate with varieties of material enjoyment. As soon as the concoctions of material enjoyment are there, because of our association we create a sort of lust or eagerness to enjoy them, and when that false enjoyment does not actually make us happy, we create another illusion known as anger, and by the manifestation of anger, the illusion becomes stronger. When we are illusioned in this way, forgetfulness of our relationship with Kṛṣṇa follows, and by thus losing Kṛṣṇa consciousness, our real intelligence is defeated. In this way we become entangled in this material world. In *Bhagavad-gītā* it is said:

> ***krodhād bhavati sammohaḥ sammohāt smṛti-vibhramaḥ***
> ***smṛti-bhraṁśād buddhi-nāśo buddhi-nāśāt praṇaśyati*** (Bg. 2.63)

By material association we lose our spiritual consciousness; consequently there is the question of the auspicious and inauspicious. But those who are *ātmārāma* or self-realized have transcended such questions. The *ātmārāmas* or self-realized persons, gradually making further progress in spiritual bliss, come to the platform of association with the Supreme Personality of Godhead. That is the perfection of life. In the beginning, the Kumāras were self-realized impersonalists, but gradually they became attracted to the personal pastimes of the Supreme Lord. The conclusion is that for those who are always engaged in the devotional service of the Personality of Godhead, the duality of the auspicious and inauspicious does not arise. Pṛthu Mahārāja is therefore asking about auspiciousness not for the sake of the Kumāras but for his own sake.

TEXT 15

तदहं कृतविश्रम्भः सुहृदो वस्तपस्विनाम् ।
संपृच्छे भव एतस्मिन् क्षेमः केनाञ्जसा भवेत् ॥१५॥

tad ahaṁ kṛta-viśrambhaḥ
su-hṛdo vas tapasvinām
sampṛcche bhava etasmin
kṣemaḥ kenāñjasā bhavet

tat—therefore; *aham*—I; *kṛta-viśrambhaḥ*—being completely assured; *su-hṛdaḥ*—friend; *vaḥ*—our; *tapasvinām*—suffering material pangs; *sampṛcche*—wish to inquire; *bhave*—in this material world; *etasmin*—this; *kṣemaḥ*—

ultimate reality; *kena*—by which means; *añjasā*—without delay; *bhavet*—can be achieved.

TRANSLATION

I am completely assured that personalities like you are the only friends for persons who are blazing in the fire of material existence. I therefore ask you how in this material world we can very soon achieve the ultimate goal of life.

PURPORT

When saintly persons go from door to door to see those who are too much materially engaged, it is to be understood that they do not go to ask anything for their personal benefit. It is a fact that saintly persons go to materialists just to give real information of the auspicious. Mahārāja Pṛthu was assured of this fact; therefore instead of wasting time by asking the Kumāras about the auspicious, he preferred to inquire from them whether he could soon be relieved from the dangerous position of materialistic existence. This was not, however, a question personally for Pṛthu Mahārāja. It was raised to teach the common man that whenever one meets a great saintly person, he should immediately surrender unto him and inquire about relief from the material pains of existence. Therefore Śrīla Narottama dāsa Ṭhākura says: *saṁsāra-viṣānale, divā-niśi hiyā jvale, juḍāite nā kainu upāya.* "We are always suffering from material pangs, and our hearts are burning, but we can not find any way out of it." The materialistic person can also be called a *tapasvī,* which means someone who is always suffering from material pains. One can only get rid of all these material pains when he takes shelter of the chanting of the Hare Kṛṣṇa *mantra.* This is also explained by Narottama dāsa Ṭhākura: *golokera prema-dhana, harināma-saṅkīrtana, rati nā janmila kene tāya.* Narottama dāsa Ṭhākura regretted that he did not pursue his attraction for the transcendental vibration of the Hare Kṛṣṇa *mantra.* The conclusion is that all persons in this material world are suffering from material pains, and if one wants to get rid of them, he must associate with saintly persons, pure devotees of the Lord, and chant the *mahā-mantra,* Hare Kṛṣṇa, Hare Kṛṣṇa, Kṛṣṇa Kṛṣṇa, Hare Hare/ Hare Rāma, Hare Rāma, Rāma Rāma, Hare Hare. That is the only auspicious way for materialistic persons.

TEXT 16

व्यक्तमात्मवतामात्मा भगवानात्मभावनः ।
स्वानामनुग्रहायेमां सिद्धरूपी चरत्यजः ॥१६॥

vyaktam ātmavatām ātmā
bhagavān ātma-bhāvanaḥ
svānām anugrahāyemāṁ
siddha-rūpī caraty ajaḥ

vyaktam—clear; *ātmavatām*—of the transcendentalists; *ātmā*—the goal of life; *bhagavān*—the Supreme Personality of Godhead; *ātma-bhāvanaḥ*—always wishing to elevate the living entities; *svānām*—whose own devotees; *anugrahāya*—just to show mercy; *imām*—this way; *siddha-rūpī*—perfectly self-realized; *carati*—travels; *ajaḥ*—Nārāyaṇa.

TRANSLATION

The Supreme Personality of Godhead is always anxious to elevate the living entities, who are His parts and parcels, and for their special benefit, the Lord travels all over the world in the form of self-realized persons like you.

PURPORT

There are different kinds of transcendentalists, namely the *jñānīs,* or impersonalists, the mystic *yogīs,* and, of course, all the devotees of the Supreme Personality of Godhead. The Kumāras, however, were both *yogīs* and *jñānīs* and finally *bhaktas* later on. In the beginning they were impersonalists, but later they developed devotional activities; therefore they are the best of the transcendentalists. The devotees are representatives of the Supreme Personality of Godhead, and to elevate the conditioned souls to their original consciousness, they travel all over the universes to enlighten the conditioned souls about Kṛṣṇa consciousness. The best devotees are *ātmavat,* or those who have fully realized the Supreme Soul. The Supreme Personality of Godhead, as Paramātmā, is sitting within everyone's heart, trying to elevate everyone to the platform of Kṛṣṇa consciousness. Therefore He is called *ātma-bhāvana.* The Supreme Personality of Godhead is always trying to give intelligence to the individual soul to understand about Himself. He is always with the individual as a friend sitting by the side of a friend, and He gives facilities to all living entities according to their desires.

The word *ātmavatām* is significant in this verse. There are three different kinds of devotees, namely *kaniṣṭha-adhikārī, madhyama-adhikārī* and *uttama-adhikārī:* the neophyte, the preacher, and the *mahā-bhāgavata* or the highly advanced devotees. The highly advanced devotee is one who knows the conclusion of the *Vedas* in full knowledge; thus he becomes a devotee.

Indeed, not only is he convinced himself, but he can convince others on the strength of Vedic evidence. The advanced devotee can also see all other living entities as part and parcel of the Supreme Lord, without discrimination. The *madhyama-adhikārī* (preacher) is also well-versed in the *śāstras* and can convince others also, but he discriminates between the favorable and the unfavorable. In other words, the *madhyama-adhikārī* does not care for the demoniac living entities, and the neophyte *kaniṣṭha-adhikārī* does not know much about *śāstra* but has full faith in the Supreme Personality of Godhead. The Kumāras were, however, *mahā-bhāgavatas* because after scrutinizingly studying the Absolute Truth, they became devotees. In other words, they were in full knowledge of the Vedic conclusion. In the *Bhagavad-gītā* it is confirmed by the Lord that there are many devotees, but a devotee who is fully conversant in the Vedic conclusion is very dear to Him. Everyone is trying to elevate himself to the highest position according to his mentality. The *karmīs,* who have a bodily concept of life, try to enjoy sense gratification to the utmost. The *jñānīs'* idea of the highest position is merging into the effulgence of the Lord. But a devotee's highest position is in preaching all over the world the glories of the Supreme Personality of Godhead. Therefore the devotees are actually the representatives of the Supreme Lord, and as such they travel all over the world directly as Nārāyaṇa because they carry Nārāyaṇa within their hearts and preach His glories. The representative of Nārāyaṇa is as good as Nārāyaṇa, but he is not to conclude, like the Māyāvādīs, that he has become Nārāyaṇa. Generally, a *sannyāsī* is addressed as Nārāyaṇa by the Māyāvādīs. Their idea is that simply by taking *sannyāsa* one becomes equal to Nārāyaṇa or becomes Nārāyaṇa Himself. The Vaiṣṇava conclusion is different, as stated by Śrīla Viśvanātha Cakravartī Ṭhākura:

sākṣād-dharitvena samasta-śāstrair
uktas tathā bhāvyata eva sadbhiḥ
kintu prabhor yaḥ priya eva tasya
vande guroḥ śrī-caraṇāravindam

According to the Vaiṣṇava philosophy, a devotee is as good as Nārāyaṇa not by becoming Nārāyaṇa but by becoming the most confidential servant of Nārāyaṇa. Such great personalities act as spiritual masters for the benefit of the people in general, and as such, a spiritual master who is preaching the glories of Nārāyaṇa should be accepted as Nārāyaṇa and be given all respects due Him.

TEXT 17

मैत्रेय उवाच
पृथोस्तत्सूक्तमाकर्ण्य सारं सुष्ठु मितं मधु ।
स्मयमान इव प्रीत्या कुमारः प्रत्युवाच ह ॥१७॥

maitreya uvāca
pṛthos tat sūktam ākarṇya
sāraṁ suṣṭhu mitaṁ madhu
smayamāna iva prītyā
kumāraḥ pratyuvāca ha

maitreyaḥ uvāca—the great sage Maitreya continued to speak; *pṛthoḥ*—of King Pṛthu; *tat*—that; *sūktam*—Vedic conclusion; *ākarṇya*—hearing; *sāram*—very substantial; *suṣṭhu*—appropriate; *mitam*—minimized; *madhu*—sweet to hear; *smayamānaḥ*—smiling; *iva*—like; *prītyā*—out of great satisfaction; *kumāraḥ*—celibate; *pratyuvāca*—replied; *ha*—thus.

TRANSLATION

Thus Sanatkumāra, the best of the celibates, after hearing the speech of Pṛthu Mahārāja, which was meaningful, appropriate, full of precise words and very sweet to hear, smiled with full satisfaction and began to speak as follows.

PURPORT

Pṛthu Mahārāja's talks before the Kumāras were very laudable because of so many qualifications. A speech should be composed of selected words, very sweet to hear and appropriate to the situation. Such speech is called meaningful. All these good qualifications are present in Pṛthu Mahārāja's speech because he is a perfect devotee. It is said, *yasyāsti bhaktir bhagavaty akiñcanā sarvair guṇais tatra samāsate surāḥ:* "For one who has unflinching devotional faith and is engaged in His service, all good qualities become manifest in his person." (*Bhāg.* 5.18.12) Thus the Kumāras were very much pleased, and Sanat-kumāra began to speak as follows.

TEXT 18

सनत्कुमार उवाच
साधु पृष्टं महाराज सर्वभूतहितात्मना ।
भवता विदुषा चापि साधूनां मतिरीदृशी ॥१८॥

sanat-kumāra uvāca
sādhu pṛṣṭaṁ mahārāja
sarvabhūta-hitātmanā
bhavatā viduṣa cāpi
sādhūnāṁ matir īdṛśī

sanat-kumāraḥ uvāca—Sanatkumāra said; *sādhu*—saintly; *pṛṣṭam*—question; *mahārāja*—my dear King; *sarva-bhūta*—all living entities; *hita-ātmanā*—by one who desires good for all; *bhavatā*—by you; *viduṣā*—well learned; *ca*—and; *api*—although; *sādhūnām*—of the saintly persons; *matiḥ*—intelligence; *īdṛśī*—like this.

TRANSLATION

Sanat-kumāra said: My dear King Pṛthu, I am very nicely questioned by you, and such questions are beneficial for all living entities, especially because they are raised by you, who are always thinking of the good of others. Although you know everything, still you ask such questions because that is the behavior of saintly persons. Such intelligence is befitting your position.

PURPORT

Mahārāja Pṛthu was well conversant in transcendental science, yet he presented himself before the Kumāras as one ignorant of it. The idea is that even if a person is very exalted and knows e erything, before his superior he should present questions. For instance, although Arjuna knew all the transcendental science, he questioned Kṛṣṇa as if he did not know. Similarly, Pṛthu Mahārāja knew everything, but he presented himself before the Kumāras as if he did not know anything. The idea is that questions by exalted persons put before the Supreme Personality of Godhead or His devotees are meant for the benefit of the general people. Therefore sometimes great personalities put themselves in that position and inquire from higher authority because they are always thinking of the benefit of others.

TEXT 19

सङ्गमः खलु साधूनामुभयेषां च सम्मतः ।
यत्सम्भाषणसम्प्रश्नः सर्वेषां वितनोति शम् ॥१९॥

saṅgamaḥ khalu sādhūnām
ubhayeṣāṁ ca sammataḥ

yat-sambhāṣaṇa-sampraśnaḥ
sarveṣāṁ vitanoti śam

saṅgamaḥ—association; *khalu*—certainly; *sādhūnām*—of devotees; *ubhayeṣām*—for both; *ca*—also; *sammataḥ*—conclusive; *yat*—which; *sambhāṣaṇa*—discussion; *sampraśnaḥ*—question and answer; *sarveṣām*—of all; *vitanoti*—expands; *śam*—real happiness.

TRANSLATION

When there is a congregation of devotees, their discussions, questions and answers become conclusive to both the speaker and the audience. Thus such a meeting is beneficial for everyone's real happiness.

PURPORT

Hearing discussions among the devotees is the only means to receive the powerful message of the Supreme Personality of Godhead. For instance, *Bhagavad-gītā* has been well known all over the world for a very long time, especially in the western world, but because the subject matter was not discussed by devotees, there was no effect. Not a single person in the West became Kṛṣṇa conscious before the Kṛṣṇa consciousness movement was founded. When the same *Bhagavad-gītā* was presented as it is through the disciplic succession, there was immediately spiritual realization.

Sanat-kumāra, one of the Kumāras, informed Pṛthu Mahārāja that his meeting with the Kumāras benefited not only Mahārāja Pṛthu but the Kumāras as well. When Nārada Muni questioned Lord Brahmā about the Supreme Personality of Godhead, Lord Brahmā thanked Nārada Muni because he gave him a chance to speak about the Supreme Lord. Therefore questions about the Supreme Personality of Godhead or about the ultimate goal of life put by a saintly person to another saintly person surcharge everything spiritually. Whoever takes advantage of such discussions is benefited both in this life and in the next.

The word *ubhayeṣām* can be described in many ways. Generally there are two classes of men, the materialist and the transcendentalist. By hearing discussions between devotees, both the materialist and transcendentalist are benefited. The materialist is benefited by association with devotees, and his life becomes regulated so that his chance of becoming a devotee or making the present life successful for understanding the real position of the living entity is increased. When one takes advantage of this opportunity, he is assured of a human form of life in the next birth, or he may be liberated completely and go back home, back to Godhead. The conclusion is that if one participates in a discussion of devotees, he is both materially and spiritually benefited. The speaker and the audience are both benefited, and the *karmīs* and *jñānīs* are benefited. The discussion of spiritual matters amongst devotees is beneficial for everyone without exception. Consequently the Kumāras admitted that not only was the King benefited by such a meeting, but the Kumāras were as well.

TEXT 20

अस्त्येव राजन् भवतो मधुद्विषः
पादारविन्दस्य गुणानुवादने ।
रतिर्दुरापा विधुनोति नैष्ठिकी
कामं कषायं मलमन्तरात्मनः ॥२०॥

asty eva rājan bhavato madhu-dviṣaḥ
pādāravindasya guṇānuvādane
ratir durāpā vidhunoti naiṣṭhikī
kāmaṁ kaṣāyaṁ malam antarātmanaḥ

asti—there is; *eva*—certainly; *rājan*—O King; *bhavataḥ*—your; *madhu-dviṣaḥ*—of the Lord; *pāda-aravindasya*—of the lotus feet; *guṇa-anuvādane*—in glorifying; *ratiḥ*—attachment; *durāpā*—very difficult; *vidhunoti*—washes; *naiṣṭhikī*—unflinching; *kāmam*—lusty; *kaṣāyam*—embellishment; *malam*—dirty; *antar-ātmanaḥ*—from the core of the heart.

TRANSLATION

Sanat-kumāra continued: My dear King, you already have an inclination to glorify the lotus feet of the Supreme Personality of Godhead. Such attachment is very difficult to achieve, but when one has attained such unflinching faith in the Lord, it automatically cleanses lusty desires from the core of the heart.

PURPORT

satāṁ prasaṅgān mama vīrya-saṁvido
bhavanti hṛt-karṇa-rasāyanāḥ kathāḥ
taj-joṣaṇād āśv apavarga-vartmani
śraddhā-ratir bhaktir anukramiṣyati (*Bhāg.* 3.25.25)

By association with devotees, dirty things within the heart of a materialistic man are gradually washed away by the grace of the Supreme Personality of Godhead. As silver becomes shiny by being polished, so lusty desires within the heart of a materialistic person are cleansed by the good association of devotees. Actually the living being has no connection with this material enjoyment nor with lusty desires. He is simply imagining or dreaming while asleep. But by the association of pure devotees, he is awakened, and immediately the spirit soul is situated in his own glory by understanding his constitutional position as the eternal servant of the Lord. Pṛthu Mahārāja was already a self-realized soul; therefore he had a natural inclination to glorify the activities of the Supreme Personality of Godhead, and the Kumāras assured him that there was no chance of his falling victim to the illusory energy of the Supreme Lord. In other words, the process of hearing and chanting about the glories of the Lord is the only means to clarify the heart of material contamination. By the process of *karma, jñāna* and *yoga,* no one will succeed in driving away contamination from the heart, but once a person takes to the shelter of the lotus feet of the Lord by devotional service, automatically all dirty things in the heart are removed without difficulty.

TEXT 21

शास्त्रेष्वियानेव सुनिश्चितो नृणां
क्षेमस्य सध्र्यग्विमृशेषु हेतुः ।
असङ्ग आत्मव्यतिरिक्त आत्मनि
दृढा रतिर्ब्रह्मणि निर्गुणे च या ॥२१॥

śāstreṣv iyān eva suniścito nṛṇāṁ
kṣemasya sadhryag-vimṛśeṣu hetuḥ
asaṅga ātma-vyatirikta ātmani
dṛḍhā ratir brahmaṇi nirguṇe ca yā

śāstreṣu—in the scriptures; *iyān eva*—this is only; *suniścitaḥ*—positively concluded; *nṛṇām*—of human society; *kṣemasya*—of the ultimate welfare; *sadhryak*—perfectly; *vimṛśeṣu*—by full consideration; *hetuḥ*—cause; *asaṅgaḥ*—unattachment; *ātma-vyatirikte*—bodily concept of life; *ātmani*—unto the Supreme Soul; *dṛḍhā*—strong; *ratiḥ*—attachment; *brahmaṇi*—transcendence; *nirguṇe*—in the Supreme, who is beyond the material modes; *ca*—and; *yā*—which.

TRANSLATION

It has been conclusively decided in the scriptures, after due consideration, that the ultimate goal for the welfare of human society is detach-

ment from the bodily concept of life and increased and steadfast attachment for the Supreme Lord, who is transcendental and beyond the modes of material nature.

PURPORT

Everyone in human society is engaged for the ultimate benefit of life, but persons who are in the bodily conception cannot achieve the ultimate goal, nor can they understand what it is. The ultimate goal of life is described in *Bhagavad-gītā. Paraṁ dṛṣṭvā nivartate* (Bg. 2.59). When one finds out the supreme goal of life, he naturally becomes detached from the bodily concept. Here in this verse the indication is that one has to steadfastly increase attachment for Transcendence *(brahmaṇi)*. As it is confirmed in the *Vedānta-sūtra, athāto brahma-jijñāsā* (*Vs.* 1.1.1): without inquiry about the Supreme or the Transcendence, one cannot give up attachment for this material world. By the evolutionary process in 8,400,000 species of life, one cannot understand the ultimate goal of life because in all those species of life, the bodily conception is very prominent. *Athāto brahma-jijñāsā* means that in order to get out of the bodily conception, one has to increase attachment or inquiry about Brahman. Then he can be situated in the transcendental devotional service–*śravaṇaṁ kīrtanaṁ viṣṇoḥ*. To increase attachment for Brahman means to engage in devotional service. Those who are attached to the impersonal form of Brahman cannot remain attached for very long. Impersonalists, after rejecting this world as *mithyā* or false *(jagan-mithyā),* come down again to this *jagan-mithyā,* although they take *sannyāsa* to increase their attachment for Brahman. Similarly, many *yogīs* who are attached to the localized aspect of Brahman as Paramātmā–great sages like Viśvāmitra–also fall down as victims of women. Therefore increased attachment for the Supreme Personality of Godhead is advised in all *śāstras.* That is the only way of detachment from material existence and is explained in *Bhagavad-gītā* as *paraṁ dṛṣṭvā nivartate* (Bg. 2.59). One can cease material activities when he actually has the taste for devotional service. Śrī Caitanya Mahāprabhu also recommended love of Godhead as the ultimate goal of life (*premā pumārtho mahān*). Without increasing love of Godhead, one cannot achieve the perfectional stage or the transcendental position.

TEXT 22

सा श्रद्धया भगवद्धर्मचर्यया
जिज्ञासयाऽऽध्यात्मिकयोगनिष्ठया ।

योगेश्वरोपासनया च नित्यं
पुण्यश्रवःकथया पुण्यया च ॥२२॥

sā śraddhayā bhagavad-dharma-caryayā
jijñāsayādhyātmika-yoga-niṣṭhayā
yogeśvaropāsanayā ca nityaṁ
puṇya-śravaḥ-kathayā puṇyayā ca

sā—that devotional service; *śraddhayā*—with faith and conviction; *bhagavat-dharma*—devotional service; *caryayā*—by discussion; *jijñāsayā*—by inquiry; *adhyātmika*—spiritual; *yoga-niṣṭhayā*—by conviction in spiritual understanding; *yogeśvara*—the Supreme Personality of Godhead; *upāsanayā*—by worship of Him; *ca*—and; *nityam*—regularly; *puṇya-śravaḥ*—by hearing which; *kathayā*—by discussion; *puṇyayā*—by pious; *ca*—also.

TRANSLATION

Attachment for the Supreme can be increased by practicing devotional service, inquiring about the Supreme Personality of God, applying bhakti-yoga in life, worshiping the Yogeśvara, the Supreme Personality of Godhead, and by hearing and chanting about the glories of the Supreme Personality of Godhead. These actions are pious in themselves.

PURPORT

The word *yogeśvara* is applicable to both the Supreme Personality of Godhead, Kṛṣṇa, and His devotees also. In *Bhagavad-gītā* this word occurs in two places. In the Eighteenth Chapter (18.78), Kṛṣṇa is described as the Supreme Personality of Godhead, Hari, who is the master of all mystic power *(yatra yogeśvaraḥ kṛṣṇo).* Yogeśvara is also described at the end of the Sixth Chapter *(sa me yuktatamo mataḥ)* (Bg. 6.47). This *yuktatama* indicates the topmost of all *yogīs*—the devotees, who can also be called *yogeśvara.* In this verse *yogeśvara-upāsanā* means to render service to a pure devotee. Thus Narottama dāsa Ṭhākura says: *chāḍiyā vaiṣṇava-sevā nistāra pāyeche kebā.* Without serving a pure devotee, one cannot advance in spiritual life. Prahlāda Mahārāja also has said:

naiṣāṁ matis tāvad urukramāṅghriṁ
spṛśaty anarthāpagamo yad arthaḥ
mahīyasāṁ pāda-rajo'bhiṣekaṁ
niṣkiñcanānāṁ na vṛṇīta yāvat. (*Bhāg.* 7.5.32)

One should take shelter of a pure devotee, who has nothing to do with this material world but is simply engaged in devotional service. By serving him only, one can transcend the qualitative material condition. In this verse it is recommended *(yogeśvara-upāsanayā)* that one serve the lotus feet of the topmost *yogī,* or the devotee. To serve the topmost devotee means to hear from him about the glories of the Supreme Personality of Godhead. To hear the glories of the Supreme Personality of Godhead from the mouth of a pure devotee is to acquire a pious life. In *Bhagavad-gītā* it is also said that without being pious one cannot engage in devotional service.

yeṣāṁ tv anta-gatam pāpaṁ janānāṁ puṇya-karmaṇām
te dvandva-moha-nirmuktā bhajante māṁ dṛḍha-vratāḥ (Bg. 7.28)

To become fixed in devotional service one has to become completely cleansed from the contamination of the material modes of nature. For work in devotional service the first item is *ādau gurvāśrayam:* one should accept a bona fide spiritual master, and from the bona fide spiritual master *(sad-dharma-pṛcchā)* inquire about his transcendental occupational duties *(sādhu-mārga-anugamanam)* and follow in the footsteps of great saintly persons, devotees. These are the instructions given in *Bhakti-rasāmṛta-sindhu* by Rūpa Gosvāmī.

The conclusion is that to increase attachment for the Supreme Personality of Godhead one has to accept a bona fide spiritual master and learn from him the methods of devotional service and hear from him about the transcendental message and glorification of the Supreme Personality of Godhead. In this way one has to increase his conviction about devotional service. Then it will be very easy to increase attachment for the Supreme Personality of Godhead.

TEXT 23

अर्थेन्द्रियारामसगोष्ठ्यतृष्णया
तत्सम्मतानामपरिग्रहेण च ।
विविक्तरुच्या परितोष आत्मनि
विना हरेर्गुणपीयूषपानात् ॥२३॥

arthendriyārāma-sagoṣṭhy-atṛṣṇayā
tat-sammatānām aparigraheṇa ca
vivikta-rucyā paritoṣa ātmani
vinā harer guṇa-pīyūṣa-pānāt

artha—riches; *indriya*—senses; *ārāma*—gratification; *sa-goṣṭhī*—with their companion; *atṛṣṇayā*—by reluctance; *tat*—that; *sammatānām*—since approved by them; *aparigraheṇa*—by nonacceptance; *ca*—also; *vivikta-rucyā*—disgusted taste; *paritoṣe*—happiness; *ātmani*—self; *vinā*—without; *hareḥ*—of the Supreme Personality of Godhead; *guṇa*—qualities; *pīyūṣa*—nectar; *pānāt*—drinking.

TRANSLATION

One has to make progress in spiritual life by not associating with persons who are simply interested in making money and sense gratification. Not only such persons, but one who associates with such persons should be avoided. One should mold his life in such a way that he cannot live in peace without drinking the nectar of the glorification of the Supreme Personality of Godhead, Hari. One can be thus elevated by losing taste for sense enjoyment.

PURPORT

In the material world everyone is interested in money and sense gratification. The only objective is to earn as much money as possible and utilize it for satisfaction of the senses. Śrīla Śukadeva Gosvāmī thus described the activities of the materialistic persons:

nidrayā hriyate naktaṁ vyavāyena ca vā vayaḥ
divā cārthehayā rājan kuṭumba-bharaṇena vā (*Bhāg.* 2.1.3)

This is a typical example of materialistic persons. At night they waste their time by sleeping more than six hours or by wasting time in sex indulgence. This is their occupation at night, and in the morning they go to their office or business place just to earn money. As soon as there is some money, they become busy in purchasing things for their children and others. Such persons are never interested in understanding the values of life—what is God, what is the individual soul, what is its relationship with God, etc. Things are degraded to such an extent that those who are supposed to be religious are also at the present moment only interested in sense gratification. The number of materialistic persons in this age of Kali has increased more than in any other age; therefore persons who are interested in going back home, back to Godhead, should not only engage in the service of realized souls but should give up the company of materialistic persons whose only aim is to earn money and employ it in sense gratification. They should also not accept the objectives of materialistic persons, namely money and sense gratification. Therefore it is stated: *bhakti–parasyānubhavaṁ viraktir anyathā syāt.* To advance in devotional service one should be uninterested in the materialistic way of life. That which is the subject matter of satisfaction for the devotees is of no interest to the nondevotees.

Simple negation, or giving up the company of materialistic persons, will not do. We must have engagements. Sometimes it is found that a person interested in spiritual advancement gives up the company of material society and goes to a secluded place as recommended for the *yogīs* especially, but that will also not help a person in spiritual advancement, for in many instances such *yogīs* also fall down. As far as *jñānīs* are concerned, generally they fall down without taking shelter of the lotus feet of the Lord. The impersonalists or the voidists can simply avoid the positive material association; they cannot remain fixed in transcendence without being engaged in devotional service. The beginning of devotional service is to hear about the glories of the Supreme Personality of Godhead. That is recommended in this verse: *vinā harer guṇa-pīyūṣa-pānāt.* One must drink the nectar of the glories of the Supreme Personality of Godhead, and this means that one must be always engaged in hearing and chanting the glories of the Lord. It is the prime method for advancing in spiritual life. Lord Caitanya Mahāprabhu also recommends this in the *Caitanya-caritāmṛta.* If one wants to make advancement in spiritual life, by great fortune he may meet a bona fide spiritual master and from him learn about Kṛṣṇa. By serving both the spiritual master and Kṛṣṇa he gets the seed of devotional service *(bhakti-latā-bīja),* and if he sows the seed within his heart and waters it by hearing and chanting, it grows into a luxuriant *bhakti-latā* or *bhakti* creeper. The creeper is so strong that it penetrates the covering of the universe and reaches the spiritual world and continues to grow on and on until it reaches and takes shelter of the lotus feet of Kṛṣṇa. An ordinary creeper also grows on and on until it takes a solid shelter on a roof; then it very steadily grows and produces the required fruit. The real cause of the growing of such fruit, which is here called nectar, is hearing and chanting the glories of the Supreme Personality of Godhead. The purport is that one cannot live outside the society of devotees; one must live in the association of devotees, where there is constant chanting and hearing of the glories of the Lord. The Kṛṣṇa consciousness movement is started for this purpose, and there are hundreds of ISKCON centers to give opportunity to all people to hear and chant and to accept the spiritual master. By not associating with persons who are materially interested, one can make solid advancement in going back home, back to Godhead.

TEXT 24

अहिंसया पारमहंस्यचर्यया
स्मृत्या मुकुन्दाचरिताग्र्यसीधुना ।
यमैरकामैर्नियमैश्चाप्यनिन्दया
निरीहया द्वन्द्वतितिक्षया च ॥२४॥

ahiṁsayā pāramahaṁsya-caryayā
smṛtyā mukundācaritāgrya-sīdhunā
yamair akāmair niyamaiś cāpy anindayā
nirīhayā dvandva-titikṣayā ca

ahiṁsayā—by nonviolence; *pāramahaṁsya-caryayā*—by following in the footsteps of great *ācāryas; smṛtyā*—by remembering; *mukunda*—the Supreme Personality of Godhead; *ācarita-agrya*—simply preaching His activities; *sīdhunā*—by the nectar; *yamaiḥ*—by following regulative principles; *akāmaiḥ*—without material desires; *niyamaiḥ*—by strictly following the rules and regulations; *ca*—also; *api*—certainly; *anindayā*—without blaspheming; *nirīhayā*—living simply, plain living; *dvandva*—duality; *titikṣayā*—by tolerance; *ca*—and.

TRANSLATION

A candidate for spiritual advancement must be nonviolent, must follow in the footsteps of great ācāryas, must always remember the nectar of the pastimes of the Supreme Personality of Godhead, must follow the regulative principles without material desire, and, while following the regulative principles, should not blaspheme others. A devotee should lead a very simple life and not be disturbed by the duality of opposing elements. He should learn to tolerate them.

PURPORT

The devotees are actually saintly persons or *sādhus*. The first qualification of a *sādhu* or devotee is *ahiṁsā* or nonviolence. Persons interested in the path of devotional service or in going back home, back to Godhead, must first practice *ahiṁsā* or nonviolence. A *sādhu* is described as *titikṣavaḥ kāruṇikāḥ* (*Bhāg.* 3.25.21). A devotee should be tolerant and should be very much compassionate toward others. For example, if he suffers personal injury, he should tolerate it, but if someone else suffers injury, he need not tolerate it. The whole world is full of violence, and a devotee's first business is to stop this violence, including the unnecessary slaughter of animals. A devotee is the friend not only of human society but of all living entities, for he sees all living entities as sons of the Supreme Personality of Godhead. He does not claim himself to be the only son of God and allow all others to be killed, thinking that they have no soul. This kind of philosophy is never advocated by a pure devotee of the Lord. *Suhṛdaḥ sarva-dehinām:* a true devotee is the friend of all living entities. Kṛṣṇa claims in *Bhagavad-gītā* to be the father of all species of living entities; consequently the devotee of Kṛṣṇa is always a friend of all. This is called *ahiṁsā.* Such nonviolence can be practiced only when we follow in the footsteps of great *ācāryas.* Therefore, according to our Vaiṣṇava philosophy, we have to follow the great *ācāryas* of the four *sampradāyas* or disciplic successions.

Trying to advance in spiritual life outside the disciplic succession is simply ludicrous. It is said, therefore: *ācāryavān puruṣo veda* (*Chānd. Up.* 6.14.2). One who follows the disciplic succession of *ācāryas* knows things as they are. *Tad-vijñānārthaṁ sa gurum evābhigacchet* (*Muṇḍ. Up.* 1.2.12). In order to understand the transcendental science, one must approach the bona fide spiritual master. The word *smṛtyā* is very important in spiritual life. *Smṛtyā* means remembering Kṛṣṇa always. Life should be molded in such a way that one cannot remain alone without thinking of Kṛṣṇa. We should live in Kṛṣṇa so that while eating, sleeping, walking and working we remain only in Kṛṣṇa. Our Kṛṣṇa consciousness society recommends that we arrange our living so that we can remember Kṛṣṇa. In our ISKCON society the devotees, while engaged in making Spiritual Sky incense, are also hearing about the glories of Kṛṣṇa or His devotees. The *śāstra* recommends: *smartavyaḥ satataṁ viṣṇuḥ.* Lord Viṣṇu should be remembered always, constantly. *Vismartavyo na jātucit:* Viṣṇu should never be forgotten. That is the spiritual way of life. *Smṛtyā.* This remembrance of the Lord can be continued if we hear about Him constantly. It is therefore recommended in this verse: *mukundācaritāgrya-sīdhunā. Sīdhu* means nectar. To hear about Kṛṣṇa from *Śrīmad-Bhāgavatam* or *Bhagavad-gītā* or similar authentic literature is to live in Kṛṣṇa consciousness. Such concentration in Kṛṣṇa consciousness can be achieved by persons who are strictly following the rules and regulative principles. We have recommended in our Kṛṣṇa consciousness movement that a devotee chant sixteen rounds on beads daily and follow the regulative principles. That will help the devotee to spiritually advance in life.

It is also stated in this verse that by controlling the senses one can become a *svāmī* or *gosvāmī.* One who is therefore enjoying this supertitle, *svāmī* or *gosvāmī*, must be very strict in controlling his senses. Indeed, he must be master of his senses. This is possible when one does not desire any material sense gratification. If, by chance, the senses want to work independently, he must control them. If we simply practice avoiding material sense gratification, controlling the senses is automatically achieved.

Another important point mentioned in this connection *(anindayā)* is that we should not criticize others' methods of religion. There are different types of religious systems operating under different qualities of material nature. Those operating in the modes of ignorance and passion cannot be as perfect as that system in the mode of goodness. In *Bhagavad-gītā* everything has been divided into three qualitative divisions; therefore religious systems are similarly categorized. When people are mostly under the modes of passion and ignorance, their system of religion will be of the same quality. A devotee, instead of criticizing such systems, will encourage the followers to stick to their principles so that gradually they can come to the platform of religion in goodness. Simply by criticizing them, a devotee's mind will be agitated. Thus a devotee should tolerate and learn to stop agitation.

Another feature of the devotee is *nirīhayā*, simple living. *Nirīhā* means gentle, meek or simple. A devotee should not live very gorgeously and imitate a materialistic person. Plain living and high thinking are recommended for a devotee. He should accept only so much as he can to keep the material body fit for the execution of devotional service. He should not eat nor sleep more than is required. Simply eating for living, and not living for eating, and sleeping only six to seven hours a day are principles to be followed by devotees. As long as the body is there it is subjected to the influence of climatic changes, disease and natural disturbances, the threefold miseries of material existence. We cannot avoid them. Sometimes we receive letters from neophyte devotees questioning why they have fallen sick, although pursuing Kṛṣṇa consciousness. They should learn from this verse that they have to become tolerant *(dvandva-titikṣayā)*. This is the world of duality. Because he has fallen sick, one should not think that he has fallen from Kṛṣṇa consciousness. Kṛṣṇa consciousness can continue without impediment from any material opposition. Lord Śrī Kṛṣṇa therefore advises in *Bhagavad-gītā, tāṁs titikṣasva bhārata:* "My dear Arjuna, please try to tolerate all these disturbances. Be fixed in your Kṛṣṇa conscious activities." (Bg. 2.14)

TEXT 25

हरेर्मुहुस्तत्परकर्णपूर-
गुणाभिधानेन विजृम्भमाणया ।
भक्त्या ह्यसङ्गः सदसत्यनात्मनि
स्यान्निर्गुणे ब्रह्मणि चाञ्जसा रतिः ॥२५॥

harer muhus tat-para-karṇa-pūra-
guṇābhidhānena vijṛmbhamāṇayā
bhaktyā hy asaṅgaḥ sad-asaty anātmani
syān nirguṇe brahmaṇi cāñjasā ratiḥ

hareḥ—of the Supreme Personality of Godhead; *muhuḥ*—constantly; *tat-para*—in relation with the Supreme Personality of Godhead; *karṇa-pūra*—decoration of the ear; *guṇa-abhidhānena*—discussing transcendental qualities; *vijṛmbhamāṇayā*—by increasing Kṛṣṇa consciousness; *bhaktyā*—by devotion; *hi*—certainly; *asaṅgaḥ*—uncontaminated; *sat-asati*—the material world; *anātmani*—opposed to spiritual understanding; *syāt*—should be; *nirguṇe*—in transcendence; *brahmaṇi*—in the Supreme Lord; *ca*—and; *añjasā*—easily; *ratiḥ*—attraction.

TRANSLATION

The devotee should gradually increase the culture of devotional service by constant hearing of the transcendental qualities of the Supreme Personality of Godhead. These pastimes are like ornamental decorations on the ears of devotees. By rendering devotional service and transcending the material qualities, one can easily be fixed in transcendence in the Supreme Personality of Godhead.

PURPORT

This verse is especially mentioned to substantiate the devotional process of hearing the subject matter. A devotee does not like to hear anything other than subjects dealing with spiritual activities, or the pastimes of the Supreme Personality of Godhead. We can increase our propensity for devotional service by hearing *Bhagavad-gītā* and *Śrīmad-Bhāgavatam* from realized souls. The more we hear from realized souls, the more we make advancement in our devotional life. The more we advance in devotional life, the more we become detached from the material world. The more we become detached from the material world, the less we associate with persons who are after money and sense gratification. This is the advice of Lord Caitanya Mahāprabhu:

niṣkiñcanasya bhagavad-bhajanonmukhasya
pāraṁ paraṁ jigamiṣor bhava-sāgarasya
sandarśanaṁ viṣayiṇām atha yoṣitāṁ ca
hā hanta hanta viṣa-bhakṣaṇato 'py asādhu.
(Cc. *Madhya* 11.8)

The word *brahmaṇi* used in this verse is commented upon by the impersonalists or professional reciters of *Bhāgavatam,* who are mainly advocates of the caste system by demoniac birthright. They say that *brahmaṇi* means the impersonal Brahman. But they cannot conclude this without reference to the context of the words *bhaktyā* and *guṇābhidhānena.* According to the impersonalists, there are no transcendental qualities in the impersonal Brahman; therefore we should understand that *brahmaṇi* means "in the Supreme Personality of Godhead." Kṛṣṇa is the Supreme Personality of Godhead, as admitted by Arjuna in *Bhagavad-gītā;* therefore wherever the word *brahma* is used, it must refer to Kṛṣṇa, not to the impersonal Brahman effulgence. *Brahmeti paramātmeti bhagavān iti śabdyate* (*Bhāg.* 1.2.11). Brahman, Paramātmā and Bhagavān can all be taken in total as Brahman, but when there is reference to the word *bhakti* or remembrance of the transcendental qualities, the word indicates the Supreme Personality of Godhead, not the impersonal Brahman.

TEXT 26

यदा रतिर्ब्रह्मणि नैष्ठिकी पुमा-
नाचार्यवान् ज्ञानविरागरंहसा ।
दहत्यवीर्यं हृदयं जीवकोशं
पञ्चात्मकं योनिमिवोत्थितोऽग्निः ॥२६॥

yadā ratir brahmaṇi naiṣṭhikī pumān
ācāryavān jñāna-virāga-raṁhasā
dahaty avīryaṁ hṛdayaṁ jīva-kośaṁ
pañcātmakaṁ yonim ivotthito 'gniḥ

yadā—when; *ratiḥ*—attachment; *brahmaṇi*—in the Supreme Personality of Godhead; *naiṣṭhikī*—fixed; *pumān*—the person; *ācāryavān*—completely surrendered to the spiritual master; *jñāna*—knowledge; *virāga*—detachment; *raṁhasā*—by the force of; *dahati*—burns; *avīryam*—impotent; *hṛdayam*—

within the heart; *jīva-kośam*—the covering of the spirit soul; *pañca-ātmakam*—five elements; *yonim*—source of birth; *iva*—like; *utthitaḥ*—emanating; *agniḥ*—fire.

TRANSLATION

Upon becoming fixed in his attachment to the Supreme Personality of Godhead by the grace of the spiritual master and by awakening knowledge and detachment, the living entity, situated within the heart of the body and covered by the five elements, burns up his material surroundings exactly as fire, arising from wood, burns the wood itself.

PURPORT

It is said that both the *jīvātmā,* the individual soul, and the Paramātmā live together within the heart. In the Vedic version it is stated, *hṛdi hy ayam ātmā:* the soul and Supersoul both live within the heart. The individual soul is liberated when it comes out of the material heart or cleanses the heart to make it spiritualized. The example given here is very appropriate: *yonim ivotthito 'gniḥ. Agni,* or fire, comes out of the wood, and by it the wood is completely destroyed. Similarly, when a living entity increases his attachment for the Supreme Personality of Godhead, he is to be considered like fire. A blazing fire is visible by its exhibition of heat and light; similarly, when the living entity within the heart becomes enlightened with full spiritual knowledge, and detached from the material world, he burns up his material covering of the five elements—earth, water, fire, air and sky—and becomes free from the five kinds of material attachments, namely, ignorance, false egoism, attachment to the material world, envy and absorption in material consciousness. Therefore *pañcātmakam,* as mentioned in this verse, refers to either the five elements or the five coverings of material contamination. When these are all burned into ashes by the blazing fire of knowledge and detachment, one is fixed firmly in the devotional service of the Supreme Personality of Godhead. Unless one takes shelter of a bona fide spiritual master and advances his attraction for Kṛṣṇa by his instructions, the five coverings of the living entity cannot be uncovered from the material heart. The living entity is centered within the heart, and to take him away from the heart is to liberate him. This is the process. One must take shelter of a bona fide spiritual master and by his instruction increase one's knowledge in devotional service, become detached from the material world and thus become liberated. An advanced devotee therefore does not live within the material body but within his spiritual body, just as a dry coconut lives detached from the coconut husk, even though within the husk. The pure devotee's body is therefore called *cinmaya-śarīra* (spiritualized body). In other words, a devotee's body is not connected with material activities, and as such, a devotee is always liberated. *Brahma-bhūyāya kalpate.* (Bg. 14.26) This is confirmed in *Bhagavad-gītā.* Śrīla Rūpa Gosvāmī also confirms this:

īhā yasya harer dāsye karmaṇā manasā vācā
nikhilāsv apy avasthāsu jīvan-muktaḥ sa ucyate.

"One who is engaged fully with his body, mind and speech in the service of the Lord is liberated even within this body, despite his condition."

TEXT 27

दग्धाशयो मुक्तसमस्ततद्गुणो
नैवात्मनो बहिरन्तर्विचष्टे ।
परात्मनोर्यद्व्यवधानं पुरस्तात्
स्वप्ने यथा पुरुषस्तद्विनाशे ॥२७॥

dagdhāśayo mukta-samasta-tad-guṇo
naivātmano bahir antar vicaṣṭe
parātmanor yad-vyavadhānaṁ purastāt
svapne yathā puruṣas tad-vināśe

dagdha-āśayaḥ—all material desires being burned; *mukta*—liberated; *samasta*—all; *tat-guṇaḥ*—qualities in connection with matter; *na*—not; *eva*—certainly; *ātmanaḥ*—the soul or the Supersoul; *bahiḥ*—external; *antaḥ*—internal; *vicaṣṭe*—acting; *para-ātmanoḥ*—of the Supersoul; *yat*—that; *vyavadhānam*—difference; *purastāt*—as it was in the beginning; *svapne*—in dream; *yathā*—as; *puruṣaḥ*—a person; *tat*—that; *vināśe*—being finished.

TRANSLATION

When a person becomes devoid of all material desires and liberated from all material qualities, he transcends distinctions between actions executed externally and internally. At that time the difference between the soul and the Supersoul, which was existing before self-realization, is annihilated. When a dream is over, there is no longer a distinction between the dream and the dreamer.

PURPORT

As described by Śrīla Rūpa Gosvāmī (*anyābhilāṣitā-śūnyam*), one must be devoid of all material desires. When a person becomes devoid of all material desires, there is no longer need for speculative knowledge or fruitive activities. In that condition it is to be understood that one is free from the material body. The example is already given above—a coconut which is dry is loosened from its outward husk. This is the stage of liberation. As said in *Śrīmad-Bhāgavatam, mukti* (liberation) means *svarūpeṇa avasthitiḥ*—being situated in one's own constitutional position. All material desires are present as long as one is in the bodily concept of life, but when one realizes that he is an eternal servant of Kṛṣṇa, his desires are no longer material. A devotee acts in this consciousness. In other words, when material desires in connection with the body are finished, one is actually liberated.

When one is liberated from the material qualities, he does not do anything for his personal sense gratification. At that time all activities performed by him are absolute. In the conditioned state there are two kinds of activities. One acts on behalf of the body, and at the same time he acts to become liberated. The devotee, when he is completely free from all material desires or all material qualities, transcends the duality of action for the body and soul. Then the bodily concept of life is completely over. Therefore Śrīla Rūpa Gosvāmī says: *īhā yasya harer dāsye karmaṇā manasā vācā/ nikhilāsv apy avasthāsu jīvan-muktaḥ sa ucyate.* When one is completely fixed in the service of the Lord, he is a liberated person in any condition of life. He is called *jīvan-muktaḥ,* liberated even within this body. In such a liberated condition, there is no distinction between actions for sense gratification and actions for liberation. When one is liberated from the desires of sense gratification, he has no longer to suffer the reactions of lamentation or illusion. Activities performed by the *karmīs* and *jñānīs* are subjected to lamentation and illusion, but a self-realized liberated person acting only for the Supreme Personality of Godhead experiences none. This is the stage of oneness, or merging into the existence of the Supreme Personality of Godhead. This means that the individual soul, while keeping his individuality, no longer has separate interests. He is fully in the service of the Lord, and he has nothing to do for his personal sense gratification; therefore he sees only the Supreme Personality of Godhead and not himself. His personal interest completely perishes. When a person comes out of a dream, the dream vanishes. While dreaming a person may consider himself a king and see the royal paraphernalia, his soldiers, etc., but when the dream is over, he does not see anything beyond himself. Similarly, a liberated person understands that he is part and parcel of the Supreme Lord acting in accordance with the desire of the Supreme Lord, and as such there is no distinction between himself and the Supreme Lord, although both of them retain their individuality. *Nityo nityānāṁ cetanaś cetanānām.* This is the perfect conception of oneness in relation to the Supersoul and the soul.

TEXT 28

आत्मानमिन्द्रियार्थं च परं यदुभयोरपि ।
सत्याशय उपाधौ वै पुमान् पश्यति नान्यदा ॥२८॥

ātmānam indriyārthaṁ ca
paraṁ yad ubhayor api
satyāśaya upādhau vai
pumān paśyati nānyadā

ātmānam—the soul; *indriya-artham*—for sense gratification; *ca*—and; *param*—transcendental; *yat*—that; *ubhayoḥ*—both; *api*—certainly; *sati*—being situated; *āśaye*—material desires; *upādhau*—designation; *vai*—certainly; *pumān*—the person; *paśyati*—sees; *nānyadā*—not otherwise.

TRANSLATION

When the soul exists for sense gratification, he creates different desires, and for that reason he becomes subjected to designations. But when one is in the transcendental position, he is no longer interested in anything except fulfilling the desires of the Lord.

PURPORT

Being covered by material desires, a spirit soul is also considered to be covered by designations belonging to a particular type of body. Thus he considers himself an animal, man, demigod, bird, beast, etc. In so many ways he is influenced by false identification caused by false egotism, and being covered by illusory material desires, he distinguishes between matter and spirit. When one is devoid of such distinctions, there is no longer a difference between matter and spirit. At that time, the spirit is the only predominating factor. As long as one is covered by material desires, he thinks himself the master or the enjoyer. Thus he acts for sense gratification and becomes subjected to material pangs, happiness and distress. But when one is freed from such a concept of life, he is no longer subjected to designations, and he envisions everything as spiritual in connection with the Supreme Lord. This is explained by Śrīla Rūpa Gosvāmī in his *Bhakti-*

rasāmṛta-sindhu: anyāsaktasya viṣayān yathārham upayuñjataḥ/ nirbandhaḥ kṛṣṇa-sambandhe yuktaṁ vairāgyam ucyate (Bh.r.s. 1.2.255).

The liberated person has no attachment for anything material or for sense gratification. He understands that everything is connected with the Supreme Personality of Godhead and that everything should be engaged in the service of the Lord. Therefore he does not give up anything. There is no question of renouncing anything because the *paramahaṁsa* knows how to engage everything in the service of the Lord. Originally everything is spiritual; nothing is material. In the *Caitanya-caritāmṛta* also it is explained that a *mahā-bhāgavata,* a highly advanced devotee, has no material vision, *sthāvara-jaṅgama dekhe, nā dekhe tāra mūrti/ sarvatra haya nija iṣṭadeva-sphūrti* (Cc. *Madhya* 8.274). Although he sees trees, mountains, and other living entities moving here and there, he sees all as the creation of the Supreme Lord, and, with reference to the context, sees only the creator and not the created. In other words, he no longer distinguishes between the created and the creator. He sees only the Supreme Personality of Godhead in everything. He sees Kṛṣṇa in everything and everything in Kṛṣṇa. This is oneness.

TEXT 29

निमित्ते सति सर्वत्र जलादावपि पूरुषः ।
आत्मनश्च परस्यापि भिदां पश्यति नान्यदा ॥२९॥

nimitte sati sarvatra
jalādāv api pūruṣaḥ
ātmanaś ca parasyāpi
bhidāṁ paśyati nānyadā

nimitte—on account of causes; *sati*—being; *sarvatra*—everywhere; *jala-ādau api*—water and other reflecting mediums; *pūruṣaḥ*—the person; *ātmanaḥ*—oneself; *ca*—and; *parasya api*—another's self; *bhidām*—differentiation; *paśyati*—sees; *nānyadā*—there is no other reason.

TRANSLATION

Only because of different causes does a person see a difference between himself and others. It is like the reflection of a body on water or oil or in a mirror appearing to be differently manifested.

PURPORT

The spirit soul is one, the Supreme Personality of Godhead. He is manifested in *svāṁśa* and *vibhinnāṁśa* expansions. The *jīvas* are *vibhinnāṁśa* expansions. The different incarnations of the Supreme

Personality of Godhead are *svāṁśa* expansions. Thus there are different potencies of the Supreme Lord, and there are different expansions of the different potencies. In this way, for different reasons there are different expansions of the same one principle, the Supreme Personality of Godhead. This understanding is real knowledge, but when the living entity is covered by the *upādhi* or designated body, he sees differences, exactly as one sees differences in reflections of oneself on water, oil or in a mirror. When something is reflected on the water, it appears to be moving. When it is reflected on ice, it appears fixed. When it is reflected on oil, it appears hazy. The subject is one, but under different conditions it appears differently. When the qualifying factor is taken away, the whole appears to be one. In other words, when one comes to the *paramahaṁsa* or perfectional stage of life by practicing *bhakti-yoga,* he sees only Kṛṣṇa everywhere. For him there is no other objective.

In conclusion, due to different causes, the living entity is visible in different forms as an animal, human being, demigod, tree, etc. Actually every living entity is the marginal potency of the Supreme Lord. In *Bhagavad-gītā,* therefore, it is explained that one who actually sees the spirit soul does not distinguish between a learned *brāhmaṇa* and a dog, an elephant or a cow. *Paṇḍitāḥ sama-darśinaḥ* (Bg. 5.18). One who is actually learned sees only the living entity, not the outward covering. Differentiation is therefore the result of different *karma* or fruitive activities, and when we stop fruitive activities, turning them into acts of devotion, we can understand that we are not different from anyone else, regardless of the form. This is only possible in Kṛṣṇa consciousness. In this movement there are many different races of men from all parts of the world participating, but because they think of themselves as servants of the Supreme Personality of Godhead, they do not differentiate between black and white, yellow and red. The Kṛṣṇa consciousness movement is therefore the only means to make the living entities transcend all designations.

TEXT 30

इन्द्रियैर्विषयाकृष्टैराक्षिप्तं ध्यायतां मनः ।
चेतनां हरते बुद्धेः स्तम्बस्तोयमिव ह्रदात् ॥३०॥

indriyair viṣayākṛṣṭair
ākṣiptaṁ dhyāyatāṁ manaḥ
cetanāṁ harate buddheḥ
stambas toyam iva hradāt

indriyaiḥ—by the senses; *viṣaya*—the sense objects; *ākṛṣṭaiḥ*—being attracted; *ākṣiptam*—agitated; *dhyāyatām*—always thinking of; *manaḥ*—mind; *cetanām*—consciousness; *harate*—becomes lost; *buddheḥ*—of intelligence; *stambaḥ*—big straws; *toyam*—water; *iva*—like; *hradāt*—from the lake.

TRANSLATION

When one's mind and senses are attracted to sense objects for enjoyment, the mind becomes agitated. As a result of continually thinking of sense objects, one's real consciousness almost becomes lost, like the water in a lake that is gradually sucked up by the big grass straws on its bank.

PURPORT

In this verse it is very nicely explained how our original Kṛṣṇa consciousness becomes polluted. Gradually we become almost completely forgetful of our relationship with the Supreme Lord. In the previous verse it is recommended that we should always keep in touch with the devotional service of the Lord so that the blazing fire of devotional service can gradually burn into ashes material desires and we can become liberated from the repetition of birth and death. This is also how we can indirectly keep our staunch faith in the lotus feet of the Supreme Personality of Godhead. When the mind is allowed to think of sense gratification continuously, it becomes the cause of our material bondage. If our mind is simply filled with sense gratification, even though we want Kṛṣṇa consciousness, by continuous practice we cannot forget the subject matter of sense gratification. If one takes up the *sannyāsa* order of life but is not able to control the mind, he will think of objects of sense gratification—namely family, society, expensive house, etc. Even though he goes to the Himalayas or the forest, his mind will continue thinking of the objects of sense gratification. In this way, gradually one's intelligence will be affected. When intelligence is affected, one loses his original taste for Kṛṣṇa consciousness.

The example given here is very appropriate. If a big lake is covered all around by long *kuśa* grass, just like columns, the waters dry up. Similarly, when the big columns of material desire increase, the clear water of consciousness is dried up. Therefore these columns of *kuśa* grass should be cut or thrown away from the very beginning. Śrī Caitanya Mahāprabhu has instructed that if from the very beginning we do not take care of unwanted grass in the paddy fields, the fertilizing agents or water will be used by them and the paddy plants will dry up. The material desire for sense enjoyment is the cause of our falldown in this material world, and thus we suffer the threefold miseries and continuous birth, death, old age and disease. However, if we turn our desires toward the transcendental loving service of the Lord, our desires become purified. We cannot kill desires. We have to purify them of different designations. If we constantly think of being a member of a particular nation, society or family and continuously think about them, we become very strongly entangled in the conditioned life of birth and death. But if our desires are applied to the service of the Lord, they become purified, and thus we become immediately freed from material contamination.

TEXT 31

भ्रश्यत्यनुस्मृतिश्चित्तं ज्ञानभ्रंशः स्मृतिक्षये ।
तद्रोधं कवयः प्राहुरात्मापह्नवमात्मनः ॥३१॥

bhraśyaty anusmṛtiś cittaṁ
jñāna-bhraṁśaḥ smṛti-kṣaye
tad-rodhaṁ kavayaḥ prāhur
ātmāpahnavam ātmanaḥ

bhraśyati—becomes destroyed; *anusmṛtiḥ*—constantly thinking; *cittam*—consciousness; *jñāna-bhraṁśaḥ*—bereft of real knowledge; *smṛti-kṣaye*—by destruction of remembrance; *tat-rodham*—choking that process; *kavayaḥ*—great learned scholars; *prāhuḥ*—have opined; *ātma*—of the soul; *apahnavam*—destruction; *ātmanaḥ*—of the soul.

TRANSLATION

When one deviates from his original consciousness, he loses the capacity to remember his previous position or recognize his present one. When remembrance is lost, all knowledge that is acquired is based on a false foundation. When this occurs, learned scholars consider that the soul is lost.

PURPORT

The living entity or the soul is ever existing and eternal. It cannot be lost, but learned scholars say that it is lost when actual knowledge is not working. That is the difference between animals and human beings. According to less intelligent philosophers, animals have no soul. But factually animals have souls. Due to the animals' gross ignorance, however, it appears that they have lost their souls. Without the soul, a body cannot move. That is the difference between a living body and a dead body. When the soul is out of the body, the body is called dead. The soul is said to be lost when there is no proper knowledge exhibited. Our original consciousness is Kṛṣṇa consciousness because we are part and parcel of Kṛṣṇa. When this consciousness is misguided and one is put into the material atmosphere, which pollutes the original consciousness, one thinks that he is a product of the material elements. Thus one loses his real remembrance of his position as part and parcel of the Supreme Personality of Godhead, just as a man who sleeps forgets himself. In this way, when the activities of proper consciousness are checked, all the activities of the lost soul are performed on a false basis. At the present moment human civilization is acting on a false platform of bodily identification; therefore it can be said that the people of the present age have lost their souls.

TEXT 32

नातः परतरो लोके पुंसः स्वार्थव्यतिक्रमः ।
यदध्यन्यस्य प्रेयस्त्वमात्मनः स्वव्यतिक्रमात् ॥३२॥

nātaḥ parataro loke
puṁsaḥ svārtha-vyatikramaḥ
yadadhy anyasya preyastvam
ātmanaḥ sva-vyatikramāt

na—not; *ataḥ*—after this; *parataraḥ*—greater; *loke*—in this world; *puṁsaḥ*—of the living entities; *sva-artha*—interest; *vyatikramaḥ*—obstruction; *yadadhi*—beyond that; *anyasya*—of others; *preyastvam*—to be more interesting; *ātmanaḥ*—for the self; *sva*—own; *vyatikramāt*—by obstruction.

TRANSLATION

There is no stronger obstruction to one's self-interest than thinking other subject matters to be more pleasing than one's self-realization.

PURPORT

Human life is especially meant for self-realization. Self refers to the Superself and the individual self, the Supreme Personality of Godhead and the living entity. When, however, one becomes more interested in the body and bodily sense gratification, he creates for himself obstructions on the path of self-realization. By the influence of *māyā,* one becomes more interested in sense gratification, which is prohibited in this world for those interested in self-realization. Instead of becoming interested in sense gratification, one should divert his activities to satisfy the senses of the Supreme Soul. Anything performed contrary to this principle is certainly against one's self-interest.

TEXT 33

अर्थेन्द्रियार्थाभिध्यानं सर्वार्थापह्नवो नृणाम् ।
भ्रंशितो ज्ञानविज्ञानाद्येनाविशति मुख्यताम् ॥३३॥

arthendriyārthābhidhyānaṁ
sarvārthāpahnavo nṛṇām
bhraṁśito jñāna-vijñānād
yenāviśati mukhyatām

artha—riches; *indriya-artha*—for the satisfaction of the senses; *abhidhyānam*—constantly thinking of; *sarva-artha*—four kinds of achievements; *apahnavaḥ*—destructive; *nṛṇām*—of human society; *bhraṁśitaḥ*—being devoid of; *jñāna*—knowledge; *vijñānāt*—devotional service; *yena*—by all this; *āviśati*—enters; *mukhyatām*—immovable life.

TRANSLATION

For human society, constantly thinking of how to earn money and apply it for sense gratification brings about the destruction of everyone's interests. When one becomes devoid of knowledge and devotional service, he enters into species of life like those of trees and stones.

PURPORT

Jñāna, or knowledge, means to understand one's constitutional position, and *vijñāna* refers to practical application of that knowledge in life. In the human form of life, one should come to the position of *jñāna* and *vijñāna,* but despite this great opportunity if one does not develop knowledge and practical application of knowledge through the help of a spiritual master and the *śāstras*—in other words, if one misuses this opportunity—then in the next life he is sure to be born in a species of nonmoving living entities. Nonmoving living entities include hills, mountains, trees, plants, etc. This stage of life is called *puṇyatām* or *mukhyatām,* namely, making all activities zero. Philosophers who support stopping all activities are called *śūnyavādī.* By nature's own way, our activities are to be gradually diverted to devotional service. But there are philosophers who, instead of purifying their activities, try to make everything zero, or void of all activities. This lack of activity is represented by the trees and the hills. This is a kind of punishment inflicted by the laws of nature. If we do not properly execute our mission of life in self-realization, nature's punishment will render us inactive by putting us in the form of trees and hills. Therefore activities directed towards sense gratification are condemned herein. One who is constantly thinking of activities to earn money and gratify the senses is following a path which is suicidal. Factually all human society is following this path. Some way or other, people are determined to earn money or get money by begging, borrowing or stealing and applying that for sense gratification. Such a civilization is the greatest obstacle in the path of self-realization.

TEXT 34

न कुर्यात्कर्हिचित्सङ्गं तमस्तीव्रं तितीरिषुः ।
धर्मार्थकाममोक्षाणां यदत्यन्तविघातकम् ॥३४॥

na kuryāt karhicit saṅgaṁ
tamas tīvraṁ titīriṣuḥ
dharmārtha-kāma-mokṣāṇāṁ
yad atyanta-vighātakam

na—do not; *kuryāt*—act; *karhicit*—at any time; *saṅgam*—association; *tamaḥ*—ignorance; *tīvram*—with great speed; *titīriṣuḥ*—persons who desire to cross over nescience; *dharma*—religion; *artha*—economic development; *kāma*—sense gratification; *mokṣāṇām*—of salvation; *yat*—that which; *atyanta*—very much; *vighātakam*—obstruction or stumbling block.

TRANSLATION

Those who strongly desire to cross the ocean of nescience must not associate with the modes of ignorance because hedonistic activities are the greatest obstructions to realization of religious principles, economic development, regulated sense gratification and, at last, liberation.

PURPORT

The four principles of life allow one to live according to religious principles, to earn money according to one's position in society, to allow the senses to enjoy the sense objects according to regulations, and to progress along the path of liberation from this material attachment. As long as the body is there, it is not possible to become completely free from all these material interests. It is not, however, recommended that one act only for sense gratification and earn money for that purpose only, sacrificing all religious principles. At the present moment, human civilization does not care for religious principles. It is, however, greatly interested in economic development without religious principles. For instance, in a slaughterhouse the butchers certainly get money easily, but such business is not based on religious principles. Similarly, there are many night clubs for sense gratification and brothels for sex. Sex, however, is allowed in married life only, and prostitution is prohibited because all our activities are ultimately aimed at liberation, at freedom from the clutches of material existence. It is advised therefore that one not act in a way that will obstruct the regular process of advancement in spiritual life and liberation. The Vedic process of sense gratification is therefore planned in such a way that one can economically develop and enjoy sense gratification and yet ultimately attain liberation. Vedic civilization offers us all knowledge in the *śāstras*, and if we live a regulated life under the direction of *śāstras* and *guru*, all our material desires will be fulfilled; at the same time we will be able to go forward to liberation.

TEXT 35

तत्रापि मोक्ष एवार्थ आत्यन्तिकतयेष्यते ।
त्रैवर्ग्योऽर्थो यतो नित्यं कृतान्तभयसंयुतः ॥३५॥

tatrāpi mokṣa evārtha
ātyantikatayeṣyate
traivargyo 'rtho yato nityaṁ
kṛtānta-bhaya-saṁyutaḥ

tatra—there; *api*—also; *mokṣaḥ*—liberation; *eva*—certainly; *arthe*—for the matter of; *ātyantikatayā*—most important; *iṣyate*—taken in that way; *traivargyaḥ*—the three others, namely, religion, economic development and sense gratification; *arthaḥ*—interest; *yataḥ*—wherefrom; *nityam*—regularly; *kṛtānta*—death; *bhaya*—fear; *saṁyutaḥ*—attached.

TRANSLATION

Out of the four principles—namely, religion, economic development, sense gratification and liberation—liberation has to be taken very seriously. The other three are subject to destruction by the stringent law of nature—death.

PURPORT

Mokṣa, or liberation, has to be taken very seriously, even at the sacrifice of the other three items. As advised by Sūta Gosvāmī in the beginning of *Śrīmad-Bhāgavatam*, religious principles are not based on success in economic development. Because we are very attached to sense gratification, we go to God, to the temple or churches, for some economic reasons. Then again, economic development does not mean sense gratification. Everything should be adjusted in such a way that we attain liberation. Therefore in this verse, liberation, *mokṣa*, is stressed. The other three items are material and therefore subject to destruction. Even if somehow we accumulate a great bank balance in this life and possess many material things, everything will be finished with death. In *Bhagavad-gītā* it is said that death is the Supreme Personality of Godhead, who ultimately takes away everything acquired by the materialistic person. Foolishly we do not care for this. Foolishly we are not afraid of death, nor do we consider that death will take away everything acquired by the process of *dharma, artha* and *kāma*. By *dharma,* or pious activities, we may be elevated to the heavenly planets, but this does not mean freedom from the clutches of birth, death, old age and disease. The purport is that we can sacrifice our interests in *traivargya,* religious principles, economic development and sense gratification, but we cannot sacrifice the cause of liberation. Regarding liberation, it is stated in *Bhagavad-gītā: tyaktvā dehaṁ punar janma naiti* (Bg. 4.9). Liberation means that after giving up this body one does not have to accept another material body. But to the impersonalists liberation means merging into the existence of impersonal Brahman. But factually this is not *mokṣa* because one has to again fall down into this material world from that impersonal position. One should therefore seek the shelter of the Supreme Personality of Godhead and engage in His devotional service. That is real liberation. The conclusion is that we should not stress pious activities, economic development and sense gratification but should concern ourselves with approaching Lord Viṣṇu in His spiritual planets, of which the topmost is Goloka Vṛndāvana where Lord Kṛṣṇa lives. Therefore this Kṛṣṇa consciousness movement is the greatest gift for persons who are actually desiring liberation.

TEXT 36

परेऽवरे च ये भावा गुणव्यतिकरादनु ।
न तेषां विद्यते क्षेममीशविध्वंसिताशिषाम् ॥३६॥

pare 'vare ca ye bhāvā
guṇa-vyatikarād anu
na teṣāṁ vidyate kṣemam
īśa-vidhvaṁsitāśiṣām

pare—in the higher status of life; *avare*—in the lower status of life; *ca*—and; *ye*—all those; *bhāvāḥ*—conceptions; *guṇa*—material qualities; *vyatikarāt*—by interaction; *anu*—following; *na*—never; *teṣām*—of them; *vidyate*—exist; *kṣemam*—correction; *īśa*—the Supreme Lord; *vidhvaṁsita*—destroyed; *āśiṣām*—of the blessings.

TRANSLATION

We accept as blessings different states of higher life, distinguishing them from lower states of life, but we should know that such distinctions exist only in relation to the interchange of the modes of material nature. Actually these states of life have no permanent existence, for all of them will be destroyed by the supreme controller.

PURPORT

In our material existence we accept a higher form of life as a blessing and a lower form as a curse. This distinction of higher and lower only exists as long as the different material qualities (*guṇas*) interact. In other words, by our good activities we are elevated to the higher planetary systems or to a higher standard of life (good education, beautiful body, etc.). These are the results of pious activities. Similarly, by impious activities we remain illiterate, get ugly bodies, a poor standard of living, etc. But all these different states of life are under the laws of material nature through the interaction of the qualities of goodness, passion and ignorance. However, all these qualities will cease to act at the time of the dissolution of the entire cosmic manifestation. The Lord therefore says in *Bhagavad-gītā:*

ābrahma-bhuvanāl lokāḥ punar āvartino 'rjuna
mām upetya tu kaunteya punar janma na vidyate
(Bg. 8.16)

Even though we elevate ourselves to the highest planetary system by the scientific advancement of knowledge or by the religious principles of life—great sacrifices and fruitive activities—at the time of dissolution these higher planetary systems and life on them will be destroyed. The words in this verse *(īśa-vidhvaṁsitāśiṣām)* indicate that all such blessings will be destroyed by the supreme controller. We will not be protected. Our bodies, either in this planet or in another planet, will be destroyed, and again we will have to remain for millions of years in an unconscious state within the body of Mahā-Viṣṇu. And again, when the creation is manifested, we have to take birth in different species of life and begin our activities. Therefore we should not be satisfied simply by a promotion to the higher planetary systems. We should try to get out of the material cosmic manifestation, go to the spiritual world and take shelter of the Supreme Personality of Godhead. That is our highest achievement. We should not be attracted by anything material, higher or lower, but should consider them all on the same level. Our real engagement should be in inquiring about the real purpose of life and rendering devotional service to the Lord. Thus we will be eternally blessed in our spiritual activities, full of knowledge and bliss.

Regulated human civilization promotes *dharma, artha, kāma* and *mokṣa.* In human society there must be religion. Without religion, human society is only animal society. Economic development and sense gratification must be based on religious principles. When religion, economic development and sense gratification are adjusted, liberation from this material birth, death, old age and disease is assured. In the present age of Kali, however, there is no question of religion and liberation. People have taken interest in economic development and sense gratification. Therefore, despite sufficient economic development all over the world, dealings in human society have become almost animalistic. When everything becomes grossly animalistic, dissolution takes place. This dissolution is to be accepted as *īśa-vidhvaṁsitāśiṣām.* The Lord's so-called blessings of economic development and sense gratification will be conclusively dissolved by destruction. At the end of this Kali-yuga, the Lord will appear as the incarnation of Kalki, and His only business will be to kill all human beings on the surface of the globe. After that killing, another golden age will begin. We should therefore know that our material activities are just like childish play. Children may play on the beach and the father will sit and watch this childish play, the construction of buildings with sand, the construction of walls and so many things, but finally the father will ask the children to come home. Then everything is destroyed. Persons who are too much addicted to the childish activities of economic development and sense gratification are sometimes especially favored by the Lord when He destroys their construction of these things.

It is said by the Lord: *yasyāham anugṛhṇāmi hariṣye tad-dhanaṁ śanaiḥ.* The Lord told Yudhiṣṭhira Mahārāja that His special favor is shown to His devotee when He takes away all his material opulences. Generally, therefore, it is experienced that Vaiṣṇavas are not very opulent in the material sense. When a Vaiṣṇava, pure devotee, tries to be materially opulent and at the same time desires to serve the Supreme Lord, his devotional service is checked. The Lord, in order to show him a special favor, destroys his so-called economic development and material opulences. Thus the devotee, being frustrated in his repeated attempts at economic development, ultimately takes solid shelter under the lotus feet of the Lord. This kind of action may also be accepted as *īśa-vidhvaṁsitāśiṣām,* whereby the Lord destroys one's material opulences but enriches him in spiritual understanding. In the course of our preaching work, we sometimes see that materialistic persons come to us and offer their obeisances to take blessings, which means they want more and more material opulences. If such material opulences are checked, such persons are no longer interested in offering obeisances to the devotees. Such materialistic persons are always concerned about their economic development. They offer obeisances to saintly persons or the Supreme Lord and give something in charity for preaching work with a view that they will be rewarded with further economic development.

However, when one is sincere in his devotional service, the Lord obliges the devotee to give up his material development and completely surrender unto Him. Because the Lord does not give blessings of material opulence to His devotee, people are afraid of worshiping Lord Viṣṇu because they see that the Vaiṣṇavas, who are worshipers of Lord Viṣṇu, are poor in superficial material opulences. Such materialistic persons, however, get immense opportunity for economic development by worshiping Lord Śiva, for Lord Śiva is the husband of the goddess Durgā, and Durgā is the proprietor of this universe. By the grace of Lord Śiva, a devotee gets the opportunity to be blessed by the goddess Durgā. Rāvaṇa, for example, was a great worshiper and devotee of Lord Śiva, and in return he got all the blessings of goddess Durgā, so much so that his whole kingdom was constructed of golden buildings. In Brazil, in this present age, huge quantities of gold have been found, and from historical references in the *Purāṇas,* we can guess safely that this was Rāvaṇa's kingdom. This kingdom was, however, destroyed by Lord Rāmacandra.

By studying such incidents, we can understand the full meaning of *īśa-vidhvaṁsitāśiṣām.* The Lord does not bestow material blessings upon the devotees, for they may be entrapped again in this material world by continuous birth, death, old age, and disease. Due to materialistic opulences, persons like Rāvaṇa become puffed up for sense gratification. Rāvaṇa even dared kidnap Sītā, who was both the wife of Lord Rāmacandra and the goddess of fortune, thinking that he would be able to enjoy the pleasure potency of the Lord. But actually, by such action, Rāvaṇa became *vidhvaṁsita* or ruined. At the present moment human civilization is too much attached to economic development and sense gratification and is therefore nearing the path of ruination.

TEXT 37

तत्त्वं नरेन्द्र जगतामथ तस्थूषां च
देहेन्द्रियासुधिषणात्मभिरावृतानाम् ।

यः क्षेत्रवित्तपतया हृदि विश्वगाविः
प्रत्यक् चकास्ति भगवांस्तमवेहि सोऽस्मि ॥ ३७ ॥

tat tvaṁ narendra jagatām atha tasthūṣāṁ ca
dehendriyāsu-dhiṣaṇātmabhir āvṛtānām
yaḥ kṣetravit-tapatayā hṛdi viśvag āviḥ
pratyak cakāsti bhagavāṁs tam avehi so 'smi

tat—therefore; *tvam*—you; *narendra*—O best of the kings; *jagatām*—of the moving; *atha*—therefore; *tasthūṣām*—the immovable; *ca*—also; *deha*—body; *indriya*—senses; *asu*—life air; *dhiṣaṇā*—by consideration; *ātmabhiḥ*—self-realization; *āvṛtānām*—those who are covered in that way; *yaḥ*—one who; *kṣetra-vit*—knower of the field; *tapatayā*—by controlling; *hṛdi*—within the heart; *viśvak*—everywhere; *āviḥ*—manifest; *pratyak*—in every hair follicle; *cakāsti*—shining; *bhagavān*—the Supreme Personality of Godhead; *tam*—unto Him; *avehi*—try to understand; *saḥ asmi*—I am that.

TRANSLATION

Sanat-kumāra advised the King: My dear King Pṛthu, try to understand the Supreme Personality of Godhead, who is living within everyone's heart along with the individual soul, in each and every body, either moving or not moving. They are fully covered by the gross material body and subtle body made of the life air and intelligence.

PURPORT

In this verse it is specifically advised that instead of wasting time in the human form of life endeavoring for economic development and sense gratification, one should try to cultivate spiritual values by understanding the Supreme Personality of Godhead who is existing within the individual soul within everyone's heart. The individual soul and the Supreme Personality of Godhead in His Paramātmā feature are both sitting within this body, which is covered by gross and subtle elements. To understand this is to attain actual spiritual culture. There are two ways of advancing in spiritual culture—by the method of the impersonalist philosophers and by devotional service. The impersonalist comes to the conclusion that he and the Supreme Spirit are one, whereas devotees or personalists realize the Absolute Truth by understanding that the Absolute Truth is the supreme predominator and we living entities are predominated; therefore our duty is to serve Him. The Vedic injunctions say: *tat tvam asi,* "You are the same," and *so 'ham,* "I am the same." The impersonalist conception of these *mantras* is that the Supreme Lord or the Absolute Truth and the living entity are one, but from the devotee's point of view these *mantras* assert that both the Supreme Lord and ourselves are of the same quality. *Tat tvam asi, ayam ātmā brahma.* Both the Supreme Lord and the living entity are spirit. Understanding this is self-realization. The human form of life is meant for understanding the Supreme Lord and oneself by spiritual cultivation of knowledge. One should not waste valuable life simply engaged in economic development and sense gratification.

In this verse the word *kṣetra-vit* is also important. This word is explained in *Bhagavad-gītā: idaṁ śarīraṁ kaunteya kṣetram ity abhidhīyate* (Bg.13.2). This body is called *kṣetra,* or the field of activities, and the proprietors of the body, the individual soul and the Supersoul sitting within the body, are both called *kṣetra-vit.* But there is a difference between the two kinds of *kṣetra-vit.* One *kṣetra-vit,* or knower of the body, namely the Paramātmā or the Supersoul, is directing the individual soul. When we rightly take the direction of the Supersoul, our life becomes successful. He is directing from within and from without. From within He is directing as *caitya-guru,* or the spiritual master sitting within the heart. Indirectly He is also helping the living entity by manifesting Himself as the spiritual master outside. In both ways the Lord is giving directions to the living entity so that he may finish up his material activities and come back home, back to Godhead. The presence of the Supreme Soul and the individual soul within the body can be perceived by anyone by the fact that as long as the individual soul and the Supersoul are both living within the body, the body is always shining and fresh. But as soon as the Supersoul and the individual soul give up possession of the gross body, it immediately decomposes. One who is spiritually advanced can thus understand the real difference between a dead body and a living body. In conclusion, one should not waste his time by so-called economic development and sense gratification but should cultivate spiritual knowledge to understand the Supersoul and the individual soul and their relationship. In this way, by advancement of knowledge, one can achieve liberation and the ultimate goal of life. It is said that if one takes to the path of liberation, even rejecting his so-called duties in the material world, he is not a loser at all. But a person who does not take to the path of liberation yet carefully executes economic development and sense gratification, loses everything. Nārada's statement before Vyāsadeva is appropriate in this connection:

tyaktvā sva-dharmaṁ caraṇāmbujaṁ harer
bhajann apakvo'tha patet tato yadi
yatra kva vābhadram abhūd amuṣya kiṁ
ko vārtha āpto'bhajatāṁ sva-dharmataḥ

(*Bhāg.* 1.5.17)

If a person, out of sentiment or for some other reason, takes to the shelter of the lotus feet of the Lord and in due course of time does not succeed in coming to the ultimate goal of life or falls down due to lack of experience, there is no loss. But for a person who does not take to the devotional service, yet executes his material duties very nicely, there is no gain.

TEXT 38

यस्मिन्निदं सदसदात्मतया विभाति
माया विवेकविधुति स्रजि वाहिबुद्धिः ।
तं नित्यमुक्तपरिशुद्धविशुद्धतत्त्वं
प्रत्यूढकर्मकलिलप्रकृतिं प्रपद्ये ॥३८॥

yasminn idaṁ sad-asad-ātmatayā vibhāti
māyā viveka-vidhuti sraji vāhi-buddhiḥ
taṁ nitya-mukta-pariśuddha-viśuddha-tattvaṁ
pratyūḍha-karma-kalila-prakṛtiṁ prapadye

yasmin—in which; *idam*—this; *sat-asat*—the Supreme Lord and His different energies; *ātmatayā*—being the root of all cause and effect; *vibhāti*—manifests; *māyā*—illusion; *viveka-vidhuti*—liberated by deliberate consideration; *sraji*—on the rope; *vā*—or; *ahi*—serpent; *buddhiḥ*—intelligence; *tam*—unto Him; *nitya*—eternally; *mukta*—liberated; *pariśuddha*—uncontaminated; *viśuddha*—pure; *tattvam*—truth; *pratyūḍha*—transcendental; *karma*—fruitive activities; *kalila*—impurities; *prakṛtim*—situated in spiritual energy; *prapadye*—surrender.

TRANSLATION

The Supreme Personality of Godhead manifests Himself as one with the cause and effect within this body and also as one who has transcended the illusory energy. This clears the misconception of a snake for a rope. Thus one can understand that the Paramātmā is eternally transcendental to the material creation and situated in pure internal energy. Thus He is transcendental to all material contamination. Unto Him only must one surrender.

PURPORT

This verse is specifically stated to defy the Māyāvāda conclusion of oneness without differentiation between the individual soul and the Supersoul. The Māyāvāda conclusion is that the living entity and the Supersoul are one; there is no difference. They proclaim that there is no separate existence outside the impersonal Brahman and that the feeling of separation is *māyā* or an illusion by which one considers a rope to be a snake. The rope and the snake argument is generally offered by the Māyāvādī philosophers. Therefore these words, which represent *vivarta-vāda,* are specifically mentioned herein. Actually Paramātmā, the Supersoul, is the Supreme Personality of Godhead, and He is eternally liberated. In other words, the Supreme Personality of Godhead is living within this body along with the individual soul, and this is confirmed in the *Vedas.* They are likened to two friends sitting on the same tree. Yet Paramātmā is above the illusory energy. The illusory energy is called *bahiraṅgā śakti* or external energy, and the living entity is called *taṭasthā śakti* or marginal potency. As stated in *Bhagavad-gītā,* the material energy, represented as earth, water, air, fire, sky, etc., and the spiritual energy, the living entity, are both energies of the Supreme Lord. Even though the energies and the energetic are identical, the living entity, individual soul, being prone to be influenced by the external energy, considers the Supreme Personality of Godhead as one with himself.

The word *prapadye* is also significant in this verse, for it refers to the conclusion of the *Bhagavad-gītā: sarva-dharmān parityajya mām ekaṁ śaraṇaṁ vraja* (Bg. 18.66). In another place the Lord says: *bahūnāṁ janmanām ante jñānavān māṁ prapadyate* (Bg. 7.19). This *prapadye* or *śaraṇaṁ vraja* refers to the individual's surrender to the Supersoul. The individual soul, when surrendered, can understand that the Supreme Personality of Godhead, although situated within the heart of the individual soul, is superior to the individual soul. The Lord is always transcendental to the material manifestation, even though it appears that the Lord and the material manifestation are one and the same. According to the Vaiṣṇava philosophy, He is one and different simultaneously. The material energy is a manifestation of His external potency, and since the potency is identical with the potent, it appears that the Lord and individual soul are one, but actually the individual soul is under the influence of material energy, and the Lord is always transcendental to it. Unless the Lord is superior to the individual soul, there is no question of *prapadye* or surrender unto Him. This word *prapadye* refers to the process of devotional service. Simply by nondevotional speculation on the rope and the snake, one cannot approach the Absolute Truth. Therefore devotional service is stressed as more important than deliberation or mental speculation to understand the Absolute Truth.

TEXT 39

यत्पादपङ्कजपलाशविलासभक्त्या
कर्माशयं ग्रथितमुद्ग्रथयन्ति सन्तः ।
तद्वन्न रिक्तमतयो यतयोऽपि रुद्ध-
स्रोतोगणास्तमरणं भज वासुदेवम् ॥३९॥

yat-pāda-paṅkaja-palāśa-vilāsa-bhaktyā
karmāśayaṁ grathitam udgrathayanti santaḥ
tadvan na rikta-matayo yatayo 'pi ruddha-
srotogaṇās tam araṇaṁ bhaja vāsudevam

yat—whose; *pāda*—feet; *paṅkaja*—lotus; *palāśa*—petals or toes; *vilāsa*—enjoyment; *bhaktyā*—by devotional service; *karma*—fruitive activities; *āśayam*—desire; *grathitam*—hard knot; *udgrathayanti*—roots out; *santaḥ*—devotees; *tat*—that; *vat*—like; *na*—never; *rikta-matayaḥ*—person devoid of devotional service; *yatayaḥ*—ever increasingly trying; *api*—even though; *ruddha*—stopped; *srotogaṇāḥ*—the waves of sense enjoyment; *tam*—unto Him; *araṇam*—worthy to take shelter; *bhaja*—engage in devotional service; *vāsudevam*—unto Kṛṣṇa, the son of Vasudeva.

TRANSLATION

The devotees, who are always engaged in the service of the toes of the lotus feet of the Lord, can very easily overcome hard-knotted desires for fruitive activities. Because this is very difficult, the nondevotees—the jñānīs and yogīs—although trying to stop the waves of sense gratification, cannot do so. Therefore you are advised to engage in the devotional service of Kṛṣṇa, the son of Vasudeva.

PURPORT

There are three kinds of transcendentalists trying to overcome the influence of the modes of material nature—the *jñānīs, yogīs* and *bhaktas.* All of them attempt to overcome the influence of the senses, which is compared to the incessant waves of a river. The waves of a river flow incessantly, and it is very difficult to stop them. Similarly, the waves of desire for material enjoyment are so strong that they cannot be stopped by any process other than *bhakti-yoga.* The *bhaktas,* by their transcendental devotional service unto the lotus feet of the Lord, become so overwhelmed with transcendental bliss that automatically their desires for material enjoyment stop. The *jñānīs* and *yogīs,* who are not attached to the lotus feet of the Lord, simply struggle against the waves of desire. They are described in this verse as *rikta-matayaḥ,* which means devoid of devotional service. In other words, the *jñānīs* and *yogīs,* although trying to be free from the desires of material activities, actually become more and more entangled in false philosophical speculation or strenuous attempts to stop the activities of the senses. As stated previously:

vāsudeve bhagavati bhakti-yogaḥ prayojitaḥ
janayaty āśu vairāgyaṁ jñānaṁ ca yad ahaitukam
(*Bhāg.* 1.2.7)

Here also the same point is stressed. *Bhaja vāsudevam* indicates that one who is engaged in the loving service of Kṛṣṇa, the son of Vasudeva, can very easily stop the waves of desires. As long as one will continue to try to artificially stop the waves of desires, he will certainly be defeated. That is indicated in this verse. Desires for fruitive activities are strongly rooted, but the trees of desire can be uprooted completely by devotional service because devotional service employs superior desire. One can give up inferior desires when engaged in superior desires. To try to stop desires is impossible. One has to desire the Supreme in order not to be entangled in inferior desires. *Jñānīs* also maintain a desire to become one with the Supreme, but such desire is also considered to be *kāma,* lust. Similarly, the *yogīs* desire mystic power, and that is also *kāma.* And the *bhaktas,* not being desirous of any sort of material enjoyment, become purified. There is no artificial attempt to stop desire. Desire becomes a source of spiritual enjoyment under the protection of the toes of the lotus feet of the Lord. It is stated herein by the Kumāras that the lotus feet of the Lord Kṛṣṇa are the ultimate reservoir of all pleasure. One should therefore take shelter of the lotus feet of the Lord instead of trying unsuccessfully to stop desires for material enjoyment. As long as one is unable to stop the desire for material enjoyment, there is no possibility of becoming liberated from the entanglement of material existence. It may be argued that the waves of a river are incessantly flowing and that they cannot be stopped, but the waves of the river flow towards the sea. When the tide comes over the river, it overwhelms the flowing of the river, and the river itself becomes overflooded, and the waves from the sea become more prominent than the waves from the river. Similarly, a devotee with intelligence plans so many things for the service of the Lord in Kṛṣṇa consciousness that stagnant material desires become overflooded by the desire to serve the Lord. As confirmed by Yāmunācārya, since he has been engaged in the service of the lotus feet of the Lord, there is always a current of newer and newer desires flowing to serve the Lord, so much so that the stagnant desire of sex life becomes very insignificant. Yāmunācārya even says that he spits on such desires. *Bhagavad-gītā* also confirms: *paraṁ dṛṣṭvā nivartate* (*Bg.* 2.59). The conclusion is that by developing a loving desire for the service of the lotus feet of the Lord, we subdue all material desires for sense gratification.

TEXT 40

कृच्छ्रो महानिह भवार्णवमप्लवेशां
षड्वर्गनक्रमसुखेन तितीर्षन्ति ।
तत्त्वं हरेर्भगवतो भजनीयमङ्घ्रिं
कृत्वोडुपं व्यसनमुत्तर दुस्तरार्णम् ॥४०॥

kṛcchro mahān iha bhavārṇavam aplaveśāṁ
ṣaḍ-varga-nakram asukhena titīrṣanti
tat tvaṁ harer bhagavato bhajanīyam aṅghriṁ
kṛtvoḍupaṁ vyasanam uttara dustarārṇam

kṛcchraḥ—troublesome; *mahān*—very great; *iha*—here in this life; *bhava-arṇavam*—ocean of material existence; *aplava-īśām*—of the nondevotees, who have not taken shelter of the lotus feet of the Supreme Personality of Godhead; *ṣaṭ-varga*—six senses; *nakram*—sharks; *asukhena*—with great difficulty; *titīrṣanti*—cross over; *tat*—therefore; *tvam*—you; *hareḥ*—of the Personality of Godhead; *bhagavataḥ*—of the Supreme; *bhajanīyam*—worthy of worship; *aṅghrim*—the lotus feet; *kṛtvā*—making; *uḍupam*—boat; *vyasanam*—all kinds of dangers; *uttara*—cross over; *dustara*—very difficult; *arṇam*—the ocean.

TRANSLATION

The ocean of nescience is very difficult to cross because it is infested with many dangerous sharks. Although those who are nondevotees undergo severe austerities and penances to cross that ocean, we recommend that you simply take shelter of the lotus feet of the Lord, which are like boats for crossing the ocean. Although the ocean is difficult to cross, by taking shelter of His lotus feet you will overcome all dangers.

PURPORT

Material existence is compared herein with the great ocean of nescience. Another name of this ocean is Vaitaraṇī. In that Vaitaraṇī ocean, which is the Causal Ocean, there are innumerable universes floating like footballs. On the other side of the ocean is the spiritual world of Vaikuṇṭha, which is described in *Bhagavad-gītā* as *paras tasmāt tu bhāvo'nyo* (Bg. 8.20). Thus there is an ever-existing spiritual nature which is beyond this material nature. Even though all the material universes are annihilated again and again in the Causal Ocean, the Vaikuṇṭha planets, which are spiritual, exist eternally and are not subject to dissolution. The human form of life gives the living entity a chance to cross the ocean of nescience, which is this material universe, and enter into the spiritual sky. Although there are many methods or boats by which one can cross the ocean, the Kumāras recommend that the King take shelter of the lotus feet of the Lord, just as one would take shelter of a good boat. Nondevotees, who do not take shelter of the Lord's lotus feet, try to cross the ocean of nescience by other methods *(karma, jñāna* and *yoga),* but they have a great deal of trouble. Indeed, sometimes they become so busy simply enjoying their troubles that they never cross the ocean. There is no guarantee that the nondevotees will cross the ocean, but even though they manage to cross, they have to undergo severe austerities and penances. On the other hand, anyone who takes to the process of devotional service and has faith that the lotus feet of the Lord are safe boats to cross that ocean is certain to cross very easily and comfortably.

Pṛthu Mahārāja is therefore advised to take the boat of the lotus feet of the Lord to easily cross over all dangers. Dangerous elements in the universe are compared to sharks in the ocean. Even though one may be a very expert swimmer, he cannot possibly survive if he is attacked by sharks. One often sees that many so called *svāmīs* and *yogīs* sometimes advertise themselves as competent to cross the ocean of nescience and to help others cross, but in actuality they are found to be simply victims of their own senses. Instead of helping their followers to cross the ocean of nescience, such *svāmīs* and *yogīs* fall prey to *māyā*, represented by the fair sex, woman, and are thus devoured by the sharks in that ocean.

TEXT 41

मैत्रेय उवाच
स एवं ब्रह्मपुत्रेण कुमारेणात्ममेधसा ।
दर्शितात्मगतिः सम्यक्प्रशस्योवाच तं नृपः ॥४१॥

maitreya uvāca
sa evaṁ brahma-putreṇa
kumāreṇātma-medhasā

darśitātma-gatiḥ samyak
praśasyovāca taṁ nṛpaḥ

maitreyaḥ uvāca—the great sage Maitreya continued to say; *saḥ*—the King; *evam*—thus; *brahma-putreṇa*—by the son of Lord Brahmā; *kumāreṇa*—by one of the Kumāras; *ātma-medhasā*—well versed in spiritual knowledge; *darśita*—being shown; *ātma-gatiḥ*—spiritual advancement; *samyak*—completely; *praśasya*—worshiping; *uvāca*—said; *tam*—unto him; *nṛpaḥ*—the King.

TRANSLATION

Being thus enlightened to complete spiritual knowledge by the son of Brahmā—one of the Kumāras, who was complete in spiritual knowledge—the King worshiped them in the following words.

PURPORT

In this verse the word *ātma-medhasā* is commented upon by Śrīpāda Viśvanātha Cakravartī Ṭhākura, who says that *ātmani* means unto Lord Kṛṣṇa, *paramātmani.* Lord Kṛṣṇa is Paramātmā (*īśvaraḥ paramaḥ kṛṣṇaḥ, Brahma-saṁhitā,* 5.1); therefore one whose mind is acting fully in Kṛṣṇa consciousness is called *ātma-medhāḥ.* This may be contrasted to the word *gṛha-medhī,* which refers to one whose brain is always engrossed with thoughts of material activities. The *ātma-medhāḥ* is always thinking of Kṛṣṇa's activities in Kṛṣṇa consciousness. Since Sanat-kumāra, who was a son of Lord Brahmā, was fully Kṛṣṇa conscious, he could point out the path of spiritual advancement. The word *ātma-gatiḥ* refers to that path of activities by which one can make progress in understanding Kṛṣṇa.

TEXT 42

राजोवाच
कृतो मेऽनुग्रहः पूर्वं हरिणाऽऽर्तानुकम्पिना ।
तमापादयितुं ब्रह्मन् भगवन् यूयमागताः ॥४२॥

rājovāca
kṛto me 'nugrahaḥ pūrvaṁ
hariṇārtānukampinā
tam āpādayituṁ brahman
bhagavan yūyam āgatāḥ

rājā uvāca—the King said; *kṛtaḥ*—done; *me*—unto me; *anugrahaḥ*—causeless mercy; *pūrvam*—formerly; *hariṇā*—by the Supreme Personality of Godhead, Lord Viṣṇu; *ārta-anukampinā*—compassionate for persons in distress; *tam*—that; *āpādayitum*—to confirm it; *brahman*—O *brāhmaṇa; bhagavan*—O powerful one; *yūyam*—all of you; *āgatāḥ*—have arrived here.

TRANSLATION

The King said: O brāhmaṇa, O powerful one, formerly Lord Viṣṇu showed me His causeless mercy, indicating that you would come to my house, and to confirm that blessing, you have all come.

PURPORT

When Lord Viṣṇu appeared on the great arena of sacrifice at the time when King Pṛthu was performing a great sacrifice (*aśvamedha*), He predicted that the Kumāras would very soon come and advise the King. Therefore Pṛthu Mahārāja remembered the causeless mercy of the Lord and thus welcomed the arrival of the Kumāras, who were fulfilling the Lord's prediction. In other words, when the Lord makes a prediction, He fulfills that prediction through some of His devotees. Similarly, Lord Caitanya Mahāprabhu predicted that both His glorious names and the Hare Kṛṣṇa *mahā-mantra* would be broadcast in all the towns and villages of the world. Śrīla Bhaktivinoda Ṭhākura and Śrīla Bhaktisiddhānta Sarasvatī Prabhupāda desired to fulfill this great prediction, and we are following in their footsteps.

Regarding His devotees, Lord Kṛṣṇa told Arjuna, *kaunteya pratijānīhi na me bhaktaḥ praṇaśyati:* "O son of Kuntī, declare it boldly that My devotee will never perish." (Bg. 9.31) The point is that the Lord Himself could declare such things, but it was His desire to make the declaration through Arjuna and thus doubly assure that His promise would never be broken. The Lord Himself promises, and His confidential devotees execute the promise. The Lord makes so many promises for the benefit of suffering humanity. Although the Lord is very compassionate upon suffering humanity, human beings are generally not very anxious to serve Him. The relationship is something like that between the father and the son; the father is always anxious for the welfare of the son, even though the son forgets or neglects the father. The word *anukampinā* is significant; the Lord is so compassionate upon the living entities that He comes Himself into this world in order to benefit fallen souls.

yadā yadā hi dharmasya
glānir bhavati bhārata

abhyutthānam adharmasya
tadātmānaṁ sṛjāmy aham

"Whenever and wherever there is a decline in religious practice, O descendant of Bharata, and a predominant rise of irreligion—at that time I descend Myself." (Bg. 4.7)

Thus it is out of compassion that the Lord appears in His different forms. Lord Śrī Kṛṣṇa appeared on this planet out of compassion for fallen souls; Lord Buddha appeared out of compassion for the poor animals who were being killed by the demons; Lord Nṛsiṁhadeva appeared out of compassion for Prahlāda Mahārāja. The conclusion is that the Lord is so compassionate upon the fallen souls within this material world that He comes Himself or sends His devotees and His servants to fulfill His desire to have all the fallen souls come back home, back to Godhead. Thus Lord Śrī Kṛṣṇa instructed *Bhagavad-gītā* to Arjuna for the benefit of the entire human society. Intelligent men should therefore seriously consider this Kṛṣṇa consciousness movement and fully utilize the instructions of *Bhagavad-gītā* as preached without adulteration by His pure devotees.

TEXT 43

निष्पादितश्च कार्त्स्न्येन भगवद्भिर्घृणालुभिः ।
साधूच्छिष्टं हि मे सर्वमात्मना सह किं ददे ॥४३॥

niṣpāditaś ca kārtsnyena
bhagavadbhir ghṛṇālubhiḥ
sādhūcchiṣṭaṁ hi me sarvam
ātmanā saha kiṁ dade

niṣpāditaḥ ca—also the order is properly carried out; *kārtsnyena*—in full; *bhagavadbhiḥ*—by the representatives of the Supreme Personality of Godhead; *ghṛṇā-ālubhiḥ*—by the most compassionate; *sādhu-ucchiṣṭam*—remnants of the foodstuffs of saintly persons; *hi*—certainly; *me*—mine; *sarvam*—everything; *ātmanā*—heart and soul; *saha*—with; *kim*—what; *dade*—shall give.

TRANSLATION

My dear brāhmaṇa, you have carried out the order thoroughly because you are also as compassionate as the Lord. It is my duty, therefore, to offer you something, but I only possess remnants of food taken by great saintly persons. What shall I give?

PURPORT

The word *sādhūcchiṣṭam* is significant in this verse. Pṛthu Mahārāja got his kingdom from great saintly persons like Bhṛgu and others just as one gets remnants of food. After the death of King Vena, the whole world was bereft of a popular ruler. There were so many catastrophes occurring that the great saintly persons, headed by Bhṛgu, created the body of King Pṛthu out of the body of his dead father, King Vena. Since King Pṛthu was thus offered the kingdom by the virtue of the mercy of great saintly persons, he did not want to divide his kingdom among saints like the Kumāras. When a father is eating food, he may, out of compassion, offer the remnants of his food to his son. Although such food may be already chewed by the father, it cannot be offered to the father again. Pṛthu Mahārāja's position was something like this; whatever he possessed had already been chewed, and therefore he could not offer it to the Kumāras. Indirectly, however, he offered everything he possessed to the Kumāras, and consequently they utilized his possessions in whatever way they liked. The next verse clarifies this matter.

TEXT 44

प्राणा दाराः सुता ब्रह्मन् गृहाश्च सपरिच्छदाः ।
राज्यं बलं मही कोश इति सर्वं निवेदितम् ॥४४॥

prāṇā dārāḥ sutā brahman
gṛhāś ca sa-paricchadāḥ
rājyaṁ balaṁ mahī kośa
iti sarvaṁ niveditam

prāṇāḥ—life; *dārāḥ*—wife; *sutāḥ*—children; *brahman*—O great *brāhmaṇa;* *gṛhāḥ*—home; *ca*—also; *sa*—with; *paricchadāḥ*—all paraphernalia; *rājyam*—kingdom; *balam*—strength; *mahī*—land; *kośaḥ*—treasury; *iti*—thus; *sarvam*—everything; *niveditam*—offered.

TRANSLATION

The King continued: Therefore, my dear brāhmaṇas, my life, wife, children, home, furniture and household paraphernalia, my kingdom, strength, land, and especially my treasury, are all offered unto you.

PURPORT

In some readings, the word *dārāḥ* is not used, but the word used then is *rāyaḥ,* which means wealth. In India there are still wealthy persons who are recognized by the state as *rāya.* A great devotee of Lord Caitanya Mahāprabhu was called Rāmānanda Rāya because he was governor of Madras and very rich. There are still many holders of the title *rāya*—Rāya Bāhādur, Rāya Chaudhuri and so on. The *dārāḥ,* or wife, is not permitted to be offered to the *brāhmaṇas.* Everything is offered to worthy persons who are able to accept charity, but nowhere is it found that one offers his wife; therefore in this case the reading *rāyaḥ* is more accurate than *dārāḥ.* Also, since Pṛthu Mahārāja offered everything to the Kumāras, the word *kośaḥ* (treasury) need not be separately mentioned. Kings and emperors used to keep a private treasury which was known as *ratna-bhāṇḍa.* The *ratna-bhāṇḍa* was a special treasury room which contained special jewelries, such as bangles, necklaces and so on, which were presented to the king by the citizens. This jewelry was kept separate from the regular treasury house where all the collected revenues were kept. Thus Pṛthu Mahārāja offered his stock of private jewelry to the lotus feet of the Kumāras. It has already been admitted that all the King's property belonged to the *brāhmaṇas* and that Pṛthu Mahārāja was simply using it for the welfare of the state. If it were actually the property of the *brāhmaṇas,* how could it be offered again to them? In this regard, Śrīpāda Śrīdhara Svāmī has explained that this offering is just like the servant's offering of food to his master. The food already belongs to the master, for the master has purchased it, but the servant, by preparing food, makes it acceptable to the master and thus offers it to him. In this way, everything belonging to Pṛthu Mahārāja was offered to the Kumāras.

TEXT 45

सैनापत्यं च राज्यं च दण्डनेतृत्वमेव च ।
सर्वलोकाधिपत्यं च वेदशास्त्रविदर्हति ॥४५॥

sainābpatyaṁ ca rājyaṁ ca
daṇḍa-netṛtvam eva ca
sarva-lokādhipatyaṁ ca
veda-śāstra-vid arhati

sainābpatyam—post of commander-in-chief; *ca*—and; *rājyam*—post of ruler over the kingdom; *ca*—and; *daṇḍa*—ruling; *netṛtvam*—leadership; *eva*—certainly; *ca*—and; *sarva*—all; *loka-adhipatyam*—proprietorship of the planet; *ca*—and; *veda-śāstra-vit*—one who knows the purport of Vedic literature; *arhati*—deserves.

TRANSLATION

Since only a person who is completely educated according to the principles of Vedic knowledge deserves to be commander-in-chief, ruler of the state, the first to chastise and the proprietor of the whole planet, Pṛthu Mahārāja offered everything to the Kumāras.

PURPORT

In this verse it is very clearly stated that a kingdom, state or empire must be governed under the instructions of saintly persons and *brāhmaṇas* like the Kumāras. When monarchy ruled throughout the world, the monarch was actually directed by a board of *brāhmaṇas* and saintly persons. The king, as the administrator of the state, executed his duties as a servant of the *brāhmaṇas.* It was not that the kings or *brāhmaṇas* were dictators, nor did they consider themselves proprietors of the state. The kings were also well versed in Vedic literatures and thus were familiar with the injunction of *Śrī Īśopaniṣad: īśāvāsyam idaṁ sarvam*—everything that exists belongs to the Supreme Personality of Godhead. In *Bhagavad-gītā* Lord Kṛṣṇa also claims that He is the proprietor of all planetary systems *(sarva-loka-maheśvaram).* Since this is the case, no one can claim to be proprietor of the state. The king, president or head of the state should always remember that he is not the proprietor but the servant.

In the present age, the king or president forgets that he is the servant of God and thinks of himself as servant of the people. The present democratic government is proclaimed to be a people's government, a government by the people and for the people, but this type of government is not sanctioned by the *Vedas.* The *Vedas* maintain that a kingdom should be governed for the purpose of satisfying the Supreme Personality of Godhead and should therefore be ruled by a representative of the Lord. The head of a state should not be appointed if he is bereft of all Vedic knowledge. In this verse it is clearly stated *(veda-śāstra-vid arhati)* that all high government posts are especially meant for persons who are well conversant with the teachings of the *Vedas.* In the *Vedas* there are definite instructions defining how a king, commander-in-chief, soldier and citizen should behave. Unfortunately there are many so-called philosophers in the present age who give instruction without citing authority, and many leaders follow their unauthorized instruction. Consequently people are not happy.

The modern theory of dialectic communism, set forth by Karl Marx and followed by communist governments, is not perfect. According to Vedic communism, no one in the state should ever starve. Presently there are many bogus institutions which are collecting funds from the public for the purpose of giving food to starving people, but these funds are invariably misused. According to the Vedic instructions, the government should arrange things in such a way that there will be no question of starvation. In the *Śrīmad-Bhāgavatam* it is stated that a householder must see to it that even a lizard or a snake does not starve. They also must be given food. In actuality, however, there is no question of starvation because everything is the property of the Supreme Lord, and He sees to it that there is ample arrangement for feeding everyone. In the *Vedas* it is said: *eko bahūnāṁ yo vidadhāti kāmān* (*Kaṭha Up.* 2.2.13). The Supreme Lord supplies the necessities of life to everyone, and there is no question of starvation. If anyone starves, it is due to the mismanagement of the so-called ruler, governor or president.

It is clear therefore that a person who is not well versed in the Vedic injunctions *(veda-śāstra-vit)* should not run for election as president, governor, etc. Formerly kings were *rājarṣis,* which meant that although they were serving as kings, they were as good as saintly persons because they would not transgress any of the injunctions of the Vedic scriptures and would rule under the direction of great saintly persons and *brāhmaṇas.* According to this arrangement, modern presidents, governors and chief executive officers are all unworthy of their posts because they are not conversant with Vedic administrative knowledge and they do not take direction from great saintly persons and *brāhmaṇas.* Because of his disobedience to the orders of the *Vedas* and the *brāhmaṇas,* King Vena, Pṛthu Mahārāja's father, was killed by the *brāhmaṇas.* Pṛthu Mahārāja therefore knew very well that it behooved him to rule the planet as the servant of saintly persons and *brāhmaṇas.*

TEXT 46

स्वमेव ब्राह्मणो भुङ्क्ते स्वं वस्ते स्वं ददाति च ।
तस्यैवानुग्रहेणान्नं भुञ्जते क्षत्रियादयः ॥४६॥

svam eva brāhmaṇo bhuṅkte
svaṁ vaste svaṁ dadāti ca
tasyaivānugraheṇānnaṁ
bhuñjate kṣatriyādayaḥ

svam—own; *eva*—certainly; *brāhmaṇaḥ*—the *brāhmaṇas; bhuṅkte*—enjoy; *svam*—own; *vaste*—clothing; *svam*—own; *dadāti*—gives in charity; *ca*—and; *tasya*—his; *eva*—certainly; *anugraheṇa*—by the mercy of; *annam*—food grains; *bhuñjate*—eats; *kṣatriya-ādayaḥ*—other divisions of the society, headed by the *kṣatriyas.*

TRANSLATION

The kṣatriyas, vaiśyas and śūdras eat their food by virtue of the brāhmaṇas' mercy. It is the brāhmaṇas who enjoy their own property, clothe themselves with their own property and give charity with their own property.

PURPORT

The Supreme Personality of Godhead is worshiped with the words *namo brahmaṇya-devāya,* which indicate that the Supreme Lord accepts the *brāhmaṇas* as worshipable gods. The Supreme Lord is worshiped by everyone, yet to teach others He worships the *brāhmaṇas.* Everyone should follow the instructions of the *brāhmaṇas,* for their only business is to spread *śabda-brahma* or Vedic knowledge all over the world. Whenever there is a scarcity of *brāhmaṇas* to spread Vedic knowledge, chaos throughout human society results. Since *brāhmaṇas* and Vaiṣṇavas are direct servants of the Supreme Personality of Godhead, they do not depend on others. In actuality, everything in the world belongs to the *brāhmaṇas,* and out of their humility the *brāhmaṇas* accept charity from the *kṣatriyas,* or kings, and the *vaiśyas,* or merchants. Although everything belongs to the *brāhmaṇas,* the *kṣatriyas* and *vaiśyas* keep everything in custody, and whenever the *brāhmaṇas* need money, they supply it. It is like a savings account with money which the depositor can draw out at his will. The *brāhmaṇas,* being engaged in the service of the Lord, have very little time to handle the finances of the world, and therefore the riches are kept by the *kṣatriyas* or the kings, who are to produce money upon the *brāhmaṇas'* demand. Actually the *brāhmaṇas* or Vaiṣṇavas do not live at others' cost; they live by spending their own money, although it appears that they are collecting this money from others. *Kṣatriyas* and *vaiśyas* have no right to give charity because whatever they possess belongs to the *brāhmaṇas.* Therefore charity should be given by the *kṣatriyas* and *vaiśyas* under the instructions of the *brāhmaṇas*. Unfortunately at the present moment there is a scarcity of *brāhmaṇas,* and since there is no one to advise the *kṣatriyas* and *vaiśyas*, the world is in a chaotic condition.

The second line of this verse indicates that the *kṣatriyas, vaiśyas* and *śūdras* eat only by virtue of the *brāhmaṇa's* mercy; in other words, they should not eat anything which is forbidden by the *brāhmaṇas.* The *brāhmaṇas* and Vaiṣṇavas know what to eat, and by their personal example they do not eat anything which is not offered first to the Supreme Personality of Godhead. They eat only *prasāda,* or remnants of the food offered to the Lord. The *kṣatriyas, vaiśyas* and *śūdras* should eat only Kṛṣṇa-*prasādam,* which is afforded them by the mercy of the *brāhmaṇas.* They cannot open slaughterhouses and eat meat, fish or eggs, or drink liquor, or earn money for this purpose without authorization. In the present age, because society is not guided by brahminical instruction, the whole population is only absorbed in sinful activities. Consequently everyone is deservedly being punished by the laws of nature. This is the situation in this age of Kali.

TEXT 47

यैरीदृशी भगवतो गतिरात्मवाद
एकान्ततो निगमिभिः प्रतिपादिता नः ।
तुष्यन्त्वदभ्रकरुणाः स्वकृतेन नित्यं
को नाम तत्प्रतिकरोति विनोदपात्रम् ॥४७॥

yair īdṛśī bhagavato gatir ātma-vāda
ekāntato nigamibhiḥ pratipāditā naḥ
tuṣyantv adabhra-karuṇāḥ sva-kṛtena nityam
ko nāma tat pratikaroti vinoda-pātram

yaiḥ—by those; *īdṛśī*—such kind of; *bhagavataḥ*—of the Supreme Personality of Godhead; *gatiḥ*—progress; *ātma-vāde*—spiritual consideration; *ekāntataḥ*—in complete understanding; *nigamibhiḥ*—by Vedic evidences; *pratipāditā*—conclusively established; *naḥ*—unto us; *tuṣyantu*—be satisfied; *adabhra*—unlimited; *karuṇāḥ*—mercy; *sva-kṛtena*—by your own activity; *nityam*—eternal; *kaḥ*—who; *nāma*—no one; *tat*—that; *pratikaroti*—counteracts; *vinā*—without; *uda-pātram*—offering of water in cupped hands.

TRANSLATION

Pṛthu Mahārāja continued: How can such persons, who have rendered unlimited service by explaining the path of self-realization in relation to the Supreme Personality of Godhead, and whose explanations are given for our enlightenment with complete conviction and Vedic evidence, be repaid except by folded palms containing water for their satisfaction? Such great personalities can be satisfied only by their own activities, which are distributed amongst human society out of their unlimited mercy.

PURPORT

Great personalities of the material world are very eager to render welfare service to human society, but actually no one can render better service than one who distributes the knowledge of spiritual realization in relation with the Supreme Personality of Godhead. All living entities are within the clutches of the illusory energy. Forgetting their real identity, they hover in material existence, transmigrating from one body to another in search of a peaceful life. Since these living entities have very little knowledge of self-realization, they are not getting any relief, although they are very anxious to attain peace of mind and some substantial happiness. Saintly persons like the Kumāras, Nārada, Prahlāda, Janaka, Śukadeva Gosvāmī, Kapiladeva, as well as the followers of such authorities as the Vaiṣṇava *ācāryas* and their servants, can render a valuable service to humanity by disseminating knowledge of the relationship between the Supreme Personality of Godhead and the living entity. Such knowledge is the perfect benediction for humanity.

Knowledge of Kṛṣṇa is such a great gift that it is impossible to repay the benefactor. Therefore Pṛthu Mahārāja requested the Kumāras to be satisfied by their own benevolent activities, which involved delivering souls from the clutches of *māyā.* The King saw that there was no other way to satisfy them for their exalted activities. The word *vinodapātram* can be divided into two words, *vinā* and *uda-pātram,* or can be understood as one word, *vinoda-pātram,* which means joker. A joker's activities simply arouse laughter, and a person who tries to repay the spiritual master or teacher of the transcendental message of Kṛṣṇa becomes a laughing stock just like a joker because it is not possible to repay such a debt. The best friend and benefactor of all people is one who awakens humanity to its original Kṛṣṇa consciousness.

TEXT 48

मैत्रेय उवाच
त आत्मयोगपतय आदिराजेन पूजिताः ।
शीलं तदीयं शंसन्तः खेऽभवन्मिषतां नृणाम् ॥४८॥

maitreya uvāca
ta ātma-yoga-pataya
ādi-rājena pūjitāḥ
śīlaṁ tadīyaṁ śaṁsantaḥ
khe 'bhavan miṣatāṁ nṛṇām

maitreyaḥ uvāca—the great sage Maitreya continued to speak; *te*—they; *ātma-yoga-patayaḥ*—the masters of self-realization by devotional service;

ādi-rājena—by the original King (Pṛthu); *pūjitāḥ*—being worshiped; *śīlam*—character; *tadīyam*—of the King; *śaṁsantaḥ*—eulogizing; *khe*—in the sky; *abhavan*—appeared; *miṣatām*—while observing; *nṛṇām*—of the people.

TRANSLATION

Being thus worshiped by Mahārāja Pṛthu, the four Kumāras, who were masters of devotional service, became very pleased. Indeed, they appeared in the sky and praised the character of the King, and everyone observed them.

PURPORT

It is said that the demigods never touch the surface of the earth. They walk and travel in space only. Like the great sage Nārada, the Kumāras do not require any machine to travel in space. There are also residents of Siddhaloka who can travel in space without machines. Since they can go from one planet to another, they are called *siddhas;* that is to say they have acquired all mystic and yogic powers. Such great saintly persons who have attained complete perfection in mystic *yoga* are not visible in this age on earth because humanity is not worthy of their presence. The Kumāras, however, praised the characteristics of Mahārāja Pṛthu and his great devotional attitude and humility. The Kumāras were greatly satisfied by King Pṛthu's method of worship. It was by the grace of Mahārāja Pṛthu that the common citizens in his domain could see the Kumāras flying in outer space.

TEXT 49

वैन्यस्तु धुर्यो महतां संस्थित्याध्यात्मशिक्षया ।
आप्तकाममिवात्मानं मेन आत्मन्यवस्थितः ॥४९॥

vainyas tu dhuryo mahatāṁ
saṁsthityādhyātma-śikṣayā
āpta-kāmam ivātmānaṁ
mena ātmany avasthitaḥ

vainyaḥ—the son of Vena Mahārāja (Pṛthu); *tu*—of course; *dhuryaḥ*—the chief; *mahatām*—of great personalities; *saṁsthityā*—being completely fixed; *ādhyātma-śikṣayā*—in the matter of self-realization; *āpta*—achieved; *kāmam*—desires; *iva*—like; *ātmānam*—in self-satisfaction; *mene*—considered; *ātmani*—in the self; *avasthitaḥ*—situated.

TRANSLATION

Amongst great personalities, Mahārāja Pṛthu was the chief by virtue of his fixed position in relation to spiritual enlightenment. He remained satisfied as one who has achieved all success in spiritual understanding.

PURPORT

Remaining fixed in devotional service gives one the utmost in self-satisfaction. Actually self-satisfaction can be achieved only by pure devotees who have no desire other than to serve the Supreme Personality of Godhead. Since the Supreme Personality of Godhead has nothing to desire, He is fully satisfied with Himself. Similarly, a devotee who has no desire other than to serve the Supreme Personality of Godhead is as self-satisfied as the Supreme Lord. Everyone is hankering after peace of mind and self-satisfaction, but these can only be achieved by becoming a pure devotee of the Lord.

King Pṛthu's statements in previous verses regarding his vast knowledge and perfect devotional service are justified here, for he is considered best amongst all *mahātmās*. In *Bhagavad-gītā* Śrī Kṛṣṇa speaks of *mahātmās* in this way:

mahātmānas tu māṁ pārtha
daivīm prakṛtim āśritāḥ
bhajanty ananya-manaso
jñātvā bhūtādim avyayam

"O son of Pṛthā, those who are not deluded, the great souls, are under the protection of the divine nature. They are fully engaged in devotional service because they know Me as the Supreme Personality of Godhead, original and inexhaustible." (Bg. 9.13)

The *mahātmās* are not under the clutches of the illusory energy but are under the protection of the spiritual energy. Because of this, the real *mahātmā* is always engaged in the devotional service of the Lord. Pṛthu Mahārāja exhibited all the symptoms of a *mahātmā;* therefore he is mentioned in this verse as *dhuryo mahatām*, best of the *mahātmās.*

TEXT 50

कर्माणि च यथाकालं यथादेशं यथाबलम् ।
यथोचितं यथावित्तमकरोद्ब्रह्मसात्कृतम् ॥५०॥

karmāṇi ca yathā-kālaṁ
yathā-deśaṁ yathā-balam
yathocitaṁ yathā-vittam
akarod brahma-sāt-kṛtam

karmāṇi—activities; *ca*—also; *yathā-kālam*—befitting time and circumstances; *yathā-deśam*—befitting the place and situation; *yathā-balam*—befitting one's own strength; *yathā-ucitam*—as far as possible; *yathā-vittam*—as far as one can spend money in this connection; *akarot*—performed; *brahma-sāt*—in the Absolute Truth; *kṛtam*—did.

TRANSLATION

Being self-satisfied, Mahārāja Pṛthu executed his duties as perfectly as possible according to the time and his situation, strength and financial position. His only aim in all his activities was to satisfy the Absolute Truth. In this way, he duly acted.

PURPORT

Mahārāja Pṛthu was a responsible monarch, and he had to execute the duties of a *kṣatriya,* a king and a devotee at the same time. Being perfect in the Lord's devotional service, he could execute his prescribed duties with complete perfection as befitted the time and circumstance and his financial strength and personal ability. In this regard, the word *karmāṇi* in this verse is significant. Pṛthu Mahārāja's activities were not ordinary because they were in relationship with the Supreme Personality of Godhead. Śrīla Rūpa Gosvāmī has advised that things which are favorable to devotional service should not be rejected, nor should activity favorable for devotional service be considered ordinary work or fruitive activity. For example, an ordinary worker conducts business in order to earn money for his sense gratification. A devotee may perform the same work in exactly the same way, but his aim is to satisfy the Supreme Lord. Consequently his activities are not ordinary.

Pṛthu Mahārāja's activities were therefore not ordinary but were all spiritual and transcendental, for his aim was to satisfy the Lord. Just as Arjuna, who was a warrior, had to fight to satisfy Kṛṣṇa, Pṛthu Mahārāja performed his royal duties as king for the satisfaction of Kṛṣṇa. Indeed, whatever he did as emperor of the whole world was perfectly befitting a pure devotee. It is therefore said by a Vaiṣṇava poet, *vaiṣṇavera kriyā mūḍha vijñe nā bujhāya:* no one can understand the activities of a pure devotee. A pure devotee's activities may appear like ordinary activities, but behind them there is profound significance—the satisfaction of the Lord. In order to understand the activities of a Vaiṣṇava, one has to become very expert. Mahārāja Pṛthu did not allow himself to function outside the institution of four *varṇas* and four *āśramas,* although as a Vaiṣṇava he was a *paramahaṁsa,* transcendental to all material activities. He remained at his position as a *kṣatriya* to rule the world and at the same time remained transcendental to such activities by satisfying the Supreme Personality of Godhead. Concealing himself as a pure devotee, he externally manifested himself as a very powerful and dutiful king. In other words, none of his activities were carried out for his own sense gratification; everything he did was meant for the satisfaction of the senses of the Lord. This is clearly explained in the next verse.

TEXT 51

फलं ब्रह्मणि संन्यस्य निर्विषङ्गः समाहितः ।
कर्माध्यक्षं च मन्वान आत्मानं प्रकृतेः परम् ॥५१॥

phalaṁ brahmaṇi sannyasya
nirviṣaṅgaḥ samāhitaḥ
karmādhyakṣaṁ ca manvāna
ātmānaṁ prakṛteḥ param

phalam—result; *brahmaṇi*—in the Absolute Truth; *sannyasya*—giving up; *nirviṣaṅgaḥ*—without being contaminated; *samāhitaḥ*—completely dedicated; *karma*—activity; *adhyakṣam*—superintendent; *ca*—and; *manvānaḥ*—always thinking of; *ātmānam*—the Supersoul; *prakṛteḥ*—of material nature; *param*—transcendental.

TRANSLATION

Mahārāja Pṛthu completely dedicated himself to be an eternal servant of the Supreme Personality of Godhead, transcendental to material nature. Consequently all the fruits of his activities were dedicated to the Lord, and he always thought of himself as the servant of the Supreme Personality of Godhead, who is the proprietor of everything.

PURPORT

The life and dedication of Mahārāja Pṛthu in the transcendental loving service of the Supreme Personality of Godhead serve as a good example of *karma-yoga.* The term *karma-yoga* is often used in *Bhagavad-gītā,* and herein Mahārāja Pṛthu is giving a practical example of what *karma-yoga* actually is. The first requirement for the proper execution of *karma-yoga* is given herein. *Phalaṁ brahmaṇi sannyasya* (or *vinyasya*): One must give the fruits of his activities to the Supreme Brahman, Parabrahman, Kṛṣṇa. By doing so, one actually situates himself in the renounced order of life, *sannyāsa.* As stated in *Bhagavad-gītā,* giving up the fruits of one's activities to the Supreme Personality of Godhead is called *sannyāsa.* Although he was living as a householder, Pṛthu Mahārāja was actually in the renounced order of life, *sannyāsa.* This will be clearer in the following verses.

The word *nirviṣaṅgaḥ* (uncontaminated) is very significant because Mahārāja Pṛthu was not attached to the results of his activities. In this material world a person is always thinking of the proprietorship of everything he accumulates or works for. When the fruits of one's activities are rendered to the service of the Lord, one is actually practicing *karma-yoga.* Anyone can practice *karma-yoga,* but it is especially easy for the householder who can install the Deity of the Lord in the home and worship Him according to the methods of *bhakti-yoga.* This method includes nine items: hearing, chanting, remembering, serving, worshiping the Deity, praying, carrying out orders, serving Kṛṣṇa as friend and sacrificing everything for Him. These methods of *karma-yoga* and *bhakti-yoga* are being broadcast all over the world by the International Society for Krishna Consciousness. Anyone can learn these methods simply by following the examples of the members of the Society.

In one's home or a temple, the Deity is considered the proprietor of everything, and everyone is considered the Deity's eternal servant. The Lord is transcendental, for He is not part of this material creation. The words *prakṛteḥ param* are used in this verse because everything within this material world is created by the external material energy of the Lord, but the Lord Himself is not a creation of this material energy. The Lord is the supreme superintendent of all material creations, as confirmed in *Bhagavad-gītā:*

mayādhyakṣeṇa prakṛtiḥ
sūyate sa-carācaram
hetunānena kaunteya
jagad viparivartate

"This material nature is working under My direction, O son of Kuntī, producing all the moving and unmoving beings, and by its rule this manifestation is created and annihilated again and again." (Bg. 9.10)

All material changes and material progress taking place by the wonderful interaction of matter are under the superintendence of the Supreme Personality of Godhead, Kṛṣṇa. Events in the material world are not taking place blindly. If one always remains as a servant of Kṛṣṇa and engages everything in His service, he is accepted as *jīvan-mukta,* a liberated soul, even during his lifetime within the material world. Generally liberation takes place after one gives up this body, but one who lives according to the example of Pṛthu Mahārāja is liberated even in this lifetime. In Kṛṣṇa consciousness the results of one's activities depend on the will of the Supreme Person. Indeed, in all cases the result is not dependent on one's own personal dexterity but is completely dependent on the will of the Supreme. This is the real significance of *phalaṁ brahmaṇi sannyasya.* A soul dedicated to the service of the Lord should never think of himself as the personal proprietor or the superintendent. A dedicated devotee should prosecute his work according to the rules and regulations described in devotional service. The results of his activities are completely dependent on the supreme will of the Lord.

TEXT 52

गृहेषु वर्तमानोऽपि स साम्राज्यश्रियान्वितः ।
नासज्जतेन्द्रियार्थेषु निरहंमतिरर्कवत् ॥५२॥

gṛheṣu vartamāno 'pi
sa sāmrājya-śriyānvitaḥ
nāsajjatendriyārtheṣu
nirahaṁ-matir arka-vat

gṛheṣu—at home; *vartamānaḥ*—being present; *api*—although; *saḥ*—the King, Pṛthu; *sāmrājya*—the entire empire; *śriyā*—opulence; *anvitaḥ*—being absorbed in; *na*—never; *asajjata*— became attracted; *indriya-artheṣu*—for sense gratification; *nir*—nor; *aham*—I am; *matiḥ*—consideration; *arka*—the sun; *vat*—like.

TRANSLATION

Mahārāja Pṛthu, who was very opulent due to the prosperity of his entire empire, remained at home as a householder. Since he was never inclined to utilize his opulences for the gratification of his senses, he remained unattached, exactly like the sun, which is unaffected in all circumstances.

PURPORT

The word *gṛheṣu* is significant in this verse. Out of the four *āśramas*—the *brahmacarya, gṛhastha, vānaprastha* and *sannyāsa*—only a *gṛhastha* or householder is allowed to associate with women; therefore the *gṛhastha-āśrama* is a kind of license for sense gratification given to the devotee. Pṛthu Mahārāja was special in that although he was given license to remain a householder, and although he possessed immense opulences in his kingdom, he never engaged in sense gratification. This was a special sign that indicated him to be a pure devotee of the Lord. A pure devotee is never attracted by sense gratification, and consequently he is liberated. In material life a person engages in sense gratification for his own personal satisfaction, but in the devotional or liberated life one aims to satisfy the senses of the Lord.

In this verse Mahārāja Pṛthu is likened to the sun *(arka-vat)*. Sometimes the sun shines on stool, urine and so many other polluted things, but since the sun is all-powerful, it is never affected by the polluted things with which it associates. On the contrary, the sunshine sterilizes and purifies polluted and dirty places. Similarly, a devotee may engage in so many material activities, but because he has no desire for sense gratification, they never affect him. On the contrary, he dovetails all material activities for the service of the Lord. Since a pure devotee knows how to utilize everything for the Lord's service, he is never affected by material activities. Instead, by his transcendental plans he purifies such activities. This is described in *Bhakti-rasāmṛta-sindhu. Sarvopādhi-vinirmuktaṁ tat-paratvena nirmalam:* his aim is to become completely purified in the service of the Lord without being affected by material designations.

TEXT 53

एवमध्यात्मयोगेन कर्माण्यनुसमाचरन् ।
पुत्रानुत्पादयामास पञ्चार्चिष्यात्मसम्मतान् ॥५३॥

evam adhyātma-yogena
karmāṇy anusamācaran
putrān utpādayāmāsa
pañcārciṣy ātma-sammatān

evam—thus; *adhyātma-yogena*—by the means of *bhakti-yoga; karmāṇi*—activities; *anu*—always; *samācaran*—executing; *putrān*—sons; *utpādayāmāsa*—

begotten; *pañca*—five in number; *arciṣi*—in his wife, Arci; *ātma*—own; *sammatān*—according to his desire.

TRANSLATION

Being situated in the liberated position of devotional service, Pṛthu Mahārāja not only performed all fruitive activities but also begot five sons by his wife Arci. Indeed, all his sons were begotten according to his own desire.

PURPORT

As a householder, Pṛthu Mahārāja had five sons by his wife Arci, and all these sons were begotten as he desired them. They were not born whimsically or by accident. How one can beget children according to one's own desire is practically unknown in the present age (Kali-yuga). In this regard the secret of success depends on the parents' acceptance of the various purificatory methods known as *saṁskāras.* The first *saṁskāra,* the *garbhādhāna-saṁskāra* or child-begetting *saṁskāra,* is compulsory, especially for the higher castes, the *brāhmaṇas* and the *kṣatriyas.* As stated in *Bhagavad-gītā,* sex life which is not against religious principles is Kṛṣṇa Himself, and according to religious principles when one wants to beget a child he must perform the *garbhādhāna-saṁskāra* before having sex. The mental state of the father and mother before sex will certainly affect the mentality of the child to be begotten. A child who is begotten out of lust may not turn out as the parents desire. As stated in the *śāstras, yathā yonir yathā bījam. Yathā yonih* indicates the mother, and *yathā bījam* indicates the father. If the mental state of the parents is prepared before they have sex, the child which they will beget will certainly reflect their mental condition. It is therefore understood by the words *ātma-sammatān* that both Pṛthu Mahārāja and Arci underwent the *garbhādhāna* purificatory process before begetting children, and thus they begot all their sons according to their desires and purified mental states. Pṛthu Mahārāja did not beget his children out of lust, nor was he attracted to his wife for sense gratificatory purposes. He begot the children as a *gṛhastha* for the future administration of his government all over the world.

TEXT 54

विजिताश्वं धूम्रकेशं हर्यक्षं द्रविणं वृकम् ।
सर्वेषां लोकपालानां दधारैकः पृथुर्गुणान् ॥५४॥

vijitāśvaṁ dhūmrakeśaṁ
haryakṣaṁ draviṇaṁ vṛkam
sarveṣāṁ loka-pālānāṁ
dadhāraikaḥ pṛthur guṇān

vijitāśvam—of the name Vijitāśva; *dhūmrakeśam*—of the name Dhūmrakeśa; *haryakṣam*—of the name Haryakṣa; *draviṇam*—of the name Draviṇa; *vṛkam*—of the name Vṛka; *sarveṣām*—of all; *loka-pālānām*—the governing heads of all planets; *dadhāra*—accepted; *ekaḥ*—one; *pṛthuḥ*—King Pṛthu Mahārāja; *guṇān*—all qualities.

TRANSLATION

After begetting five sons named Vijitāśva, Dhūmrakeśa, Haryakṣa, Draviṇa and Vṛka, Pṛthu Mahārāja continued to rule the planet. He accepted all the qualities of the deities who governed all other planets.

PURPORT

In each and every planet there is a predominating deity. It is understood from *Bhagavad-gītā* that in the sun there is a predominating deity named Vivasvān. Similarly, there is a predominating deity of the moon and of the various planets. Actually the predominating deities in all the other planets are descendants from the predominating deities of the sun and moon. On this planet earth there are two *kṣatriya* dynasties, and one comes from the predominating deity of the sun and the other from the predominating deity of the moon, known as *Sūrya-vaṁśa* and *Candra-vaṁśa* respectively. When monarchy existed on this planet, the chief member was one of the members of the *Sūrya* dynasty or *Sūrya-vaṁśa,* and the subordinate kings belonged to the *Candra-vaṁśa.* However, Mahārāja Pṛthu was so powerful that he could exhibit all the qualities of the predominating deities in other planets.

TEXT 55

गोपीथाय जगत्सृष्टेः काले स्वे स्वेऽच्युतात्मकः ।
मनोवाग्वृत्तिभिः सौम्यैर्गुणैः संरञ्जयन् प्रजाः ॥५५॥

gopīthāya jagat-sṛṣṭeḥ
kāle sve sve 'cyutātmakaḥ
mano-vāg-vṛttibhiḥ saumyair
guṇaiḥ saṁrañjayan prajāḥ

gopīthāya—for the protection of; *jagat-sṛṣṭeḥ*—of the supreme creator; *kāle*—in due course of time; *sve sve*—own; *acyuta-ātmakaḥ*—being Kṛṣṇa conscious; *manaḥ*—mind; *vāk*—words; *vṛttibhiḥ*—by occupation; *saumyaiḥ*—very gentle; *guṇaiḥ*—by qualification; *saṁrañjayan*—pleasing; *prajāḥ*—the citizens.

TRANSLATION

Since Mahārāja Pṛthu was a perfect devotee of the Supreme Personality of Godhead, he wanted to protect the Lord's creation by pleasing the various citizens according to their various desires. Therefore Pṛthu Mahārāja used to please them in all respects by his words, mentality, works and gentle behavior.

PURPORT

As will be explained in the next verse, Pṛthu Mahārāja used to please all kinds of citizens by his extraordinary capacity to understand the mentality of others. Indeed, his dealings were so perfect that every one of the citizens was very much satisfied and lived in complete peace. The word *acyutātmakaḥ* is significant in this verse, for Mahārāja Pṛthu used to rule this planet as the representative of the Supreme Personality of Godhead. He knew he was the representative of the Lord and that the Lord's creation must be protected intelligently. Atheists cannot understand the purpose behind the creation. Although this material world is condemned when it is compared to the spiritual world, there is still some purpose behind it. Modern scientists and philosophers cannot understand that purpose, nor do they believe in the existence of a creator. They try to establish everything by their so-called scientific research, but they do not center anything around the supreme creator. A devotee, however, can understand the purpose of creation, which is to give facilities to the individual living entities who want to lord it over material nature. The ruler of this planet should therefore know that all the inhabitants, especially human beings, have come to this material world for sense enjoyment. It is therefore the duty of the ruler to satisfy them in their sense enjoyment as well as to elevate them to Kṛṣṇa consciousness so that they all can ultimately return home, back to Godhead.

With this idea in mind, the king or government head should rule the world. In this way, everyone will be satisfied. How can this be accomplished? There are many examples like Pṛthu Mahārāja, and the history of his regency on this planet is elaborately described in *Śrīmad-Bhāgavatam*.

Even in this fallen age if the rulers, governors and presidents take advantage of Pṛthu Mahārāja's example, there will certainly be a reign of peace and prosperity throughout the world.

TEXT 56

राजेत्यधान्नामधेयं सोमराज इवापरः ।
सूर्यवद्विसृजन् गृह्णन् प्रतपंश्च भुवो वसु ॥५६॥

rājety adhān nāma-dheyaṁ
soma-rāja ivāparaḥ
sūrya-vad visṛjan gṛhṇan
pratapaṁś ca bhuvo vasu

rājā—the King; *iti*—thus; *adhāt*—took up; *nāma-dheyam*—of the name; *soma-rājaḥ*—the king of the moon planet; *iva*—like; *aparaḥ*—on the other hand; *sūrya-vat*—like the sun-god; *visṛjan*—distributing; *gṛhṇan*—exacting; *pratapan*—by strong ruling; *ca*—also; *bhuvaḥ*—of the world; *vasu*—revenue.

TRANSLATION

Mahārāja Pṛthu became as celebrated a king as Somarāja, the king of the moon. He was also powerful and exacting, just like the sun-god who distributes heat and light and at the same time exacts all the planetary waters.

PURPORT

In this verse Mahārāja Pṛthu is compared to the kings of the moon and sun. The king of the moon and the king of the sun serve as examples of how the Lord desires the universe to be ruled. The sun distributes heat and light and at the same time exacts water from all planets. The moon is very pleasing at night, and when one becomes fatigued after a day's labor in the sun, he can enjoy the moonshine. Like the sun-god, Pṛthu Mahārāja distributed his heat and light to give protection to his kingdom, for without heat and light no one can exist. Similarly, Pṛthu Mahārāja exacted taxes and gave such strong orders to the citizens and government that no one had the power to disobey him. On the other hand, he pleased everyone just like the moonshine. Both the sun and the moon have particular influences by which they maintain order in the universe, and modern scientists and philosophers should become familiar with the Supreme Lord's perfect plan for universal maintenance.

TEXT 57

दुर्धर्षस्तेजसेवाग्निर्महेन्द्र इव दुर्जयः ।
तितिक्षया धरित्रीव द्यौरिवाभीष्टदो नृणाम् ॥५७॥

durdharṣas tejasevāgnir
mahendra iva durjayaḥ
titikṣayā dharitrīva
dyaur ivābhīṣṭa-do nṛṇām

durdharṣaḥ—unconquerable; *tejasā*—by prowess; *iva*—like; *agniḥ*—fire; *mahendraḥ*—the king of heaven; *iva*—likened; *durjayaḥ*—insuperable; *titikṣayā*—by tolerance; *dharitrī*—the earth; *iva*—like; *dyauḥ*—the heavenly planets; *iva*—like; *abhīṣṭa-daḥ*—fulfilling desires; *nṛṇām*—of human society.

TRANSLATION

Mahārāja Pṛthu was so strong and powerful that no one could disobey his orders any more than one could conquer fire itself. He was so strong that he was compared to Indra, the king of heaven, whose power is insuperable. On the other hand, Mahārāja Pṛthu was also as tolerant as the earth, and in fulfilling various desires of human society, he was like heaven itself.

PURPORT

It is the duty of a king to give protection to the citizens and to fulfill their desires. At the same time, the citizens must obey the laws of the state. Mahārāja Pṛthu maintained all the standards of good government, and he was so invincible that no one could disobey his orders any more than a person could stop heat and light emanating from a fire. He was so strong and powerful that he was compared to the king of heaven, Indra. In this age modern scientists have been experimenting with nuclear weapons, and in a former age they used to release *brahmāstras,* but all these *brahmāstras* and nuclear weapons are insignificant compared to the thunderbolt of the king of heaven. When Indra releases a thunderbolt, even the biggest hills and mountains crack. On the other hand, Mahārāja Pṛthu was as tolerant as the earth itself, and he fulfilled all the desires of his citizens, just as torrents of rain from the sky fulfill the need of the earth for water. Without rainfall, it is not possible to survive on this planet. As stated in *Bhagavad-gītā* (*parjanyād anna-sambhavaḥ,* Bg. 3.14), food grains are produced only because rain falls from the sky, and without grains, no one on the earth can survive. Consequently an unlimited distribution of mercy is compared with the water falling from the clouds. Mahārāja Pṛthu distributed his mercy incessantly, much like rainfall. In other words, Mahārāja Pṛthu was softer than a rose flower and harder than a thunderbolt. In this way he ruled over his kingdom.

TEXT 58

वर्षति स्म यथाकामं पर्जन्य इव तर्पयन् ।
समुद्र इव दुर्बोधः सत्त्वेनाचलराडिव ॥५८॥

varṣati sma yathā-kāmaṁ
parjanya iva tarpayan
samudra iva durbodhaḥ
sattvenācala-rāḍ iva

varṣati—pouring; *sma*—used to; *yathā-kāmam*—as much as one can desire; *parjanyaḥ*—water; *iva*—like; *tarpayan*—pleasing; *samudraḥ*—the sea; *iva*—likened; *durbodhaḥ*—not understandable; *sattvena*—by existential position; *acala*—the hills; *rāṭ iva*—like the king of.

TRANSLATION

Just as rainfall satisfies everyone's desires, Mahārāja Pṛthu used to satisfy everyone. He was like the sea in that no one could understand his depths, and he was like Meru, the king of hills, in the fixity of his purpose.

PURPORT

Mahārāja Pṛthu used to distribute his mercy to suffering humanity, and it was like rainfall after excessive heat. The ocean is wide and expansive, and it is very difficult to measure its length and breadth; similarly, Pṛthu Mahārāja was so deep and grave that no one could fathom his purposes. The hill known as Meru is fixed in the universe as a universal pivot, and no one can move it an inch from its position; similarly, no one could ever dissuade Mahārāja Pṛthu when he was determined.

TEXT 59

धर्मराडिव शिक्षायामाश्चर्ये हिमवानिव ।
कुवेर इव कोशाढ्यो गुप्तार्थो वरुणो यथा ॥५९॥

dharma-rāḍ iva śikṣāyām
āścarye himavān iva

kuvera iva kośāḍhyo
guptārtho varuṇo yathā

dharma-rāṭ iva—like King Yamarāja (the superintendent of death); *śikṣāyām*—in education; *āścarye*—in opulence; *himavān iva*—like the Himalayan Mountains; *kuveraḥ*—the treasurer of the heavenly planets; *iva*—like; *kośa-āḍhyaḥ*—in the matter of possessing wealth; *gupta-arthaḥ*—secrecy; *varuṇaḥ*—the demigod named Varuṇa; *yathā*—like.

TRANSLATION

Mahārāja Pṛthu's intelligence and education were exactly like that of Yamarāja, the superintendent of death. His opulence was comparable to the Himalayan Mountains, where all valuable jewels and metals are stocked. He possessed great riches like Kuvera, the treasurer of the heavenly planets, and no one could reveal his secrets, for they were like the demigod Varuṇa's.

PURPORT

Yamarāja or Dharmarāja, as the superintendent of death, has to judge the criminal living entities who have committed sinful activities throughout their lives. Consequently Yamarāja is expected to be most expert in judicial matters. Pṛthu Mahārāja was also highly learned and exceedingly exact in delivering his judgment upon the citizens. No one could excel him in opulence any more than estimate the stock of minerals and jewels in the Himalayan Mountains; therefore he is compared to Kuvera, the treasurer of the heavenly planets. Nor could anyone discover the secrets of his life any more than learn the secrets of Varuṇa, the demigod presiding over the water, the night, and the western sky. Varuṇa is omniscient, and since he punishes sins, he is prayed to for forgiveness. He is also the sender of disease and is often associated with Mitra and Indra.

TEXT 60

मातरिश्वेव सर्वात्मा बलेन महसौजसा ।
अविषह्यतया देवो भगवान् भूतराडिव ॥६०॥

mātariśveva sarvātmā
balena mahasaujasā
aviṣahyatayā devo
bhagavān bhūta-rāḍ iva

mātariśvā—the air; *iva*—like; *sarva-ātmā*—all-pervading; *balena*—by bodily strength; *mahasā ojasā*—by courage and power; *aviṣahyatayā*—by intolerance; *devaḥ*—the demigod; *bhagavān*—the most powerful; *bhūta-rāṭ iva*—like Rudra or Sadāśiva.

TRANSLATION

In his bodily strength and in the strength of his senses, Mahārāja Pṛthu was as strong as the wind, which can go anywhere and everywhere. As far as his intolerance was concerned, he was just like the all-powerful Rudra expansion of Lord Śiva, or Sadāśiva.

TEXT 61

कन्दर्प इव सौन्दर्ये मनस्वी मृगराडिव ।
वात्सल्ये मनुवन्नृणां प्रभुत्वे भगवानजः ॥६१॥

kandarpa iva saundarye
manasvī mṛga-rāḍ iva
vātsalye manuvan nṛṇāṁ
prabhutve bhagavān ajaḥ

kandarpaḥ—Cupid; *iva*—like; *saundarye*—in beauty; *manasvī*—in thoughtfulness; *mṛga-rāṭ iva*—like the king of the animals, the lion; *vātsalye*—in affection; *manu-vat*—like Svāyambhuva Manu; *nṛṇām*—of human society; *prabhutve*—in the matter of controlling; *bhagavān*—the lord; *ajaḥ*—Brahmā.

TRANSLATION

In his bodily beauty he was just like Cupid, and in his thoughtfulness he was like a lion. In his affection he was just like Svāyambhuva Manu, and in his ability to control he was like Lord Brahmā.

TEXT 62

बृहस्पतिर्ब्रह्मवादे आत्मवत्त्वे स्वयं हरिः
भक्त्या गोगुरुविप्रेषु विष्वक्सेनानुवर्तिषु ।
ह्रिया प्रश्रयशीलाभ्यामात्मतुल्यः परोद्यमे ॥६२॥

bṛhaspatir brahma-vāde
ātmavattve svayaṁ hariḥ
bhaktyā go-guru-vipreṣu
viṣvaksenānuvartiṣu
hriyā praśraya-śīlābhyām
ātma-tulyaḥ parodyame

bṛhaspatiḥ—the priest of the heavenly planets; *brahma-vāde*—in the matter of spiritual understanding; *ātmavattve*—in the matter of self-control; *svayam*—personally; *hariḥ*—the Supreme Personality of Godhead; *bhaktyā*—in devotion; *go*—cow; *guru*—spiritual master; *vipreṣu*—unto the *brāhmaṇas; viṣvaksena*—the Personality of Godhead; *anuvartiṣu*—followers; *hriyā*—by shyness; *praśraya-śīlābhyām*—by most gentle behavior; *ātma-tulyaḥ*—exactly like his personal interest; *para-udyame*—in the matter of philanthropic work.

TRANSLATION

In his personal behavior, Pṛthu Mahārāja exhibited all good qualities, and in spiritual knowledge he was exactly like Bṛhaspati. In self-control he was like the Supreme Personality of Godhead Himself. As far as his devotional service was concerned, he was a great follower of devotees who were attached to cow protection and the rendering of all service to the spiritual master and the brāhmaṇas. He was perfect in his shyness and in his gentle behavior, and when he engaged in some philanthropic activity, he worked as if he were working for his own personal self.

PURPORT

When Lord Caitanya talked to Sārvabhauma Bhaṭṭācārya, the Lord gave him the honor of becoming the incarnation of Bṛhaspati. Bṛhaspati is the chief priest of the heavenly kingdom, and he is a follower of the philosophy known as Brahmavāda or Māyāvāda. Bṛhaspati is also a great logician. It appears from this statement that Mahārāja Pṛthu, although a great devotee constantly engaged in the loving service of the Lord, could defeat all kinds of impersonalists and Māyāvādīs by his profound knowledge of Vedic scriptures. We should learn from Mahārāja Pṛthu that a Vaiṣṇava or devotee must not only be fixed in the service of the Lord, but, if required, must be prepared to argue with the impersonalist Māyāvādīs with all logic and philosophy and defeat their contention that the Absolute Truth is impersonal.

The Supreme Personality of Godhead is the ideal self-controller or *brahmacārī*. When Kṛṣṇa was elected to be president of the Rājasūya *yajña* performed by Mahārāja Yudhiṣṭhira, Grandfather Bhīṣmadeva praised Lord Kṛṣṇa as the greatest *brahmacārī*. Because Grandfather Bhīṣmadeva was a *brahmacārī*, he was quite fit to distinguish a *brahmacārī* from a *vyabhicārī*. Although Pṛthu Mahārāja was a householder and father of five children, he was still considered to be most controlled. One who begets Kṛṣṇa conscious children for the benefit of humanity is actually a *brahma-*

cārī. One who simply begets children like cats and dogs is not a proper father. The word *brahmacārī* also refers to one who acts on the platform of Brahman or devotional service. In the impersonal Brahman conception, there is no activity, yet when one performs activities in connection with the Supreme Personality of Godhead, he is to be known as *brahmacārī.* Thus Pṛthu Mahārāja was an ideal *brahmacārī* and *gṛhastha* simultaneously. *Viṣvaksenānuvartiṣu* refers to those devotees who are constantly engaged in the service of the Lord. Other devotees must follow in their footsteps. Śrīla Narottama dāsa Ṭhākura said, *ei chaya gosāñi yāṅra, mui tāṅra dāsa.* He is prepared to become anyone's disciple who follows in the footsteps of the six Gosvāmīs.

Also, like all Vaiṣṇavas, Mahārāja Pṛthu was devoted to cow protection, spiritual masters and qualified *brāhmaṇas.* Pṛthu Mahārāja was also very humble, meek and gentle, and whenever he performed any philanthropic work or welfare activity for the general public, he would labor exactly as if he were tending to his own personal necessities. In other words, his philanthropic activities were not for the sake of show but were performed out of personal feeling and commitment. All philanthropic activities should be thus performed.

TEXT 63

कीर्त्योर्ध्वगीतया पुम्भिस्त्रैलोक्ये तत्र तत्र ह ।
प्रविष्टः कर्णरन्ध्रेषु स्त्रीणां रामः सतामिव ॥६३॥

kīrtyordhva-gītayā pumbhis
trailokye tatra tatra ha
praviṣṭaḥ karṇa-randhreṣu
strīṇāṁ rāmaḥ satām iva

kīrtyā—by reputation; *ūrdhva-gītayā*—by loud declaration; *pumbhiḥ*—by the general public; *trailokye*—all over the universe; *tatra tatra*—here and there; *ha*—certainly; *praviṣṭaḥ*—entering; *karṇa-randhreṣu*—in the aural holes; *strīṇām*—of the women; *rāmaḥ*—Lord Rāmacandra; *satām*—of the devotees; *iva*—like.

TRANSLATION

Throughout the whole universe—in the higher, lower and middle planetary systems—Pṛthu Mahārāja's reputation was loudly declared, and all ladies and devotees heard his glories, which were as sweet as the glories of Lord Rāmacandra.

PURPORT

In this verse the words *strīṇām* and *rāmaḥ* are significant. It is the practice amongst ladies to hear and enjoy the praises of certain heroes. From this verse it appears that Pṛthu Mahārāja's reputation was so great that ladies all over the universe would hear of it with great pleasure. At the same time, his glories were heard all over the universe by the devotees, and they were as pleasing as Lord Rāmacandra's glories. Lord Rāmacandra's kingdom is still existing, and recently there was a political party in India named the Rāmarājya Party, which wanted to establish a kingdom resembling the kingdom of Rāma. Unfortunately, modern politicians want the kingdom of Rāma without Rāma Himself. Although they have banished the idea of God consciousness, they still expect to establish the kingdom of Rāma. Such a proposal is rejected by devotees. Pṛthu Mahārāja's reputation was heard by saintly persons because he exactly represented Lord Rāmacandra, the ideal king.

Thus end the Bhaktivedanta purports of the Fourth Canto, Twenty-second Chapter, of the Śrīmad-Bhāgavatam, *entitled "King Pṛthu Mahārāja's Meeting with the Four Kumāras."*

CHAPTER TWENTY-THREE

Mahārāja Pṛthu's Going Back Home

TEXTS 1-3

मैत्रेय उवाच
दृष्ट्वाऽऽत्मानं प्रवयसमेकदा वैन्य आत्मवान् ।
आत्मना वर्धिताशेषस्वानुसर्गः प्रजापतिः ॥ १ ॥
जगतस्तस्थुषश्चापि वृत्तिदो धर्मभृत्सताम् ।
निष्पादितेश्वरादेशो यदर्थमिह जज्ञिवान् ॥ २ ॥
आत्मजेष्वात्मजां न्यस्य विरहाद्रुदतीमिव ।
प्रजासु विमनःस्वेकः सदारोऽगात्तपोवनम् ॥ ३ ॥

maitreya uvāca
dṛṣṭvātmānaṁ pravayasam
ekadā vainya ātmavān
ātmanā vardhitāśeṣa-
svānusargaḥ prajāpatiḥ

jagatas tasthuṣaś cāpi
vṛtti-do dharma-bhṛt satām
niṣpāditeśvarādeśo
yad-artham iha jajñivān

ātma-jeṣv ātma-jāṁ nyasya
virahād rudatīm iva
prajāsu vimanaḥsv ekaḥ
sa-dāro 'gāt tapo-vanam

maitreyaḥ uvāca—the sage Maitreya continued to speak; *dṛṣṭvā*—after seeing; *ātmānam*—of the body; *pravayasam*—old age; *ekadā*—once upon a time; *vainyaḥ*—King Pṛthu; *ātmavān*—fully conversant in spiritual education; *ātmanā*—by oneself; *vardhita*—increased; *aśeṣa*—unlimitedly; *sva-*

anusargaḥ—creation of material opulences; *prajā-patiḥ*—a protector of citizens; *jagataḥ*—moving; *tasthuṣaḥ*—not moving; *ca*—also; *api*—certainly; *vṛtti-daḥ*—one who gives pensions; *dharma-bhṛt*—one who observes the religious principles; *satām*—of the devotees; *niṣpādita*—fully executed; *īśvara*—of the Supreme Personality of Godhead; *ādeśaḥ*—order; *yat-artham*—in coordination with Him; *iha*—in this world; *jajñivān*—performed; *ātma-jeṣu*—unto his sons; *ātma-jām*—the earth; *nyasya*—indicating; *virahāt*—out of separation; *rudatīm iva*—just like lamenting; *prajāsu*—unto the citizens; *vimanaḥsu*—unto the aggrieved; *ekaḥ*—alone; *sa-dāraḥ*—with his wife; *agāt*—went; *tapaḥ-vanam*—in the forest where one can execute austerities.

TRANSLATION

At the last stage of his life, when Mahārāja Pṛthu saw himself getting old, that great soul, who was King of the world, divided whatever opulence he had accumulated amongst all kinds of living entities, moving and nonmoving. He arranged pensions for everyone according to religious principles, and after executing the orders of the Supreme Personality of Godhead, in complete coordination with Him, he dedicated his sons unto the earth, which was considered to be his daughter. Then Mahārāja Pṛthu left the presence of his citizens, who were almost lamenting and crying from feeling separation from the King, and went to the forest alone with his wife to perform austerities.

PURPORT

Mahārāja Pṛthu was one of the *śaktyāveśa* incarnations of the Supreme Personality of Godhead, and as such he appeared on the surface of the earth to execute the orders of the Supreme. As stated in *Bhagavad-gītā*, the Supreme Lord is the proprietor of all planets, and He is always anxious to see that in each and every planet the living entities are happily living and executing their duties. As soon as there is some discrepancy in the execution of duties, the Lord appears on earth, as confirmed in *Bhagavad-gītā: yadā yadā hi dharmasya glānir bhavati bhārata* (Bg. 4.7).

Since there were so many discrepancies during the reign of King Vena, the Lord sent His most confidential devotee, Mahārāja Pṛthu, to settle things. Therefore, after executing the orders of the Supreme Personality of Godhead and settling the affairs of the world, Mahārāja Pṛthu was ready to retire. He had been exemplary in his governmental administration, and now he was to become exemplary in his retirement. He divided all his property amongst his sons and appointed them to rule the world, and then he went to the forest with his wife. It is significant in this connection that it is said that Mahārāja Pṛthu retired alone and at the same time took his wife with him. According to Vedic principles, when retiring from family life, one can take his wife with him, for the husband and wife are considered to be one unit. Thus they can both combinedly perform austerities for liberation. This is the path that Mahārāja Pṛthu, who was an exemplary character, followed, and this is also the way of Vedic civilization. One should not simply remain at home until the time of death but should separate from family life at a timely moment and prepare himself to go back to Godhead. As a *śaktyāveśa* incarnation of God who had actually come from Vaikuṇṭha as a representative of Kṛṣṇa, Mahārāja Pṛthu was certain to go back to Godhead. Nonetheless in order to set the example in all ways, he also underwent severe austerities in the *tapo-vana.* It appears that in those days there were many *tapo-vanas,* or forests especially meant for retirement and the practice of austerities. Indeed, it was compulsory for everyone to go to the *tapo-vana* to fully accept the shelter of the Supreme Personality of Godhead, for it is very difficult to retire from family life and at the same time remain at home.

TEXT 4

तत्राप्यदाभ्यनियमो वैखानससुसम्मते ।
आरब्ध उग्रतपसि यथा स्वविजये पुरा ॥ ४ ॥

tatrāpy adābhya-niyamo
vaikhānasa-susammate
ārabdha ugra-tapasi
yathā sva-vijaye purā

tatra—there; *api*—also; *adābhya*—severe; *niyamaḥ*—austerities; *vaikhānasa*—rules and regulations of retired life; *susammate*—perfectly recognized; *ārabdhaḥ*—beginning; *ugra*—severe; *tapasi*—austerity; *yathā*—as much as; *sva-vijaye*—in conquering the world; *purā*—formerly.

TRANSLATION

After retiring from family life, Mahārāja Pṛthu strictly followed the regulations of retired life and underwent severe austerities in the forest. He engaged in these activities as seriously as he had formerly engaged in leading the government and conquering everyone.

PURPORT

As it is necessary for one to become very active in family life, similarly, after retirement from family life, it is necessary to control the mind and senses. This is possible when one engages himself fully in the devotional service of the Lord. Actually the whole purpose of the Vedic system, the Vedic social order, is to enable one to ultimately return home, back to Godhead. The *gṛhastha-āśrama* is a sort of concession combining sense gratification with a regulative life. It is to enable one to easily retire in the middle of life and engage fully in austerities in order to transcend material sense gratification once and for all. Therefore in the *vānaprastha* stage of life, *tapasya,* or austerity, is strongly recommended. Mahārāja Pṛthu followed exactly all the rules of *vānaprastha* life, which is technically known as *vaikhānasa-āśrama.* The word *vaikhānasa-susammate* is significant because in *vānaprastha* life the regulative principles are also to be strictly followed. In other words, Mahārāja Pṛthu was an ideal character in every sphere of life. *Mahājano yena gataḥ sa panthāḥ:* one should follow in the footsteps of great personalities. Thus by following the exemplary character of Mahārāja Pṛthu, one can become perfect in all respects while living this life or while retiring from active life. Thus after giving up this body, one can become liberated and go back to Godhead.

TEXT 5

कन्दमूलफलाहारः शुष्कपर्णाशनः क्वचित् ।
अब्भक्षः कतिचित्पक्षान् वायुभक्षस्ततः परम् ॥ ५ ॥

kanda-mūla-phalāhāraḥ
śuṣkaparṇāśanaḥ kvacit
ab-bhakṣaḥ katicit pakṣān
vāyu-bhakṣas tataḥ param

kanda—trunk; *mūla*—roots; *phala*—fruits; *āhāraḥ*—eating; *śuṣka*—dry; *parṇa*—leaves; *āśanaḥ*—eating; *kvacit*—sometimes; *ap-bhakṣaḥ*—drinking water; *katicit*—for several; *pakṣān*—fortnights; *vāyu*—the air; *bhakṣaḥ*—breathing; *tataḥ param*—thereafter.

TRANSLATION

In the tapo-vana, Mahārāja Pṛthu sometimes ate the trunks and roots of trees, and sometimes he ate fruit and dried leaves, and for some weeks he drank only water. Finally he lived simply by breathing air.

PURPORT

In *Bhagavad-gītā yogīs* are advised to go to a secluded place in the forest and live alone in a sanctified spot there. By Pṛthu Mahārāja's behavior we can understand that when he went to the forest, he did not eat any cooked food sent from the city by some devotees or disciples. As soon as one takes a vow to live in the forest, he must simply eat roots, tree trunks, fruits, dried leaves or whatever nature provides in that way. Pṛthu Mahārāja strictly adopted these principles for living in the forest, and sometimes he ate nothing but dried leaves and drank nothing but a little water. Sometimes he lived on nothing but air, and sometimes he ate some fruit from the trees. In this way he lived in the forest and underwent severe austerity, especially in regards to eating. In other words, overeating is not at all recommended for one who wants to progress in spiritual life. Śrī Rūpa Gosvāmī also warns *(atyāhāraḥ prayāsaś ca)* that too much eating and too much endeavor are against the principles by which one can advance in spiritual life.

It is also notable that according to Vedic injunction, to live in the forest is to live in the mode of complete goodness, whereas to live in the city is to live in the mode of passion, and to live in a brothel or drinking house is to live in the mode of ignorance. However, to live in a temple is to live in Vaikuṇṭha, which is transcendental to all the modes of material nature. This Kṛṣṇa consciousness movement affords one the opportunity to live in the temple of the Lord, which is as good as Vaikuṇṭha. Consequently a Kṛṣṇa conscious person does not need to go to the forest and artificially try to imitate Mahārāja Pṛthu or the great sages and *munis* who used to live in the forest.

Śrīla Rūpa Gosvāmī, after retiring from his minister's seat in the government, went to Vṛndāvana and lived beneath a tree, like Mahārāja Pṛthu. Since then, many people have gone to Vṛndāvana to imitate Rūpa Gosvāmī's behavior. Instead of advancing in spiritual life, many have fallen into material habits and even in Vṛndāvana have become victims of illicit sex, gambling and intoxication. This Kṛṣṇa consciousness movement has been introduced in the Western countries, but it is not possible for Westerners to go to the forest and practice the severe austerities which were ideally practiced by Pṛthu Mahārāja or Rūpa Gosvāmī. However, Westerners or anyone else can follow in the footsteps of Śrīla Bhaktisiddhānta Sarasvatī Ṭhākura by living in a temple, which is transcendental to residence in a forest, and to vow to accept Kṛṣṇa *prasāda* and nothing else, follow the regulative principles, and chant sixteen rounds daily of the Hare Kṛṣṇa *mantra.* In this way, one's spiritual life will never be disturbed.

TEXT 6

ग्रीष्मे पञ्चतपा वीरो वर्षास्वासारषाण्मुनिः ।
आकण्ठमग्नः शिशिरे उदके स्थण्डिलेशयः ॥ ६ ॥

grīṣme pañca-tapā vīro
varṣāsv āsāraṣāṇ muniḥ
ākaṇṭha-magnaḥ śiśire
udake sthaṇḍileśayaḥ

grīṣme—in the summer season; *pañca-tapāḥ*—five kinds of heating; *vīraḥ*—the hero; *varṣāsu*—in the rainy season; *āsāraṣāṭ*—being situated within the torrents of rain; *muniḥ*—like the great sages; *ākaṇṭha*—up to the neck; *magnaḥ*—drowned; *śiśire*—in winter; *udake*—within water; *sthaṇḍile-śayaḥ*—lying down on the floor.

TRANSLATION

Following the principles of forest living and the footsteps of the great sages and munis, Pṛthu Mahārāja accepted five kinds of heating processes during the summer season, exposed himself to torrents of rain in the rainy season, and, in the winter, stood in water up to his neck. He also used to simply lie down on the floor to sleep.

PURPORT

These are some of the austerities executed by the *jñānīs* and *yogīs,* who cannot accept the process of *bhakti-yoga.* They must undergo such severe types of austerity in order to become purified from material contamination. *Pañca-tapāḥ* refers to five kinds of heating processes. One is also enjoined to sit within a circle of fire, with flames blazing from four sides and the sun blazing directly overhead. This is one kind of *pañca-tapāḥ* recommended for austerity. Similarly, in the rainy season one is enjoined to expose himself to torrents of rain and in winter to sit in cold water up to the neck. As far as bedding is concerned, the ascetic should be content with simply lying on the floor. The purpose for undergoing such severe austerities is to become a devotee of the Supreme Personality of Godhead, Kṛṣṇa, as explained in the next verse.

TEXT 7

तितिक्षुर्यतवाग्दान्त ऊर्ध्वरेता जितानिलः ।
आरिराधयिषुः कृष्णमचरत्तप उत्तमम् ॥ ७ ॥

titikṣur yata-vāg dānta
ūrdhva-retā jitānilaḥ
ārirādhayiṣuḥ kṛṣṇam
acarat tapa uttamam

titikṣuḥ—tolerating; *yata*—controlling; *vāk*—words; *dāntaḥ*—controlling the senses; *ūrdhva-retāḥ*—without discharge of semen; *jita-anilaḥ*—controlling the life air; *ārirādhayiṣuḥ*—simply desiring; *kṛṣṇam*—Lord Kṛṣṇa; *acarat*—practice; *tapaḥ*—austerities; *uttamam*—the best.

TRANSLATION

Mahārāja Pṛthu underwent all these severe austerities in order to control his words and his senses, to refrain from discharging his semina and to control the life air within his body. All this he did for the satisfaction of Kṛṣṇa. He had no other purpose.

PURPORT

In Kali-yuga the following is recommended:

harer nāma harer nāma harer nāmaiva kevalam
kalau nāsty eva nāsty eva nāsty eva gatir anyathā.
(*Bṛhan-nāradīya Purāṇa*)

In order to be recognized by Kṛṣṇa, the Supreme Personality of Godhead, one should chant the holy name of the Lord continuously, twenty-four hours a day. Unfortunate persons who cannot accept this formula prefer to execute some type of pseudo-meditation without accepting the other processes of austerity. The fact is, however, that one must accept either the severe method of austerity described above to become purified or take to the process of devotional service recommended for pleasing the Supreme Lord, Kṛṣṇa. The person who is Kṛṣṇa conscious is most intelligent because in Kali-yuga it is not at all possible to undergo such severe austerities. We need only follow great personalities like Lord Caitanya Mahāprabhu. In His *Śikṣāṣṭaka,* Lord Caitanya Mahāprabhu wrote, *paraṁ vijayate śrī-kṛṣṇa-saṅkīrtanam:* all glories to the holy names of Lord Kṛṣṇa, which from the very beginning purify the heart and immediately liberate one. *Bhava-mahādāvāgni-nirvāpanam.* If the real purpose of all *yoga* is to please Lord Kṛṣṇa, then this simple *bhakti-yoga* system recommended for this age is sufficient. It is necessary, however, to engage constantly in the service of the Lord. Although Pṛthu Mahārāja executed his austerities long before the appearance of Lord Kṛṣṇa on this planet, his purpose was still to please Kṛṣṇa.

There are many fools who claim that worship of Kṛṣṇa began only about five thousand years ago, after the appearance of Lord Kṛṣṇa in India, but this is not a fact. Pṛthu Mahārāja worshiped Kṛṣṇa millions of years ago, for Pṛthu happened to be a descendant of the family of Mahārāja Dhruva, who reigned for 36,000 years during the Satya-yuga age. Unless his total life span was 100,000 years, how could Dhruva Mahārāja reign over the world for 36,000 years? The point is that Kṛṣṇa worship existed at the beginning of creation and has continued to exist throughout Satya-yuga, Tretā-yuga and Dvāpara-yuga, and now it is continuing in Kali-yuga. As stated in *Bhagavad-gītā,* Kṛṣṇa not only appears in this millennium of Brahmā's life, but in every millennium. Therefore worship of Kṛṣṇa is conducted in all millenniums. It is not that Kṛṣṇa worship began only when Kṛṣṇa appeared on this planet five thousand years ago. This is a foolish conclusion that is not substantiated by Vedic literatures.

Also of significance in this verse are the words *ārirādhayiṣuḥ kṛṣṇam acarat tapa uttamam.* Mahārāja Pṛthu underwent severe types of austerities for the express purpose of worshiping Kṛṣṇa. Kṛṣṇa is so kind, especially in this age, that He appears in the transcendental vibration of His holy name. As is said in the *Nārada-pañcarātra, ārādhito yadi haris tapasā tataḥ kim.* If Kṛṣṇa is worshiped, if He is the goal of advancement, there is no need for one to execute severe types of *tapasya,* because one has already reached his destination. If, after executing all types of *tapasya,* one cannot reach Kṛṣṇa, all his *tapasya* has no value, for without Kṛṣṇa all austerity is simply wasted labor. *Śrama eva hi kevalam* (*Bhāg.* 1.2.8). We should therefore not be discouraged just because we cannot go to the forest and practice severe austerities. Our life is so short that we must strictly adhere to the principles laid down by the Vaiṣṇava *ācāryas* and peacefully execute Kṛṣṇa consciousness. There is no need to become despondent. Narottama dāsa Ṭhākura recommends: *ānande bala hari, bhaja vṛndāvana, śrī-guru-vaiṣṇava-pade majāiyā mana.* For a transcendental blissful life, chant the Hare Kṛṣṇa *mantra,* come worship the holy place of Vṛndāvana, and always engage in the service of the Lord, of the spiritual master, and of the Vaiṣṇavas. This Kṛṣṇa consciousness movement is therefore very safe and easy. We have only to execute the order of the Lord and fully surrender unto Him. We have only to execute the order of the spiritual master, preach Kṛṣṇa consciousness and follow in the path of the Vaiṣṇavas. The spiritual master represents both Lord Kṛṣṇa and the Vaiṣṇavas; therefore by following the instructions of the spiritual master and by chanting Hare Kṛṣṇa, everything will be all right.

TEXT 8

तेन क्रमानुसिद्धेन ध्वस्तकर्ममलाशयः ।
प्राणायामैः सन्निरुद्धषड्वर्गश्छिन्नबन्धनः ॥ ८ ॥

tena kramānusiddhena
dhvasta-karma-malāśayaḥ
prāṇāyāmaiḥ sanniruddha-
ṣaḍ-vargaś chinna-bandhanaḥ

tena—thus by practicing such austerities; *krama*—gradually; *anu*—constantly; *siddhena*—by perfection; *dhvasta*—smashed; *karma*—fruitive activities; *mala*—dirty things; *āśayaḥ*—desire; *prāṇayamaiḥ*—by practice of *prāṇāyāma-yoga,* breathing exercises; *san*—being; *niruddha*—stopped; *ṣaṭ-vargaḥ*—the mind and the senses; *chinna-bandhanaḥ*—completely cut off from all bondage.

TRANSLATION

By thus practicing severe austerities, Mahārāja Pṛthu gradually became steadfast in spiritual life and completely free of all desires for fruitive activities. He also practiced breathing exercises to control his mind and senses, and by such control he became completely free from all desires for fruitive activity.

PURPORT

The word *prāṇāyamaiḥ* is very important in this verse because the *haṭha-yogīs* and *aṣṭāṅga-yogīs* practice *prāṇāyāma,* but generally they do not know the purpose behind it. The purpose of *prāṇāyāma,* or mystic *yoga,* is to stop the mind and senses from engaging in fruitive activities. The so-called *yogīs* who practice in Western countries have no idea of this. The aim of *prāṇayāma* is not to make the body strong and fit for working hard. The aim is worship of Kṛṣṇa. In the previous verse it was specifically mentioned that whatever austerity, *prāṇāyāma* and mystic *yoga* practices Pṛthu Mahārāja performed were performed for the sake of worshiping Kṛṣṇa. Thus Pṛthu Mahārāja serves as a perfect example for *yogīs* also. Whatever he did, he did to please the Supreme Personality of Godhead, Kṛṣṇa.

The minds of those who are addicted to fruitive activity are always filled with unclean desires. Fruitive activities are symptomatic of our polluted desire to dominate material nature. As long as one continues to be subject to polluted desires, he has to accept one material body after another. So-called *yogīs,* without knowledge of the real purpose of *yoga,* practice it in order to keep the body fit. Thus they engage themselves in fruitive activities, and thus they are bound by desire to accept another body. They are not aware that the ultimate goal of life is to approach Kṛṣṇa. In order to save such *yogīs* from wandering throughout the different species of life, the *śāstras* warn that in this age such yogic practice is simply a waste of time. The only means of elevation is the chanting of the Hare Kṛṣṇa *mahā-mantra.*

King Pṛthu's activities took place in Satya-yuga, and in this age this practice of *yoga* is misunderstood by fallen souls who are not capable of practicing anything. Consequently the *śāstras* enjoin: *kalau nāsty eva nāsty eva nāsty eva gatir anyathā.* The conclusion is that unless the *karmīs, jñānīs* and *yogīs* come to the point of devotional service to Lord Kṛṣṇa, their so-called austerities and *yoga* have no value. *Nārādhitaḥ:* if Hari, the Supreme Personality of Godhead, is not worshiped, there is no point in practicing meditational *yoga,* performing *karma-yoga* or culturing empiric knowledge. As far as *prāṇāyāma* is concerned, chanting of the holy name of the Lord and dancing in ecstasy are also considered *prāṇāyāma.* In a previous verse, Sanatkumāra instructed Mahārāja Pṛthu to engage constantly in the service of the Supreme Lord, Vāsudeva:

yat pāda-paṅkaja-palāśa-vilāsa-bhaktyā
karmāśayaṁ grathitam udgrathayanti santaḥ

Only by worshiping Vāsudeva can one become free from the desires of fruitive activities. Outside of worshiping Vāsudeva, the *yogīs* and *jñānīs* cannot attain freedom from such desires. *Tadvan na rikta-matayo yatayo'pi ruddha-srotogaṇās tam araṇaṁ bhaja vāsudevam* (*Bhāg.* 4.22.39). Here the word *prāṇāyāma* does not refer to any ulterior motive. The actual aim is to strengthen the mind and senses in order to engage them in devotional service. In the present age this determination can be very easily acquired simply by chanting the holy names—Hare Kṛṣṇa, Hare Kṛṣṇa, Kṛṣṇa Kṛṣṇa, Hare Hare/ Hare Rāma, Hare Rāma, Rāma Rāma, Hare Hare.

TEXT 9

सनत्कुमारो भगवान् यदाहाध्यात्मिकं परम् ।
योगं तेनैव पुरुषमभजत्पुरुषर्षभः ॥ ९ ॥

sanat-kumāro bhagavān
yad āhādhyātmikaṁ param

yogaṁ tenaiva puruṣam
abhajat puruṣarṣabhaḥ

sanat-kumāraḥ—Sanat-kumāra; *bhagavān*—most powerful; *yat*—that which; *āha*—said; *ādhyātmikam*—spiritual advancement of life; *param*—ultimate; *yogam*—mysticism; *tena*—by that; *eva*—certainly; *puruṣam*—Supreme Person; *abhajat*—worshiped; *puruṣa-ṛṣabhaḥ*—the best of the human beings.

TRANSLATION

Thus the best amongst human beings, Mahārāja Pṛthu, followed that path of spiritual advancement which was advised by Sanat-kumāra. That is to say, he worshiped the Supreme Personality of Godhead, Kṛṣṇa.

PURPORT

In this verse it is clearly said that Mahārāja Pṛthu, practicing the *prāṇāyāma-yoga* system, engaged in the service of the Supreme Personality of Godhead as advised by the saint Sanat-kumāra. In this verse the words *puruṣam abhajat puruṣarṣabhaḥ* are significant: *puruṣarṣabha* refers to Mahārāja Pṛthu, the best amongst human beings, and *puruṣam* refers to the Supreme Personality of Godhead. The conclusion is that the best man amongst all men engages in the service of the Supreme Person. One *puruṣa* is worshipable, and the other *puruṣa* is the worshiper. When the *puruṣa* who worships, the living entity, thinks of becoming one with the Supreme Person, he simply becomes bewildered and falls into the darkness of ignorance. As stated by Lord Kṛṣṇa in *Bhagavad-gītā*, all living entities assembled in the battlefield, as well as Kṛṣṇa Himself, were also present in the past as individuals and would continue to be present in the future as individuals also (Bg. 2.12). Therefore the two *puruṣas*, the living entity and the Supreme Personality of Godhead, never lose their respective identities.

Actually one who is self-realized engages himself in the service of the Lord perpetually, both in this life and in the next. Indeed, for devotees there is no difference between this life and the next. In this life a neophyte devotee is trained to serve the Supreme Personality of Godhead, and in the next life he approaches that Supreme Person in Vaikuṇṭha and renders the same devotional service. Even for the neophyte devotee, devotional service is considered *brahma-bhūyāya kalpate*. Devotional service to the Lord is never considered a material activity. Since he is acting on the *brahma-bhūta* platform, a devotee is already liberated. He therefore has no need to practice any other type of *yoga* in order to approach the *brahma-bhūta* stage. If the devotee adheres strictly to the orders of the spiritual master, follows the rules and regulations and chants the Hare Kṛṣṇa *mantra*, it should be concluded that he is already at the *brahma-bhūta* stage, as confirmed in *Bhagavad-gītā:*

māṁ ca yo 'vyabhicāreṇa
bhakti-yogena sevate
sa guṇān samatītyaitān
brahma-bhūyāya kalpate

"One who is engaged in full devotional service, unfailing in all circumstances, at once transcends the modes of material nature and thus comes to the level of Brahman." (Bg. 14.26)

TEXT 10

भगवद्धर्मिणः साधोः श्रद्धया यततः सदा ।
भक्तिर्भगवति ब्रह्मण्यनन्यविषयाभवत् ॥१०॥

bhagavad-dharmiṇaḥ sādhoḥ
śraddhayā yatataḥ sadā
bhaktir bhagavati brahmaṇy
ananya-viṣayābhavat

bhagavat-dharmiṇaḥ—one who executes devotional service; *sādhoḥ*—of the devotee; *śraddhayā*—with faith; *yatataḥ*—endeavoring; *sadā*—always; *bhaktiḥ*—devotion; *bhagavati*—unto the Personality of Godhead; *brahmaṇi*—the origin of impersonal Brahman; *ananya-viṣayā*—firmly fixed without deviation; *abhavat*—became.

TRANSLATION

Mahārāja Pṛthu thus engaged completely in devotional service, executing the rules and regulations strictly according to principles, twenty-four hours daily. Thus his love and devotion unto the Supreme Personality of Godhead, Kṛṣṇa, developed and became unflinching and fixed.

PURPORT

The word *bhagavad-dharmiṇaḥ* indicates that the religious process practiced by Mahārāja Pṛthu was beyond all pretentions. As stated in the beginning of *Śrīmad-Bhāgavatam, dharmaḥ projjhita-kaitavo 'tra* (*Bhāg.* 1.1.2): Religious principles which are simply pretentious are actually nothing but cheating. *Bhagavad-dharmiṇaḥ* is described by Vīrarāghavācārya as *nivṛtta-dharmeṇa,* which indicates that it cannot be contaminated by material aspiration. As described by Śrīla Rūpa Gosvāmī:

anyābhilāṣitā-śūnyaṁ jñāna-karmādy-anāvṛtam
ānukūlyena kṛṣṇānuśīlanaṁ bhaktir uttamā

When one is not inspired by material desires and is not contaminated by the processes of fruitive activity and empiric speculation, he fully engages in the favorable service of the Lord. That is called *bhagavad-dharma,* or pure devotional service. In this verse the word *brahmaṇi* does not refer to the impersonal Brahman. Impersonal Brahman is a subordinate feature of the Supreme Personality of Godhead, and since impersonal Brahman worshipers desire to merge into the Brahman effulgence, they cannot be considered followers of *bhagavad-dharma.* After being baffled in his material enjoyment, the impersonalist may desire to merge into the existence of the Lord, but a pure devotee of the Lord has no such desire. Therefore a pure devotee is really *bhagavad-dharmī.*

It is clear from this verse that Mahārāja Pṛthu was never a worshiper of the impersonal Brahman but was at all times a pure devotee of the Supreme Personality of Godhead. *Bhagavati brahmaṇi* refers to one who is engaged in devotional service to the Personality of Godhead. A devotee's knowledge of the impersonal Brahman is automatically revealed, and he is not interested in merging into the impersonal Brahman. Mahārāja Pṛthu's activities in devotional service enabled him to become fixed and steady in the discharge of devotional activities without having to take recourse to *karma, jñāna* or *yoga.*

TEXT 11

तस्यानया भगवतः परिकर्मशुद्ध-
सत्त्वात्मनस्तदनुसंस्मरणानुपूर्त्या ।
ज्ञानं विरक्तिमदभून्निशितेन येन
चिच्छेद संशयपदं निजजीवकोशम् ॥११॥

tasyānayā bhagavataḥ parikarma-śuddha-
sattvātmanas tad-anusaṁsmaraṇānupūrtyā
jñānaṁ viraktimad abhūn niśitena yena
ciccheda saṁśaya-padaṁ nija-jīva-kośam

tasya—his; *anayā*—by this; *bhagavataḥ*—of the Supreme Personality of Godhead; *parikarma*—activities in devotional service; *śuddha*—pure, transcendental; *sattva*—existence; *ātmanaḥ*—of the mind; *tat*—of the Supreme Personality of Godhead; *anusaṁsmaraṇa*—constantly remembering; *anupūrtyā*—being perfectly done; *jñānam*—knowledge; *virakti*—nonattachment; *mat*—possessing; *abhūt*—became manifested; *niśitena*—by sharpened activities; *yena*—by which; *ciccheda*—become separated; *saṁśaya-padam*—position of doubtfulness; *nija*—own; *jīva-kośam*—engagement of the living entity.

TRANSLATION

By regularly discharging devotional service, Pṛthu Mahārāja became transcendental in mind and could therefore constantly think of the lotus feet of the Lord. Because of this, he became completely detached and attained perfect knowledge by which he could transcend all doubt. Thus he was freed from the clutches of false ego and the material conception of life.

PURPORT

In the *Nārada-pañcarātra,* devotional service to the Lord is likened unto a queen. When a queen gives an audience, many maidservants follow her. The maidservants of devotional service are material opulence, liberation and mystic powers. The *karmīs* are very much attached to material enjoyment; the *jñānīs* are very anxious to become freed from material clutches; and the *yogīs* are very fond of attaining the eight kinds of mystic perfection. From the *Nārada-pañcarātra* we understand that if one attains the stage of pure devotional service, he also attains all the opulences derived from fruitive activities, empiric philosophical speculation and mystic yogic practice. Śrīla Bilvamaṅgala Ṭhākura therefore prayed in his *Kṛṣṇa-karṇāmṛta:* "My dear Lord, if I have unflinching devotion to You, You become manifest before me personally, and the results of fruitive activity and empiric philosophical speculation—namely religion, economic development, sense gratification and liberation—become like personal attendants and remain standing before me as if awaiting my order." The idea here is that the *jñānīs,* by culture of *brahma-vidyā,* spiritual knowledge, struggle very hard to get out of the clutches of material nature, but a devotee, by dint of his advancement in devotional service, automatically becomes detached from his material body. When the devotee's spiritual body begins to manifest, he actually enters into his activities in transcendental life.

At present we have contacted a material body, material mind and material intelligence, but when we become free from these material conditions, our spiritual body, spiritual mind and spiritual intelligence become manifest. In that transcendental state, a devotee attains all the benefits of *karma, jñāna* and *yoga.* Although he never engages in fruitive activities or empiric speculation to attain mystic powers, automatically mystic powers appear in his service. A devotee does not want any kind of material opulence, but such opulence appears before him automatically. He does not have to endeavor for it. Because of his devotional service, he automatically becomes *brahma-bhūta.* As stated before, this is confirmed in *Bhagavad-gītā:*

māṁ ca yo 'vyabhicāreṇa
bhakti-yogena sevate
sa guṇān samatītyaitān
brahma-bhūyāya kalpate

"One who is engaged in full devotional service, unfailing in all circumstances, at once transcends the modes of material nature and thus comes to the level of Brahman." (Bg. 14.26)

Because of his regular discharge of devotional service, a devotee attains the transcendental stage of life. Since his mind is transcendentally situated, he cannot think of anything but the lotus feet of the Lord. This is the meaning of the word *saṁsmaraṇa-anupūrtyā.* By constantly thinking of the lotus feet of the Lord, the devotee immediately becomes situated in *śuddha-sattva. Śuddha-sattva* refers to that platform which is above the modes of material nature, including the mode of goodness. In the material world, the mode of goodness is considered to be representative of the highest perfection, but one has to transcend this mode and come to the stage of *śuddha-sattva,* or pure goodness, where the three qualities of material nature cannot act.

Śrīla Viśvanātha Cakravartī Ṭhākura gives the following example: If one has strong digestive power, after eating he automatically lights a fire within his stomach to digest everything and does not need to take medicine to aid his digestion. Similarly, the fire of devotional service is so strong that a devotee does not need to act separately to attain perfect knowledge or detachment from material attractions. A *jñānī* may become detached from material attractions by prolonged discussions on subjects of knowledge and may in this way finally come to the *brahma-bhūta* stage, but a devotee does not have to undergo so much trouble. By virtue of his devotional service, he attains the *brahma-bhūta* stage without a doubt. The *yogīs* and *jñānīs* are always doubtful about their constitutional position; therefore they mistakenly think of becoming one with the Supreme. However, a devotee's relationship with the Supreme becomes manifest beyond all doubt, and he immediately understands that his position is that of eternal servant of the Lord. The *jñānīs* and *yogīs* may think of attaining liberation without rendering devotional service, but actually this is not possible because their intelligence is not as pure as that of a pure devotee. In other words, the *jñānīs* and *yogīs* cannot become factually liberated unless they become elevated to the position of devotees.

Āruhya kṛcchreṇa paraṁ padaṁ tataḥ patanty adho 'nādṛta-yuṣmad-aṅghrayaḥ (*Bhāg.* 10.2.32). The *jñānīs* and *yogīs* may rise to the highest position, Brahman realization, but because of their lack of devotion unto the lotus feet of the Lord, they again fall down into material nature. Therefore *jñāna* and *yoga* should not be accepted as the real processes for liberation. By discharging devotional service, Mahārāja Pṛthu automatically transcended all these positions. Since Mahārāja Pṛthu was a *śaktyāveśa* incarnation of the Supreme Lord, he did not have to act in any way to attain liberation. He came from the Vaikuṇṭha world, or spiritual sky, in order to execute the will of the Supreme Lord on earth. Consequently he was to return home, back to Godhead, without having to execute *jñāna*, *yoga* or *karma*. Although Pṛthu Mahārāja was eternally a pure devotee of the Lord, he nonetheless adopted the process of devotional service in order to teach the people in general the proper process for executing the duties of life and ultimately returning home, back to Godhead.

TEXT 12

छिन्नान्यधीरधिगतात्मगतिर्निरीह-
स्तत्तत्यजेऽच्छिनदिदं वयुनेन येन ।
तावन्न योगगतिभिर्यतिरप्रमत्तो
यावद्गदाग्रजकथासु रतिं न कुर्यात् ॥१२॥

chinnānya-dhīr adhigatātma-gatir nirīhas
tat tatyaje 'cchinad idaṁ vayunena yena
tāvan na yoga-gatibhir yatir apramatto
yāvad gadāgraja-kathāsu ratiṁ na kuryāt

chinna—being separated; *anya-dhīḥ*—all other concepts of life (the bodily concept of life); *adhigata*—being firmly convinced; *ātma-gatiḥ*—ultimate goal of spiritual life; *nirīhaḥ*—desireless; *tat*—that; *tatyaje*—gave up; *acchinat*—he had cut; *idam*—this; *vayunena*—with the knowledge; *yena*—by which; *tāvat*—so long; *na*—never; *yoga-gatibhiḥ*—the practice of the mystic *yoga* system; *yatiḥ*—the practicer; *apramattaḥ*—without any illusion; *yāvat*—so long; *gadāgraja*—of Kṛṣṇa; *kathāsu*—words; *ratim*—attraction; *na*—never; *kuryāt*—do it.

TRANSLATION

When he became completely free from the conception of bodily life, Mahārāja Pṛthu realized Lord Kṛṣṇa sitting in everyone's heart as the Paramātmā. Being thus able to get all instructions from Him, he gave up all other practices of yoga and jñāna. He was not even interested in the perfection of the yoga and jñāna systems, for he thoroughly realized that devotional service to Kṛṣṇa is the ultimate goal of life and that unless the yogīs and jñānīs become attracted to Kṛṣṇa-kathā [narrations about Kṛṣṇa], their illusions concerning existence can never be dispelled.

PURPORT

As long as one is too much absorbed in the bodily conception of life, he becomes interested in many different processes of self-realization, such as the mystic *yoga* system or the system utilizing the speculative empiric methods. However, when one understands that the ultimate goal of life is to approach Kṛṣṇa, he realizes Kṛṣṇa within everyone's heart and therefore helps everyone who is interested in Kṛṣṇa consciousness. Actually the perfection of life depends on one's inclination to hear about Kṛṣṇa. It is therefore mentioned in this verse: *yāvad gadāgraja-kathāsu ratiṁ na kuryāt.* Unless one becomes interested in Kṛṣṇa, in His pastimes and activities, there is no question of liberation by means of *yoga* practice or speculative knowledge.

Having attained to the stage of devotion, Mahārāja Pṛthu became uninterested in the practices of *jñāna* and *yoga* and abandoned them. This is the stage of pure devotional life as described by Rūpa Gosvāmī: *anyābhilāṣitā-śūnyaṁ jñāna-karmādy-anāvṛtam/ ānukūlyena kṛṣṇānuśīlanaṁ bhaktir uttamā.* Real *jñāna* means understanding that the living entity is the eternal servant of the Lord. This knowledge is attained after many, many births, as confirmed in *Bhagavad-gītā: bahūnāṁ janmanām ante jñānavān māṁ prapadyate* (Bg. 7.19). In the *paramahaṁsa* stage of life, one fully realizes Kṛṣṇa as everything: *vāsudevaḥ sarvam iti sa mahātmā sudurlabhaḥ.* When one understands fully that Kṛṣṇa is everything and that Kṛṣṇa consciousness is the highest perfection of life, he becomes a *paramahaṁsa,* or *mahātmā.* Such a *mahātmā* or *paramahaṁsa* is very rare to find. A *paramahaṁsa* or pure devotee is never attracted by *haṭha-yoga* or speculative knowledge. He is simply interested in the unalloyed devotional service of the Lord. Sometimes one who is formally addicted to these processes tries to perform devotional service and the *jñāna* and *yoga* practices at the same time, but as soon as one comes to the unalloyed stage of devotional service, he is able to give up all other methods of self-realization. In other words, when one firmly realizes Kṛṣṇa as the supreme goal, he is no longer attracted by mystic *yoga* practice or the speculative empirical methods of knowledge.

TEXT 13

एवं स वीरप्रवरः संयोज्यात्मानमात्मनि ।
ब्रह्मभूतो दृढं काले तत्याज स्वं कलेवरम् ॥१३॥

evaṁ sa vīra-pravaraḥ
saṁyojyātmānam ātmani
brahma-bhūto dṛḍhaṁ kāle
tatyāja svaṁ kalevaram

evam—thus; *saḥ*—he; *vīra-pravaraḥ*—the chief of the heroes; *saṁyojya*—applying; *ātmānam*—mind; *ātmani*—unto the Supersoul; *brahma-bhūtaḥ*—being liberated; *dṛḍham*—firmly; *kāle*—in due course of time; *tatyāja*—gave up; *svam*—own; *kalevaram*—body.

TRANSLATION

In due course of time, Pṛthu Mahārāja was able to fix his mind firmly upon the lotus feet of Kṛṣṇa, and thus, completely situated on the brahma-bhūta platform, he gave up the material body.

PURPORT

According to a Bengali proverb, whatever spiritual progress one makes in life will be tested at the time of death. In *Bhagavad-gītā* it is also confirmed: *yaṁ yaṁ vāpi smaran bhāvaṁ tyajaty ante kalevaram/ taṁ tam evaiti kaunteya sadā tad-bhāva-bhāvitaḥ* (Bg. 8.6). Those who are practicing Kṛṣṇa consciousness know that their examination will be held at the time of death. If one can remember Kṛṣṇa at death, he is immediately transferred to Goloka Vṛndāvana, or Kṛṣṇaloka, and thus his life becomes successful. Pṛthu Mahārāja, by the grace of Kṛṣṇa, could understand that the end of his life was near, and thus he became very jubilant and proceeded to completely give up his body on the *brahma-bhūta* stage by practicing the yogic process. It is thoroughly described in the following verses how one can voluntarily give up this body and return home, back to Godhead. The yogic process practiced by Pṛthu Mahārāja at the time of death accelerates the giving up of this body while one is in sound health physically and mentally. Every devotee desires to give up the body while it is sound physically and mentally. This desire was also expressed by King Kulaśekhara in his *Mukunda-mālā-stotra:*

kṛṣṇa tvadīya-padapaṅkaja-pañjarāntam
adyaiva me viśatu mānasa-rāja-haṁsaḥ
prāṇa-prayāṇa-samaye kapha-vāta-pittaiḥ
kaṇṭhāvarodhana-vidhau smaraṇaṁ kutas te

King Kulaśekhara wanted to give up his body while in a healthy state, and he thus prayed to Kṛṣṇa to let him die immediately while he was in good health and while his mind was sound. When a man dies, he is generally overpowered by mucus and bile, and thus he chokes. Since it is very difficult to vibrate any sound while choking, it is simply by Kṛṣṇa's grace that one can chant Hare Kṛṣṇa at the time of death. However, by situating oneself in the *muktāsana* position, a *yogī* can immediately give up his body and go to whatever planet he desires. A perfect *yogī* can give up his body whenever he desires through the practice of *yoga.*

TEXT 14

सम्पीड्य पायुं पार्ष्णिभ्यां वायुमुत्सारयञ्छनैः ।
नाभ्यां कोष्ठेष्ववस्थाप्य हृदुरःकण्ठशीर्षणि ॥१४॥

sampīḍya pāyuṁ pārṣṇibhyāṁ
vāyum utsārayañ chanaiḥ
nābhyāṁ koṣṭheṣv avasthāpya
hṛd-uraḥ-kaṇṭha-śīrṣaṇi

sampīḍya—by blocking; *pāyum*—the door of the anus; *pārṣṇibhyām*—by the calves; *vāyum*—the air which goes up; *utsārayan*—pushing upward; *śanaiḥ*—gradually; *nābhyām*—by the navel; *koṣṭheṣu*—in the heart and in the throat; *avasthāpya*—fixing up; *hṛt*—in the heart; *uraḥ*—upwards; *kaṇṭha*—throat; *śīrṣaṇi*—between the two eyebrows.

TRANSLATION

When Mahārāja Pṛthu practiced a particular yogic sitting posture, he blocked the doors of his anus with his ankles, pressed his right and left calves and gradually raised his life air upward, passing it on to the circle of his navel, up to his heart and throat, and finally pushed it upward to the central position between his two eyebrows.

PURPORT

The sitting posture described herein is called *muktāsana.* In the *yoga* process, after following the strict regulative principles controlling sleeping, eating and mating, one is allowed to practice the different sitting postures. The ultimate aim of *yoga* is to enable one to give up this body according to his own free will. One who has attained the ultimate summit of *yoga* practice can live in the body as long as he likes, or, as long as he is not completely perfect, leave the body to go anywhere within or outside the universe. Some *yogīs* leave their bodies to go to the higher planetary systems and enjoy the material facilities therein. However, intelligent *yogīs* do not wish to waste their time within this material world at all; they do not care for the material facilities in higher planetary systems but are interested in going directly to the spiritual sky, back home, back to Godhead.

From the description in this verse, it appears that Mahārāja Pṛthu had no desire to promote himself to the higher planetary systems. He wanted to return home immediately, back to Godhead. Although Mahārāja Pṛthu stopped all practice of mystic *yoga* after realizing Kṛṣṇa consciousness, he nonetheless took advantage of his previous practice and immediately placed himself on the *brahma-bhūta* platform in order to accelerate his return to Godhead. The aim of this particular system of *āsana,* known as the sitting posture for liberation, or *muktāsana,* is to attain success in *kuṇḍalinī-cakra* and gradually raise the life from the *mūlādhāra-cakra* to the *svādhiṣṭhāna-cakra,* then to the *maṇipūra-cakra,* the *anāhata-cakra,* the *viśuddha-cakra,* and finally to the *ājñā-cakra.* When the *yogī* reaches the *ājñā-cakra,* between the two eyebrows, he is able to penetrate the *brahma-randhra,* or the hole in his skull, and go to any planet he desires up to the spiritual kingdom of Vaikuṇṭha, or Kṛṣṇaloka. The conclusion is that one has to come to the *brahma-bhūta* stage for going back to Godhead. However, those who are in Kṛṣṇa consciousness, or who are practicing *bhakti-yoga (śravaṇaṁ kīrtanaṁ viṣṇoḥ smaraṇaṁ pāda-sevanam)*, can return to Godhead without even practicing the *muktāsana* process. The purpose of *muktāsana* practice is to come to the *brahma-bhūta* stage, for without being on the *brahma-bhūta* stage, one cannot be promoted to the spiritual sky. As stated in *Bhagavad-gītā: māṁ ca yo 'vyabhicāreṇa bhakti-yogena sevate/ sa guṇān samatītyaitān brahma-bhūyāya kalpate* (Bg. 14.26). The *bhakti-yogī,* practicing *bhakti-yoga,* is always situated on the *brahma-bhūta* stage *(brahma-bhūyāya kalpate).* If a devotee is able to continue on the *brahma-bhūta* platform, he enters the spiritual sky automatically after death and returns to Godhead. Consequently a devotee need not feel sorry for not having practiced the *kuṇḍalinī-cakra* or not penetrating the six *cakras* one after another. As far as Mahārāja Pṛthu was concerned, he had already practiced this process, and since he did not want to wait for the time when his death would occur naturally, he took advantage of the *ṣaṭ-*

cakra penetration process and thus gave up the body according to his own free will and immediately entered the spiritual sky.

TEXT 15

उत्सर्पयंस्तु तं मूर्ध्नि क्रमेणावेश्य निःस्पृहः
वायुं वायौ क्षितौ कायं तेजस्तेजस्ययूयुजत् ॥१५॥

utsarpayaṁs tu taṁ mūrdhni
krameṇāveśya niḥspṛhaḥ
vāyuṁ vāyau kṣitau kāyaṁ
tejas tejasy ayūyujat

utsarpayan—thus placing; *tu*—but; *tam*—the air; *mūrdhni*—on the head; *krameṇa*—gradually; *āveśya*—placing; *niḥspṛhaḥ*—being freed from all material desires; *vāyum*—the air portion of the body; *vāyau*—in the total air covering the universe; *kṣitau*—in the total covering of earth; *kāyam*—this material body; *tejaḥ*—the fire in the body; *tejasi*—in the total fire of the material covering; *ayūyujat*—mixed.

TRANSLATION

In this way, Pṛthu Mahārāja gradually raised his air of life up to the hole in his skull, whereupon he lost all desire for material existence. Gradually he merged his air of life with the totality of air, his body with the totality of earth, and the fire within his body with the totality of fire.

PURPORT

When the spiritual spark, which is described as one ten-thousandth part of the tip of a hair, is forced into material existence, that spark is covered by gross and subtle material elements. The material body is composed of five gross elements—earth, water, fire, air and ether—and three subtle elements—mind, intelligence and ego. When one attains liberation, he is freed from these material coverings. Indeed, success in *yoga* involves getting free from these material coverings and entering into spiritual existence. Lord Buddha's teachings of *nirvāṇa* are based on this principle. Lord Buddha instructed his followers to give up these material coverings by means of meditation and *yoga*. Lord Buddha did not give any information about the soul, but if one follows his instructions strictly, he will ultimately become free from the material coverings and attain *nirvāṇa*.

When a living entity gives up the material coverings, he remains a spirit soul. This spirit soul must enter into the spiritual sky to merge into the Brahman effulgence. Unfortunately, unless the living entity has information of the spiritual world and the Vaikuṇṭhas, there is a 99.9 percent chance of his falling down again into material existence. There is, however, a small chance of being promoted to a spiritual planet from the Brahman effulgence, or the *brahmajyoti.* This *brahmajyoti* is considered by impersonalists to be without variety, and the Buddhists consider it to be void. In either case, whether one accepts the spiritual sky as being without variety or void, there is none of the spiritual bliss which is enjoyed in the spiritual planets, Vaikuṇṭhas or Kṛṣṇaloka. In the absence of varieties of enjoyment, the spirit soul gradually feels an attraction to enjoy a life of bliss, and not having any information of Kṛṣṇaloka or Vaikuṇṭhaloka, he naturally falls down to material activities in order to enjoy material varieties.

TEXT 16

खान्याकाशे द्रवं तोये यथास्थानं विभागशः ।
क्षितिमम्भसि तत्तेजस्यदो वायौ नभस्यमुम् ॥१६॥

khāny ākāśe dravaṁ toye
yathā-sthānaṁ vibhāgaśaḥ
kṣitim ambhasi tat tejasy
ado vāyau nabhasy amum

khāni—the different holes in the body for the sense organs; *ākāśe*—in the sky; *dravam*—the liquid substance; *toye*—in the water; *yathā-sthānam*—according to proper situation; *vibhāgaśaḥ*—as they are divided; *kṣitim*—earth; *ambhasi*—in the water; *tat*—that; *tejasi*—in the fire; *adaḥ*—the fire; *vāyau*—in the air; *nabhasi*—in the sky; *amum*—that.

TRANSLATION

In this way, according to the different positions of the various parts of the body, Pṛthu Mahārāja merged his bodily air with the air of the sky, his bodily liquids, such as blood and various secretions, with the totality of water, and he merged earth with water, then water with fire, fire with air, air with sky, and so on.

PURPORT

In this verse two words are very important: *yathā-sthānaṁ vibhāgaśaḥ.* In *Śrīmad-Bhāgavatam,* Second Canto, Chapter Five, Lord Brahmā clearly explained to Nārada how the creation took place, and he explained one step after another the proper divisions of the senses, the controller of the senses, the objects of the senses, and the material elements, and he also explained how they are created one after another: the air from the sky, the fire from the air, the water from the fire, the earth from the water, etc. It is important to know thoroughly the process of creation as it applies to this cosmic manifestation. Similarly, this body is also created according to the same process by the Supreme Lord. The Personality of Godhead, after entering the universe, creates the cosmic manifestations one after another. Similarly, the living entity, after entering a womb of a mother, also collects his gross and subtle bodies, taking ingredients from the totality of sky, air, fire, water and earth. The words *yathā-sthānaṁ vibhāgaśaḥ* indicate that one should know the process of creation and should meditate upon the creative process inversely and thus become free from material contamination.

TEXT 17

इन्द्रियेषु मनस्तानि तन्मात्रेषु यथोद्भवम् ।
भूतादिनामून्युत्कृष्य महत्यात्मनि सन्दधे ॥१७॥

indriyeṣu manas tāni
tanmātreṣu yathodbhavam
bhūtādināmūny utkṛṣya
mahaty ātmani sandadhe

indriyeṣu—in the sense organs; *manaḥ*—the mind; *tāni*—the sense organs; *tanmātreṣu*—in the objects of the senses; *yathā-udbhavam*—wherefrom they generated; *bhūta-ādinā*—by the five elements; *amūni*—all those sense objects; *utkṛṣya*—taking out; *mahati*—in the *mahat-tattva; ātmani*—unto the ego; *sandadhe*—amalgamated.

TRANSLATION

He amalgamated the mind with the senses and the senses with the sense objects, according to their respective positions, and he also amalgamated the material ego with the total material energy, mahat-tattva.

PURPORT

In respect to the ego, the total material energy is sundered in two parts—one agitated by the mode of ignorance, and the other agitated by the modes of passion and goodness. Due to agitation by the mode of ignorance, the five gross elements are created. Due to agitation by the mode of passion, the mind is created, and due to agitation by the mode of goodness, false egoism or identification with matter is created. The mind is protected by a particular type of demigod. Sometimes the mind *(manaḥ)* is also understood to have a controlling deity or demigod. In this way the total mind, namely the material mind controlled by material demigods, was amalgamated with the senses. The senses, in turn, were amalgamated with the sense objects. The sense objects are forms, tastes, smells, sounds, etc. Sound is the ultimate source of the sense objects. The mind was attracted by the senses and the senses by the sense objects, and all of them were ultimately amalgamated in the sky. The creation is so arranged that cause and effect follow one after the other. The merging process involves amalgamating the effect with the original cause. Since the ultimate cause in the material world is the *mahat-tattva,* everything was gradually wound up and amalgamated with the *mahat-tattva.* This may be compared to *śūnyavāda,* or voidism, in that this is the process for cleansing the real spiritual mind, or consciousness.

When the mind is completely washed of all material contamination, the pure consciousness acts. The sound vibration from the spiritual sky can automatically cleanse all material contaminations, as confirmed by Caitanya Mahāprabhu: *ceto-darpaṇa-mārjanam.* We need only take the advice of Lord Caitanya Mahāprabhu and chant the Hare Kṛṣṇa *mantra* to cleanse the mind of all material contamination, and this may be considered the summary of this difficult verse. As soon as the whole material contamination is washed away by this process of chanting, all desires and reactions to material activities become immediately vanquished, and real life, peaceful existence, begins. In this age of Kali it is very difficult to adopt the yogic process mentioned in this verse. Unless one is very expert in such *yoga,* the best course is to adopt the ways and means of Lord Caitanya Mahāprabhu, *śrī-kṛṣṇa-saṅkīrtanam.* Thus one can gloriously become freed from all material contamination by the simple process of chanting Hare Kṛṣṇa, Hare Kṛṣṇa, Kṛṣṇa Kṛṣṇa, Hare Hare/ Hare Rāma, Hare Rāma, Rāma Rāma, Hare Hare. Just as life in this material world has its beginning in material sound, similarly a spiritual life has its beginning in this spiritual sound vibration.

TEXT 18

तं सर्वगुणविन्यासं जीवे मायामये न्यधात् ।
तं चानुशयमात्मस्थमसावनुशयी पुमान् ।
ज्ञानवैराग्यवीर्येण स्वरूपस्थोऽजहात्प्रभुः ॥१८॥

taṁ sarva-guṇa-vinyāsaṁ
jīve māyāmaye nyadhāt

taṁ cānuśayam ātma-stham
asāv anuśayī pumān
jñāna-vairāgya-vīryeṇa
svarūpa-stho 'jahāt prabhuḥ

tam—unto Him; *sarva-guṇa-vinyāsam*—the reservoir of all qualities; *jīve*—unto the designations; *māyāmaye*—the reservoir of all potencies; *nyadhāt*—placed; *tam*—that; *ca*—also; *anuśayam*—designation; *ātma-stham*—situated in self-realization; *asau*—he; *anuśayī*—the living entity; *pumān*—the enjoyer; *jñāna*—knowledge; *vairāgya*—renunciation; *vīryeṇa*—by the prowess of; *svarūpa-sthaḥ*—being situated in one's constitutional position; *ajahāt*—returned back home; *prabhuḥ*—the controller.

TRANSLATION

Pṛthu Mahārāja then offered the total designation of the living entity unto the supreme controller of illusory energy. Being released from all the designations by which the living entity became entrapped, he became free by knowledge and renunciation and by the spiritual force of his devotional service. In this way, being situated in his original constitutional position of Kṛṣṇa consciousness, he gave up this body as a prabhu, or controller of the senses.

PURPORT

As stated in the *Vedas,* the Supreme Personality of Godhead is the source of material energy. Consequently He is sometimes called *māyāmaya,* or the Supreme Person who can create His pastimes through His potency known as the material energy. The *jīva,* or the individual living entity, becomes entrapped by the material energy by the supreme will of the Supreme Personality of Godhead. In *Bhagavad-gītā* we understand:

īśvaraḥ sarva-bhūtānāṁ
hṛd-deśe 'rjuna tiṣṭhati
bhrāmayan sarva-bhūtāni
yantrārūḍhāni māyayā

"The Supreme Lord is situated in everyone's heart, O Arjuna, and is directing the wanderings of all living entities, who are seated as on a machine, made of the material energy." (Bg. 18.61)

Īśvara, the Supreme Personality of Godhead, is situated within the heart of all conditioned souls, and by His supreme will the living entity or individual soul gets the facility to lord it over material nature in various types of bodies, which are known as *yantra,* or the moving vehicle offered by the total material energy, *māyā.* Although the individual living entity *(jīva)* and the Lord are both situated within the material energy, the Lord is directing the movements of the *jīva* soul by offering him different types of bodies through the material energy, and thus the living entity is wandering throughout the universes in various forms of body and becomes implicated in different situations, partaking of the reactions of fruitive activities.

When Pṛthu Mahārāja became spiritually powerful by the enhancement of his spiritual knowledge, *jñāna* and renunciation of material desires, he became a *prabhu,* or master of his senses (sometimes called *gosvāmī* or *svāmī).* This means that he was no longer controlled by the influence of material energy. When one is strong enough to give up the influence of material energy, he is called *prabhu.* In this verse the word *svarūpasthaḥ* is also very significant. The real identity of the individual soul lies in understanding or attaining the knowledge that he is eternally a servant of Kṛṣṇa. This understanding is called *svarūpopalabdhi.* By culturing devotional service, the devotee gradually comes to understand his actual relationship with the Supreme Personality of Godhead. This understanding of one's pure spiritual position is called *svarūpopalabdhi,* and when one attains that stage he can understand how he is related with the Supreme Personality of Godhead as a servant or friend, or as a parent or conjugal lover. This stage of understanding is called *svarūpasthaḥ.* Pṛthu Mahārāja realized this *svarūpa* completely, and it will be clear in the later chapters that he personally left this world, or this body, by riding on a chariot sent from Vaikuṇṭha.

In this verse the word *prabhu* is also significant. As stated before, when one is completely self-realized and acts according to that position, he can be called *prabhu.* The spiritual master is addressed as "Prabhupāda" because he is a completely self-realized soul. The word *pāda* means "position," and Prabhupāda indicates that he is given the position of *prabhu,* or the Supreme Personality of Godhead, for he acts on behalf of the Supreme Personality of Godhead. Unless one is a *prabhu,* or controller of the senses, he cannot act as spiritual master. He is authorized by the Supreme Prabhu, or Lord Kṛṣṇa. In his verses praising the spiritual master, Śrīla Viśvanātha Cakravartī Ṭhākura writes:

sākṣād-dharitvena samasta-śāstrair
uktas tathā bhāvyata eva sadbhiḥ

"The spiritual master is honored as much as the Supreme Lord because he is the most confidential servitor of the Lord." Thus Pṛthu Mahārāja can also be called Prabhupāda, or, as described herein, *prabhu.* Another question may be raised in this connection. Since Pṛthu Mahārāja was a power incarnation of the Supreme Personality of Godhead, *śaktyāveśa-avatāra,* why did he have to execute the regulative principles in order to become a *prabhu*? Because he appeared on this earth as an ideal king and because it is the duty of the king to instruct the citizens in the execution of devotional service, he followed all the regulative principles of devotional service in order to teach others. Similarly, Caitanya Mahāprabhu, although Kṛṣṇa Himself, taught us how to approach Kṛṣṇa as a devotee. It is said: *āpani ācari' bhakti śikhāinu savāre.* Lord Caitanya Mahāprabhu instructed others in the process of devotional service by setting the example Himself through His own personal actions. Similarly, Pṛthu Mahārāja, although a *śaktyāveśa-avatāra* incarnation, still behaved exactly as a devotee in order to achieve the position of *prabhu.* Furthermore, *svarūpasthaḥ* means complete liberation. As it is said, *hitvānyathā rūpaṁ svarūpena avasthitiḥ:* when a living entity abandons the activities of *māyā* and attains the position from which he can execute devotional service, his state is called *svarūpasthaḥ,* or complete liberation.

TEXT 19

अर्चिर्नाम महाराज्ञी तत्पत्न्यनुगता वनम् ।
सुकुमार्यतदर्हा च यत्पद्भ्यां स्पर्शनं भुवः ॥१९॥

arcir nāma mahā-rājñī
tat-patny anugatā vanam
sukumāry atad-arhā ca
yat-padbhyāṁ sparśanaṁ bhuvaḥ

arciḥ nāma—of the name Arci; *mahā-rājñī*—the Queen; *tat-patnī*—the wife of Mahārāja Pṛthu; *anugatā*—who followed her husband; *vanam*—in the forest; *sukumārī*—very delicate body; *a-tat-arhā*—who did not deserve; *ca*—also; *yat-padbhyām*—by the touch of whose feet; *sparśanam*—touching; *bhuvaḥ*—on the earth.

TRANSLATION

The Queen, the wife of Pṛthu Mahārāja, whose name was Arci, followed her husband into the forest. Since she was a queen, her body was very delicate. Although she did not deserve to live in the forest, still she voluntarily touched her lotus feet to the ground.

PURPORT

Because Pṛthu Mahārāja's wife was the Queen and also a daughter of a king, she never experienced walking on the ground because queens used to never come out of the palace. They certainly never went to the forests and tolerated all the difficulties of living in the wilderness. In Vedic civilization there are hundreds of similar examples of such renunciation on the part of queens and dedication to the husband. The goddess of fortune, mother Sītā, followed her husband Rāmacandra when He went to the forest. Lord Rāmacandra went to the forest in compliance to the order of His father Mahārāja Daśaratha, but mother Sītā was not so ordered. Nonetheless, she voluntarily accepted the path of her husband. Similarly, Gāndhārī, the wife of King Dhṛtarāṣṭra, also followed her husband into the forest. Being the wives of great personalities like Pṛthu, Lord Rāmacandra and Dhṛtarāṣṭra, these were ideal, chaste women. Such queens also instructed the general people by showing them how to become a chaste wife and follow the husband in every stage of life. When the husband is king, she sits beside him as the queen, and when he goes to the forest, she also follows, despite having to tolerate all kinds of difficulties in living in the forest. Therefore it is said here *(a-tad-arhā)* that although she did not want to touch her feet to the ground, she nonetheless accepted all difficulties when she went to the forest with her husband.

TEXT 20

अतीव भर्तुर्व्रतधर्मनिष्ठया
शुश्रूषया चार्षदेहयात्रया ।
नाविन्दतार्तिं परिकर्शितापि सा
प्रेयस्करस्पर्शनमाननिर्वृतिः ॥२०॥

atīva bhartur vrata-dharma-niṣṭhayā
śuśrūṣayā cārṣa-deha-yātrayā
nāvindatārtiṁ parikarśitāpi sā
preyaskara-sparśana-māna-nirvṛtiḥ

atīva—very much; *bhartuḥ*—of the husband; *vrata-dharma*—vow to serve him; *niṣṭhayā*—by determination; *śuśrūṣayā*—by serving; *ca*—also; *ārṣa*—like the great saintly sages; *deha*—body; *yātrayā*—living condition; *na*—did not; *avindata*—perceive; *ārtim*—any difficulty; *parikarśitā api*—although transformed to become lean and thin; *sā*—she; *preyaskara*—very pleasing; *sparśana*—touching; *māna*—engaged; *nirvṛtiḥ*—pleasure.

TRANSLATION

Although she was not accustomed to such difficulties, Queen Arci followed her husband in the regulative principles of living in the forest like great sages. She lay down on the ground and ate only fruits, flowers and leaves, and because she was not fit for these activities, she became frail and thin. Yet because of the pleasure she derived in serving her husband, she did not feel any difficulties.

PURPORT

The words *bhartur vrata-dharma-niṣṭhayā* indicate that a woman's duty or religious principle is to serve her husband in all conditions. In Vedic civilization a man is taught from the beginning of his life to become a *brahmacārī,* then an ideal *gṛhastha,* then *vānaprastha,* then *sannyāsī,* and the wife is taught just to follow the husband strictly in all conditions of life. After the period of *brahmacarya,* a man accepts a householder's life, and the woman is also taught by her parents to be a chaste wife. Thus when a girl and boy are united, both are trained for a life dedicated to a higher purpose. The boy is trained to execute his duty in accordance with the higher purpose of life, and the girl is trained to follow him. The chaste wife's duty is to keep her husband pleased in householder life in all respects, and when the husband retires from family life, she is to go to the forest and adopt the life of *vānaprastha,* or *vana-vāsī.* At that time the wife is to follow her husband and take care of him, just as she took care of him in householder life. But when the husband takes the renounced order of life, namely *sannyāsa,* the wife is to return home and become a saintly woman, setting an example for her children and daughters-in-law and showing them how to live a life of austerity.

When Caitanya Mahāprabhu took *sannyāsa,* His wife, Viṣṇupriyā-devī, although only sixteen years old, also took the vow of austerity due to her husband's leaving home. She chanted her beads, and after finishing one round, she collected one grain of rice. In this way, as many rounds as she chanted, she would receive the same number of rice grains and then cook them and so take *prasāda.* This is called austerity. Even today in India, widows, or women whose husbands have taken *sannyāsa,* follow the principles of austerity, even though they live with their children. Pṛthu Mahārāja's wife, Arci, was steadily determined to execute the duty of a wife, and while her husband was in the forest, she followed him in eating only fruits and leaves and lying down on the ground. Since a woman's body is considerably more delicate than a man's, Queen Arci became very frail and thin. *Parikarśitā.* When one engages in austerities, his body generally becomes lean and thin. Becoming fat is not a very good qualification in spiritual life because a person who is engaged in spiritual life must reduce the comforts of the body—namely eating, sleeping and mating—to a minimum. Although Queen Arci became very thin from living in the forest according to regulative principles, she was not unhappy because she was enjoying the honor of serving her great husband.

TEXT 21

देहं विपन्नाखिलचेतनादिकं
पत्युः पृथिव्या दयितस्य चात्मनः ।
आलक्ष्य किञ्चिच्च विलप्य सा सती
चितामथारोपयदद्रिसानुनि ॥२१॥

deham vipannākhila-cetanādikam
patyuḥ pṛthivyā dayitasya cātmanaḥ
ālakṣya kiñcic ca vilapya sā satī
citām athāropayad adrisānuni

deham—body; *vipanna*—completely failing; *akhila*—all; *cetana*—feeling; *ādikam*—symptoms; *patyuḥ*—of her husband; *pṛthivyāḥ*—the world; *dayitasya*—of the merciful; *ca ātmanaḥ*—also of herself; *ālakṣya*—by seeing; *kiñcit*—very little; *ca*—and; *vilapya*—lamenting; *sā*—she; *satī*—the chaste; *citām*—unto the fire; *atha*—now; *āropayat*—placed; *adri*—hill; *sānuni*—on the top.

TRANSLATION

When Queen Arci saw that her husband, who had been so merciful to her and the earth, no longer showed symptoms of life, she lamented for a little while and then built a fiery pyre on top of a hill and placed the body of her husband on it.

PURPORT

After seeing all the life symptoms in her husband stop, the Queen lamented for a while. The word *kiñcit* means "for a little while." The Queen was completely aware that her husband was not dead, although the symptoms of life—action, intelligence and sense perception—had ceased. As stated in *Bhagavad-gītā:*

dehino 'smin yathā dehe
kaumāram yauvanam jarā
tathā dehāntara-prāptir
dhīras tatra na muhyati

"As the embodied soul continually passes, in this body, from boyhood to youth to old age, the soul similarly passes into another body at death. The self-realized soul is not bewildered by such a change." (Bg. 2.13)

When a living entity transfers from one body to another, a process generally known as death, a sane man does not lament, for he knows that the living entity is not dead but is simply transferred from one body to another. The Queen should have been afraid of being alone in the forest with the body of her husband, but since she was a great wife of a great personality, she lamented for a while but immediately understood that she had many duties to perform. Thus instead of wasting her time in lamentation, she immediately prepared a fiery pyre on top of a hill and then placed the body of her husband on it to be burned.

Mahārāja Pṛthu is described here as *dayita,* for he was not only the king of the earth, but he treated the earth as his protected child. Similarly, he protected his wife also. It was the duty of the king to give protection to everyone, especially to the earth or land which he ruled, as well as the citizens and his family members. Since Pṛthu Mahārāja was a perfect king, he gave protection to everyone, and therefore he is described here as *dayita.*

TEXT 22

विधाय कृत्यं ह्रदिनीजलाप्लुता
दत्त्वोदकं भर्तुरुदारकर्मणः ।
नत्वा दिविस्थांस्त्रिदशांस्त्रिः परीत्य
विवेश वह्निं ध्यायती भर्तृपादौ ॥२२॥

vidhāya kṛtyaṁ hradinī-jalāplutā
dattvodakaṁ bhartur udāra-karmaṇaḥ
natvā divi-sthāṁs tri-daśāṁs triḥ parītya
viveśa vahniṁ dhyāyatī bhartṛ-pādau

vidhāya—executing; *kṛtyam*—the regulative function; *hradinī*—in the water of the river; *jala-āplutā*—taking bath completely; *dattvā udakam*—offering oblations of water; *bhartuḥ*—of her husband; *udāra-karmaṇaḥ*—who was so liberal; *natvā*—offering obeisances; *divi-sthān*—situated in the sky; *tri-daśān*—the thirty million demigods; *triḥ*—three times; *parītya*—circumambulating; *viveśa*—entered; *vahnim*—the fire; *dhyāyatī*—while thinking of; *bhartṛ*—of her husband; *pādau*—the two lotus feet.

TRANSLATION

After this, the Queen executed the necessary funerary functions and offered oblations of water. After bathing in the river, she offered obeisances to various demigods situated in the sky in the different planetary systems. She then circumambulated the fire and, while thinking of the lotus feet of her husband, entered its flames.

PURPORT

The entrance of a chaste wife into the flames of the pyre of her dead husband is known as *saha-gamana.* This means that it is customary for the wife to die with her husband. This system of *saha-gamana* has been practiced in Vedic civilization from time immemorial. Even after the British period in India this practice was rigidly observed, but soon it degraded to the point that even when the wife was not strong enough to enter the fire of her dead husband the relatives would force her to enter. Thus this practice had to be stopped, but even today there are still some solitary cases where a wife will voluntarily enter the fire and die with her husband. Even after 1940 we personally knew of a chaste wife who died in this way.

TEXT 23

विलोक्यानुगतां साध्वीं पृथुं वीरवरं पतिम् ।
तुष्टुवुर्वरदा देवैर्देवपत्न्यः सहस्रशः ॥२३॥

vilokyānugatāṁ sādhvīṁ
pṛthuṁ vīra-varaṁ patim
tuṣṭuvur vara-dā devair
deva-patnyaḥ sahasraśaḥ

vilokya—by observing; *anugatām*—dying after the husband; *sādhvīm*—the chaste woman; *pṛthum*—of King Pṛthu; *vīra-varam*—the great warrior; *patim*—husband; *tuṣṭuvuḥ*—offered prayers; *vara-dāḥ*—able to give benediction; *devaiḥ*—by the demigods; *deva-patnyaḥ*—the wives of the demigods; *sahasraśaḥ*—in thousands.

TRANSLATION

After observing this brave act performed by the chaste wife Arci, the wife of the great King Pṛthu, many thousands of the wives of the demigods, along with their husbands, offered prayers to the Queen, for they were very much satisfied.

TEXT 24

कुर्वत्यः कुसुमासारं तस्मिन्मन्दरसानुनि ।
नदत्स्वमरतूर्येषु गृणन्ति स्म परस्परम् ॥२४॥

kurvatyaḥ kusumāsāraṁ
tasmin mandara-sānuni
nadatsv amara-tūryeṣu
gṛṇanti sma parasparam

kurvatyaḥ—just showering; *kusuma-āsāram*—showers of flowers; *tasmin*—in that; *mandara*—of the Mandara hill; *sānuni*—on the top; *nadatsu*—vibrating; *amara-tūryeṣu*—beating of the drums of the demigods; *gṛṇanti sma*—they were talking; *parasparam*—amongst themselves as follows.

TRANSLATION

At that time the demigods were situated on the top of Mandara Hill, and all their wives began to shower flowers on the funeral pyre and began to talk amongst themselves as follows.

TEXT 25

देव्य ऊचुः
अहो इयं वधूर्धन्या या चैवं भूभुजां पतिम् ।
सर्वात्मना पतिं भेजे यज्ञेशं श्रीर्वधूरिव ॥२५॥

devya ūcuḥ
aho iyaṁ vadhūr dhanyā
yā caivaṁ bhū-bhujāṁ patim
sarvātmanā patiṁ bheje
yajñeśaṁ śrīr vadhūr iva

devyaḥ ūcuḥ—the wives of the demigods said; *aho*—alas; *iyam*—this; *vadhūḥ*—the wife; *dhanyā*—most glorious; *yā*—who; *ca*—also; *evam*—as; *bhū*—of the world; *bhujām*—of all the kings; *patim*—the king; *sarvātmanā*—with full understanding; *patim*—unto the husband; *bheje*—worshiped; *yajñeśam*—unto Lord Viṣṇu; *śrīḥ*—the goddess of fortune; *vadhūḥ*—wife; *iva*—like.

TRANSLATION

The wives of the demigods said: All glories to Queen Arci! We can see that this Queen of the great King Pṛthu, the Emperor of all the kings of the world, has served her husband with mind, speech and body exactly as the goddess of fortune serves the Supreme Personality of Godhead, Yajñeśa or Viṣṇu.

PURPORT

In this verse the words *yajñeśaṁ śrīr vadhūr iva* indicate that Queen Arci served her husband just as the goddess of fortune serves the Supreme Personality of Godhead Viṣṇu. We can observe that even in the history of this world, when Lord Kṛṣṇa, the Supreme Viṣṇu, was ruling over Dvārakā, Queen Rukmiṇī, who was the chief of all Kṛṣṇa's queens, used to serve Lord Kṛṣṇa personally in spite of having many hundreds of maidservants to assist her. Similarly, the goddess of fortune in the Vaikuṇṭha planets also serves Nārāyaṇa personally, although there are many thousands of devotees prepared to serve the Lord. This practice is also followed by the wives of the demigods, and in days past the wives of men also followed this same principle. In Vedic civilization the husband and wife were not separated by such man-made laws as divorce. We should understand the necessity for maintaining family life in human society and should thus abolish this artificial law known as divorce. The husband and wife should live in Kṛṣṇa consciousness and follow the footsteps of Lakṣmī-Nārāyaṇa, or Kṛṣṇa-Rukmiṇī. In this way peace and harmony can be possible within this world.

TEXT 26

सैषा नूनं व्रजत्यूर्ध्वमनु वैन्यं पतिं सती ।
पश्यतास्मानतीत्यार्चिर्दुर्विभाव्येन कर्मणा ॥२६॥

saiṣā nūnaṁ vrajaty ūrdhvam
anu vainyaṁ patiṁ satī
paśyatāsmān atītyārcir
durvibhāvyena karmaṇā

sā—she; *eṣā*—this; *nūnam*—certainly; *vrajati*—going; *ūrdhvam*—upwards; *anu*—following; *vainyam*—the son of Vena; *patim*—husband; *satī*—chaste; *paśyata*—just see; *asmān*—us; *atītya*—overpassing; *arciḥ*—of the name Arci; *durvibhāvyena*—by inconceivable; *karmaṇā*—activities.

TRANSLATION

The wives of the demigods continued: Just see how this chaste lady, Arci, by dint of her inconceivable pious activities, is still following her husband upwards, as far as we can see.

PURPORT

Both Pṛthu Mahārāja's airplane and the airplane carrying Queen Arci were passing out of the vision of the ladies of the higher planetary systems. These ladies were simply astonished to see how Pṛthu Mahārāja and his wife achieved such an exalted position. Although they were the wives of the denizens of the higher planetary system and Pṛthu Mahārāja was an inhabitant of an inferior planetary system (the Earth), the King, along with his wife, passed beyond the realms of the demigods and went upward to Vaikuṇṭhaloka. The word *ūrdhvam* (upwards) is significant here, for the ladies speaking were from the higher planetary systems, which include the moon, sun and Venus up to Brahmaloka, or the highest planet. Beyond Brahmaloka is the spiritual sky, and in that spiritual sky there are innumerable Vaikuṇṭhalokas. Thus the word *ūrdhvam* indicates that the Vaikuṇṭha planets are beyond or above these material planets, and it was to these Vaikuṇṭha planets that Pṛthu Mahārāja and his wife were going. This also indicates that when Pṛthu Mahārāja and his wife, Arci, abandoned their material bodies in the material fire, they immediately developed their spiritual bodies and entered into spiritual airplanes which could penetrate the material elements and reach the spiritual sky. Since they were carried by two separate airplanes, it may be concluded that even after being burnt in the funeral pyre they remained separate individual persons. In other words, they never lost their identity or became void, as imagined by the impersonalists.

The ladies in the higher planetary systems were capable of seeing both downwards and upwards. When they looked down they could see that the body of Pṛthu Mahārāja was being burnt and that his wife, Arci, was entering into the fire, and when they looked upwards they could see how they were being carried in two airplanes to the Vaikuṇṭhalokas. All of this is possible simply by *durvibhāvyena karmaṇā*, inconceivable activity. Pṛthu Mahārāja was a pure devotee, and his wife, Queen Arci, simply followed her husband. Thus they can both be considered pure devotees, and thus they are capable of performing inconceivable activities. Such activities are not possible for ordinary men. Indeed, ordinary men cannot even take to the devotional service of the Lord, nor can ordinary women maintain such vows of chastity and follow their husbands in all respects. A woman does not need to attain high qualifications, but if she simply follows in the footsteps of her husband, who must be a devotee, then both husband and wife attain liberation and are promoted to the Vaikuṇṭhalokas. This is evinced by the inconceivable activities of Mahārāja Pṛthu and his wife.

TEXT 27

तेषां दुरापं किं त्वन्यन्मर्त्यानां भगवत्पदम् ।
भुवि लोलायुषो ये वै नैष्कर्म्यं साधयन्त्युत ॥२७॥

teṣāṁ durāpaṁ kiṁ tv anyan
martyānāṁ bhagavat-padam
bhuvi lolāyuṣo ye vai
naiṣkarmyaṁ sādhayanty uta

teṣām—of them; *durāpam*—difficult to obtain; *kim*—what; *tu*—but; *anyat*—anything else; *martyānām*—of the human beings; *bhagavat-padam*—the kingdom of God; *bhuvi*—in the world; *lola*—flickering; *āyuṣaḥ*—span of life; *ye*—those; *vai*—certainly; *naiṣkarmyam*—the path of liberation; *sādhayanti*—execute; *uta*—exactly.

TRANSLATION

In this material world, every human being has a short span of life, but those who are engaged in devotional service go back home, back to Godhead, for they are actually on the path of liberation. For such persons, there is nothing which is not available.

PURPORT

In *Bhagavad-gītā* Lord Kṛṣṇa says: *anityam asukhaṁ lokam imaṁ prāpya bhajasva mām* (Bg. 9.33). The Lord here declares that this material world is full of miseries (*asukham*) and at the same time is very flickering (*anityam*). Therefore one's only duty is to engage himself in devotional service. This is the best end to which human life can be put. Those devotees who are constantly engaged in the service of the lotus feet of the Lord achieve not only all material benefits but also all spiritual benefits, for at the end of life they go back home, back to Godhead. Their destination is described in this verse as *bhagavat-padam*. The word *padam* means "abode," and *bhagavat* means "the Supreme Personality of Godhead." Thus the destination of the devotees is the abode of the Supreme Personality of Godhead.

In this verse the word *naiṣkarmyam,* which means transcendental knowledge, is also significant. Unless one comes to the platform of transcendental knowledge and offers devotional service to the Lord, he is not perfect. Generally the processes of *jñāna, yoga* and *karma* are executed life after life before one gets a chance to render pure devotional service to the Lord. This chance is given by the grace of a pure devotee, and it is in this way only that one can actually attain liberation. In the context of this narration, the wives of the demigods repented because although they had the opportunity of a birth in a higher planetary system, a lifetime spanning many millions of years and all material comforts, they were not as fortunate as Pṛthu Mahārāja and his wife, who were actually surpassing them. In other words, Pṛthu Mahārāja and his wife scorned promotion to the higher planetary systems and even to Brahmaloka because the position which they were attaining was incomparable. In *Bhagavad-gītā* the Lord affirms, *ābrahma-bhuvanāl lokāḥ punar āvartino 'rjuna:* "From the highest planet in the material world to the lowest, all are places of misery wherein repeated birth and death take place." (Bg. 8.16) In other words, even if one goes to the highest planet, Brahmaloka, he has to return to the miseries of birth and death. In the Ninth Chapter of *Bhagavad-gītā,* Lord Kṛṣṇa also asserts:

te taṁ bhuktvā svarga-lokaṁ viśālaṁ
kṣīṇe puṇye martya-lokaṁ viśanti

"When they have thus enjoyed heavenly sense pleasure, they return to this mortal planet again." (Bg. 9.21) Thus after exhausting the results of pious activities, one has to come again to the lower planetary systems and begin a new chapter of pious activities. It is therefore said in *Śrīmad-Bhāgavatam, naiṣkarmyam apy acyuta-bhāva-varjitam:* "The path of liberation is not at all secure unless one attains the devotional service of the Lord." (*Bhāg.* 1.5.12) Even if one is promoted to the impersonal *brahmajyoti,* he runs every chance of falling down into this material world. If it is possible to fall down from the *brahmajyoti,* which is beyond the higher planetary systems in this material world, then what can be said of the ordinary *yogīs* and *karmīs* who can only be elevated to the higher material planets? Thus the wives of the denizens of the higher planetary systems did not very much appreciate the results of *karma, jñāna* and *yoga.*

TEXT 28

**स वञ्चितो बतात्मध्रुक् कृच्छ्रेण महता भुवि ।
लब्ध्वापवर्ग्यं मानुष्यं विषयेषु विषज्जते ॥२८॥**

*sa vañcito batātma-dhruk
kṛcchreṇa mahatā bhuvi
labdhvāpavargyaṁ mānuṣyaṁ
viṣayeṣu viṣajjate*

saḥ—he; *vañcitaḥ*—cheated; *bata*—certainly; *ātma-dhruk*—envious of himself; *kṛcchreṇa*—with great difficulty; *mahatā*—by great activities; *bhuvi*—in this world; *labdhvā*—by achieving; *āpavargyam*—the path of liberation; *mānuṣyam*—in the human form of life; *viṣayeṣu*—in the matter of sense gratification; *viṣajjate*—becomes engaged.

TRANSLATION

Any person who engages himself within this material world in performing activities that necessitate great struggle, and who, after obtaining a human form of life—which is a chance to attain liberation from miseries—undertakes the difficult tasks of fruitive activities, must be considered to be cheated and envious of his own self.

PURPORT

In this material world people are engaged in different activities simply to achieve a little success in sense gratification. The *karmīs* are engaged in performing very difficult activities, and thus they open gigantic factories, build huge cities, make big scientific discoveries, etc. In other words, they are engaged in performing very costly sacrifices in order to be promoted to the higher planetary systems. Similarly, *yogīs* are engaged in achieving a similar goal by accepting the tedious practices of mystic *yoga. Jñānīs* are engaged in philosophical speculation in order to gain release from the clutches of material nature. In these ways everyone is engaged in performing very difficult tasks simply for the gratification of the senses. All of these are considered to be engaged in sense gratificatory activities (or *viṣaya*) because they all demand some facility for material existence. Actually the results of such activities are temporary, as Kṛṣṇa Himself proclaims in *Bhagavad-gītā: antavat tu phalaṁ teṣām:* "The fruits [of those who worship the demigods] are limited and temporary." (Bg. 7.23) Thus the fruits of the activities of the *yogīs, karmīs* and *jñānīs* are ephemeral. Moreover, Kṛṣṇa says, *tad bhavaty alpa-medhasām:* "They are simply meant for men of small intelligence." (Bg. 7.23) The word *viṣaya* denotes sense gratification. The *karmīs* flatly state that they want sense gratification. The *yogīs* also want sense gratification, but they want it to a higher degree. It is their desire to show some miraculous results through the practice of *yoga*. Thus they strive very hard to achieve success in becoming smaller than the smallest or greater than the greatest, or in creating a planet like the earth, or, as scientists, by inventing so many wonderful machines. Similarly, the *jñānīs* are also engaged in sense gratification, for they are simply interested in becoming one with the Supreme. Thus the aim of all these activities is sense gratification to a higher or a lower degree. The *bhaktas*, however, are not interested in sense gratificatory practices; they are simply satisfied to get an opportunity to serve the Lord. Although they are satisfied in any condition, there is nothing they cannot obtain because they are purely engaged in the service of the Lord.

The wives of the demigods condemn the performers of sense gratificatory activities as *vañcita,* cheated. Those so engaged are actually killing themselves (*ātma-hā*). As stated in *Śrīmad-Bhāgavatam:*

nṛ-deham ādyaṁ su-labhaṁ su-durlabhaṁ
plavaṁ su-kalpaṁ guru-karṇa-dhāram
mayānukūlena nabhasvateritaṁ
pumān bhavābdhiṁ na taret sa ātma-hā
(*Bhāg.* 11.20.17)

When one wants to cross a large ocean, he requires a strong boat. It is said that this human form of life is a good boat by which one can cross the ocean of nescience. In the human form of life one can obtain the guidance of a good navigator, the spiritual master. He also gets a favorable wind by the mercy of Kṛṣṇa, and that wind is the instructions of Kṛṣṇa. The human body is the boat, the instructions of Lord Kṛṣṇa are the favorable winds, and the spiritual master is the navigator. The spiritual master knows well how to adjust the sails to catch the winds favorably and steer the boat to its destination. If, however, one does not take advantage of this opportunity, he wastes the human form of life. Wasting time and life in this way is the same as committing suicide.

The word *labdhvāpavargyam* is significant in this verse because, according to Jīva Gosvāmī, *āpavargyam,* or the path of liberation, does not refer to merging into the impersonal Brahman but to *sālokyādi-siddhi* which means attaining the very planet where the Supreme Personality of Godhead resides. There are five kinds of liberation, and one is called *sāyujya-mukti,* or merging into the existence of the Supreme or the impersonal Brahman effulgence. However, since there is a chance of one's falling down again into the material sky from the Brahman effulgence, Śrīla Jīva Gosvāmī advises that in this human form of life one's only aim should be to go back home, back to Godhead. The words *sa vañcitaḥ* indicate that once a person has obtained the human form of life, he is actually cheated if he does not make preparations to go back home, back to Godhead. The position of all nondevotees who are not interested in going back to Godhead is very much lamentable, for the human form of life is meant for executing devotional service and nothing else.

TEXT 29

मैत्रेय उवाच

स्तुवतीष्वमरस्त्रीषु पतिलोकं गता वधूः ।
यं वा आत्मविदां धुर्यो वैन्यः प्रापाच्युताश्रयः ॥२९॥

maitreya uvāca
stuvatīṣv amara-strīṣu
pati-lokaṁ gatā vadhūḥ
yaṁ vā ātma-vidāṁ dhuryo
vainyaḥ prāpācyutāśrayaḥ

maitreyaḥ uvāca—the great sage Maitreya continued to speak; *stuvatīṣu*—while glorifying; *amara-strīṣu*—by the wives of the denizens of heaven; *pati-lokam*—the planet where the husband had gone; *gatā*—reaching; *vadhūḥ*—the wife; *yam*—where; *vā*—or; *ātma-vidām*—of the self-realized souls; *dhuryaḥ*—the topmost; *vainyaḥ*—the son of King Vena (Pṛthu Mahārāja); *prāpa*—obtained; *acyuta-āśrayaḥ*—under the protection of the Supreme Personality of Godhead.

TRANSLATION

The great sage Maitreya continued speaking: My dear Vidura, when the wives of the denizens of heaven were thus talking amongst themselves, Queen Arci reached the planet which her husband, Mahārāja Pṛthu, the topmost self-realized soul, had attained.

PURPORT

According to Vedic scriptures, a woman who dies with her husband, or enters into the fire in which her husband is burning, also enters the same planet her husband attains. In this material world there is a planet known as Patiloka, just as there is a planet known as Pitṛloka. But in this verse the word *pati-loka* does not refer to any planet within this material universe, for Pṛthu Mahārāja, being topmost amongst self-realized souls, certainly returned home, back to Godhead, and attained one of the Vaikuṇṭha planets. Queen Arci also entered *patiloka,* but this planet is not in the material universe, for she actually entered the planet which her husband attained. In the material world also, when a woman dies with her husband, she again unites with him in the next birth. Similarly, Mahārāja Pṛthu and Queen Arci united in the Vaikuṇṭha planets. In the Vaikuṇṭha planets there are husbands and wives, but there is no question of their giving birth to children nor having sex life. In the Vaikuṇṭha planets both husbands and wives are extraordinarily beautiful, and they are attracted to one another, but they do not enjoy sex life. Indeed, they consider sex not to be very relishable because both husband and wife are always absorbed in Kṛṣṇa consciousness and in glorifying and chanting the glories of the Lord.

According to Bhaktivinoda Ṭhākura also, a husband and wife can turn the home into a place as good as Vaikuṇṭha, even while in this material world. Being absorbed in Kṛṣṇa consciousness, even in this world husband and wife can live in Vaikuṇṭha simply by installing the Deity of the Lord within the home and serving the Deity according to the directions of the *śāstras.* In this way, they will never feel the sex urge. That is the test of advancement in devotional service. One who is advanced in devotional service is never attracted by sex life, and as soon as one becomes detached from sex life and proportionately attached to the service of the Lord, he actually experiences living in the Vaikuṇṭha planets. In the ultimate issue, there is actually no material world, but when one forgets the service of the Lord and engages himself in the service of his senses, he is said to be living in the material world.

TEXT 30

इत्थंभूतानुभावोऽसौ पृथुः स भगवत्तमः ।
कीर्तितं तस्य चरितमुद्दामचरितस्य ते ॥३०॥

itthambhūtānubhāvo 'sau
pṛthuḥ sa bhagavattamaḥ

kīrtitaṁ tasya caritam
uddāma-caritasya te

itthambhūta—thus; *anubhāvaḥ*—very great, powerful; *asau*—that; *pṛthuḥ*—King Pṛthu; *saḥ*—he; *bhagavattamaḥ*—the best among the lords; *kīrtitam*—described; *tasya*—his; *caritam*—character; *uddāma*—very great; *caritasya*—one who possesses such qualities; *te*—to you.

TRANSLATION

Maitreya continued: The greatest of all devotees, Mahārāja Pṛthu, was very powerful, and his character was liberal, magnificent and magnanimous. Thus I have described him to you as far as possible.

PURPORT

In this verse the word *bhagavattamaḥ* is very significant, for the word *bhagavat* is used especially to refer to the Supreme Personality of Godhead, as the word *bhagavān* (the Supreme Personality of Godhead) is derived from the word *bhagavat.* Sometimes, however, we see that the word *bhagavān* is used for great personalities like Lord Brahmā, Lord Śiva and Nārada Muni. This is the case with Pṛthu Mahārāja, who is described here as the best of the *bhagavāns,* or the best of the lords. A person can be so addressed only if he is a great personality who exhibits extraordinary and uncommon features, or who attains the greatest goal after his disappearance, or who knows the difference between knowledge and ignorance. In other words, the word *bhagavān* should not be used for ordinary persons.

TEXT 31

य इदं सुमहत्पुण्यं श्रद्धयावहितः पठेत् ।
श्रावयेच्छृणुयाद्वापि स पृथोः पदवीमियात् ॥३१॥

ya idaṁ su-mahat puṇyaṁ
śraddhayāvahitaḥ paṭhet
śrāvayec chṛṇuyād vāpi
sa pṛthoḥ padavīm iyāt

yaḥ—anyone; *idam*—this; *su-mahat*—very great; *puṇyam*—pious; *śraddhayā*—with great faith; *avahitaḥ*—with great attention; *paṭhet*—reads; *śrāvayet*—explains; *śṛṇuyāt*—hears; *vā*—or; *api*—certainly; *saḥ*—that person; *pṛthoḥ*—of King Pṛthu; *padavīm*—situation; *iyāt*—attains.

TRANSLATION

Any person who describes the great characteristics of King Pṛthu with faith and determination—whether he reads or hears of them himself or helps others to hear of them—is certain to attain the very planet which Mahārāja Pṛthu attained. In other words, such a person also returns home to the Vaikuṇṭha planets, back to Godhead.

PURPORT

In the execution of devotional service, *śravaṇaṁ kīrtanaṁ viṣṇoḥ* is especially stressed. This means that *bhakti,* or devotional service, begins by hearing and chanting about Viṣṇu. When we speak of Viṣṇu, we also refer to that which relates to Viṣṇu. In the *Śiva Purāṇa,* Lord Śiva recommends Viṣṇu worship to be the topmost worship, and better than Viṣṇu worship is worship of the Vaiṣṇava or anything that is related to Viṣṇu. The fact is explained herein that hearing and chanting about a Vaiṣṇava is as good as hearing and chanting about Viṣṇu, for Maitreya has explained that anyone who hears about Pṛthu Mahārāja with attention also attains the planet which Mahārāja Pṛthu attained. There is no duality between Viṣṇu and the Vaiṣṇava, and this is called *advaya-jñāna.* A Vaiṣṇava is as important as Viṣṇu, and therefore Śrīla Viśvanātha Cakravartī Ṭhākura wrote in his *Gurv-aṣṭaka:*

sākṣād-dharitvena samasta-śāstrair
uktas tathā bhāvyata eva sadbhiḥ
kintu prabhor yaḥ priya eva tasya
vande guroḥ śrī-caraṇāravindam

"The spiritual master is honored as much as the Supreme Lord because he is the most confidential servitor of the Lord. This is acknowledged in all revealed scriptures and is followed by all authorities. Therefore I offer my respectful obeisances unto the lotus feet of my spiritual master, who is a bona fide representative of Śrī Hari."

The supreme Vaiṣṇava is the spiritual master, and he is nondifferent from the Supreme Personality of Godhead. It is said that sometimes Lord Caitanya Mahāprabhu used to chant the names of the *gopīs.* Some of the Lord's students tried to advise Him to chant the name of Kṛṣṇa instead, but upon hearing this Caitanya Mahāprabhu became very angry with His students. The controversy on this subject reached such a point that after this incident Caitanya Mahāprabhu decided to take *sannyāsa* because He was not taken very seriously in His *gṛhastha-āśrama.* The point is that since Śrī Caitanya Mahāprabhu chanted the names of the *gopīs,* worship of the *gopīs* or the devotees of the Lord is as good as devotional service rendered directly to the Lord. It is also stated by the Lord Himself that devotional service to His devotees is better than service offered directly to Him. Sometimes the *sahajiyā* class of devotees are only interested in Kṛṣṇa's personal pastimes to the exclusion of the activities of the devotees. This type of devotee is not on a very high level; one who sees the devotee and the Lord on the same level has further progressed.

TEXT 32

ब्राह्मणो ब्रह्मवर्चस्वी राजन्यो जगतीपतिः ।
वैश्यः पठन् विट्पतिः स्याच्छूद्रः सत्तमतामियात् ॥३२॥

brāhmaṇo brahma-varcasvī
rājanyo jagatī-patiḥ
vaiśyaḥ paṭhan viṭ-patiḥ syāc
chūdraḥ sattamatām iyāt

brāhmaṇaḥ—the brāhmaṇas; *brahma-varcasvī*—one who has attained the power of spiritual success; *rājanyaḥ*—the royal order; *jagatī-patiḥ*—the king of the world; *vaiśyaḥ*—the mercantile class of men; *paṭhan*—by reading; *viṭ-patiḥ*—becomes master of the animals; *syāt*—becomes; *śūdraḥ*—the laborer class of men; *sattamatām*—the position of a great devotee; *iyāt*—attains.

TRANSLATION

If one hears of the characteristics of Pṛthu Mahārāja and is a brāhmaṇa, he becomes perfectly qualified with brahminical powers; if he is a kṣatriya, he becomes a king of the world; if he is a vaiśya, he becomes a master of other vaiśyas and many animals; and if he is a śūdra, he becomes the topmost devotee.

PURPORT

In *Śrīmad-Bhāgavatam* it is recommended that one should become a devotee regardless of one's condition. Whether one is without desire (*akāma*), or with desire (*sakāma*), or whether one desires liberation (*mokṣa-kāma*), he is advised to worship the Supreme Lord and execute devotional service unto Him. By so doing, one attains all perfection in any field of life. The process of devotional service—especially hearing and chanting—is so powerful that it can bring a person to the perfectional stage. In this verse *brāhmaṇas, kṣatriyas, vaiśyas* and *śūdras* are mentioned, but here it should be understood that that reference is to the *brāhmaṇa* who is born in a brahminical family, the *kṣatriya* who is born in a *kṣatriya* family, the *vaiśya* who is born in a *vaiśya* family and the *śūdra* in a *śūdra* family. But whether one is a *brāhmaṇa, kṣatriya, vaiśya* or *śūdra,* he can attain perfection simply by hearing and chanting.

To take birth in a family of *brāhmaṇas* is not the ultimate finishing touch; one must have the power of a *brāhmaṇa,* which is called *brahma-tejas.* Similarly, taking birth in a royal family is not the all in all; one must possess the power to rule the world. Similarly, taking birth as a *vaiśya* is not all; one must possess hundreds or thousands of animals (specifically cows) and rule over other *vaiśyas* as Nanda Mahārāja did in Vṛndāvana. Nanda Mahārāja was a *vaiśya* who possessed 900,000 cows and ruled over many cowherd men and boys. A person who is born in a *śūdra* family can become greater than a *brāhmaṇa* simply by accepting devotional service and giving aural reception to the pastimes of the Lord and His devotees.

TEXT 33

त्रिः कृत्व इदमाकर्ण्य नरो नार्यथवाऽऽदृता ।
अप्रजः सुप्रजतमो निर्धनो धनवत्तमः ॥३३॥

triḥ kṛtva idam ākarṇya
naro nāry athavādṛtā
aprajaḥ su-prajatamo
nirdhano dhanavattamaḥ

triḥ—thrice; *kṛtvaḥ*—repeating; *idam*—this; *ākarṇya*—hearing; *naraḥ*—man; *nārī*—woman; *athavā*—or; *ādṛtā*—in great respect; *aprajaḥ*—one who has no children; *su-prajatamaḥ*—surrounded by many children; *nirdhanaḥ*—without any money; *dhanavat*—rich; *tamaḥ*—the greatest.

TRANSLATION

It doesn't matter whether one is a man or woman. Anyone who, with great respect, hears this narration of Mahārāja Pṛthu, will become the father of many children if he is without children, and will become the richest of men if he is without money.

PURPORT

Materialistic persons who are very fond of money and great families worship different demigods to attain their desires, especially Goddess Durgā, Lord Śiva and Lord Brahmā. Such materialistic persons are called *śry-aiśvarya-prajepsavaḥ. Śrī* means beauty, *aiśvarya* means riches, *prajā* means children and *īpsavaḥ* means desiring. As described in the Second Canto of *Śrīmad-Bhāgavatam,* one has to worship various demigods for different types of benedictions. However, here it is indicated that simply by hearing of the life and character of Mahārāja Pṛthu, one can have both riches and children in enormous quantities. One simply has to read and understand the history, the life and activities of Pṛthu Mahārāja. It is advised that one read them at least three times. Those who are materially afflicted will so benefit by hearing of the Supreme Lord and His devotees that they need not go to any demigod. The word *su-prajatamaḥ* (surrounded by many children) is very significant in this verse, for one may have many children but may not have any qualified children. Here, however, it is stated *(su-prajatamaḥ)* that all the children thus attained would be qualified in education, wealth, beauty and strength—everything complete.

TEXT 34

अस्पष्टकीर्तिः सुयशा मूर्खो भवति पण्डितः ।
इदं स्वस्त्ययनं पुंसाममङ्गल्यनिवारणम् ॥३४॥

aspaṣṭa-kīrtiḥ su-yaśā
mūrkho bhavati paṇḍitaḥ
idaṁ svasty-ayanaṁ puṁsām
amaṅgalya-nivāraṇam

aspaṣṭa-kīrtiḥ—unmanifested reputation; *su-yaśāḥ*—very famous; *mūrkhaḥ*—illiterate; *bhavati*—becomes; *paṇḍitaḥ*—learned; *idam*—this; *svasti-ayanam*—auspiciousness; *puṁsām*—of the men; *amaṅgalya*—inauspiciousness; *nivāraṇam*—prohibiting.

TRANSLATION

Also, one who hears this narration three times will become very reputable if he is not recognized in society, and he will become a great scholar if he is illiterate. In other words, hearing of the narrations of Pṛthu Mahārāja is so auspicious that it drives away all bad luck.

PURPORT

In the material world, everyone wants some profit, some adoration and some reputation. By associating in different ways with the Supreme Personality of Godhead or His devotee, one can very easily become opulent in every respect. Even if one is not known or recognized by society, he becomes very famous and important if he takes to devotional service and preaching. As far as education is concerned, one can become recognized in society as a great learned scholar simply by hearing *Śrīmad-Bhāgavatam* and *Bhagavad-gītā*, wherein the pastimes of the Lord and His devotees are described. This material world is full of dangers at every step, but a devotee has no fear because devotional service is so auspicious that it automatically counteracts all kinds of bad luck. Since hearing about Pṛthu Mahārāja is one of the items of devotional service *(śravaṇam)*, naturally hearing about him brings all good fortune.

TEXT 35

धन्यं यशस्यमायुष्यं स्वर्ग्यं कलिमलापहम् ।
धर्मार्थकाममोक्षाणां सम्यक्सिद्धिमभीप्सुभिः ।
श्रद्धयैतदनुश्राव्यं चतुर्णां कारणं परम् ॥३५॥

dhanyaṁ yaśasyam āyuṣyaṁ
svargyaṁ kali-malāpaham
dharmārtha-kāma-mokṣāṇāṁ
samyak siddhim abhīpsubhiḥ
śraddhayaitad anuśrāvyaṁ
caturṇāṁ kāraṇaṁ param

dhanyam—the source of riches; *yaśasyam*—the source of reputation; *āyuṣyam*—the source of an increased span of life; *svargyam*—the source of elevation to the heavenly planets; *kali*—of the age of Kali; *mala-apaham*—decreasing the contamination; *dharma*—religion; *artha*—economic development; *kāma*—sense gratification; *mokṣāṇām*—of liberation; *samyak*—completely; *siddhim*—perfection; *abhīpsubhiḥ*—by those desiring; *śraddhayā*—with great respect; *etat*—this narration; *anuśrāvyam*—must one hear; *caturṇām*—of the four; *kāraṇam*—cause; *param*—ultimate.

TRANSLATION

By hearing the narration of Pṛthu Mahārāja, one can become great, increase his duration of life, gain promotion to the heavenly planets and counteract the contaminations of this age of Kali. In addition, one can promote the causes of religion, economic development, sense gratification and liberation. Therefore from all sides it is advisable for a materialistic person who is interested in such things to read and hear the narrations of the life and character of Pṛthu Mahārāja.

PURPORT

By reading and hearing the narrations of the life and character of Pṛthu Mahārāja, one naturally becomes a devotee, and as soon as one becomes a devotee, his material desires automatically become fulfilled. Therefore it is recommended in *Śrīmad-Bhāgavatam: akāmaḥ sarva-kāmo vā mokṣa-kāma udāra-dhīḥ/ tīvreṇa bhakti-yogena yajeta puruṣaṁ param* (*Bhāg.* 2.3.10). It is recommended that if a person wants to return home, back to Godhead, or wants to become a pure devotee *(akāma)*, or wants some material prosperity *(sakāma* or *sarva-kāma)*, or wants to merge into the existence of the Supreme Brahman effulgence *(mokṣa-kāma)*, he is recommended to take to the path of devotional service and hear and chant of Lord Viṣṇu or of His devotee. This is the sum and substance of all Vedic literatures. *Vedaiś ca sarvair aham eva vedyo* (Bg. 15.15). The purpose of Vedic knowledge is to understand Kṛṣṇa and His devotees. Whenever we speak of Kṛṣṇa, we refer to His devotees also, for He is not alone. He is never *nirviśeṣa* or *śūnya,* without variety or zero. Kṛṣṇa is full of variety, and as soon as Kṛṣṇa is present, there cannot be any question of void.

TEXT 36

विजयाभिमुखो राजा श्रुत्वैतदभियाति यान् ।
बलिं तस्मै हरन्त्यग्रे राजानः पृथवे यथा ॥३६॥

vijayābhimukho rājā
śrutvaitad abhiyāti yān
baliṁ tasmai haranty agre
rājānaḥ pṛthave yathā

vijaya-abhimukhaḥ—one who is about to start for victory; *rājā*—king; *śrutvā*—hearing; *etat*—this; *abhiyāti*—starts; *yān*—on the chariot; *balim*—taxes; *tasmai*—unto him; *haranti*—present; *agre*—before; *rājānaḥ*—other kings; *pṛthave*—unto King Pṛthu; *yathā*—as it was done.

TRANSLATION

If a king, who is desirous of attaining victory and ruling power, chants the narration of Pṛthu Mahārāja three times before going forth on his chariot, all subordinate kings will automatically render all kinds of taxes unto him—as they rendered them unto Mahārāja Pṛthu—simply upon his order.

PURPORT

Since a *kṣatriya* king naturally desires to rule the world, he wishes to make all other kings subordinate to him. This was also the position many years ago when Pṛthu Mahārāja was ruling over the earth. At that time he was the only emperor on this planet. Even five thousand years ago, Mahārāja Yudhiṣṭhira and Mahārāja Parīkṣit were the sole emperors of this planet. Sometimes the subordinate kings rebelled, and it was necessary for the emperor to go and chastise them. This process of chanting the narrations of the life and character of Pṛthu Mahārāja is recommended for conquering kings if they want to fulfill their desire to rule the world.

TEXT 37

मुक्तान्यसङ्गो भगवत्यमलां भक्तिमुद्वहन् ।
वैन्यस्य चरितं पुण्यं शृणुयाच्छ्रावयेत्पठेत् ॥३७॥

muktānya-saṅgo bhagavaty
amalāṁ bhaktim udvahan
vainyasya caritaṁ puṇyaṁ
śṛṇuyāc chrāvayet paṭhet

mukta-anya-saṅgaḥ—being freed from all material contamination; *bhagavati*—unto the Supreme Personality of Godhead; *amalām*—unalloyed; *bhaktim*—devotional service; *udvahan*—carrying out; *vainyasya*—of the son of Mahārāja Vena; *caritam*—character; *puṇyam*—pious; *śṛṇuyāt*—must hear; *śrāvayet*—must induce others to hear; *paṭhet*—and go on reading.

TRANSLATION

A pure devotee who is executing the different processes of devotional service may be situated in the transcendental position, being completely absorbed in Kṛṣṇa consciousness, but even he, while discharging devotional service, must hear, read and induce others to hear about the character and life of Pṛthu Mahārāja.

PURPORT

There is a type of neophyte devotee who is very anxious to hear about the pastimes of the Lord, especially the *rāsa-līlā* chapters in *Śrīmad-Bhāgavatam.* Such a devotee should know by this instruction that the pastimes of Pṛthu Mahārāja are nondifferent from the pastimes of the Supreme Personality of Godhead. An ideal king, Pṛthu Mahārāja exhibited all talents in showing how to rule the citizens, how to educate them, how to develop the state economically, how to fight enemies, how to perform great sacrifices (*yajñas*), etc. Thus it is recommended for the *sahajiyā*, or the neophyte devotee, to hear, chant and get others to hear about the activities of Pṛthu Mahārāja, even though one may think himself to be in the transcendental position of advanced devotional service.

TEXT 38

वैचित्रवीर्याभिहितं महन्माहात्म्यसूचकम्
अस्मिन् कृतमतिमर्त्यम् पार्थवीं गतिमाप्नुयात् ॥३८॥

vaicitravīryābhihitaṁ
mahan-māhātmya-sūcakam
asmin kṛtam atimartyaṁ
pārthavīṁ gatim āpnuyāt

vaicitravīrya—O son of Vicitravīrya (Vidura); *abhihitam*—explained; *mahat*—great; *māhātmya*—greatness; *sūcakam*—awakening; *asmin*—in this; *kṛtam*—performed; *atimartyam*—uncommon; *pārthavīm*—in connection with Pṛthu Mahārāja; *gatim*—advancement, destination; *āpnuyāt*—one should achieve.

TRANSLATION

The great sage Maitreya continued: My dear Vidura, I have as far as possible spoken the narrations about Pṛthu Mahārāja, which enrich one's devotional attitude. Whoever takes advantage of these benefits also goes back home, back to Godhead, like Mahārāja Pṛthu.

PURPORT

The word *śrāvayet*, mentioned in a previous verse, indicates that one should not only read for himself, but should also induce others to read and hear. That is called preaching. Caitanya Mahāprabhu recommended this practice: *yāre dekha, tāre kaha 'kṛṣṇa'-upadeśa* (Cc. *Madhya* 7.128). "Whomever you meet, simply talk with him about the instructions given by Kṛṣṇa or tell him of narrations about Kṛṣṇa." Pṛthu Mahārāja's history of devotional service is as potent as narrations about the activities of the Supreme Personality of Godhead. One should not make distinctions between the pastimes of the Lord and the activities of Pṛthu Mahārāja, and whenever it is possible a devotee should attempt to induce others to hear about Pṛthu Mahārāja. One should not only read of his pastimes for one's own benefit but should induce others to read and hear about them also. In this way everyone can be benefited.

TEXT 39

अनुदिनमिदमादरेण शृण्वन्
पृथुचरितं प्रथयन् विमुक्तसङ्गः ।
भगवति भवसिन्धुपोतपादे
स च निपुणां लभते रतिं मनुष्यः ॥३९॥

anudinam idam ādareṇa śṛṇvan
pṛthu-caritaṁ prathayan vimukta-saṅgaḥ
bhagavati bhava-sindhu-pota-pāde
sa ca nipuṇāṁ labhate ratiṁ manuṣyaḥ

anudinam—day after day; *idam*—this; *ādareṇa*—with great respect; *śṛṇvan*—hearing; *pṛthu-caritam*—the narration of Pṛthu Mahārāja; *prathayan*—chanting; *vimukta*—liberated; *saṅgaḥ*—association; *bhagavati*—unto the Supreme Personality of Godhead; *bhava-sindhu*—the ocean of nescience; *pota*—the boat; *pāde*—whose lotus feet; *saḥ*—he; *ca*—also; *nipuṇām*—complete; *labhate*—achieves; *ratim*—attachment; *manuṣyaḥ*—the person.

TRANSLATION

Whoever, with great reverence and adoration, regularly reads, chants and describes the history of Mahārāja Pṛthu's activities will certainly increase unflinching faith and attraction for the lotus feet of the Lord. The Lord's lotus feet are the boat by which one can cross the ocean of nescience.

PURPORT

The word *bhava-sindhu-pota-pāde* is significant in this verse. The lotus feet of the Lord are known as *mahat-padam;* this means that the total source of material existence rests on the lotus feet of the Lord. As stated in *Bhagavad-gītā* (Bg. 10.8), *ahaṁ sarvasya prabhavaḥ:* everything is emanating from Him. This cosmic manifestation, which is compared to an ocean of nescience, is also resting on the lotus feet of the Lord. As such, this great ocean of nescience is minimized by a person who is a pure devotee. One who has taken shelter of the lotus feet of the Lord need not cross over the ocean because he has already crossed it by virtue of his position at the Lord's lotus feet. By hearing and chanting of the glories of the Lord or the Lord's devotee, one can become firmly fixed in the service of the lotus feet of the Lord. This position can also be achieved very easily by narrating the history of the life of Pṛthu Mahārāja regularly every day. The word *vimukta-saṅgaḥ* is also significant in this connection. Because we associate with the three qualities of material nature, our position in this material world is full of dangers, but when we engage in the devotional service of the Lord by the process of *śravaṇam* and *kīrtanam,* we immediately become *vimukta-saṅga,* or liberated.

Thus end the Bhaktivedanta purports of Fourth Canto, Twenty-third Chapter, of the Śrīmad-Bhāgavatam, *entitled* "Mahārāja Pṛthu's Going Back Home."

CHAPTER TWENTY-FOUR

Chanting the Song Sung by Lord Śiva

TEXT 1

मैत्रेय उवाच
विजिताश्वोऽधिराजाऽऽसीत्पृथुपुत्रः पृथुश्रवाः ।
यवीयोभ्योऽददात्काष्ठा भ्रातृभ्यो भ्रातृवत्सलः ॥ १ ॥

maitreya uvāca
vijitāśvo 'dhirājāsīt
pṛthu-putraḥ pṛthu-śravāḥ
yavīyobhyo 'dadāt kāṣṭhā
bhrātṛbhyo bhrātṛ-vatsalaḥ

maitreyaḥ uvāca—Maitreya continued to speak; *vijitāśvaḥ*—of the name Vijitāśva; *adhirājā*—the emperor; *āsīt*—became; *pṛthu-putraḥ*—the son of Mahārāja Pṛthu; *pṛthu-śravāḥ*—of great activities; *yavīyobhyaḥ*—unto the younger brothers; *adadāt*—offered; *kāṣṭhāḥ*—different directions; *bhrātṛbhyaḥ*—unto the brothers; *bhrātṛ-vatsalaḥ*—very affectionate to the brothers.

TRANSLATION

The great sage Maitreya continued: Vijitāśva, the eldest son of Mahārāja Pṛthu, who had a reputation like his father, became emperor and gave his younger brothers different directions of the world to govern, for he was very affectionate toward his brothers.

PURPORT

After describing the life and character of Mahārāja Pṛthu in the previous chapter, the great sage Maitreya began to speak about the sons and grandsons in the genealogical line of the Pṛthu dynasty. After the death of Mahārāja Pṛthu, his eldest son, Vijitāśva, became emperor of the world.

King Vijitāśva was very affectionate toward his younger brothers, and therefore he wanted them to rule different directions of the world. From time immemorial the eldest son generally becomes king after the death of the previous king. When the Pāṇḍavas ruled the earth, Mahārāja Yudhiṣṭhira, the eldest son of King Pāṇḍu, became emperor, and his younger brothers assisted him. Similarly, King Vijitāśva's younger brothers were appointed to govern the different directions of the world.

TEXT 2

हर्यक्षायादिशत्प्राचीं धूम्रकेशाय दक्षिणाम् ।
प्रतीचीं वृकसंज्ञाय तुर्यां द्रविणसे विभुः ॥ २ ॥

haryakṣāyādiśat prācīṁ
dhūmrakeśāya dakṣiṇām
pratīcīṁ vṛka-saṁjñāya
turyāṁ draviṇase vibhuḥ

haryakṣāya—unto Haryakṣa; *adiśat*—delivered; *prācīm*—eastern; *dhūmrakeśāya*—unto Dhūmrakeśa; *dakṣiṇām*—the southern side; *pratīcīm*—the western side; *vṛka-saṁjñāya*—unto his brother whose name was Vṛka; *turyām*—the northern side; *draviṇase*—unto another brother of his named Draviṇa; *vibhuḥ*—the master.

TRANSLATION

Mahārāja Vijitāśva offered the eastern part of the world to his brother Haryakṣa, the southern part to Dhūmrakeśa, the western part to Vṛka, and the northern part to Draviṇa.

TEXT 3

अन्तर्धानगतिं शक्राल्लब्ध्वान्तर्धानसंज्ञितः ।
अपत्यत्रयमाधत्त शिखण्डिन्यां सुसम्मतम् ॥ ३ ॥

antardhāna-gatiṁ śakrāl
labdhvāntardhāna-saṁjñitaḥ
apatya-trayam ādhatta
śikhaṇḍinyāṁ su-sammatam

antardhāna—of disappearance; *gatim*—achievement; *śakrāt*—from King Indra; *labdhvā*—getting; *antardhāna*—of the name; *saṁjñitaḥ*—so nominated; *apatya*—children; *trayam*—three; *ādhatta*—begot; *śikhaṇḍinyām*—in Śikhaṇḍinī, his wife; *su-sammatam*—approved by everyone.

TRANSLATION

Formerly, Mahārāja Vijitāśva pleased the King of heaven, Indra, and from him received the title Antardhāna. His wife's name was Śikhaṇḍinī, and by her he begot three good sons.

PURPORT

Mahārāja Vijitāśva was known as Antardhāna, which means "disappearance." He received this title from Indra, and it refers to the time when Indra stole Mahārāja Pṛthu's horse from the sacrificial arena. Indra was not visible to others when he was stealing the horse, but Mahārāja Pṛthu's son, Vijitāśva, could see him. Yet despite his knowing that Indra was taking away his father's horse, he did not attack him. This indicates that Mahārāja Vijitāśva respected the right persons. Although Indra was stealing the horse from his father, Vijitāśva knew perfectly well that Indra was not an ordinary thief. Since Indra was a great and powerful demigod and servant of the Supreme Personality of Godhead, Vijitāśva purposefully excused him due to sentiment only, even though Indra was acting wrongly. Thus Indra became very pleased with Vijitāśva at that time. The demigods have the great mystic power of being able to appear and disappear according to their will, and since Indra was very pleased with Vijitāśva, he bestowed this mystic power upon him. Thus Vijitāśva became known as Antardhāna.

TEXT 4

पावकः पवमानश्च शुचिरित्यग्नयः पुरा ।
वसिष्ठशापादुत्पन्नाः पुनर्योगगतिं गताः ॥ ४ ॥

pāvakaḥ pavamānaś ca
śucir ity agnayaḥ purā
vasiṣṭha-śāpād utpannāḥ
punar yoga-gatiṁ gatāḥ

pāvakaḥ—of the name Pāvaka; *pavamānaḥ*—of the name Pavamāna; *ca*—also; *śuciḥ*—of the name Śuci; *iti*—thus; *agnayaḥ*—the fire-gods; *purā*—

formerly; *vasiṣṭha*—the great sage Vasiṣṭha; *śāpāt*—by being cursed; *utpannāḥ*—now born as such; *punaḥ*—again; *yoga-gatim*—the destination of mystic *yoga* practice; *gatāḥ*—attained.

TRANSLATION

The three sons of Mahārāja Antardhāna were named Pāvaka, Pavamāna and Śuci. Formerly these three personalities were the demigods of fire, but due to the curse of the great sage Vasiṣṭha, they became the sons of Mahārāja Antardhāna. As such, they were as powerful as the fire-gods, and they attained the destination of mystic yoga power, being again situated as the demigods of fire.

PURPORT

In *Bhagavad-gītā* it is stated (Bg. 6.41-43) that one who falls down from *yoga* practice is elevated to the heavenly planets, and after enjoying the material facilities there he again comes down to the earthly planet and takes birth in a very rich family or a very pious *brāhmaṇa* family. Thus it is to be understood that when demigods fall down, they come to earth as sons of very rich and pious families. In such families, the living entity gets an opportunity to execute Kṛṣṇa consciousness and thereby gain promotion to his desired goal. The sons of Mahārāja Antardhāna had been the demigods in charge of fire, and they again regained their former position and by mystic power returned to the heavenly planets.

TEXT 5

अन्तर्धानो नभस्वत्यां हविर्धानमविन्दत ।
य इन्द्रमश्वहर्तारं विद्वानपि न जघ्निवान् ॥ ५ ॥

antardhāno nabhasvatyāṁ
havirdhānam avindata
ya indram aśva-hartāraṁ
vidvān api na jaghnivān

antardhānaḥ—the king of the name Antardhāna; *nabhasvatyām*—unto his wife Nabhasvatī; *havirdhānam*—of the name Havirdhāna; *avindata*—obtained; *yaḥ*—who; *indram*—King Indra; *aśva-hartāram*—who was stealing the horse of his father; *vidvān api*—although he knew it; *na jaghnivān*—did not kill.

TRANSLATION

Mahārāja Antardhāna had another wife named Nabhasvatī, and by her he was happy to beget another son named Havirdhāna. Since Mahārāja Antardhāna was very liberal, he did not kill Indra while the demigod was stealing his father's horse at the sacrifice.

PURPORT

It is understood from various scriptures and *Purāṇas* that the King of heaven, Indra, was very expert in stealing and kidnapping. He could steal anything without being visible to the proprietor, and he could kidnap anyone's wife without being detected. Once he raped the wife of Gautama Muni by using his disappearing art, and similarly by becoming invisible he stole the horse of Mahārāja Pṛthu. Although in human society such activities are considered abominable, the demigod Indra was not considered to be degraded by them. Although Antardhāna could understand that King Indra was stealing the horse from his father, he did not kill him, for he knew that if one who is very powerful sometimes commits an abominable act, it should be disregarded. In *Bhagavad-gītā* it is clearly stated:

api cet sudurācāro
bhajate mām ananya-bhāk
sādhur eva sa mantavyaḥ
samyag vyavasito hi saḥ

"Even if one commits the most abominable actions, if he is engaged in devotional service, he is to be considered saintly because he is properly situated." (Bg. 9.30)

Thus even if a devotee commits an abominable act, he should be considered a *sādhu,* or a pious man, because of his unflinching devotion to the Lord. The devotees of the Lord never willingly commit any sinful act, but sometimes they commit something abominable due to their previous habits. Such acts should not be taken very seriously, however, because the devotees of the Lord are very powerful, whether they are on the heavenly planets or on this planet. If by chance they commit something abominable, it should not be taken into account but should be overlooked.

TEXT 6

राज्ञां वृत्तिं करादानदण्डशुल्कादिदारुणाम् ।
मन्यमानो दीर्घसत्रव्याजेन विससर्ज ह ॥ ६ ॥

rājñāṁ vṛttiṁ karādāna-
daṇḍa-śulkādi-dāruṇām
manyamāno dīrgha-sattra-
vyājena visasarja ha

rājñām—of the kings; *vṛttim*—source of livelihood; *kara*—taxes; *ādāna*—realization; *daṇḍa*—punishment; *śulka*—fines; *ādi*—etc.; *dāruṇām*—which are very severe; *manyamānaḥ*—thinking like that; *dīrgha*—long; *sattra*—sacrifice; *vyājena*—on the plea; *visasarja*—gave up; *ha*—in the past.

TRANSLATION

Whenever Antardhāna, the supreme royal power, had to exact taxes, punish his citizens, and fine them severely, he was not willing to do so. Consequently he retired from the execution of such duties and engaged himself in the performance of different sacrifices.

PURPORT

It is clear herein that the king sometimes has to perform duties which are not very desirable just because he is the king. Similarly, Arjuna was not at all willing to fight because fighting or killing one's own kinsmen and family members is not at all desirable. Nonetheless the *kṣatriyas* had to perform such undesirable actions as a matter of duty. Mahārāja Antardhāna was not very happy while exacting taxes or punishing the citizens for their criminal activities; therefore, on the plea of performing sacrifices, he retired from the royal majestic power at a very early age.

TEXT 7

तत्रापि हंसं पुरुषं परमात्मानमात्मदृक् ।
यजंस्तल्लोकतामाप कुशलेन समाधिना ॥ ७ ॥

tatrāpi haṁsaṁ puruṣaṁ
paramātmānam ātma-dṛk
yajaṁs tal-lokatām āpa
kuśalena samādhinā

tatrāpi—despite his engagement; *haṁsam*—one who kills the distress of his kinsmen; *puruṣam*—unto the Supreme Person; *paramātmānam*—the most beloved Supersoul; *ātma-dṛk*—one who has seen or acquired self-realization; *yajan*—by worshiping; *tat-lokatām*—achieved the same planet; *āpa*—achieved; *kuśalena*—very easily; *samādhinā*—always keeping himself in ecstasy.

TRANSLATION

Although Mahārāja Antardhāna was engaged in performing sacrifices, because he was a self-realized soul he very intelligently rendered devotional service to the Lord, who eradicates all the fears of His devotees. By thus worshiping the Supreme Lord, Mahārāja Antardhāna, rapt in ecstasy, attained His planet very easily.

PURPORT

Since sacrifices are generally performed by fruitive actors, it is especially mentioned here *(tatrāpi)* that although Mahārāja Antardhāna was externally engaged in performing sacrifices, his real business was rendering devotional service by hearing and chanting. In other words, he was performing the usual sacrifices by the method of *saṅkīrtana-yajña*, as recommended herein:

śravaṇaṁ kīrtanaṁ viṣṇoḥ smaraṇaṁ pāda-sevanam
arcanaṁ vandanaṁ dāsyaṁ sakhyam ātma-nivedanam (*Bhāg*. 7.5.23)

Devotional service is called *kīrtana-yajña*, and by practicing the *saṅkīrtana-yajña*, one is very easily elevated to the planet where the Supreme Lord resides. Out of the five kinds of liberations, achieving the same planet where the Lord resides and living with the Lord there is called *sālokya* liberation.

TEXT 8

हविर्धानाद्धविर्धानी विदुरासूत षट् सुतान् ।
बर्हिषदं गयं शुक्लं कृष्णं सत्यं जितव्रतम् ॥ ८ ॥

havirdhānād dhavirdhānī
vidurāsūta ṣaṭ sutān
barhiṣadaṁ gayaṁ śuklaṁ
kṛṣṇaṁ satyaṁ jitavratam

havirdhānāt—from Havirdhāna; *havirdhānī*—the name of the wife of Havirdhāna; *vidura*—O Vidura; *asūta*—gave birth; *ṣaṭ*—six; *sutān*—sons;

barhiṣadam—of the name Barhiṣat; *gayam*—of the name Gaya; *śuklam*—of the name Śukla; *kṛṣṇam*—of the name Kṛṣṇa; *satyam*—of the name Satya; *jitavratam*—of the name Jitavrata.

TRANSLATION

Havirdhāna, the son of Mahārāja Antardhāna, had a wife named Havirdhānī, who gave birth to six sons named Barhiṣat, Gaya, Śukla, Kṛṣṇa, Satya and Jitavrata.

TEXT 9

बर्हिषत् सुमहाभागो हाविर्धानिः प्रजापतिः ।
क्रियाकाण्डेषु निष्णातो योगेषु च कुरूद्वह ॥ ९ ॥

barhiṣat su-mahābhāgo
hāvirdhāniḥ prajāpatiḥ
kriyā-kāṇḍeṣu niṣṇāto
yogeṣu ca kurūdvaha

barhiṣat—of the name Barhiṣat; *su-mahābhāgaḥ*—very fortunate; *hāvirdhāniḥ*—of the name Hāvirdhāni; *prajāpatiḥ*—the post of Prajāpati; *kriyā-kāṇḍeṣu*—in the matter of fruitive activities; *niṣṇātaḥ*—being merged in; *yogeṣu*—in mystic *yoga* practices; *ca*—also; *kurūdvaha*—O best of the Kurus (Vidura).

TRANSLATION

The great sage Maitreya continued: My dear Vidura, Havirdhāna's very powerful son named Barhiṣat was very expert in performing various kinds of fruitive sacrifices, and he was also expert in the practice of mystic yoga. By his great qualifications, he became known as Prajāpati.

PURPORT

In the beginning of the creation there were not many living entities, and consequently the very powerful living entities or demigods were appointed as *prajāpatis* in order to beget children and increase the population. There are many *prajāpatis*—Brahmā, Dakṣa and Manu are sometimes known as *prajāpatis*—and Barhiṣat, the son of Havirdhāna, became one of them.

TEXT 10

यस्येदं देवयजनमनुयज्ञं वितन्वतः ।
प्राचीनाग्रैः कुशैरासीदास्तृतं वसुधातलम् ॥१०॥

yasyedaṁ deva-yajanam
anuyajñaṁ vitanvataḥ
prācīnāgraiḥ kuśair āsīd
āstṛtaṁ vasudhā-talam

yasya—whose; *idam*—this; *deva-yajanam*—satisfying the demigods by sacrifices; *anuyajñam*—continually sacrificing; *vitanvataḥ*—executing; *prācīna-agraiḥ*—keeping the *kuśa* grass facing towards the eastern side; *kuśaiḥ*—the *kuśa* grass; *āsīt*—remained; *āstṛtam*—scattered; *vasudhā-talam*—all over the surface of the globe.

TRANSLATION

Mahārāja Barhiṣat executed many sacrifices all over the world. He scattered kuśa grasses and kept the tops of the grasses pointed eastward.

PURPORT

As stated in the previous verse (*kriyā-kāṇḍeṣu niṣṇātaḥ*), Mahārāja Barhiṣat dived very deeply into the fruitive activities of sacrifice. This means that as soon as he finished one *yajña* in one place, he began performing another *yajña* in the immediate vicinity. At the present moment there is a similar need to perform *saṅkīrtana-yajña* all over the world. The Kṛṣṇa consciousness movement has started performing *saṅkīrtana-yajña* in different places, and it has been experienced that wherever *saṅkīrtana-yajña* is performed, many thousands of people gather and take part in it. Imperceptible auspiciousness achieved in this connection should be continued all over the world. The members of the Kṛṣṇa consciousness movement should perform *saṅkīrtana-yajña* one after another, so much so that all the people of the world will either jokingly or seriously chant Hare Kṛṣṇa, Hare Kṛṣṇa, Kṛṣṇa Kṛṣṇa, Hare Hare/ Hare Rāma, Hare Rāma, Rāma Rāma, Hare Hare, and thus they will derive the benefit of cleansing the heart. The holy name of the Lord (*Harer nāma*) is so powerful that whether it is chanted jokingly or seriously the effect of vibrating this transcendental sound will be equally distributed. It is not possible at the present moment to perform repeated *yajñas* as Mahārāja Barhiṣat performed, but it is within our means to perform *saṅkīrtana-yajña*, which does not cost anything. One can sit down anywhere and chant Hare Kṛṣṇa, Hare Kṛṣṇa, Kṛṣṇa Kṛṣṇa, Hare Hare/ Hare Rāma, Hare Rāma, Rāma Rāma, Hare Hare. If the surface of the globe is overflooded with the chanting of the Hare Kṛṣṇa *mantra*, the people of the world will be very, very happy.

TEXT 11

सामुद्रीं देवदेवोक्तामुपयेमे शतद्रुतिम् ।
यां वीक्ष्य चारुसर्वाङ्गीं किशोरीं सुष्ठ्वलङ्कृताम् ।
परिक्रमन्तीमुद्वाहे चकमेऽग्निः शुकीमिव ॥११॥

sāmudrīṁ devadevoktām
upayeme śatadrutim
yāṁ vīkṣya cāru-sarvāṅgīṁ
kiśorīṁ suṣṭhv-alaṅkṛtām
parikramantīm udvāhe
cakame 'gniḥ śukīm iva

sāmudrīm—unto the daughter of the ocean; *devadeva-uktām*—being advised by the supreme demigod, Lord Brahmā; *upayeme*—married; *śatadrutim*—of the name Śatadruti; *yām*—whom; *vīkṣya*—seeing; *cāru*—very attractive; *sarva-aṅgīm*—all the features of the body; *kiśorīm*—youthful; *suṣṭhu*—sufficiently; *alaṅkṛtām*—decorated with ornaments; *parikramantīm*—circumambulating; *udvāhe*—in the marriage ceremony; *cakame*—became attracted; *agniḥ*—the fire-god; *śukīm*—unto Śukī; *iva*—like.

TRANSLATION

Mahārāja Barhiṣat—henceforward known as Prācīnabarhi—was ordered by the supreme demigod Lord Brahmā to marry the daughter of the ocean named Śatadruti. Her bodily features were completely beautiful, and she was very young. She was decorated with the proper garments, and when she came into the marriage arena and began circumambulating it, the fire-god Agni became so attracted to her that he desired her company, exactly as he had formerly desired to enjoy Śukī.

PURPORT

In this verse the word *suṣṭhv-alaṅkṛtām* is significant. According to the Vedic system, when a girl is married, she is very profusely and gorgeously decorated with costly saris and jewelry, and during the marriage ceremony the bride circumambulates the bridegroom seven times. After this, the bridegroom and bride look at one another and become attracted for life. When the bridegroom finds the bride very beautiful, the attraction between them immediately becomes very strongly fixed. As stated in *Śrīmad-Bhāgavatam*, men and women are naturally attracted to one another, and when they are united by marriage that attraction becomes very strong. Being so strongly attracted, the bridegroom attempts to set up a nice homestead and eventually a good field for producing grains. Then children come, then friends and then wealth. In this way the male becomes more and more entangled in the material conceptions of life, and he begins to think, "This is mine," and "It is I who am acting." In this way the illusion of material existence is perpetuated.

The words *śukīm iva* are also significant, for the fire-god Agni became attracted by the beauty of Śatadruti while she was circumambulating the bridegroom Prācīnabarhi, just as he had previously been attracted to the beauty of Śukī, the wife of Saptarṣi. When the fire-god had been present long ago at the assembly of Saptarṣi, he was attracted by the beauty of Śukī when she was circumambulating in the same way. Agni's wife, named Svāhā, took the form of Śukī and enjoyed sex life with Agni. Not only the fire-god Agni but the heavenly god Indra and sometimes even Lord Brahmā and Lord Śiva—all very highly situated demigods—are subject to being attracted by sex at any time. The sex drive is so strong in the living entities that the whole material world is running on sex attraction only, and it is due to sex attraction that one remains in the material world and is obliged to accept different types of bodies. The attraction of sex life is more clearly explained in the next verse.

TEXT 12

विबुधासुरगन्धर्वमुनिसिद्धनरोरगाः ।
विजिताः सूर्यया दिक्षु क्वणयन्त्यैव नूपुरैः ॥१२॥

vibudhāsura-gandharva-
muni-siddha-naroragāḥ
vijitāḥ sūryayā dikṣu
kvaṇayantyaiva nūpuraiḥ

vibudha—learned; *asura*—the demons; *gandharva*—the denizens of Gandharvaloka; *muni*—great sages; *siddha*—the denizens of Siddhaloka; *nara*—the inhabitants of the earthly planets; *uragāḥ*—denizens of Nāgaloka; *vijitāḥ*—captivated; *sūryayā*—by the new bride; *dikṣu*—in all directions; *kvaṇayantyā*—tinkling; *eva*—only; *nūpuraiḥ*—by her ankle bells.

TRANSLATION

While Śatadruti was thus being married, the demons, the denizens of Gandharvaloka, the great sages, and the denizens of Siddhaloka, the earthly planets and Nāgaloka, although highly exalted, were all captivated by the tinkling of her ankle bells.

PURPORT

Generally a woman becomes more beautiful when, after an early marriage, she gives birth to a child. To give birth to a child is the natural function of a woman, and therefore a woman becomes more and more beautiful as she gives birth to one child after another. In the case of Śatadruti, however, she was so beautiful that she attracted the whole universe at her marriage ceremony. Indeed, she attracted all the learned and exalted demigods simply by the tinkling of her ankle bells. This indicates that all the demigods wanted to see her beauty completely, but they were not able to see it because she was fully dressed and covered with ornaments. Since they could only see the feet of Śatadruti, they became attracted by her ankle bells, which tinkled as she walked. In other words, the demigods became captivated by her simply by hearing the tinkling of her ankle bells. They did not have to see her complete beauty. It is sometimes understood that a person becomes lusty just by hearing the tinkling of bangles on the hands of women, or the tinkling of ankle bells, or just by seeing a woman's sari. Thus it is concluded that woman is the complete representation of *māyā.* Although Viśvāmitra Muni was engaged in practicing mystic *yoga* with closed eyes, his transcendental meditation was broken when he heard the tinkling of bangles on the hands of Menakā. In this way Viśvāmitra Muni became a victim of Menakā and fathered a child who is universally celebrated as Śakuntalā. The conclusion is that no one can save himself from the attraction of woman, even though he be an exalted demigod or an inhabitant of the higher planets. Only a devotee of the Lord, who is attracted by Kṛṣṇa, can escape the lures of woman. Once one is attracted by Kṛṣṇa, the illusory energy of the world cannot attract him.

TEXT 13

प्राचीनबर्हिषः पुत्राः शतद्रुत्यां दशाभवन् ।
तुल्यनामव्रताः सर्वे धर्मस्नाताः प्रचेतसः ॥१३॥

prācīnabarhiṣaḥ putrāḥ
śatadrutyāṁ daśābhavan
tulya-nāma-vratāḥ sarve
dharma-snātāḥ pracetasaḥ

prācīnabarhiṣaḥ—of King Prācīnabarhi; *putrāḥ*—sons; *śatadrutyām*—in the womb of Śatadruti; *daśa*—ten; *abhavan*—became manifest; *tulya*—equally; *nāma*—name; *vratāḥ*—vow; *sarve*—all; *dharma*—religiosity; *snātāḥ*—completely merged in; *pracetasaḥ*—all of them being designated as Pracetās.

TRANSLATION

King Prācīnabarhi begot ten children in the womb of Śatadruti, and all of them were equally endowed with religiosity, and all of them were known as the Pracetās.

PURPORT

The word *dharma-snātāḥ* is significant, for the ten children were all merged in the practice of religion. In addition, they possessed all good qualities. One is supposed to be perfect when one is perfectly religious, perfect in the execution of one's vows to render devotional service, perfect in knowledge, perfect in good behavior and so on. All the Pracetās were on the same level of perfection.

TEXT 14

पित्राऽऽदिष्टाः प्रजासर्गे तपसेऽर्णवमाविशन् ।
दशवर्षसहस्राणि तपसाऽऽर्चंस्तपस्पतिम् ॥१४॥

pitrādiṣṭāḥ prajā-sarge
tapase 'rṇavam āviśan
daśa-varṣa-sahasrāṇi
tapasārcaṁs tapas-patim

pitrā—by the father; *ādiṣṭāḥ*—being ordered by; *prajā-sarge*—in the matter of begetting children; *tapase*—for executing austerity; *arṇavam*—in the ocean; *āviśan*—entered; *daśa-varṣa*—ten years; *sahasrāṇi*—such thousands; *tapasā*—by their austerity; *ārcan*—worshiped; *tapaḥ*—of austerity; *patim*—the master.

TRANSLATION

When all these Pracetās were ordered by their father to marry and beget children, they all entered the ocean and practiced austerities and penances for ten thousand years. Thus they worshiped the master of all austerity, the Supreme Personality of Godhead.

PURPORT

Sometimes great sages and ascetics enter the Himalayan Mountains in order to find seclusion from the turmoil of the world. It appears, however, that all the Pracetās, the sons of Prācīnabarhi, entered the depths of the ocean to perform austerity in a secluded place. Since they performed austerities for ten thousand years, this incident took place in the Satya-yuga, when people used to live for a hundred thousand years. It is also significant that by their austerity they worshiped the master of austerity Śrī Kṛṣṇa, the Supreme Personality of Godhead. If one wants to perform austerities and penances in order to attain the supreme goal, one must attain the favor of the Supreme Personality of Godhead. If one achieves the favor of the

Supreme Lord, it is to be understood that he has finished all kinds of austerities and penances and has attained efficiency in their execution. On the other hand, if one does not attain the perfect stage of devotional service, all austerities and penances actually have no meaning, for without the Supreme Lord no one can attain the highest results derived from performing them. As stated in *Bhagavad-gītā,* Lord Śrī Kṛṣṇa is the master of all penances and sacrifices.

bhoktāraṁ yajña-tapasāṁ
sarva-loka-maheśvaram
suhṛdaṁ sarva-bhūtānāṁ
jñātvā māṁ śāntim ṛcchati

"The sages, knowing Me as the ultimate purpose of all sacrifices and austerities, the Supreme Lord of all planets and demigods, and the benefactor and well-wisher of all living entities, attain peace from the pangs of material miseries." (Bg. 5.29)

In *Śrīmad-Bhāgavatam* it is also stated that even if a person is born in a family of *caṇḍālas*—the lowest birth one can get in human society—he is glorious if he chants the holy names of the Lord, for it is to be understood that by such chanting a devotee definitely proves that he underwent all kinds of austerities in his previous life. By the grace of Lord Caitanya, one who chants the *mahā-mantra* (Hare Kṛṣṇa, Hare Kṛṣṇa, Kṛṣṇa Kṛṣṇa, Hare Hare/ Hare Rāma, Hare Rāma, Rāma Rāma, Hare Hare) attains the highest perfectional stage which had previously been attained by people who entered the ocean and executed austerities for ten thousand years. In this age of Kali, if a person does not take advantage of chanting the Hare Kṛṣṇa *mantra,* which is offered as a great concession to the fallen human beings of this age, it is to be understood that he will become very much bewildered by the illusory energy of the Lord.

TEXT 15

यदुक्तं पथि दृष्टेन गिरिशेन प्रसीदता ।
तद्ध्यायन्तो जपन्तश्च पूजयन्तश्च संयताः ॥१५॥

yad uktaṁ pathi dṛṣṭena
giriśena prasīdatā
tad dhyāyanto japantaś ca
pūjayantaś ca saṁyatāḥ

yat—that; *uktam*—said; *pathi*—on the way; *dṛṣṭena*—while meeting; *giriśena*—by Lord Śiva; *prasīdatā*—being very much satisfied; *tat*—that; *dhyāyantaḥ*—meditating; *japantaḥ ca*—chanting also; *pūjayantaḥ ca*—worshiping also; *saṁyatāḥ*—with great control.

TRANSLATION

When all the sons of Prācīnabarhi left home to execute austerities, they met Lord Śiva, who, out of great mercy, instructed them about the Absolute Truth. All the sons of Prācīnabarhi meditated upon the instructions, chanting and worshiping them with great care and attention.

PURPORT

It is clear that to perform austerities or penances, or, for that matter, any form of devotional service, one has to be guided by a spiritual master. Here it is clearly stated that the ten sons of Mahārāja Prācīnabarhi were favored by an appearance of Lord Śiva, who, out of great kindness, gave them instructions regarding the execution of austerities. Lord Śiva actually became the spiritual master of the ten sons, and in turn his disciples took his words so seriously that simply by meditating upon his instructions (*dhyāyantaḥ*) they became perfect. This is the secret of success. After being initiated and receiving the orders of the spiritual master, the disciple should unhesitatingly think about the instructions or orders of the spiritual master and should not allow himself to be disturbed by anything else. This is also the verdict of Śrīla Viśvanātha Cakravartī Ṭhākura, who, while explaining a verse of *Bhagavad-gītā* (*vyavasāyātmikā buddhir ekeha kuru-nandana*, Bg. 2.41), points out that the order of the spiritual master is the life substance of the disciple. The disciple shouldn't consider whether he is going back home, back to Godhead; his first business should be to execute the order of his spiritual master. Thus a disciple should always meditate on the order of the spiritual master, and that is perfectional meditation. Not only should he meditate upon that order, but he should find out the means by which he can perfectly worship and execute it.

TEXT 16

विदुर उवाच

प्रचेतसां गिरित्रेण यथाऽऽसीत्पथि सङ्गमः ।
यदुताह हरः प्रीतस्तन्नो ब्रह्मन् वदार्थवत् ॥१६॥

vidura uvāca
pracetasāṁ giritreṇa
yathāsīt pathi saṅgamaḥ
yad utāha haraḥ prītas
tan no brahman vadārthavat

viduraḥ uvāca—Vidura inquired; *pracetasām*—of all the Pracetās; *giritreṇa*—by Lord Śiva; *yathā*—as and as; *āsīt*—it was; *pathi*—on the road; *saṅgamaḥ*—meeting; *yat*—which; *utāha*—said; *haraḥ*—Lord Śiva; *prītaḥ*—being pleased; *tat*—that; *naḥ*—unto us; *brahman*—O great *brāhmaṇa; vada*—speak; *arthavat*—with clear meaning.

TRANSLATION

Vidura asked Maitreya: My dear brāhmaṇa, why did the Pracetās meet Lord Śiva on the way? Please tell me how the meeting happened, how Lord Śiva became very pleased with them, and how he instructed them. Certainly such talks are important, and I wish that you will please be merciful upon me and describe them.

PURPORT

Whenever there are some important talks between a devotee and the Lord or between exalted devotees, one should be very much curious to hear them. At the meeting of Naimiṣāraṇya, where Sūta Gosvāmī spoke *Śrīmad-Bhāgavatam* to all the great sages, Sūta Gosvāmī was also asked about the talks between Mahārāja Parīkṣit and Śukadeva Gosvāmī, for the sages believed that the talks between Śukadeva Gosvāmī and Mahārāja Parīkṣit must have been as important as the talks between Lord Kṛṣṇa and Arjuna. As everyone is still eager to learn the subject of *Bhagavad-gītā* in order to become perfectly enlightened, Vidura was similarly eager to learn from the great sage Maitreya about the talks between Lord Śiva and the Pracetās.

TEXT 17

सङ्गमः खलु विप्रर्षे शिवेनेह शरीरिणाम् ।
दुर्लभो मुनयो दध्युरसङ्गाद्यमभीप्सितम् ॥१७॥

saṅgamaḥ khalu viprarṣe
śiveneha śarīriṇām
durlabho munayo dadhyur
asaṅgād yam abhīpsitam

saṅgamaḥ—association; *khalu*—certainly; *viprarṣe*—O best of the *brāhmaṇas; śivena*—along with Lord Śiva; *iha*—in this world; *śarīriṇām*—those who are encaged in material bodies; *durlabhaḥ*—very rare; *munayaḥ*—great sages; *dadhyuḥ*—engaged themselves in meditation; *asaṅgāt*—being detached from anything else; *yam*—unto whom; *abhīpsitam*—desiring.

TRANSLATION

The great sage Vidura continued: O best of the brāhmaṇas, it is very difficult for living entities encaged within this material body to have personal contact with Lord Śiva. Even great sages who have no material attachments do not contact him, despite their always being absorbed in meditation to attain his personal contact.

PURPORT

Since Lord Śiva does not incarnate himself unless there is some special reason, it is very difficult for an ordinary person to contact him. However, Lord Śiva does descend on a special occasion when he is ordered by the Supreme Personality of Godhead. In this regard, it is stated in the *Padma Purāṇa* that Lord Śiva appeared as a *brāhmaṇa* in the age of Kali to preach the Māyāvāda philosophy, which is nothing but a type of Buddhist philosophy. It is stated in *Padma Purāṇa*:

māyāvādam asac-chāstraṁ pracchannaṁ bauddham ucyate
mayaiva vihitaṁ devi kalau brāhmaṇa-mūrtinā

Lord Śiva, speaking to Pārvatī Devī, foretold that he would spread the Māyāvāda philosophy in the guise of a *sannyāsī brāhmaṇa* just to eradicate Buddhist philosophy. This *sannyāsī* was Śrīpāda Śaṅkarācārya. In order to overcome the effects of Buddhist philosophy and spread Vedānta philosophy, Śrīpāda Śaṅkarācārya had to make some compromise with the Buddhist philosophy, and as such he preached the philosophy of monism, for it was required at that time. Otherwise there was no need for his preaching Māyāvāda philosophy. At the present moment there is no need for Māyāvāda philosophy nor Buddhist philosophy, and Lord Caitanya rejected both of them. This Kṛṣṇa consciousness movement is spreading the philosophy of Lord Caitanya and rejecting the philosophy of both classes of Māyāvāda. Strictly speaking, both Buddhist philosophy and Śaṅkara's philosophy are but different types of Māyāvāda dealing on the platform of material existence. Neither of these philosophies has spiritual significance. There is spiritual significance only after one accepts the philosophy of

Bhagavad-gītā, which culminates in surrendering unto the Supreme Personality of Godhead. Generally people worship Lord Śiva for some material benefit, and although they cannot see him personally, they nonetheless derive great material profit by worshiping him.

TEXT 18

आत्मारामोऽपि यस्त्वस्य लोककल्पस्य राधसे ।
शक्त्या युक्तो विचरति घोरया भगवान् भवः ॥१८॥

ātmārāmo 'pi yas tv asya
loka-kalpasya rādhase
śaktyā yukto vicarati
ghorayā bhagavān bhavaḥ

ātmārāmaḥ—self-satisfied; *api*—although he is; *yaḥ*—one who is; *tu*—but; *asya*—this; *loka*—material world; *kalpasya*—when manifested; *rādhase*—for the matter of helping its existence; *śaktyā*—potencies; *yuktaḥ*—being engaged; *vicarati*—he acts; *ghorayā*—very dangerous; *bhagavān*—His Lordship; *bhavaḥ*—Śiva.

TRANSLATION

Lord Śiva, the most powerful demigod, second only to Lord Viṣṇu, is self-sufficient. Although he has nothing to aspire for in the material world, for the benefit of those in the material world he is always busily engaged everywhere and is accompanied by his dangerous energies like Goddess Kālī and Goddess Durgā.

PURPORT

Lord Śiva is known as the greatest devotee of the Supreme Personality of Godhead. He is also known as *vaiṣṇavānāṁ yathā śambhuḥ,* the best of all types of Vaiṣṇavas. Consequently Lord Śiva has a Vaiṣṇava *sampradāya,* the disciplic succession known as Rudra-sampradāya. Just as there is a Brahma-sampradāya coming directly from Lord Brahmā, the Rudra-sampradāya comes directly from Lord Śiva. As stated in *Śrīmad-Bhāgavatam,* Lord Śiva is one of the twelve great personalities. This refers to the twelve great authorities who preach God consciousness. The name Śambhu means Lord Śiva. His disciplic succession is also known as the Viṣṇusvāmi-sampradāya, and the current Viṣṇusvāmi-sampradāya is also known as the Vallabha-sampradāya. The current Brahma-sampradāya is known as the Madhva-Gauḍīya-sampradāya. Even though Lord Śiva appeared to preach Māyāvāda philosophy, at the end of his pastime in the form of Śaṅkarācārya, he preached the Vaiṣṇava philosophy: *bhaja govindaṁ bhaja govindaṁ bhaja govindaṁ mūḍha-mate.* He stressed worshiping Lord Kṛṣṇa or Govinda three times in this verse and especially warned his followers that they could not possibly achieve deliverance or *mukti* simply by word jugglery and grammatical puzzles. If one is actually serious to attain *mukti,* he must worship Lord Kṛṣṇa. That is Śrīpāda Śaṅkarācārya's last instruction.

Herein it is mentioned that Lord Śiva is always accompanied by his material energy (*śaktyā ghorayā*). Material energy—Goddess Durgā or Goddess Kālī—is always under his control. Goddess Kālī and Durgā serve him by killing all the *asuras* or demons. Sometimes Kālī becomes so infuriated that she indiscriminately kills all kinds of *asuras.* There is a popular picture of Goddess Kālī in which she wears a garland composed of the heads of the *asuras* and holds in her left hand a captured head and in her right hand a great *khaḍga,* or chopper, for killing *asuras.* Great wars are symbolic representations of Kālī's devastation of the *asuras* and are actually conducted by the Goddess Kālī.

sṛṣṭi-sthiti-pralaya-sādhana-śaktir ekā
chāyeva yasya bhuvanāni bibharti durgā (Bs. 5.44)

Asuras, however, try to pacify the Goddess Kālī or Durgā by worshiping her in material opulence, but when the *asuras* become too intolerable, Goddess Kālī does not discriminate in killing them wholesale. *Asuras* do not know the secret of the energy of Lord Śiva, and they prefer to worship Goddess Kālī or Durgā or Lord Śiva for material benefit. Due to their demonic character, they are reluctant to surrender to Lord Kṛṣṇa, as indicated by *Bhagavad-gītā:*

na māṁ duṣkṛtino mūḍhāḥ
prapadyante narādhamāḥ
māyayāpahṛta-jñānā
āsuraṁ bhāvam āśritāḥ (Bg. 7.15)

Lord Śiva's duty is very dangerous because he has to employ the energy of Goddess Kālī (or Durgā). In another popular picture the Goddess Kālī is sometimes seen standing on the prostrate body of Lord Śiva, which indicates that sometimes Lord Śiva has to fall down flat in order to stop Goddess Kālī from killing the *asuras.* Since Lord Śiva controls the great material energy (Goddess Durgā), worshipers of Lord Śiva attain very opulent positions within this material world. Under Lord Śiva's direction, a worshiper of Lord Śiva gets all kinds of material facilities. In contrast, a Vaiṣṇava, or worshiper of Lord Viṣṇu, gradually becomes poorer in material possessions because Lord Viṣṇu does not trick His devotees into becoming materially entangled by possessions. Lord Viṣṇu gives His devotees intelligence from within, as stated in *Bhagavad-gītā:*

teṣāṁ satata-yuktānāṁ
bhajatāṁ prīti-pūrvakam
dadāmi buddhi-yogaṁ taṁ
yena mām upayānti te

"To those who are constantly devoted and worship Me with love, I give the understanding by which they can come to Me." (Bg. 10.10)

Thus Lord Viṣṇu gives intelligence to His devotee so that the devotee can make progress on the path back home, back to Godhead. Since a devotee has nothing to do with any kind of material possession, he does not come under the control of Goddess Kālī or the Goddess Durgā.

Lord Śiva is also in charge of the *tamo-guṇa,* or the mode of ignorance in this material world. Both Lord Brahmā and Lord Śiva are incarnations of Lord Viṣṇu, but Lord Brahmā is in charge of the creation whereas Lord Śiva is in charge of the destruction, which he carries out with the help of his material energy, Goddess Kālī or Goddess Durgā. Thus in this verse Lord Śiva is described as being accompanied by dangerous potencies (*śaktyā ghorayā*), and that is the actual position of Lord Śiva.

TEXT 19

मैत्रेय उवाच
प्रचेतसः पितुर्वाक्यं शिरसाऽऽदाय साधवः ।
दिशं प्रतीचीं प्रययुस्तपस्यादृतचेतसः ॥१९॥

maitreya uvāca
pracetasaḥ pitur vākyaṁ
śirasādāya sādhavaḥ
diśaṁ pratīcīṁ prayayus
tapasy ādṛta-cetasaḥ

maitreyaḥ uvāca—the great sage Maitreya continued to speak; *pracetasaḥ*—all the sons of King Prācīnabarhi; *pituḥ*—of the father; *vākyam*—words; *śirasā*—on the head; *ādāya*—accepting; *sādhavaḥ*—all pious; *diśam*—

direction; *pratīcīm*—western; *prayayuḥ*—went away; *tapasi*—in austerities; *ādṛta*—accepting seriously; *cetasaḥ*—in the heart.

TRANSLATION

The great sage Maitreya continued: My dear Vidura, because of their pious nature, all the sons of Prācīnabarhi very seriously accepted the words of their father with heart and soul, and with these words on their heads, they went toward the west to execute their father's order.

PURPORT

In this verse *sādhavaḥ* (meaning pious or well behaved) is very important, especially at the present moment. It is derived from the word *sādhu.* A perfect *sādhu* is one who is always engaged in the devotional service of the Supreme Personality of Godhead. Prācīnabarhi's sons are described as *sādhavaḥ* because of their complete obedience to their father. The father, king and spiritual master are supposed to be representatives of the Supreme Personality of Godhead, and as such they have to be respected as the Supreme Lord. It is the duty of the father, the spiritual master and the king to regulate their subordinates in such a way that they ultimately become fully unalloyed devotees of the Supreme Lord. That is the duty of the superiors, and it is the duty of the subordinates to obey their orders perfectly and in a disciplined way. The word *śirasā* (on their heads) is also significant, for the Pracetās accepted the orders of their father and carried them on their heads, which means they accepted them in complete surrender.

TEXT 20

स समुद्रमुप विस्तीर्णमपश्यन् सुमहत्सरः ।
महन्मन इव स्वच्छं प्रसन्नसलिलाशयम् ॥२०॥

sa samudram upa vistīrṇam
apaśyan su-mahat saraḥ
mahan-mana iva svacchaṁ
prasanna-salilāśayam

sa samudram—almost near the ocean; *upa*—more or less; *vistīrṇam*—very wide and long; *apaśyan*—they saw; *su-mahat*—very great; *saraḥ*—reservoir of water; *mahat*—great soul; *manaḥ*—mind; *iva*—like; *su-accham*—clear; *prasanna*—joyful; *salila*—water; *āśayam*—taken shelter of.

TRANSLATION

While traveling, the Pracetās happened to see a great reservoir of water which seemed almost as big as the ocean. The water of this lake was so calm and quiet that it seemed like the mind of a great soul, and its inhabitants, the aquatics, appeared to be very peaceful and happy to be under the protection of such a watery reservoir.

PURPORT

The word *sa samudra* means "near the sea." The reservoir of water was like a bay, for it was not very far from the sea. The word *upa,* meaning "more or less," is used in many ways, as in the word *upapati,* which indicates a husband "more or less," that is to say a lover who is acting like a husband. *Upa* also means greater, smaller or nearer. Considering all these points, the reservoir of water which was seen by the Pracetās while they were traveling was actually a large bay or lake. And unlike the sea or ocean, which has turbulent waves, this reservoir was very calm and quiet. Indeed, the water was so clear that it seemed like the mind of some great soul. There may be many great souls–*jñānīs, yogīs* and *bhaktas,* or pure devotees, are also called great souls–but they are very rarely found. One can find many great souls amongst *yogīs* and *jñānīs,* but a truly great soul, a pure devotee of the Lord who is fully surrendered to the Lord, is very rarely found (*sa mahātmā sudurlabhaḥ,* Bg. 7.19). A devotee's mind is always calm, quiet and desireless because he is always *anyābhilāṣitā-śūnyam,* and he has no desire other than to serve Kṛṣṇa as His personal servant, friend, father, mother or conjugal lover. Due to his association with Kṛṣṇa, a devotee is always very calm and cool. It is also significant that within that reservoir all the aquatics were also very calm and quiet. Because the disciples of a devotee have taken shelter of a great man, they become very calm and quiet and are not agitated by the waves of the material world.

This material world is often described as an ocean of nescience. In such an ocean, everything is agitated. The mind of a great devotee is also like an ocean or a very large lake, but there is no agitation. As stated in *Bhagavad-gītā: vyavasāyātmikā buddhir ekeha kuru-nandana* (Bg. 2.41). Those who are fixed in the service of the Lord are not agitated by anything. It is also stated in *Bhagavad-gītā: yasmin sthito na duḥkhena guruṇāpi vicālyate* (Bg. 6.22). Even if he suffers some reversals in life, a devotee is never agitated. Therefore whoever takes shelter of a great soul or a great devotee becomes pacified. In the *Caitanya-caritāmṛta* it is stated:

kṛṣṇa-bhakta——niṣkāma, ataeva 'śānta' (Cc. *Madhya* 19.149). A devotee of Lord Kṛṣṇa is always peaceful because he has no desire, whereas the *yogīs, karmīs* and *jñānīs* have so many desires to fulfill. One may argue that the devotees have desires, for they wish to go home, back to Godhead, but such a desire does not agitate the mind. Although he wishes to go back to Godhead, a devotee is satisfied in any condition of life. Consequently the word *mahan-manaḥ* is used in this verse to indicate that the reservoir of water was as calm and quiet as the mind of a great devotee.

TEXT 21

नीलरक्तोत्पलाम्भोजकह्लारेन्दीवराकरम् ।
हंससारसचक्राह्वकारण्डवनिकूजितम् ॥२१॥

nīla-raktotpalāmbhoja-
kahlārendīvarākaram
haṁsa-sārasa-cakrāhva-
kāraṇḍava-nikūjitam

nīla—blue; *rakta*—red; *utpala*—lotus; *ambhoja*—born from the water; *kahlāra*—another kind of lotus; *indīvara*—another kind of lotus; *ākaram*—the mine; *haṁsa*—swans; *sārasa*—cranes; *cakrāhva*—the ducks of the name; *kāraṇḍava*—birds of the name; *nikūjitam*—vibrated by their sounds.

TRANSLATION

In that great lake there were different types of lotus flowers. Some of them were bluish, and some of them were red. Some of them grew at night, some in the day, and some, like the indīvara lotus flower, in the evening. Combined together, the lotus flowers filled the lake so full that the lake appeared to be a great mine of such flowers. Consequently on the shores there were swans and cranes, cakravāka, kāraṇḍava and other beautiful water birds, standing about.

PURPORT

The word *ākaram* (mine) is significant in this verse, for the reservoir of water appeared like a mine from which different types of lotus flowers were produced. Some of the lotus flowers grew during the day, some at night and some in the evening, and accordingly they had different names and different colors. All these flowers were present on that lake, and because the lake was so calm and quiet and filled with lotus flowers, superior birds, like swans, *cakravākas* and *kāraṇḍavas,* stood on the shores and vibrated their different songs, making the entire scene attractive and beautiful. As there are different types of human beings, according to the association of the three qualities of material nature, there are similarly different types of birds, bees, trees, etc. Everything is divided according to the three qualities of material nature. Birds like swans and cranes, who enjoy clear waters and lotus flowers, are different from crows, who enjoy filthy places. Similarly, there are persons who are controlled by the modes of ignorance and passion and those who are controlled by the mode of goodness. The creation is so varied that there are always varieties found in every society. Thus on the bank of this lake all the superior birds lived to enjoy that atmosphere created by that great reservoir filled with lotus flowers.

TEXT 22

मत्तभ्रमरसौस्वर्यहृष्टरोमलताङ्घ्रिपम् ।
पद्मकोशरजो दिक्षु विक्षिपत्पवनोत्सवम् ॥२२॥

matta-bhramara-sausvarya-
hṛṣṭa-roma-latāṅghripam
padma-kośa-rajo dikṣu
vikṣipat-pavanotsavam

matta—mad; *bhramara*—bumblebees; *sausvarya*—with great humming; *hṛṣṭa*—joyfully; *roma*—hair on the body; *latā*—creepers; *aṅghri-pam*—trees; *padma*—lotus flower; *kośa*—whorl; *rajaḥ*—saffron; *dikṣu*—in all directions; *vikṣipat*—throwing away; *pavana*—air; *utsavam*—festival.

TRANSLATION

There were various trees and creepers on all sides of the lake, and there were mad bumblebees humming all about them. The trees appeared to be very jolly due to the sweet humming of the bumblebees, and the saffron, which was contained in the lotus flowers, was being thrown into the air. These all created such an atmosphere that it appeared as though a festival were taking place there.

PURPORT

Trees and creepers are also different types of living beings. When bumblebees come upon trees and creepers to collect honey, certainly such plants become very happy. On such an occasion the wind also takes advantage of the situation by throwing pollen or saffron contained in the lotus flowers. All this combines with the sweet vibration created by the swans and the calm of the water. The Pracetās consider such a place to be like a continuous festival. From this description it appears that the Pracetās reached Śivaloka, which is supposed to be situated near the Himalayan Mountains.

TEXT 23

तत्र गान्धर्वमाकर्ण्य दिव्यमार्गमनोहरम् ।
विसिस्म्यू राजपुत्रास्ते मृदङ्गपणवाद्यनु ॥२३॥

tatra gāndharvam ākarṇya
divya-mārga-manoharam
visismyū rāja-putrās te
mṛdaṅga-paṇavādy anu

tatra—there; *gāndharvam*—musical sounds; *ākarṇya*—hearing; *divya*—heavenly; *mārga*—symmetrical; *manoharam*—beautiful; *visismyuḥ*—they became amazed; *rāja-putrāḥ*—all the sons of King Barhiṣat; *te*—all of them; *mṛdaṅga*—drums; *paṇava*—kettledrums; *ādi*—all together; *anu*—always.

TRANSLATION

The sons of the king became very much amazed when they heard vibrations from various drums and kettledrums along with other orderly musical sounds pleasing to the ear.

PURPORT

In addition to the various flowers and living entities about the lake, there were also many musical vibrations. The void of the impersonalists, which has no variegatedness, is not at all pleasing compared to such a scene. Actually one has to attain the perfection of *sac-cid-ānanda,* eternity, bliss and knowledge. Because the impersonalists deny these varieties of creation, they cannot actually enjoy transcendental bliss. The place where the Pracetās arrived was the abode of Lord Śiva. Impersonalists are generally worshipers of Lord Śiva, but Lord Śiva is never without variety in his abode. Thus wherever one goes, whether to the planet of Lord Śiva, Lord Viṣṇu or Lord Brahmā, there is variety to be enjoyed by persons full in knowledge and bliss.

TEXT 24-25

तर्ह्येव सरसस्तस्मान्निष्क्रामन्तं सहानुगम् ।
उपगीयमानममरप्रवरं विबुधानुगैः ॥२४॥
तप्तहेमनिकायाभं शितिकण्ठं त्रिलोचनम् ।
प्रसादसुमुखं वीक्ष्य प्रणेमुर्जातकौतुकाः ॥२५॥

tarhy eva sarasas tasmān
niṣkrāmantaṁ sahānugam
upagīyamānam amara-
pravaraṁ vibudhānugaiḥ

tapta-hema-nikāyābhaṁ
śiti-kaṇṭhaṁ tri-locanam
prasāda-sumukhaṁ vīkṣya
praṇemur jāta-kautukāḥ

tarhi—in that very moment; *eva*—certainly; *sarasaḥ*—from the water; *tasmāt*—therefrom; *niṣkrāmantam*—coming out; *sahānugam*—accompanied by great souls; *upagīyamānam*—glorified by the followers; *amara-pravaram*—the chief of the demigods; *vibudha-anugaiḥ*—followed by his associates; *tapta-hema*—molten gold; *nikāyābham*—bodily features; *śiti-kaṇṭham*—blue throat; *tri-locanam*—with three eyes; *prasāda*—merciful; *su-mukham*—beautiful face; *vīkṣya*—seeing; *praṇemuḥ*—offered obeisances; *jāta*—aroused; *kautukāḥ*—being amazed by the situation.

TRANSLATION

The Pracetās were fortunate to see Lord Śiva, the chief of the demigods, emerging from the water with his associates. His bodily luster was just like molten gold, his throat was bluish, and he had three eyes, which looked very mercifully upon his devotees. He was accompanied by many musicians who were glorifying him. As soon as the Pracetās saw Lord Śiva, they immediately offered their obeisances in great amazement and fell down at the lotus feet of the lord.

PURPORT

The word *vibudhānugaiḥ* indicates that Lord Śiva is always accompanied by the denizens of the higher planets, known as Gandharvas and Kinnaras. They are very expert in musical science, and Lord Śiva is worshiped by them constantly. In pictures, Lord Śiva is generally painted white, but here we find that the color of his skin is not exactly white but is like molten gold, or a glowing yellowish color. Because Lord Śiva is always very, very merciful, his name is Āśutoṣa. Amongst all the demigods, Lord Śiva can be pacified even by the lowest class of men, who need only offer him obeisances and leaves of a *bael* tree. Thus his name is Āśutoṣa, which means that he is pleased very quickly.

Generally those who are very fond of material prosperity approach Lord Śiva for such benediction. The lord, being very merciful, quickly awards all the blessings the devotee asks of him. The demons take advantage of this leniency and sometimes take benedictions from Lord Śiva which can be very dangerous to others. For instance, Vṛkāsura took a benediction from Lord Śiva by which he could kill everyone he touched on the head. Although Lord Śiva sometimes very liberally gives such benedictions to his devotees, the difficulty is that the demons, being very cunning, sometimes want to experiment improperly with such benedictions. For instance, after receiving his benediction, Vṛkāsura tried to touch the head of Lord Śiva. Devotees of Lord Viṣṇu, however, have no desire for such benedictions, and Lord Viṣṇu does not give His devotees benedictions which would cause disturbance to the whole world.

TEXT 26

स तान् प्रपन्नार्तिहरो भगवान्धर्मवत्सलः ।
धर्मज्ञान् शीलसम्पन्नान् प्रीतः प्रीतानुवाच ह ॥२६॥

sa tān prapannārti-haro
bhagavān dharma-vatsalaḥ
dharma-jñān śīla-sampannān
prītaḥ prītān uvāca ha

saḥ—Lord Śiva; *tān*—them; *prapanna-ārti-haraḥ*—one who drives away all kinds of dangers; *bhagavān*—the lord; *dharma-vatsalaḥ*—very much fond of religious principles; *dharma-jñān*—persons who are aware of religious principles; *śīla-sampannān*—very well behaved; *prītaḥ*—being pleased; *prītān*—of very gentle behavior; *uvāca*—talked with them; *ha*—in the past.

TRANSLATION

Lord Śiva became very pleased with the Pracetās because generally Lord Śiva is the protector of pious persons and persons of gentle behavior. Being very much pleased with the princes, he began to speak as follows.

PURPORT

The Supreme Personality of Godhead, Viṣṇu or Kṛṣṇa, is known as *bhakta-vatsala,* and herein we find Lord Śiva described as *dharma-vatsala.* Of course the word *dharma-vatsala* refers to a person who lives according to religious principles. That is understood. Nonetheless, these two words have additional significance. Sometimes Lord Śiva has to deal with persons who are in the modes of passion and ignorance. Such persons are not always very much religious and pious in their activities, but since they worship Lord Śiva for some material profit, they sometimes obey the religious principles. As soon as Lord Śiva sees that his devotees are following religious principles, he benedicts them. The Pracetās, sons of Prācīnabarhi, were naturally very pious and gentle, and consequently Lord Śiva was immediately pleased with them. Lord Śiva could understand that the princes were sons of Vaiṣṇavas, and as such Lord Śiva offered prayers to the Supreme Personality of Godhead as follows.

TEXT 27

श्रीरुद्र उवाच
यूयं वेदिषदः पुत्रा विदितं वश्चिकीर्षितम् ।
अनुग्रहाय भद्रं व एवं मे दर्शनं कृतम् ॥२७॥

śrī-rudra uvāca
yūyaṁ vediṣadaḥ putrā
viditaṁ vaś cikīrṣitam
anugrahāya bhadraṁ va
evaṁ me darśanaṁ kṛtam

śrī-rudraḥ uvāca—Lord Śiva began to speak; *yūyam*—all of you; *vediṣadaḥ*—of King Prācīnabarhi; *putrāḥ*—sons; *viditam*—knowing; *vaḥ*—your; *cikīrṣitam*—desires; *anugrahāya*—for the matter of showing you mercy; *bhadram*—all good fortune unto you; *vaḥ*—all of you; *evam*—thus; *me*—my; *darśanam*—audience; *kṛtam*—you have done.

TRANSLATION

Lord Śiva said: You are all the sons of King Prācīnabarhi, and I wish all good fortune to you. I also know what you are going to do, and therefore I am visible to you just to show my mercy upon you.

PURPORT

By these words Lord Śiva indicates that what the princes were going to do was known to him. It is a fact that they were going to worship Lord Viṣṇu by severe austerities and penances. Knowing this fact, Lord Śiva immediately became very pleased, as apparent by the next verse. This indicates that a person who is not yet a devotee of the Supreme Personality of Godhead but who desires to serve the Supreme Lord receives the benedictions of the demigods, headed by the chief demigod, Lord Śiva. Thus a devotee of the Lord does not need to try to please the demigods separately. Simply by worshiping the Supreme Lord, a devotee can please all of them. Nor does he have to ask the demigods for material benedictions, for the demigods, being pleased with the devotee, automatically offer him everything that he needs. The demigods are servants of the Lord, and they are always prepared to help a devotee in all circumstances. Therefore Śrīla Bilvamaṅgala Ṭhākura said that if one has unalloyed devotion for the Supreme Lord, the goddess of liberation is ready to serve him, to say nothing of the gods of material opulences. Indeed, all the demigods are simply waiting for an opportunity to serve the devotee. Thus there is no need for a devotee of Kṛṣṇa to endeavor for material opulence or liberation. By being situated in the transcendental position of devotional service, he receives all the benefits of *dharma, artha, kāma* and *mokṣa.*

TEXT 28

यः परं रंहसः साक्षात्त्रिगुणाज्जीवसंज्ञितात् ।
भगवन्तं वासुदेवं प्रपन्नः स प्रियो हि मे ॥२८॥

yaḥ paraṁ raṁhasaḥ sākṣāt
tri-guṇāj jīva-saṁjñitāt
bhagavantaṁ vāsudevaṁ
prapannaḥ sa priyo hi me

yaḥ—anyone; *param*—transcendental; *raṁhasaḥ*—of the controller; *sākṣāt*—directly; *tri-guṇāt*—from the three modes of material nature; *jīva-saṁjñitāt*—living entities called by the name *jīvas*; *bhagavantam*—unto the Supreme Personality of Godhead; *vāsudevam*—unto Kṛṣṇa; *prapannaḥ*—surrendered; *saḥ*—he; *priyaḥ*—very dear; *hi*—undoubtedly; *me*—of me.

TRANSLATION

Lord Śiva continued: Any person who is surrendered to the Supreme Personality of Godhead, Kṛṣṇa, the controller of everything—material nature as well as the living entity—is actually very dear to me.

PURPORT

Now Lord Śiva explains the reason he has personally come before the princes. It is because all the princes are devotees of Lord Kṛṣṇa. As stated in *Bhagavad-gītā:*

bahūnāṁ janmanām ante
jñānavān māṁ prapadyate
vāsudevaḥ sarvam iti
sa mahātmā sudurlabhaḥ

"After many births and deaths, he who is actually in knowledge surrenders unto Me, knowing Me to be the cause of all causes and all that is. Such a great soul is very rare." (Bg. 7.19)

Lord Śiva is rarely seen by common men, and similarly a person who is fully surrendered unto Vāsudeva, Kṛṣṇa, is also very rarely seen because a person who is fully surrendered unto the Supreme Lord is very rare (*sa mahātmā sudurlabhaḥ).* Consequently Lord Śiva came especially to see the Pracetās because they were fully surrendered unto the Supreme Personality of Godhead, Vāsudeva. Vāsudeva is also mentioned in the beginning of *Śrīmad-Bhāgavatam* in the *mantra: oṁ namo bhagavate vāsudevāya.* Since Vāsudeva is the ultimate truth, Lord Śiva openly proclaims that one who is a devotee of Lord Vāsudeva, who is surrendered to Lord Kṛṣṇa, is actually very dear to him. Lord Vāsudeva, Kṛṣṇa, is worshipable not only by ordinary living entities but by demigods like Lord Śiva, Lord Brahmā and others. *Yaṁ brahmā varuṇendra-rudra-marutaḥ stunvanti divyaiḥ stavaiḥ* (*Bhāg.* 12.13.1). Kṛṣṇa is worshiped by Lord Brahmā, Śiva, Varuṇa, Indra, Candra and all other demigods. That is also the situation with a devotee. Indeed, one who takes to Kṛṣṇa consciousness immediately becomes very dear to anyone who is simply finding out and beginning to understand what Kṛṣṇa consciousness actually is. Similarly, all the demigods are also trying to find out who is actually surrendered to Lord Vāsudeva. Because the Pracetā princes were surrendered to Vāsudeva, Lord Śiva willingly came forth to see them.

Lord Vāsudeva, or Kṛṣṇa, is described in *Bhagavad-gītā* as Puruṣottama. Actually He is the enjoyer *(puruṣa)* and the Supreme *(uttama)* as well. He is the enjoyer of everything—the *prakṛti* and the *puruṣa.* Being influenced by the three modes of material nature, the living entity tries to dominate material nature, but actually he is not the *puruṣa* (enjoyer) but is *prakṛti,* as described in *Bhagavad-gītā:*

apareyam itas tv anyāṁ
prakṛtiṁ viddhi me parām
jīva-bhūtāṁ mahā-bāho
yayedaṁ dhāryate jagat

"Besides this inferior nature, O mighty-armed Arjuna, there is a superior energy of Mine, which are all living entities who are struggling with material nature and are sustaining the universe." (Bg. 7.5)

Thus the *jīva,* or living entity, is actually *prakṛti,* or the marginal energy of the Supreme Lord. Being associated with material energy, he tries to lord it over the material nature. This is also confirmed in *Bhagavad-gītā:*

mamaivāṁśo jīva-loke
jīva-bhūtaḥ sanātanaḥ
manaḥ ṣaṣṭhānīndriyāṇi
prakṛti-sthāni karṣati

"The living entities in this conditioned world are My eternal, fragmental parts. Due to conditioned life, they are struggling very hard with the six senses, which include the mind." (Bg. 15.7)

By endeavoring to dominate material nature, the living entity simply struggles hard for existence. Indeed, he struggles so hard to enjoy himself that he cannot even enjoy the material resources. Thus he is sometimes called *prakṛti,* or *jīva,* for he is situated in the marginal potency. When the living entity is covered with the three modes of material nature, he is called *jīva-saṁjñita.* There are two kinds of living entities: one is called *kṣara,* and the other is *akṣara. Kṣara* refers to those who have fallen down and become conditioned, and *akṣara* refers to those who are not conditioned. The vast majority of living entities live in the spiritual world and are called *akṣara.* They are in the position of Brahman, pure spiritual existence. They are different from those who have been conditioned by the three modes of material nature.

Being above both the *kṣara* and *akṣara,* Lord Kṛṣṇa is described in *Bhagavad-gītā* as Puruṣottama:

yasmāt kṣaram atīto 'ham
akṣarād api cottamaḥ
ato 'smi loke vede ca
prathitaḥ puruṣottamaḥ

"Because I am transcendental, beyond both the fallible and the infallible, and because I am the greatest, I am celebrated both in the world and in the *Vedas* as that Supreme Person." (Bg. 15.18)

The impersonalists may say that Kṛṣṇa is the impersonal Brahman, but actually the impersonal Brahman is subordinate to Kṛṣṇa, as also confirmed in *Bhagavad-gītā:*

brahmaṇo hi pratiṣṭhāham
amṛtasyāvyayasya ca
śāśvatasya ca dharmasya
sukhasyaikāntikasya ca

"And I am the basis of the impersonal Brahman, which is the constitutional position of ultimate happiness, and which is immortal, imperishable and eternal." (Bg. 14.27)

That Kṛṣṇa is the source of the impersonal Brahman is also confirmed in *Brahma-saṁhitā: yasya prabhā prabhavato jagadaṇḍa-koṭi* (Bs. 5.40). The impersonal Brahman is nothing but the effulgence or bodily rays of Kṛṣṇa, and in those bodily rays there are innumerable universes floating. Thus in all respects Kṛṣṇa is the Supreme Lord, and Lord Śiva is very satisfied with those who are completely surrendered to Him. Complete surrender is desired by Kṛṣṇa, as He indicates in the last chapter of *Bhagavad-gītā:*

sarva-dharmān parityajya
māṁ ekaṁ śaraṇaṁ vraja
ahaṁ tvāṁ sarva-pāpebhyo
mokṣayiṣyāmi mā śucaḥ

"Abandon all varieties of religion and just surrender unto Me. I shall deliver you from all sinful reaction. Do not fear." (Bg. 18.66)

The word *sākṣāt,* meaning "directly," is very significant. There are many so-called devotees, but actually they are only *karmīs* and *jñānīs,* for they are not directly devotees of Lord Kṛṣṇa. The *karmīs* sometimes offer the results of their activities to Lord Vāsudeva, and this offering is called *karmārpaṇam.* These are considered to be fruitive activities, for the *karmīs* consider Lord Viṣṇu to be one of the demigods like Lord Śiva and Lord Brahmā. Because they consider Lord Viṣṇu to be on the same level with the demigods, they contend that surrendering to the demigods is as good as surrendering unto Vāsudeva. This contention is denied herein because if it were true, Lord Śiva would have said that surrender unto him, Lord Vāsudeva, Viṣṇu or Brahmā is the same. However, Lord Śiva does not say this because he himself surrenders unto Vāsudeva, and whoever else surrenders unto Vāsudeva is very, very dear to him. This is expressed herein openly. The conclusion is that a devotee of Lord Śiva is not dear to Lord Śiva, but a devotee of Lord Kṛṣṇa is very dear to Lord Śiva.

TEXT 29

स्वधर्मनिष्ठः शतजन्मभिः पुमान्
विरिञ्चतामेति ततः परं हि माम् ।
अव्याकृतं भागवतोऽथ वैष्णवं
पदं यथाहं विबुधाः कलात्यये ॥२९॥

sva-dharma-niṣṭhaḥ śata-janmabhiḥ pumān
viriñcatām eti tataḥ paraṁ hi mām
avyākṛtaṁ bhāgavato 'tha vaiṣṇavaṁ
padaṁ yathāhaṁ vibudhāḥ kalātyaye

sva-dharma-niṣṭhaḥ—one who is situated in his own *dharma* or occupation; *śata-janmabhiḥ*—for one hundred births; *pumān*—a living entity; *viriñcatām*—the post of Lord Brahmā; *eti*—gets; *tataḥ*—thereafter; *param*—above; *hi*—certainly; *mām*—attains Me; *avyākṛtam*—without deviation; *bhāgavataḥ*—unto the Supreme Personality of Godhead; *atha*—therefore; *vaiṣṇavam*—a pure devotee of the Lord; *padam*—post; *yathā*—as; *aham*—I; *vibudhāḥ*—demigods; *kalā-atyaye*—after the annihilation of the material world.

TRANSLATION

A person who executes his occupational duty properly for one hundred births becomes qualified to occupy the post of Brahmā, and if he becomes more qualified, he can approach Lord Śiva. A person who is directly surrendered to Lord Kṛṣṇa or Viṣṇu in unalloyed devotional service is immediately promoted to the spiritual planets. Lord Śiva and other demigods attain these planets after the destruction of this material world.

PURPORT

The highest perfection of the evolutionary process, as described by the Vaiṣṇava poet Jayadeva Gosvāmī, is given herein. *Pralaya-payodhi-jale dhṛtavān asi vedam.* The evolutionary process begins from the point of devastation *(pralaya)* when the whole universe is filled with water. At that time there are many fishes and other aquatics, and from these aquatics evolve creepers, trees, etc. From these, insects and reptiles evolve, and from them birds, beasts, and then human beings. Finally civilized human beings evolve, and at present these civilized human beings are at a junction where they can make further evolutionary progress in spiritual life. Here it is stated *(sva-dharma-niṣṭhaḥ)* that when a living entity comes to a civilized form of life, there must be *sva-dharma,* social divisions according to one's work and qualifications. This is indicated in *Bhagavad-gītā:*

cātur-varṇyaṁ mayā sṛṣṭaṁ
guṇa-karma-vibhāgaśaḥ

"According to the three modes of material nature and the work ascribed to them, the four divisions of human society were created by Me." (Bg. 4.13)

In civilized human society there are the divisions of *brāhmaṇa, kṣatriya, vaiśya* and *śūdra,* and everyone must properly execute his occupational duty in accordance to his division. Here it is described *(sva-dharma-niṣṭhaḥ)* that it doesn't matter whether one is a *brāhmaṇa, kṣatriya, vaiśya* or *śūdra.* If one sticks to his position and properly executes his particular duty, he is considered a civilized human being. Otherwise he is no better than an animal. It is also mentioned herein that whoever executes his occupational duty *(sva-dharma)* for one hundred births (for instance, if a *brāhmaṇa* continues to act as a *brāhmaṇa*), becomes eligible for promotion to Brahmaloka, the planet where Lord Brahmā lives. There is also a planet called Śivaloka, or Sadāśivaloka, which is situated in a marginal position between the spiritual and material worlds. If, after being situated in Brahmaloka, one becomes more qualified, he is promoted to Sadāśivaloka. Similarly, when one becomes even more qualified, he can attain the Vaikuṇṭhalokas. The Vaikuṇṭhalokas are targets for everyone, even the demigods, and they can be attained by a devotee who has no desire for material benefit. As indicated in *Bhagavad-gītā,* one does not escape material miseries even if he is elevated to Brahmaloka.

ābrahma-bhuvanāl lokāḥ
punar āvartino 'rjuna
mām upetya tu kaunteya
punar janma na vidyate

"From the highest planet in the material world down to the lowest, all are places of misery wherein repeated birth and death take place. But one who attains to My abode, O son of Kuntī, never takes birth again." (Bg. 8.16)

Similarly, one is not very safe even if he is promoted to Śivaloka, because the planet of Śivaloka is marginal. However, if one attains Vaikuṇṭhaloka (*mām upetya tu kaunteya punar janma na vidyate,* Bg. 8.16), he attains the highest perfection of life and the end of the evolutionary process. In other words, it is confirmed herein that a person in human society who has developed consciousness must take to Kṛṣṇa consciousness in order to be promoted to Vaikuṇṭhaloka, or Kṛṣṇaloka, immediately after leaving the body. As stated in *Bhagavad-gītā:*

janma karma ca me divyam
evaṁ yo vetti tattvataḥ
tyaktvā dehaṁ punar janma
naiti mām eti so 'rjuna

"One who knows the transcendental nature of My appearance and activities does not, upon leaving the body, take his birth again in this material world, but attains My eternal abode, O Arjuna." (Bg. 4.9)

A devotee who is fully in Kṛṣṇa consciousness, who is not attracted by any other *loka,* or planet, including Brahmaloka and Śivaloka, is immediately transferred to Kṛṣṇaloka *(mām eti).* That is the highest perfection of life and the perfection of the evolutionary process.

TEXT 30

अथ भागवता यूयं प्रियाः स्थ भगवान् यथा ।
न मद्भागवतानां च प्रेयानन्योऽस्ति कर्हिचित् ॥३०॥

atha bhāgavatā yūyaṁ
priyāḥ stha bhagavān yathā
na mad bhāgavatānāṁ ca
preyān anyo 'sti karhicit

atha—therefore; *bhāgavatāḥ*—devotees; *yūyam*—all of you; *priyāḥ*—very dear to me; *stha*—you are; *bhagavān*—the Supreme Personality of Godhead; *yathā*—as; *na*—neither; *mat*—than me; *bhāgavatānām*—of the devotees; *ca*—also; *preyān*—very dear; *anyaḥ*—others; *asti*—there is; *karhicit*—at any time.

TRANSLATION

You are all devotees of the Lord, and as such I appreciate that you are as respectable as the Supreme Personality of Godhead Himself. I know in this way that the devotees also respect me and that I am dear to them. Thus no one can be as dear to the devotees as I am.

PURPORT

It is said *(vaiṣṇavānāṁ yathā śambhuḥ)* that Lord Śiva is the best of all devotees; therefore all devotees of Lord Kṛṣṇa are also devotees of Lord Śiva. In Vṛndāvana there is Lord Śiva's temple called Gopīśvara. The *gopīs* used to worship not only Lord Śiva but Kātyāyanī or Durgā as well, but their aim was to attain the favor of Lord Kṛṣṇa. A devotee of Lord Kṛṣṇa does not disrespect Lord Śiva but worships Lord Śiva as the most exalted devotee of Lord Kṛṣṇa. Consequently whenever a devotee worships Lord Śiva, he prays to him to achieve the favor of Kṛṣṇa, and he does not request material profit. In *Bhagavad-gītā* it is said that generally people worship demigods for some material profit. *Kāmais tais tair hṛtajñānāḥ* (Bg. 7.20). Driven by material lust, they worship demigods, but a devotee never does so, for he is never driven by material lust. That is the difference between a devotee's respect for Lord Śiva and an *asura's* respect for him. The *asura* worships Lord Śiva, takes some benediction from him, misuses the benediction and ultimately is killed by the Supreme Personality of Godhead, who awards him liberation.

Because Lord Śiva is a great devotee of the Supreme Personality of Godhead, he loves all the devotees of the Supreme Lord. Lord Śiva told the Pracetās that because they were devotees of the Lord, he loved them very much. Lord Śiva was not only kind and merciful to the Pracetās; anyone who is a devotee of the Supreme Personality of Godhead is very dear to Lord Śiva. Not only are the devotees dear to Lord Śiva, but he respects them as much as he respects the Supreme Personality of Godhead. Similarly, devotees of the Supreme Lord also worship Lord Śiva as the most dear devotee of Lord Kṛṣṇa. They do not worship him as a separate Personality of Godhead. It is stated in the list of *nāma-aparādhas* that it is an offense to think that the chanting of the name of Hari and the chanting of Hara or Śiva are the same. The devotees must always know that Lord Viṣṇu is the Supreme Personality of Godhead and that Lord Śiva is His devotee.

A devotee should be offered respect on the level of the Supreme Personality of Godhead, and sometimes even more respect. Indeed, Lord Rāma, the Personality of Godhead Himself, sometimes worshiped Lord Śiva. If a devotee is worshiped by the Lord, why should a devotee not be worshiped by other devotees on the same level with the Lord? This is the conclusion. From this verse it appears that Lord Śiva benedicts the *asuras* simply for the sake of formality. Actually he loves one who is devoted to the Supreme Personality of Godhead.

TEXT 31

इदं विविक्तं जप्तव्यं पवित्रं मङ्गलं परम् ।
निःश्रेयसकरं चापि श्रूयतां तद्वदामि वः ॥३१॥

idaṁ viviktaṁ japtavyaṁ
pavitraṁ maṅgalaṁ param
niḥśreyasa-karaṁ cāpi
śrūyatāṁ tad vadāmi vaḥ

idam—this; *viviktam*—very, particular; *japtavyam*—always to be chanted; *pavitram*—very pure; *maṅgalam*—auspicious; *param*—transcendental; *niḥśreyasa-karam*—very beneficial; *ca*—also; *api*—certainly; *śrūyatām*—please hear; *tat*—that; *vadāmi*—I am speaking; *vaḥ*—unto you.

TRANSLATION

Now I shall chant one mantra which is not only transcendental, pure and auspicious but is the best prayer for anyone who is aspiring to attain the ultimate goal of life. When I chant this mantra, please hear it carefully and attentively.

PURPORT

The word *viviktam* is very significant. No one should think of the prayers recited by Lord Śiva as being sectarian; rather, they are very confidential, so much so that anyone desiring the ultimate prosperity or auspicious goal of life must take the instructions of Lord Śiva and pray to and glorify the Supreme Personality of Godhead as Lord Śiva himself did.

TEXT 32

मैत्रेय उवाच

इत्यनुक्रोशहृदयो भगवानाह ताञ्छिवः ।
बद्धाञ्जलीन् राजपुत्रान्नारायणपरो वचः ॥३२॥

maitreya uvāca
ity anukrośa-hṛdayo
bhagavān āha tāñ chivaḥ
baddhāñjalīn rāja-putrān
nārāyaṇa-paro vacaḥ

maitreyaḥ uvāca—the great saint Maitreya continued to speak; *iti*—thus; *anukrośa-hṛdayaḥ*—very kindhearted; *bhagavān*—the lord; *āha*—said; *tān*—unto the Pracetās; *śivaḥ*—Lord Śiva; *baddha-añjalīn*—who were standing with folded hands; *rāja-putrān*—the sons of the king; *nārāyaṇa-paraḥ*—Lord Śiva, the great devotee of Nārāyaṇa; *vacaḥ*—words.

TRANSLATION

The great sage Maitreya continued: Out of his causeless mercy, the exalted personality, Lord Śiva, a great devotee of Lord Nārāyaṇa, continued to speak to the King's sons, who were standing with folded hands.

PURPORT

Lord Śiva voluntarily came to benedict the sons of the King as well as do something beneficial for them. He personally chanted the *mantra* so that the *mantra* would be more powerful, and he advised that the *mantra* be chanted by the King's sons *(rāja-putras)*. When a *mantra* is chanted by a great devotee, the *mantra* becomes more powerful. Although the Hare Kṛṣṇa *mahā-mantra* is powerful in itself, a disciple upon initiation receives the *mantra* from his spiritual master, for when the *mantra* is chanted by the spiritual master, it becomes more powerful. Lord Śiva advised the sons of the King to hear him attentively, for inattentive hearing is offensive.

TEXT 33

श्रीरुद्र उवाच
जितं त आत्मविद्वर्यस्वस्तये स्वस्तिरस्तु मे ।
भवताराधसा राद्धं सर्वात्मा आत्मने नमः ॥३३॥

śrī-rudra uvāca
jitaṁ ta ātma-vid-varya-
svastaye svastir astu me
bhavatārādhasā rāddhaṁ
sarvātmā ātmane namaḥ

śrī-rudraḥ uvāca—Lord Śiva began to speak; *jitam*—all glories; *te*—unto You; *ātma-vit*—self-realized; *varya*—the best; *svastaye*—unto the auspicious; *svastiḥ*—auspiciousness; *astu*—let there be; *me*—of me; *bhavatā*—by You; *ārādhasā*—by the all-perfect; *rāddham*—worshipable; *sarvātmā*—the Supreme Soul; *ātmane*—unto the Supreme Soul; *namaḥ*—obeisances.

TRANSLATION

Lord Śiva addressed the Supreme Personality of Godhead with the following prayer: O Supreme Personality of Godhead, all glories unto You. You are the most exalted of all self-realized souls. Since You are always auspicious for the self-realized, I wish that You will be auspicious for me. You are worshipable by virtue of the all-perfect instructions which You give. You are the Supersoul; therefore I offer my obeisances unto You as the supreme living being.

PURPORT

As long as a devotee is inspired by the Lord to offer the Lord a prayer, the devotee immediately glorifies the Lord in the beginning by saying, "All glories unto You, my Lord." The Lord is glorified because He is considered to be the chief of all self-realized souls. As said in the *Vedas (nityo nityānāṁ cetanaś cetanānām, Kaṭha,* 2.2.13), the Supreme Being, the Personality of Godhead, is the chief living being amongst all living beings. There are different kinds of individual living beings—some of them are in this material world, and some are in the spiritual world. Those who are in the spiritual world are known to be completely self-realized because on the spiritual platform the living entity is not forgetful of his service to the Lord. Therefore in the spiritual world all those who are in the devotional service of the Lord are eternally fixed, for they understand the position of the Supreme Being, as well as their individual constitution. Thus amongst self-realized souls, the Lord is known as the perfectly self-realized soul. *Nityo nityānāṁ cetanaś cetanānām.* When the individual soul is fixed in his knowledge of the Lord as the Supreme Being, he actually becomes established in an all-auspicious position. Lord Śiva prays herein that his auspicious position will continue eternally by virtue of the Lord's mercy upon him.

The Supreme Lord is all-perfect, and the Lord instructs that one who worships Him also becomes perfect. As stated in *Bhagavad-gītā: mattaḥ smṛtir jñānam apohanaṁ ca* (Bg. 15.15). The Lord is situated as the Supersoul in everyone's heart, but He is so kind to His devotees that He gives them instructions by which they may continue to progress. When they receive instructions from the all-perfect, there is no chance of their being misled. This is also confirmed in *Bhagavad-gītā: dadāmi buddhi-yogaṁ taṁ yena mām upayānti te* (Bg. 10.10). The Lord is always ready to give instructions to the pure devotee so that the devotee can advance further and further in devotional service. Since the Lord gives instructions as Sarvātmā, the Supersoul, Lord Śiva offers Him respect with the words *sarvātmā ātmane namaḥ*. The individual soul is called *ātmā*, and the Lord is also called *ātmā* as well as Paramātmā. Being situated in everyone's heart, the Lord is known as the supreme *ātmā*. Therefore all obeisances are offered unto Him. In this regard, one may refer to the prayers of Kuntī in the First Canto of *Śrīmad-Bhāgavatam:*

tathā paramahaṁsānāṁ munīnām amalātmanām
bhaktiyoga-vidhānārthaṁ kathaṁ paśyema hi striyaḥ (Bhāg. 1.8.20*)*

The Lord is always ready to give instructions to the *paramahaṁsas*, or the topmost devotees of the Lord who are completely liberated from all contaminations of the material world. The Lord always gives instructions to such exalted devotees to inform them how they can remain fixed in devotional service. Similarly, it is stated in the *ātmārāma* verse:

ātmārāmāś ca munayo nirgranthā apy urukrame
kurvanty ahaitukīṁ bhaktim itthambhūta-guṇo hariḥ (Bhāg. 1.7.10*)*

The word *ātmārāma* refers to those who are not interested in the material world but are simply engaged in spiritual realization. Such self-realized persons are generally considered in two categories—impersonal and personal. However, impersonalists also become devotees when they are attracted by the personal transcendental qualities of the Lord. The conclusion is that Lord Śiva wanted to remain a fixed devotee of the Supreme Personality of Godhead, Vāsudeva. As explained in the following verses, Lord Śiva never desires to merge into the existence of the Supreme Lord like the impersonalists. Rather, he thinks that it would be good fortune for him to continue to be fixed in the understanding of the Lord as the Supreme Being. By this understanding, one realizes that all living entities—including Lord Śiva, Lord Brahmā and other demigods—are servants of the Supreme Lord.

TEXT 34

नमः पङ्कजनाभाय भूतसूक्ष्मेन्द्रियात्मने ।
वासुदेवाय शान्ताय कूटस्थाय स्वरोचिषे ॥३४॥

namaḥ paṅkaja-nābhāya
bhūta-sūkṣmendriyātmane
vāsudevāya śāntāya
kūṭasthāya sva-rociṣe

namaḥ—all obeisances unto You; *paṅkaja-nābhāya*—unto the Supreme Personality of Godhead from whose navel the lotus flower emanates; *bhūta-sūkṣma*—the sense objects; *indriya*—the senses; *ātmane*—the origin; *vāsudevāya*—unto Lord Vāsudeva; *śāntāya*—always peaceful; *kūṭasthāya*—without being changed; *sva-rociṣe*—unto the supreme illumination.

TRANSLATION

My Lord, You are the origin of the creation by virtue of the lotus flower which sprouts from Your navel. You are the supreme controller of the senses and the sense objects, and You are also the all-pervading Vāsudeva. You are most peaceful, and because of Your self-illuminated existence, You are not disturbed by the six kinds of transformations.

PURPORT

The Lord as Garbhodakaśāyī Viṣṇu lies in the ocean of Garbha within this universe, and from His navel the lotus flower sprouts. Lord Brahmā is generated from that lotus flower, and from Lord Brahmā the creation of this material world begins. As such, the Supreme Personality of Godhead, Garbhodakaśāyī Viṣṇu, is the origin of the material senses and sense objects. Since Lord Śiva considers himself to be one of the products of the material world, his senses are under the control of the supreme creator. The Supreme Lord is also known as Hṛṣīkeśa, master of the senses, which indicates that our senses and sense objects are formed by the Supreme Lord. As such, He can control our senses and out of His mercy engage them in the service of the master of the senses. In the conditioned state, the living entity struggles in this material world and engages his senses for material satisfaction. However, if the living entity is graced by the Supreme Personality of Godhead, he can engage these very senses in the service of the Lord. Lord Śiva desires not to be misled by the material senses but to engage always in the service of the Lord without being subject to contamination by materialistic influences. By the grace and help of Lord Vāsudeva, who is all-pervading, one can engage his senses in devotional service without deviation, just as the Lord acts without deviation.

The words *śāntāya kūṭasthāya sva-rociṣe* are very significant. Although the Lord is within this material world, He is not disturbed by the waves of material existence. However, conditioned souls are agitated by six kinds of transformations; namely, they become agitated when they are hungry, when they are thirsty, when they are aggrieved, when they are illusioned, when they grow old, and when they are on the deathbed. Although conditioned souls become very easily illusioned by these conditions in the material world, the Supreme Personality of Godhead, as the Supersoul, Vāsudeva, is never agitated by these transformations. Therefore it is said here *(kūṭasthāya)* that He is always peaceful and devoid of agitation because of His prowess, which is described herein as *sva-rociṣe,* indicating that He is illuminated by His own transcendental position. In other words, the individual soul, although within the illumination of the Supreme, sometimes falls down from that illumination because of his tiny position, and when he falls down he enters into material conditional life. The Lord, however, is not subject to such conditioning; therefore He is described as self-illuminated. Consequently any conditioned soul within this material universe can remain completely perfect when he is under the protection of Vāsudeva or when he is engaged in devotional service.

TEXT 35

सङ्कर्षणाय सूक्ष्माय दुरन्तायान्तकाय च ।
नमो विश्वप्रबोधाय प्रद्युम्नायान्तरात्मने ॥३५॥

saṅkarṣaṇāya sūkṣmāya
durantāyāntakāya ca
namo viśva-prabodhāya
pradyumnāyāntarātmane

saṅkarṣaṇāya—unto the master of integration; *sūkṣmāya*—unto the subtle unmanifested material ingredients; *durantāya*—unto the unsurpassable; *antakāya*—unto the master of disintegration; *ca*—also; *namaḥ*—obeisances; *viśva-prabodhāya*—unto the master of the development of the universe; *pradyumnāya*—unto Lord Pradyumna; *antarātmane*—unto the Supersoul in everyone's heart.

TRANSLATION

My dear Lord, You are the origin of the subtle material ingredients, the master of all integration as well as the master of all disintegration, the predominating Deity named Saṅkarṣaṇa, and the master of all intelligence,

known as the predominating Deity Pradyumna. Therefore, I offer my respectful obeisances unto You.

PURPORT

The whole universe is maintained by the integrating power of the Supreme Lord, who is known in that capacity by the name of Saṅkarṣaṇa. The material scientists might have discovered the law of gravity which maintains the integration of objects within the material energy, yet the master of all integration can create devastation by the disintegrating blazing fire emanating from His mouth. A description of this can be found in the Eleventh Chapter of *Bhagavad-gītā* wherein the universal form of the Lord is described. The master of integration is also the destroyer of this world by virtue of His disintegrating energy. Saṅkarṣaṇa is the master of integration and disintegration, whereas Pradyumna, another feature of Lord Vāsudeva, is responsible for universal growth and maintenance. The word *sūkṣmāya* is significant because within this gross material body there are subtle material bodies—namely mind, intelligence and ego. The Lord in His different features (Vāsudeva, Aniruddha, Pradyumna and Saṅkarṣaṇa) maintains both the material and subtle elements of this world. As mentioned in *Bhagavad-gītā,* the material elements are earth, water, fire, air and ether, and the material subtle elements are mind, intelligence and ego. All of them are controlled by the Supreme Personality of Godhead as Vāsudeva, Saṅkarṣaṇa, Pradyumna and Aniruddha, and this will be further explained in the following verse.

TEXT 36

नमो नमोऽनिरुद्धाय हृषीकेशेन्द्रियात्मने ।
नमः परमहंसाय पूर्णाय निभृतात्मने ॥३६॥

namo namo 'niruddhāya
hṛṣīkeśendriyātmane
namaḥ paramahaṁsāya
pūrṇāya nibhṛtātmane

namaḥ—all my obeisances unto You; *namaḥ*—obeisances again; *aniruddhāya*—unto Lord Aniruddha; *hṛṣīkeśa*—the master of the senses; *indriya-ātmane*—the director of the senses; *namaḥ*—all obeisances unto You; *paramahaṁsāya*—unto the Supreme Perfect; *pūrṇāya*—unto the Supreme Complete; *nibhṛta-ātmane*—who is situated apart from this material creation.

TRANSLATION

My Lord, as the supreme directing Deity known as Aniruddha, You are the master of the senses and the mind. I therefore offer my obeisances unto You again and again. You are known as Ananta as well as Saṅkarṣaṇa because of Your ability to destroy the whole creation by the blazing fire from Your mouth.

PURPORT

Hṛṣīkeśendriyātmane. The mind is the director of the senses, and Lord Aniruddha is the director of the mind. In order to execute devotional service, one has to fix his mind on the lotus feet of Kṛṣṇa; therefore Lord Śiva prays to the controller of the mind, Lord Aniruddha, to be pleased and to help him engage his mind on the lotus feet of the Lord. It is stated in *Bhagavad-gītā: man-manā bhava mad-bhakto mad-yājī māṁ namaskuru* (Bg. 9.34). The mind has to be engaged in meditation on the lotus feet of the Lord in order to execute devotional service. It is also stated in *Bhagavad-gītā:*

sarvasya cāhaṁ hṛdi sanniviṣṭo
mattaḥ smṛtir jñānam apohanaṁ ca
vedaiś ca sarvair aham eva vedyo
vedānta-kṛd veda-vid eva cāham

"I am seated in everyone's heart, and from Me come remembrance, knowledge and forgetfulness. By all the *Vedas* am I to be known; indeed I am the compiler of *Vedānta,* and I am the knower of the *Vedas.*" (Bg. 15.15)

Thus if Lord Aniruddha is pleased, He can help the mind engage in the service of the Lord. It is also indicated in this verse that Lord Aniruddha is the sun-god by virtue of His expansions. Since the predominating deity of the sun is an expansion of Lord Aniruddha, Lord Śiva also prays to the sun-god in this verse.

Lord Kṛṣṇa, by His quadruple expansion (Vāsudeva, Saṅkarṣaṇa, Pradyumna and Aniruddha), is the Lord of psychic action—namely, thinking, feeling, willing and acting. Lord Śiva prays to Lord Aniruddha as the sun-god who is the controlling deity of the external material elements which constitute the construction of the material body. According to Śrīla Viśvanātha Cakravartī Ṭhākura, the word *paramahaṁsa* is also another name for the sun-god. The sun-god is addressed herein as *nibhṛtātmane,* which indicates that he always maintains the various planets by manipulating the rainfall. The sun-god evaporates water from the seas and oceans and then forms the water into clouds and distributes it over land. When there is sufficient rainfall, grains are produced, and these grains maintain living entities in each and every planet. The sun-god is also addressed herein as *pūrṇa,* or complete, because the rays emanating from the sun have no end. For millions and millions of years since the creation of this universe, the sun-god has been supplying heat and light without diminution. The word *paramahaṁsa* is applied to persons who are completely cleansed. When there is sufficient sunshine, the mind remains clear and transparent—in other words, the sun-god helps the mind of the living entity to become situated on the platform of *paramahaṁsa.* Thus Lord Śiva prays to Aniruddha to be kind upon him so that his mind will always be in the perfect state of cleanliness and will be engaged in the devotional service of the Lord. Just as fire sterilizes all unclean things, the sun-god also keeps everything sterilized, especially dirty things within the mind, thus enabling one to attain elevation to the platform of spiritual understanding.

TEXT 37

स्वर्गापवर्गद्वाराय नित्यं शुचिषदे नमः ।
नमो हिरण्यवीर्याय चातुर्होत्राय तन्तवे ॥३७॥

svargāpavarga-dvārāya
nityaṁ śuci-ṣade namaḥ
namo hiraṇya-vīryāya
cāturhotrāya tantave

svarga—the heavenly planets; *apavarga*—the path of liberation; *dvārāya*—unto the door of; *nityam*—eternally; *śuci-ṣade*—unto the most purified; *namaḥ*—my obeisances unto You; *namaḥ*—my obeisances; *hiraṇya*—gold; *vīryāya*—semina; *cātur-hotrāya*—the Vedic sacrifices of the name; *tantave*—unto one who expands.

TRANSLATION

My Lord, O Aniruddha, You are the authority by which the doors of the higher planetary systems and liberation are opened. You are always within the pure heart of the living entity. Therefore I offer my obeisances unto You. You are the possessor of semina which is like gold, and thus, in the form of fire, You help the Vedic sacrifices, beginning with cāturhotra. Therefore I offer my obeisances unto You.

PURPORT

The word *svarga* indicates a position in the higher or heavenly planetary systems, and the word *apavarga* means liberation. Those who are attached to the *karma-kāṇḍīya* activities described in the *Vedas* are actually entangled in the three modes of material nature. The *Bhagavad-gītā* therefore says that one should be above the dominion of fruitive activities. There are different kinds of liberation, or *mukti.* The best *mukti* is engagement in the devotional service of the Supreme Lord. Lord Aniruddha not only helps fruitive actors by elevating them to the higher planetary systems, but He also helps the devotee engage in devotional service by dint of His inexhaustible energy. Just as heat is the source of material energy, the inspiration of Lord Aniruddha is the energy by which one can engage in executing devotional service.

TEXT 38

नम ऊर्ज इषे त्रय्याः पतये यज्ञरेतसे ।
तृप्तिदाय च जीवानां नमः सर्वरसात्मने ॥३८॥

nama ūrja iṣe trayyāḥ
pataye yajña-retase
tṛpti-dāya ca jīvānāṁ
namaḥ sarva-rasātmane

namaḥ—I offer all obeisances unto You; *ūrje*—unto the provider of the Pitṛloka; *iṣe*—the provider of all the demigods; *trayyāḥ*—of the three *Vedas; pataye*—unto the master; *yajña*—sacrifices; *retase*—unto the predominating deity of the moon planet; *tṛpti-dāya*—unto Him who gives satisfaction to everyone; *ca*—also; *jīvānām*—of the living entities; *namaḥ*—I offer my obeisances; *sarva-rasa-ātmane*—unto the all-pervading Supersoul.

TRANSLATION

My Lord, You are the provider of the Pitṛlokas as well as all the demigods. You are the predominating deity of the moon and the master of all three Vedas. I offer my respectful obeisances unto You because You are the original source of satisfaction for all living entities.

PURPORT

When the living entity is born within this material world—especially as a human being—he has several obligations unto the demigods, unto the saintly persons and unto living entities in general. As enjoined in the *śāstras: devarṣi-bhūtāpta-nṛṇāṁ pitṝṇām.* Thus one has an obligation to one's forefathers, the previous hierarchy. Lord Śiva prays to Lord Aniruddha to give him strength so he can become free from all obligations to the *pitās*, demigods, general living entities and saintly persons and completely engage himself in the devotional service of the Lord. As stated:

devarṣi-bhūtāpta-nṛṇāṁ pitṝṇāṁ
na kiṅkaro nāyam ṛṇī ca rājan
sarvātmanā yaḥ śaraṇaṁ śaraṇyaṁ
gato mukundaṁ parihṛtya kartam
(*Bhāg.* 11.5.41)

One becomes free from all obligations to the demigods, saintly persons, *pitās,* ancient forefathers, etc., if one is completely engaged in the devotional service of the Lord. Lord Śiva therefore prays to Lord Aniruddha to give him strength so that he can be free from such obligations and entirely engage in the Lord's service.

Soma, or the predominating deity of the moon, is responsible for the living entity's ability to relish the taste of food through the tongue. Lord Śiva prays to Lord Aniruddha to give him strength so that he will not taste anything but the *prasāda* of the Lord. Śrīla Bhaktivinoda Ṭhākura has sung a verse indicating that the tongue is the most vicious enemy and is the most voracious of all the senses. If one can control the tongue, he can easily control the other senses. The tongue can be controlled only by eating *prasāda* offered to the Deity. Lord Śiva's prayer to Lord Aniruddha is meant for this purpose *(tṛpti-dāya);* he prays to Lord Aniruddha to help him be satisfied by eating only *prasāda* offered to the Lord.

TEXT 39

सर्वसत्त्वात्मदेहाय विशेषाय स्थवीयसे ।
नमस्त्रैलोक्यपालाय सहओजोबलाय च ॥३९॥

sarva-sattvātma-dehāya
viśeṣāya sthavīyase
namas trailokya-pālāya
saha ojo-balāya ca

sarva—all; *sattva*—existence; *ātma*—soul; *dehāya*—unto the body; *viśeṣāya*—diversity; *sthavīyase*—unto the material world; *namaḥ*—offering obeisances; *trailokya*—three planetary systems; *pālāya*—maintainer; *saha*—along with; *ojaḥ*—prowess; *balāya*—unto the strength; *ca*—also.

TRANSLATION

My dear Lord, You are the gigantic universal form which contains all the individual bodies of the living entities. You are the maintainer of the

three worlds, and as such You maintain the mind, senses, body and air of life within them. I therefore offer my respectful obeisances unto You.

PURPORT

As the individual body of the living entity is composed of millions of cells, germs and microbes, the universal body of the Supreme Lord similarly contains all the individual bodies of the living entities. Lord Śiva is offering his obeisances to the universal body, which includes all other bodies, so that everyone's body may fully engage in devotional service. Since this individual body is composed of senses, all the senses should be engaged in devotional service. For instance, the smelling instrument, the nose, can engage in smelling the flowers offered to the lotus feet of the Lord, the hands can engage in cleansing the temple of the Lord, etc. Indeed, being the life air of every living entity, the Lord is the maintainer of the three worlds. Consequently He can induce every living entity to engage in his real life's duty with full bodily and mental strength. Thus every living entity should serve the Supreme Personality of Godhead by his *prāṇa* (life), *artha* (wealth), intelligence and words. As stated in the *Śrīmad-Bhāgavatam:*

etāvaj janma-sāphalyaṁ dehinām iha dehiṣu
prāṇair arthair dhiyā vācā śreya evācaret sadā (*Bhāg.* 10.22.35)

Even though one may desire to engage in the service of the Lord, without sanction one cannot do so. Lord Śiva is offering his prayers in so many different ways in order to show living entities how to engage in the devotional service of the Lord.

TEXT 40

अर्थलिङ्गाय नभसे नमोऽन्तर्बहिरात्मने ।
नमः पुण्याय लोकाय अमुष्मै भूरिवर्चसे ॥४०॥

artha-liṅgāya nabhase
namo 'ntar-bahir-ātmane
namaḥ puṇyāya lokāya
amuṣmai bhūri-varcase

artha—meaning; *liṅgāya*—revealing; *nabhase*—unto the sky; *namaḥ*—offering obeisances; *antaḥ*—within; *bahiḥ*—and without; *ātmane*—unto the self; *namaḥ*—offering obeisances; *puṇyāya*—pious activities; *lokāya*—for creation; *amuṣmai*—beyond death; *bhūri-varcase*—the supreme effulgence.

TRANSLATION

My dear Lord, by expanding Your transcendental vibrations, You reveal the actual meaning of everything. You are the all-pervading sky within and without, and You are the ultimate goal of pious activities executed both within this material world and beyond it. I therefore offer my respectful obeisances again and again unto You.

PURPORT

Vedic evidence is called *śabda-brahma.* There are many things which are beyond the perception of our imperfect senses, yet the authoritative evidence of sound vibration is perfect. The *Vedas* are known as *śabda-brahma* because evidence taken from the *Vedas* constitutes the ultimate understanding. This is because *śabda-brahma,* or the *Vedas,* represents the Supreme Personality of Godhead. However, the real essence of *śabda-brahma* is the chanting of the Hare Kṛṣṇa *mantra.* By vibrating this transcendental sound, the meaning of everything both material and spiritual is revealed. This Hare Kṛṣṇa is nondifferent from the Personality of Godhead. The meaning of everything is received through the air through sound vibration. The vibration may be material or spiritual, but without sound vibration no one can understand the meaning of anything. In the *Vedas* it is said: *antar bahiś ca tat sarvaṁ vyāpya nārāyaṇaḥ sthitaḥ.* "Nārāyaṇa is all-pervading, and He exists both within and without." This is also confirmed in *Bhagavad-gītā:*

yathā prakāśayaty ekaḥ
kṛtsnaṁ lokam imaṁ raviḥ
kṣetraṁ kṣetrī tathā kṛtsnaṁ
prakāśayati bhārata

"O son of Bharata, as the sun alone illuminates all this universe, so do the living entity and the Supersoul illuminate the entire body by consciousness." (Bg. 13.34)

In other words, the consciousness of both the soul and Supersoul is all-pervading; the limited consciousness of the living entity is pervading the entire material body, and the supreme consciousness of the Lord is pervading the entire universe. Because the soul is present within the body, consciousness pervades the entire body; similarly, because the supreme soul, or Kṛṣṇa, is present within this universe, everything is working in order. *Mayādhyakṣeṇa prakṛtiḥ sūyate sa-carācaram:* "This material nature is working under My direction, O son of Kuntī, and it is producing all moving and unmoving beings." (Bg. 9.10)

Lord Śiva is therefore praying to the Personality of Godhead to be kind to us so that simply by chanting the Hare Kṛṣṇa *mantra* we can understand everything in both the material and spiritual worlds. The word *amuṣmai* is significant in this regard because it indicates the best target one can aim for after attaining the higher planetary systems. Those who are engaged in fruitive activities *(karmīs)* attain the higher planetary systems as a result of their past activities, and the *jñānīs,* who seek unification or a monistic merging with the effulgence of the Supreme Lord, also attain their desired end, but in the ultimate issue, the devotees who desire to personally associate with the Lord are promoted to the Vaikuṇṭhalokas, or Goloka Vṛndāvana. The Lord is described in *Bhagavad-gītā* as *pavitraṁ paramam* (Bg. 10.12), the supremely pious one. This is also confirmed in this verse. Śukadeva Gosvāmī has stated that the cowherd boys who played with Lord Kṛṣṇa were not ordinary living entities. Only after accumulating many pious activities in various births does one get the opportunity to personally associate with the Supreme Personality of Godhead. Since only the pure can reach Him, He is the supreme pure.

TEXT 41

प्रवृत्ताय निवृत्ताय पितृदेवाय कर्मणे ।
नमोऽधर्मविपाकाय मृत्यवे दुःखदाय च ॥४१॥

pravṛttāya nivṛttāya
pitṛ-devāya karmaṇe
namo 'dharma-vipākāya
mṛtyave duḥkha-dāya ca

pravṛttāya—inclination; *nivṛttāya*—disinclination; *pitṛ-devāya*—unto the master of Pitṛloka; *karmaṇe*—unto the resultant action of fruitive activities; *namaḥ*—offering respects; *adharma*—irreligious; *vipākāya*—unto the result; *mṛtyave*—unto death; *duḥkha-dāya*—the cause of all kinds of miserable conditions; *ca*—also.

TRANSLATION

My dear Lord, You are the viewer of the results of pious activities. You are inclination, disinclination and their resultant activities. You are the cause of the miserable conditions of life caused by irreligion, and therefore You are death. I offer You my respectful obeisances.

PURPORT

The Supreme Personality of Godhead is situated in everyone's heart, and from Him issue a living entity's inclinations and disinclinations. This is confirmed in *Bhagavad-gītā:*

sarvasya cāhaṁ hṛdi sanniviṣṭo
mattaḥ smṛtir jñānam apohanaṁ ca

"I am seated in everyone's heart, and from Me come remembrance, knowledge and forgetfulness." (Bg. 15.15)

The Supreme Personality of Godhead causes the *asuras* to forget Him and the devotees to remember Him. One's disinclinations are due to the Supreme Personality of Godhead. According to *Bhagavad-gītā* the *asuras* do not know which way one should be inclined to act and which way one should not be inclined to act. *Pravṛttiṁ ca nivṛttiṁ ca janā na vidur āsurāḥ:* "Those who are demoniac do not know what is to be done and what is not to be done." (Bg. 16.7) Although the *asuras* oppose devotional service, it is to be understood that they are inclined that way due to the Supreme Personality of Godhead. Because the *asuras* do not like to engage in the Lord's devotional service, the Lord within gives them the intelligence to forget. Ordinary *karmīs* desire promotion to Pitṛloka, as confirmed in *Bhagavad-gītā. Yānti deva-vratā devān pitṝn yānti pitṛ-vratāḥ:* "Those who worship the demigods will take birth among the demigods, and those who worship ancestors go to the ancestors." (Bg. 9.25)

In this verse the word *duḥkha-dāya* is also very significant, for those who are nondevotees are perpetually put into the cycle of birth and death. This is a very miserable condition. Because one's position in life is attained according to one's activities, the *asuras,* or nondevotees, are put into such miserable conditions.

TEXT 42

नमस्त आशिषामीश मनवे कारणात्मने ।
नमो धर्माय बृहते कृष्णायाकुण्ठमेधसे ।
पुरुषाय पुराणाय सांख्ययोगेश्वराय च ॥४२॥

namas ta āśiṣām īśa
manave kāraṇātmane
namo dharmāya bṛhate
kṛṣṇāyākuṇṭha-medhase
puruṣāya purāṇāya
sāṅkhya-yogeśvarāya ca

namaḥ—offering obeisances; *te*—unto You; *āśiṣām īśa*—O topmost of all bestowers of benediction; *manave*—unto the supreme mind or supreme Manu; *kāraṇa-ātmane*—the supreme cause of all causes; *namaḥ*—offering obeisances; *dharmāya*—unto one who knows the best of all religion; *bṛhate*—the greatest; *kṛṣṇāya*—unto Kṛṣṇa; *akuṇṭha-medhase*—unto one whose brain activity is never checked; *puruṣāya*—the Supreme Person; *purāṇāya*—the oldest of the old; *sāṅkhya-yoga-īśvarāya*—the master of the principles of *sāṅkhya-yoga; ca*—and.

TRANSLATION

My dear Lord, You are the topmost of all bestowers of all benediction, the oldest and supreme enjoyer amongst all enjoyers. You are the master of all the worlds' metaphysical philosophy, for You are the supreme cause of all causes, Lord Kṛṣṇa. You are the greatest of all religious principles, the supreme mind, and You have a brain which is never checked by any condition. Therefore I repeatedly offer my obeisances unto You.

PURPORT

The words *kṛṣṇāya akuṇṭha-medhase* are significant in this verse. Modern scientists have stopped their brainwork by discovering the theory of uncertainty, but factually for a living being there cannot be any brain activity which is not checked by time and space limitations. A living entity is called *aṇu,* an atomic particle of the spirit soul, and therefore his brain is also atomic. It cannot accommodate unlimited knowledge. This does not mean, however, that the Supreme Personality of Godhead, Kṛṣṇa, has a limited brain. What Kṛṣṇa says and does is not limited by time and space. In *Bhagavad-gītā* it is said:

vedāhaṁ samatītāni
vartamānāni cārjuna
bhaviṣyāṇi ca bhūtāni
māṁ tu veda na kaścana

"O Arjuna, as the Supreme Personality of Godhead, I know everything that has happened in the past, all that is happening in the present, and all things that are yet to come. I also know all living entities; but Me no one knows." (Bg. 7.26)

Kṛṣṇa knows everything, but one cannot know Kṛṣṇa without being favored by Him. Thus for Kṛṣṇa and His representative there is no question of a theory of uncertainty. What Kṛṣṇa says is all perfect and certain and is applicable to the past, present and future. Nor is there any uncertainty for one who knows exactly what Kṛṣṇa says. The Kṛṣṇa consciousness movement is based on *Bhagavad-gītā* as it is, as spoken by Lord Kṛṣṇa, and for those who are engaged in this movement, there is no question of uncertainty.

Lord Kṛṣṇa is also addressed herein as *āśiṣām īśa.* The great saintly personalities, sages and demigods are able to offer benedictions to ordinary living entities, but they in turn are benedicted by the Supreme Personality of Godhead. Without being benedicted by Kṛṣṇa, one cannot offer benediction to anyone else. The word *manave,* meaning "unto the supreme Manu," is also significant. The supreme Manu in Vedic literature is Svāyambhuva Manu, who is an incarnation of Kṛṣṇa. All the Manus are empowered incarnations of Kṛṣṇa (*manvantara-avatāra*). There are fourteen Manus in one day of Brahmā, 420 in one month, 5,040 in one year, and 504,000 Manus in the lifetime of Brahmā. Since all the Manus are directors of human society, ultimately Kṛṣṇa is the supreme director of human society. In another sense, the word *manave* indicates the perfection of all kinds of *mantras.* The *mantra* delivers the conditioned soul from his bondage; so simply by chanting the *mantra* Hare Kṛṣṇa, Hare Kṛṣṇa, Kṛṣṇa Kṛṣṇa, Hare Hare/ Hare Rāma, Hare Rāma, Rāma Rāma, Hare Hare, one can gain deliverance from any condition.

Kāraṇātmane: everything has a cause. The theory of chance is repudiated in this verse. Because everything has its cause, there is no question of chance. Because so-called philosophers and scientists are unable to find the real cause, they foolishly say that everything happens by chance. In *Brahma-saṁhitā* Kṛṣṇa is described as the cause of all causes; therefore He is addressed herein as *kāraṇātmane.* His very personality is the original cause of everything, the root of everything and the seed of everything. As described in the *Vedānta-sūtra, janmādy asya yataḥ* (1.1.2): the Absolute Truth is the supreme cause of all emanations.

The word *sāṅkhya-yogeśvarāya* is also significant herein, for Kṛṣṇa is described in *Bhagavad-gītā* as Yogeśvara, the master of all mystic powers. Without possessing inconceivable mystic powers, one cannot be accepted as God. In this age of Kali, those who have a little fragmental portion of mystic power claim to be God, but such pseudo-Gods can only be accepted as fools, for only Kṛṣṇa is the Supreme Person who possesses all mystic and yogic perfections. The *sāṅkhya-yoga* system popular at the present moment was propounded by the atheist Kapila, but the original *sāṅkhya-yoga* system was propounded by an incarnation of Kṛṣṇa also named Kapila, the son of Devahūti. Similarly, Dattātreya, another incarnation of Kṛṣṇa, also explained the *sāṅkhya-yoga* system. Thus Kṛṣṇa is the origin of all *sāṅkhya-yoga* systems and mystic *yoga* powers.

The words *purāṇāya puruṣāya* are also worthy of special attention. In *Brahma-saṁhitā,* Kṛṣṇa is accepted as the *ādi-puruṣa,* the original person, or the original enjoyer. In *Bhagavad-gītā,* Lord Kṛṣṇa is also accepted as *purāṇa-puruṣa,* the oldest person. Although He is the oldest of all personalities, He is also the youngest of all, or *nava-yauvana.* Another significant word is *dharmāya.* Since Kṛṣṇa is the original propounder of all kinds of religious principles, it is said: *dharmaṁ tu sākṣād bhagavat-*

praṇītam. No one can introduce a new type of religion, for religion is already there, having been established by Lord Kṛṣṇa. In *Bhagavad-gītā* Kṛṣṇa informs us of the original *dharma* and asks us to give up all kinds of religious principles. The real *dharma* is surrender unto Him. In the *Mahābhārata,* it is also said:

ye ca veda-vido viprā ye cādhyātma-vido janāḥ
te vadanti mahātmānaṁ kṛṣṇaṁ dharmaṁ sanātanam

The purport is that one who has studied the *Vedas* perfectly, who is a perfect *vipra,* or knower of the *Vedas,* who knows what spiritual life actually is, speaks about Kṛṣṇa, the Supreme Person, as one's *sanātana-dharma.* Lord Śiva therefore teaches us the principles of *sanātana-dharma.*

TEXT 43

शक्तित्रयसमेताय मीढुषेऽहंकृतात्मने ।
चेतआकूतिरूपाय नमो वाचोविभूतये ॥४३॥

śakti-traya-sametāya
mīḍhuṣe 'haṅkṛtātmane
ceta-ākūti-rūpāya
namo vāco vibhūtaye

śakti-traya—three kinds of energies; *sametāya*—unto the reservoir; *mīḍhuṣe*—unto Rudra; *ahaṅkṛta-ātmane*—the source of egotism; *cetaḥ*—knowledge; *ākūti*—eagerness to work; *rūpāya*—unto the form of; *namaḥ*—my obeisances; *vācaḥ*—unto the sound; *vibhūtaye*—unto the different types of opulences.

TRANSLATION

My dear Lord, You are the supreme controller of the worker, sense activities, and results of sense activities [karma]. Therefore You are the controller of the body, mind and the senses. You are also the supreme controller of egotism, known as Rudra. You are the source of knowledge and the activities of the Vedic injunctions.

PURPORT

Everyone acts under the dictation of the ego. Therefore Lord Śiva is trying to purify false egotism through the mercy of the Supreme Personality of Godhead. Since Lord Śiva, or Rudra, is himself the controller of egotism, he indirectly wants to be purified by the mercy of the Lord so that his real egotism can be awakened. Of course Lord Rudra is always spiritually awake, but for our benefit he is praying in this way. For the impersonalist, pure egotism is *ahaṁ brahmāsmi*—"I am not this body; I am spirit soul." But in its actual position, the spirit soul has devotional activities to perform. Therefore Lord Śiva prays to be engaged both in mind and in action in the devotional service of the Supreme Lord according to the direction of the *Vedas.* This is the process for purifying false egotism. *Cetaḥ* means knowledge. Without perfect knowledge, one cannot act perfectly. The real source of knowledge is the *vācaḥ,* or sound vibration, given by Vedic instructions. Here the word *vācaḥ,* or vibration, means the Vedic vibration. The origin of creation is sound vibration, and if the sound vibration is clear and purified, perfect knowledge and perfect activities actually become manifest. This is enacted by the chanting of the *mahā-mantra* Hare Kṛṣṇa, Hare Kṛṣṇa, Kṛṣṇa Kṛṣṇa, Hare Hare/ Hare Rāma, Hare Rāma, Rāma Rāma, Hare Hare. Thus Lord Śiva is praying again and again for the purification of body, mind and activities through the purification of knowledge and action under the pure directions of the *Vedas.* Lord Śiva prays to the Supreme Personality of Godhead so that his mind, senses and words will all turn toward devotional activities only.

TEXT 44

दर्शनं नो दिदृक्षूणां देहि भागवतार्चितम् ।
रूपं प्रियतमं स्वानां सर्वेन्द्रियगुणाञ्जनम् ॥४४॥

darśanaṁ no didṛkṣūṇāṁ
dehi bhāgavatārcitam
rūpaṁ priyatamaṁ svānāṁ
sarvendriya-guṇāñjanam

darśanam—vision; *naḥ*—our; *didṛkṣūṇām*—desirous to see; *dehi*—kindly exhibit; *bhāgavata*—of the devotees; *arcitam*—as worshiped by them; *rūpam*—form; *priyatamam*—dearmost; *svānām*—of Your devotees; *sarva-indriya*—all the senses; *guṇa*—qualities; *añjanam*—very much pleasing.

TRANSLATION

My dear Lord, I wish to see You exactly in the form that Your very dear devotees worship. You have many other forms, but I wish to see Your form that is especially liked by the devotees. Please be merciful upon me and show me that form, for only that form worshiped by the devotees can perfectly satisfy all the demands of the senses.

PURPORT

In the *śruti,* or *Veda-mantra,* it is said that the Supreme Absolute Truth is *sarva-kāmaḥ sarva-gandhaḥ sarva-rasaḥ,* or, in other words, He is known as *raso vai saḥ,* the source of all relishable relationships *(rasas).* We have various senses—the power of seeing, tasting, smelling, touching, etc.—and all the propensities of our senses can be satisfied when the senses are engaged in the service of the Lord. *Hṛṣīkeṇa hṛṣīkeśa-sevanaṁ bhaktir ucyate (Nārada-pañcarātra).* "*Bhakti* means engaging all the senses in the service of the master of the senses, Hṛṣīkeśa." These material senses, however, cannot be engaged in the service of the Lord; therefore one has to become free from all designations. *Sarvopādhi-vinirmuktaṁ tatparatvena nirmalam.* One has to become free from all designation or false egotism and thus become purified. When we engage our senses in the service of the Lord, the desires or the inclinations of the senses can be perfectly fulfilled. Lord Śiva therefore wants to see the Lord in a form which is inconceivable to the Buddhist philosophers or the Buddhists.

The impersonalists and the voidists also have to see the form of the Absolute. In Buddhist temples there are forms of Lord Buddha in meditation, but these are not worshiped like the forms of the Lord in Vaiṣṇava temples (forms like Rādhā-Kṛṣṇa, Sītā-Rāma or Lakṣmī-Nārāyaṇa). Amongst the different *sampradāyas* (Vaiṣṇava sects) either Rādhā-Kṛṣṇa or Lakṣmī-Nārāyaṇa is worshiped. Lord Śiva wants to see that form perfectly, just as the devotees want to see it. The words *rūpaṁ priyatamaṁ svānām* are specifically mentioned here, indicating that Lord Śiva wants to see that form which is very dear to the devotees. The word *svānām* is especially significant because only the devotees are very, very dear to the Supreme Personality of Godhead. The *jñānīs, yogīs* and *karmīs* are not particularly dear, for the *karmīs* simply want to see the Supreme Personality of Godhead as their order supplier. The *jñānīs* want to see Him to become one with Him, and the *yogīs* want to see Him partially represented within their heart as Paramātmā, but the *bhaktas,* or the devotees, want to see Him in His complete perfection. As stated in *Brahma-saṁhitā:*

veṇuṁ kvaṇantam aravinda-dalāyatākṣaṁ
barhāvataṁsam asitāmbuda-sundarāṅgam
kandarpa-koṭi-kamanīya-viśeṣa-śobhaṁ
govindam ādi-puruṣaṁ tam ahaṁ bhajāmi

"I worship Govinda, the primeval Lord, who is adept at playing on His flute, whose eyes are blooming like lotus petals, whose head is bedecked with peacock feathers, whose beauty is tinged with the hue of blue clouds, and whose unique loveliness charms millions of Cupids." (Bs. 5.30) Thus Lord Śiva's desire is to see the Supreme Personality of Godhead as He is described in this way—that is, he wants to see Him as He appears to the *bhāgavatas,* the devotees. The conclusion is that Lord Śiva wants to see Him in complete perfection and not in the impersonalist or voidist way. Although the Lord is one in His various forms *(advaitam acyutam anādim)*, still His form as the young enjoyer of the *gopīs* and companion of the cowherd boys *(kiśora-mūrti)* is the most perfect form. Thus Vaiṣṇavas accept the form of the Lord in His Vṛndāvana pastimes as the chief form.

TEXTS 45-46

स्निग्धप्रावृड्घनश्यामं सर्वसौन्दर्यसंग्रहम् ।
चार्वायतचतुर्बाहु सुजातरुचिराननम् ॥४५॥
पद्मकोशपलाशाक्षं सुन्दरभ्रु सुनासिकम् ।
सुद्विजं सुकपोलास्यं समकर्णविभूषणम् ॥४६॥

snigdha-prāvṛḍ-ghanaśyāmaṁ
sarva-saundarya-saṅgraham
cārv-āyata-catur-bāhu
sujāta-rucirānanam

padma-kośa-palāśākṣaṁ
sundara-bhru su-nāsikam
su-dvijaṁ su-kapolāsyaṁ
sama-karṇa-vibhūṣaṇam

snigdha—glistening; *prāvṛṣ*—rainy season; *ghana-śyāmam*—densely cloudy; *sarva*—all; *saundarya*—beauty; *saṅgraham*—collection; *cāru*—beautiful; *āyata*—bodily feature; *cātuḥ-bāhu*—unto the four-armed; *sujāta*—ultimately beautiful; *rucira*—very pleasing; *ānanam*—face; *padma-kośa*—the whorl of the lotus flower; *palāśa*—petals; *akṣam*—eyes; *sundara*—beautiful; *bhru*—eyebrows; *su-nāsikam*—raised nose; *su-dvijam*—beautiful teeth; *su-kapola*—beautiful forehead; *āsyam*—face; *sama-karṇa*—equally beautiful ears; *vibhūṣaṇam*—fully decorated.

TRANSLATION

The Lord's beauty resembles a dark cloud during the rainy season. As the rainfall glistens, His bodily features also glisten. Indeed, He is the sum total of all beauty. The Lord has four arms and an exquisitely beautiful face with eyes like lotus petals, a beautiful highly raised nose, a mind-attracting smile, a beautiful forehead and equally beautiful and fully decorated ears.

PURPORT

After the scorching heat of the summer season, it is very pleasing to see dark clouds in the sky. As confirmed in *Brahma-saṁhitā: barhāvataṁsam asitāmbuda-sundarāṅgam.* The Lord wears a peacock feather in His hair, and His bodily complexion is just like a blackish cloud. The word *sundara,* or *snigdha,* means very pleasing, even when compared with *kandarpa-koṭi-kamanīya.* Kṛṣṇa's beauty is so pleasing that not even millions upon millions of Cupids can compare to it. The Lord's form as Viṣṇu is decorated in all opulence; therefore Lord Śiva is trying to see that most opulent form of Nārāyaṇa, or Viṣṇu. Generally the worship of the Lord begins with the worship of Nārāyaṇa or Viṣṇu, whereas the worship of Lord Kṛṣṇa and Rādhā is most confidential. Lord Nārāyaṇa is worshipable by the *Pāñcarātrika-vidhi,* or regulative principles, whereas Lord Kṛṣṇa is worshipable by the *Bhāgavata-vidhi.* No one can worship the Lord in the *Bhāgavata-vidhi* without going through the regulations of the *Pāñcarātrika-vidhi.* Actually neophyte devotees worship the Lord according to the *Pāñcarātrika-vidhi,* or the regulative principles enjoined in the *Nārada-pañcarātra.* Rādhā-Kṛṣṇa cannot be approached by the neophyte devotees; therefore temple worship according to regulative principles is offered to Lakṣmī-Nārāyaṇa. Although there may be a Rādhā-Kṛṣṇa *vigraha,* or form, the worship of the neophyte devotees is acceptable as Lakṣmī-Nārāyaṇa worship. Worship according to the *Pāñcarātrika-vidhi* is called *vidhi-mārga,* and worship according to the *Bhāgavata-vidhi* principles is called *rāga-mārga.* The principles of *rāga-mārga* are especially meant for devotees who are elevated to the Vṛndāvana platform.

The inhabitants of Vṛndāvana, the *gopīs,* mother Yaśodā, Nanda Mahārāja, the cowherd boys, the cows and everyone else, are actually on the *rāga-mārga* or *Bhāgavata-mārga* platform. However, they participate in five basic *rasas—dāsya, sakhya, vātsalya, mādhurya* and *śānta.* Although these five *rasas* are found in the *Bhāgavata-mārga,* the *Bhāgavata-mārga* is especially meant for *vātsalya* and *mādhurya,* or paternal and conjugal relationships. Yet there is the *vipralambha-sakhya,* the higher fraternal worship of the Lord especially enjoyed by the cowherd boys. Although there is friendship between Kṛṣṇa and the cowherd boys, this friendship is different from the *aiśvarya* friendship between Kṛṣṇa and Arjuna. When Arjuna saw the *viśva-rūpa,* the gigantic universal form of the Lord, he was afraid for having treated Kṛṣṇa as an ordinary friend; therefore he begged Kṛṣṇa's pardon. However, the cowherd boys who are friends of Kṛṣṇa in Vṛndāvana sometimes ride on the shoulders of Kṛṣṇa. They treat Kṛṣṇa equally, just as they treat one another, and they are never afraid of Him, nor do they ever beg His pardon. Thus the *rāga-mārga,* or *Bhāgavata-mārga,* friendship exists on a higher platform with Kṛṣṇa, namely the platform of *vipralambha* friendship. Paternal friendship, conjugal paternal service, as well as conjugal service, are visible in the Vṛndāvana *rāga-mārga* relationships.

Without serving Kṛṣṇa according to the *vidhi-mārga* regulative principles of the *Pāñcarātrika-vidhi,* unscrupulous persons want to jump immediately to the *rāga-mārga* principles. Such persons are called *sahajiyā.* There are also demons who enjoy depicting Kṛṣṇa and His pastimes with the *gopīs,* taking advantage of Kṛṣṇa by their licentious character. These demons who print books and write lyrics on the *rāga-mārga* principles are surely on the way to hell. Unfortunately, they lead others down with them. Devotees in Kṛṣṇa consciousness should be very careful to avoid such demons. One should strictly follow the *vidhi-mārga* regulative principles in the worship of Lakṣmī-Nārāyaṇa, although the Lord is present in the temple as Rādhā-Kṛṣṇa. Rādhā-Kṛṣṇa includes Lakṣmī-Nārāyaṇa; therefore when one worships the Lord according to the regulative principles, the Lord accepts the service in the role of Lakṣmī-Nārāyaṇa. In *Nectar of Devotion* full instructions are given about the *vidhi-mārga* worship of Rādhā-Kṛṣṇa or Lakṣmī-Nārāyaṇa. Although there are sixty-four kinds of offenses one can commit in *vidhi-mārga* worship, in *rāga-mārga* worship there is no consideration of such offenses because the devotees on that platform are very much elevated, and there is no question of offense. But if we do not follow the regulative principles on the *vidhi-mārga* platform and keep our eyes trained to spot offenses, we will not make progress.

In his description of Kṛṣṇa's beauty, Lord Śiva uses the words *cārv-āyata-catur-bāhu sujāta-rucirānanam,* indicating the beautiful four-armed form of Nārāyaṇa, or Viṣṇu. Those who worship Lord Kṛṣṇa describe Him as *sujāta-rucirānanam.* In the *Viṣṇu-tattva* there are hundreds and thousands and millions of forms of the Supreme Lord, but of all these forms, the form of Kṛṣṇa is the most beautiful. Thus for those who worship Kṛṣṇa, the word *sujāta-rucirānanam* is used.

The four arms of Lord Viṣṇu have different purposes. The hands holding a lotus flower and conchshell are meant for the devotees, whereas the other two hands, holding a disc and mace or club, are meant for the demons. Actually all of the Lord's arms are auspicious, whether they are holding conchshells and flowers or clubs and discs. The demons killed by Lord Viṣṇu's *cakra* disc and club are elevated to the spiritual world, just like the devotees who are protected by the hands holding the lotus flower and conchshell. However, the demons who are elevated to the spiritual world are situated in the impersonal Brahman effulgence, whereas the devotees are allowed to enter into the Vaikuṇṭha planets. Those who are devotees of Lord Kṛṣṇa are immediately elevated to the Goloka Vṛndāvana planet.

The Lord's beauty is compared to rainfall because when the rain falls in the rainy season, it becomes more and more pleasing to the people. After the scorching heat of the summer season, the people enjoy the rainy season very much. Indeed, they even come out of their doors in the villages and enjoy the rainfall directly. Thus the Lord's bodily features are compared with the clouds of the rainy season. The devotees enjoy the Lord's beauty because it is a collection of all kinds of beauties. Therefore the word *sarva-saundarya-saṅgraham* is used. No one can say that the body of the Lord is wanting in beautiful parts. It is completely *pūrṇam.* Everything is complete: God's creation, God's beauty, and God's bodily features. All these are so complete that all one's desires can become fully satisfied when one sees the beauty of the Lord. The word *sarva-saundarya* indicates that there are different types of beauties in the material and spiritual worlds, and that the Lord contains all of them. Both materialists and spiritualists can enjoy the beauty of the Lord. Because the Supreme Lord attracts everyone, including demons and devotees, materialists and spiritualists, He is called Kṛṣṇa. Similarly, His devotees also attract everyone. As mentioned in the *Ṣaḍ-gosvāmī-stotra: dhīrādhīra-jana-priyau*—the Gosvāmīs are equally dear to the *dhīra* (devotees) and *adhīra* (demons). Lord Kṛṣṇa was not very pleasing to the demons when He was present in Vṛndāvana, but the six Gosvāmīs were pleasing to the demons when they were present in Vṛndāvana. That is the beauty of the Lord's dealings with His devotees; sometimes the Lord gives more credit to His devotees than He takes for Himself. For instance, on the Battlefield of Kurukṣetra, Lord Kṛṣṇa fought simply by giving directions. Yet it was Arjuna who took the credit for fighting. *Nimitta-mātraṁ bhava savyasācin* (Bg. 11.33). "You, O Savyasācin [Arjuna], can be but an instrument in the fight." Everything was arranged by the Lord, but the credit of victory was given to Arjuna. Similarly, in the Kṛṣṇa consciousness movement, everything is happening according to the predictions of Lord Caitanya, but the credit goes to Lord Caitanya's sincere servants. Thus the Lord is described herein as *sarva-saundarya-saṅgraham.*

TEXTS 47-48

प्रीतिप्रहसितापाङ्गमलकै रूपशोभितम् ।
लसत्पङ्कजकिञ्जल्कदुकूलं मृष्टकुण्डलम् ॥४७॥

स्फुरत्किरीटवलयहारनूपुरमेखलम् ।
शङ्खचक्रगदापद्ममालामण्युत्तमर्द्धिमत् ॥४८॥

prīti-prahasitāpāṅgam
alakai rūpa-śobhitam
lasat-paṅkaja-kiñjalka-
dukūlaṁ mṛṣṭa-kuṇḍalam

sphurat-kirīṭa-valaya-
hāra-nūpura-mekhalam
śaṅkha-cakra-gadā-padma-
mālā-maṇy-uttamarddhimat

prīti—merciful; *prahasita*—smiling; *apāṅgam*—sidelong glance; *alakaiḥ*—with curling hair; *rūpa*—beauty; *śobhitam*—increased; *lasat*—glittering; *paṅkaja*—of the lotus; *kiñjalka*—saffron; *dukūlam*—clothing; *mṛṣṭa*—glittering; *kuṇḍalam*—earrings; *sphurat*—shiny; *kirīṭa*—helmet; *valaya*—bangles; *hāra*—necklace; *nūpura*—ankle bells; *mekhalam*—belt; *śaṅkha*—conchshell; *cakra*—wheel; *gadā*—club; *padma*—lotus flower; *mālā*—garland; *maṇi*—pearls; *uttama*—first class; *ṛddhimat*—still more beautified on account of this.

TRANSLATION

The Lord is superexcellently beautiful on account of His open and merciful smile and His sidelong glance upon His devotees. His black hair is curly, and His garments, waving in the wind, appear as flying saffron pollen from lotus flowers. His glittering earrings, shining helmet, bangles, garland, ankle bells, waist belt and various other bodily ornaments combine with conchshell, disc, club and lotus flower to increase the natural beauty of the Kaustubha pearl on His chest.

PURPORT

The word *prahasitāpāṅga,* referring to Kṛṣṇa's smile and sidelong glances at His devotees, specifically applies to His dealings with the *gopīs.* Kṛṣṇa is always in a joking mood when He increases the feelings of conjugal *rasa* in the hearts of the *gopīs.* The conchshell, club, disc and lotus flower can be either held in His hands or seen on the palms of His hands. According to palmistry, the signs of a conchshell, club, lotus flower and disc mark the palms of great personalities and especially indicate the Supreme Personality of Godhead.

TEXT 49

सिंहस्कन्धत्विषो बिभ्रत्सौभगग्रीवकौस्तुभम् ।
श्रियानपायिन्या क्षिप्तनिकषाश्मोरसोल्लसत् ॥४९॥

siṁha-skandha-tviṣo bibhrat
saubhaga-grīva-kaustubham
śriyānapāyinyā kṣipta-
nikaṣāśmorasollasat

siṁha—the lion; *skandha*—shoulders; *tviṣaḥ*—the coils of hair; *bibhrat*—bearing; *saubhaga*—fortunate; *grīva*—neck; *kaustubham*—the pearl of the name; *śriyā*—beauty; *anapāyinyā*—never decreasing; *kṣipta*—defeating; *nikaṣa*—the stone for testing gold; *aśma*—stone; *urasā*—with the chest; *ullasat*—glittering.

TRANSLATION

The Lord has shoulders just like a lion. Upon these shoulders are garlands, necklaces and epaulets, and all of these are always glittering. Besides these, there is the beauty of the Kaustubha maṇi pearl, and on the dark chest of the Lord there are streaks named Śrīvatsa, which are signs of the goddess of fortune. The glittering of these streaks excels the beauty of the golden streaks on a gold-testing stone. Indeed, such beauty defeats a gold-testing stone.

PURPORT

The curling hair on the shoulders of a lion always appears very, very beautiful. Similarly, the shoulders of the Lord were just like a lion's, and the necklace and garlands, along with the Kaustubha pearl necklace, combined to excel the beauty of a lion. The chest of the Lord is streaked with Śrīvatsa lines, the sign of the goddess of fortune. Consequently the Lord's chest excels the beauty of a testing stone for gold. The black siliceous stone on which gold is rubbed to test its value always looks very beautiful, being streaked with gold lines. Yet the chest of the Lord excels even such a stone in its beauty.

TEXT 50

पूररेचकसंविग्नवलिवल्गुदलोदरम् ।
प्रतिसंक्रामयद्विश्वं नाभ्याऽऽवर्तगभीरया ॥५०॥

pūra-recaka-saṁvigna-
vali-valgu-dalodaram
pratisaṅkrāmayad viśvaṁ
nābhyāvarta-gabhīrayā

pūra—inhaling; *recaka*—exhaling; *saṁvigna*—agitated; *vali*—the wrinkles on the abdomen; *valgu*—beautiful; *dala*—like the banyan leaf; *udaram*—abdomen; *pratisaṅkrāmayat*—coiling down; *viśvam*—universe; *nābhya*—navel; *āvarta*—screwing; *gabhīrayā*—by deepness.

TRANSLATION

The Lord's abdomen is beautiful due to three ripples in the flesh. Being so round, His abdomen resembles the leaf of a banyan tree, and when He exhales and inhales, the movement of the ripples appears very, very beautiful. The coils within the navel of the Lord are so deep that it appears that the entire universe sprouted out of it and yet again wishes to go back.

PURPORT

The whole universe is born out of the lotus stem which sprouted from the navel of the Lord. Lord Brahmā sat on the top of this lotus stem to create the whole universe. The navel of the Lord is so deep and coiling that it appears that the whole universe again wants to withdraw into the navel, being attracted by the Lord's beauty. The Lord's navel and the ripples on His belly always increase the beauty of His bodily features. The details of the bodily features of the Lord especially indicate the Personality of Godhead. Impersonalists cannot appreciate the beautiful body of the Lord which is described in these prayers by Lord Śiva. Although the impersonalists are always engaged in the worship of Lord Śiva, they are unable to understand the prayers offered by Lord Śiva to the bodily features of Lord Viṣṇu. Lord Viṣṇu is known as *śiva-viriñci-nutam* (*Bhāg.* 11.5.33), for He is always worshiped by Lord Brahmā and Lord Śiva.

TEXT 51

श्यामश्रोण्यधिरोचिष्णुदुकूलस्वर्णमेखलम् ।
समचार्वङ्घ्रिजङ्घोरुनिम्नजानुसुदर्शनम् ॥५१॥

śyāma-śroṇy-adhi-rociṣṇu-
dukūla-svarṇa-mekhalam
sama-cārv-aṅghri-jaṅghoru-
nimna-jānu-sudarśanam

śyāma—blackish; *śroṇi*—lower part of the waist; *adhi*—extra; *rociṣṇu*—pleasing; *dukūla*—garments; *svarṇa*—golden; *mekhalam*—belt; *sama*—symmetrical; *cāru*—beautiful; *aṅghri*—lotus feet; *jaṅgha*—calves; *ūru*—thighs; *nimna*—lower; *jānu*—knees; *su-darśanam*—very beautiful.

TRANSLATION

The lower part of the Lord's waist is dark and covered with yellow garments and a belt bedecked with golden embroidery work. His symmetrical lotus feet and the calves, thighs and joints of His legs are extraordinarily beautiful. Indeed, the Lord's entire body appears to be well built.

PURPORT

Lord Śiva is one of the twelve great authorities mentioned in *Śrīmad-Bhāgavatam* (6.3.20). These authorities are Svayambhū, Nārada, Śambhu, Kumāra, Kapila, Manu, Prahlāda, Janaka, Bhīṣma, Bali, Vaiyāsaki or Śukadeva Gosvāmī, and Yamarāja. The impersonalists who generally worship Lord Śiva should learn of the transcendental *sac-cid-ānanda-vigraha* form of the Lord. Here Lord Śiva kindly describes the details of the Lord's bodily features. Thus the impersonalists' argument that the Lord has no form cannot be accepted under any circumstance.

TEXT 52

पदा शरत्पद्मपलाशरोचिषा
नखद्युभिर्नोऽन्तरघं विधुन्वता ।
प्रदर्शय स्वीयमपास्तसाध्वसं
पदं गुरो मार्गगुरुस्तमोजुषाम् ॥५२॥

padā śarat-padma-palāśa-rociṣā
nakha-dyubhir no 'ntar-aghaṁ vidhunvatā
pradarśaya svīyam apāsta-sādhvasaṁ
padaṁ guro mārga-gurus tamo-juṣām

padā—by the lotus feet; *śarat*—autumn; *padma*—lotus flower; *palāśa*—petals; *rociṣā*—very pleasing; *nakha*—nails; *dyubhiḥ*—by the effulgence; *naḥ*—our; *antar-agham*—dirty things; *vidhunvatā*—which can cleanse; *pradarśaya*—just show; *svīyam*—Your own; *apāsta*—diminishing; *sādhvasam*—the trouble of the material world; *padam*—lotus feet; *guro*—O supreme spiritual master; *mārga*—the path; *guruḥ*—spiritual master; *tamaḥ-juṣām*—of the persons suffering in ignorance.

TRANSLATION

My dear Lord, Your two lotus feet are so beautiful that they appear like two blossoming petals of the lotus flower which grows during the autumn season. Indeed, the nails of Your lotus feet emanate such a great effulgence that they immediately dissipate all the darkness in the heart of a conditioned soul. My dear Lord, kindly show me that form of Yours which always dissipates all kinds of darkness in the heart of a devotee. My dear Lord, You are the supreme spiritual master of everyone; therefore all conditioned souls covered with the darkness of ignorance can be enlightened by You as the spiritual master.

PURPORT

Lord Śiva has thus described the bodily features of the Lord authoritatively. Now he wants to see the lotus feet of the Lord. When a devotee wants to see the transcendental form of the Lord, he begins his meditation on the Lord's body by first looking at the feet of the Lord. *Śrīmad-Bhāgavatam* is considered to be the transcendental sound form of the Lord, and the twelve cantos are divided in accordance with the transcendental form of the Lord. The First and Second Cantos of *Śrīmad-Bhāgavatam* are called the two lotus feet of the Lord. It is therefore suggested by Lord Śiva that one should first try to see the lotus feet of the Lord. This also means that if one is serious about reading *Śrīmad-Bhāgavatam,* he must begin by seriously studying the First and Second Cantos.

The beauty of the lotus feet of the Lord is compared to the petals of a lotus flower which grows in the autumn season. By nature's law, in autumn the dirty or muddy waters of rivers and lakes become very clean. At that time the lotus flowers growing in the lakes appear very bright and beautiful. The lotus flower itself is compared with the lotus feet of the Lord, and the petals are compared with the nails of the feet of the Lord. The nails of the feet of the Lord are very bright, as *Brahma-saṁhitā* testifies. *Ānanda-cinmaya-sad-ujjvala-vigrahasya:* every limb of the transcendental body of the Lord is made of *ānanda-cinmaya-sad-ujjvala.* Thus every limb is eternally bright. As sunshine dissipates the darkness of this material world, the effulgence emanating from the body of the Lord immediately dries up the darkness in the heart of the conditioned soul. In other words, everyone serious about understanding the transcendental science and seeing the transcendental form of the Lord must first of all attempt to see the lotus feet of the Lord by studying the First and Second Cantos of *Śrīmad-Bhāgavatam.* When one sees the lotus feet of the Lord, all kinds of doubts and fears within the heart are vanquished.

In *Bhagavad-gītā* it is said that in order to make spiritual progress, one must become fearless. *Abhayaṁ sattva-saṁśuddhiḥ* (Bg. 16.1). Fearfulness is the result of material involvement. It is also said in *Śrīmad-Bhāgavatam: bhayaṁ dvitīyābhiniveśataḥ syāt* (*Bhāg.* 11.2.37). Fearfulness is a creation of the bodily conception of life. As long as one is absorbed in the thought that he is this material body, he is fearful, and as soon as one is freed from this material conception, he becomes *brahma-bhūta,* or self-realized, and immediately becomes fearless. *Brahma-bhūtaḥ prasannātmā* (Bg. 18.54). Without being fearless, one cannot be joyful. The *bhaktas,* the devotees, are fearless and always joyful because they are constantly engaged in the service of the lotus feet of the Lord. It is also said:

evaṁ prasanna-manaso bhagavad-bhakti-yogataḥ
bhagavat-tattva-vijñānaṁ mukta-saṅgasya jāyate (*Bhāg.* 1.2.20)

By practicing *bhagavad-bhakti-yoga,* one becomes fearless and joyful. Unless one becomes fearless and joyful, he cannot understand the science of God. *Bhagavat-tattva-vijñānaṁ mukta-saṅgasya jāyate.* This verse refers to those who are completely liberated from the fearfulness of this material world. When one is so liberated, he can really understand the transcendental features of the form of the Lord. Lord Śiva therefore advises everyone to practice *bhagavad-bhakti-yoga.* As will be clear in the following verses, by doing so one can become really liberated and enjoy spiritual bliss.

It is also stated:

oṁ ajñāna-timirāndhasya jñānāñjana-śalākayā
cakṣur unmīlitaṁ yena tasmai śrī-gurave namaḥ

The Lord is the supreme spiritual master, and the bona fide representative of the Supreme Lord is also a spiritual master. The Lord from within enlightens the devotees by the effulgence of the nails of His lotus feet, and His representative, the spiritual master, enlightens from without. Only by thinking of the lotus feet of the Lord and always taking the spiritual master's advice can one advance in spiritual life and understand Vedic knowledge.

yasya deve parā bhaktir yathā deve tathā gurau
tasyaite kathitā hy arthāḥ prakāśante mahātmanaḥ (*Svet. Up.* 6.23)

Thus the *Vedas* enjoin that for one who has unflinching faith in the lotus feet of the Lord, as well as in the spiritual master, the real import of Vedic knowledge can be revealed.

TEXT 53

एतद्रूपमनुध्येयमात्मशुद्धिमभीप्सताम् ।
यद्भक्तियोगोऽभयदः स्वधर्ममनुतिष्ठताम् ॥५३॥

etad rūpam anudhyeyam
ātma-śuddhim abhīpsatām
yad-bhakti-yogo 'bhaya-daḥ
sva-dharmam anutiṣṭhatām

etat—this; *rūpam*—form; *anudhyeyam*—must be meditated upon; *ātma*—self; *śuddhim*—purification; *abhīpsatām*—of those who are desiring so; *yat*—that which; *bhakti-yogaḥ*—the devotional service; *abhaya-daḥ*—factual fearlessness; *sva-dharmam*—one's own occupational duties; *anutiṣṭhatām*—executing.

TRANSLATION

My dear Lord, those who desire to purify their existence must always engage in the meditation of Your lotus feet, as described above. Those who are serious about executing their occupational duties and who want freedom from fear must take to this process of bhakti-yoga.

PURPORT

It is said that the transcendental name, form, pastimes and entourage of the Lord cannot be appreciated by the blunt material senses; therefore one has to engage himself in devotional service so that the senses may be purified and one can see the Supreme Personality of Godhead. Here, however, it is indicated that those who are constantly engaged in meditating on the lotus feet of the Lord are certainly purified of the material contamination of the senses and are thus able to see the Supreme Lord eye to eye. The word "meditation" is very popular in this age amongst the common people, but they do not know the actual meaning of meditation. However, from Vedic literature we learn that the *yogīs* are always absorbed in meditation upon the lotus feet of the Lord. *Dhyānāvasthita-tad-gatena manasā paśyanti yaṁ yoginaḥ* (*Bhāg*. 12.13.1). This is the real business of the *yogīs:* to think of the lotus feet of the Lord. Lord Śiva therefore advises that one who is actually serious about purification must engage himself in this type of meditation or in the mystic *yoga* system, which will help him not only to see the Lord within constantly but to see Him eye to eye and become His associate in Vaikuṇṭhaloka or Goloka Vṛndāvana.

The word *sva-dharmam* (as in *sva-dharmam anutiṣṭhatām*) indicates that the system of *varṇāśrama*—which indicates the occupational duties of the *brāhmaṇa, kṣatriya, vaiśya* and *śūdra* and which is the perfect institution for humanity—must be supported by *bhakti-yoga* if one at all wants security in life. Generally people think that simply by executing the occupational duties of a *brāhmaṇa, kṣatriya, vaiśya* or *śūdra,* or the duty of a *brahmacārī, gṛhastha, vānaprastha* or *sannyāsī,* one becomes fearless or securely attains liberation, but factually unless all these occupational duties are accompanied by *bhakti-yoga,* one cannot become fearless. In *Bhagavad-gītā* there are descriptions of *karma-yoga, jñāna-yoga, bhakti-yoga, dhyāna-yoga,* etc., but unless one comes to the point of *bhakti-yoga,* these other *yogas* cannot help one attain the highest perfection of life. In other words, *bhakti-yoga* is the only means for liberation. We find this conclusion also in *Caitanya-caritāmṛta* in a discussion between Lord Caitanya and Rāmānanda Rāya regarding a human being's liberation from this material world. In that discussion Rāmānanda Rāya referred to the execution of *varṇāśrama-dharma,* and Lord Caitanya indicated *(eho bāhya)* that the *varṇāśrama-dharma* was simply external. Lord Caitanya wanted to impress upon Rāmānanda Rāya that simply by executing the duties of *varṇāśrama-dharma* one is not guaranteed liberation. Finally Rāmānanda Rāya referred to the process of *bhakti-yoga: sthāne sthitāḥ śruti-gatāṁ tanu-vāṅ-manobhiḥ* (*Bhāg.* 10.14.3). Regardless of one's condition of life, if he practices *bhakti-yoga,* which begins with hearing *(śruti-gatām)* the transcendental messages of the Lord through the mouths of devotees, he gradually conquers the unconquerable God.

God is known to be unconquerable, but one who submissively hears the words of a self-realized soul conquers the unconquerable. The conclusion is that if one is serious about liberation, he not only should execute the occupational duties of *varṇāśrama-dharma* but should also engage in *bhakti-yoga* by beginning hearing from a realized soul. This process will help the devotee conquer the unconquerable Supreme Personality of Godhead and become His associate after giving up the material body.

TEXT 54

भवान् भक्तिमता लभ्यो दुर्लभः सर्वदेहिनाम् ।
स्वाराज्यस्याप्यभिमत एकान्तेनात्मविद्गतिः ॥५४॥

bhavān bhaktimatā labhyo
durlabhaḥ sarva-dehinām

svārājyasyāpy abhimata
ekāntenātma-vid-gatiḥ

bhavān—Your Grace; *bhaktimatā*—by the devotee; *labhyaḥ*—obtainable; *durlabhaḥ*—very difficult to be obtained; *sarva-dehinām*—of all other living entities; *svārājyasya*—of the king of heaven; *api*—even; *abhimataḥ*—the ultimate goal; *ekāntena*—by oneness; *ātma-vit*—of the self-realized; *gatiḥ*—the ultimate destination.

TRANSLATION

My dear Lord, the king in charge of the heavenly kingdom is also desirous to obtain the ultimate goal of life—devotional service. Similarly, You are the ultimate destination of those who identify themselves with You [ahaṁ brahmāsmi]. However, it is very difficult for them to attain You, whereas a devotee can very easily attain Your Lordship.

PURPORT

As stated in *Brahma-saṁhitā: vedeṣu durlabham adurlabham ātma-bhaktau.* This indicates that it is very difficult for one to attain the ultimate goal of life and reach the supreme destination, Vaikuṇṭhaloka or Goloka Vṛndāvana, simply by studying Vedānta philosophy or Vedic literature. However, this highest perfectional stage can be attained by the devotees very easily. That is the meaning of *vedeṣu durlabham adurlabham ātma-bhaktau.* The same point is confirmed by Lord Śiva in this verse. The Lord is very difficult for the *karma-yogīs, jñāna-yogīs* and *dhyāna-yogīs* to attain. Those who are *bhakti-yogīs,* however, have no difficulty at all. In the word *svārājyasya, svar* refers to Svargaloka, the heavenly planet, and *svārājya* refers to the ruler of the heavenly planet, Indra. Generally, *karmīs* desire elevation to heavenly planets, but King Indra desires to become perfect in *bhakti-yoga.* Those who also identify themselves as *ahaṁ brahmāsmi* ("I am the Supreme Brahman, one with the Absolute Truth.") also ultimately desire to attain perfect liberation in the Vaikuṇṭha planets or Goloka Vṛndāvana. In *Bhagavad-gītā* it is said:

bhaktyā mām abhijānāti
yāvān yaś cāsmi tattvataḥ
tato māṁ tattvato jñātvā
viśate tad-anantaram

"One can understand the Supreme Personality as He is only by devotional service. And when one is in full consciousness of the Supreme Lord by such devotion, he can enter into the kingdom of God." (Bg. 18.55)

Thus if one desires to enter into the spiritual world, he must try to understand the Supreme Personality of Godhead by practicing *bhakti-yoga.* Simply by practicing *bhakti-yoga* one can understand the Supreme Lord in truth, but without such understanding, one cannot enter the spiritual kingdom. One may be elevated to the heavenly planets or may realize himself as Brahman *(ahaṁ brahmāsmi)*, but that is not the end of realization. One must realize the position of the Supreme Personality of Godhead by *bhakti-yoga;* then real perfection of life is attained.

TEXT 55

तं दुराराध्यमाराध्य सतामपि दुरापया ।
एकान्तभक्त्या को वाञ्छेत्पादमूलं विना बहिः ॥५५॥

taṁ durārādhyam ārādhya
satām api durāpayā
ekānta-bhaktyā ko vāñchet
pāda-mūlaṁ vinā bahiḥ

tam—unto You; *durārādhyam*—very difficult to worship; *ārādhya*—having worshiped; *satām api*—even for the most exalted persons; *durāpayā*—very difficult to attain; *ekānta*—pure; *bhaktyā*—by devotional service; *kaḥ*—who is that man; *vāñchet*—should desire; *pāda-mūlam*—lotus feet; *vinā*—without; *bahiḥ*—those who are outsiders.

TRANSLATION

My dear Lord, pure devotional service is even difficult for liberated persons to discharge, but devotional service alone can satisfy You. Who will take to other processes of self-realization if he is actually serious about the perfection of life?

PURPORT

The word *satām* refers to transcendentalists. There are three kinds of transcendentalists: the *jñānī, yogī* and *bhakta.* Out of these three, the *bhakta* is selected as the most suitable candidate to approach the Supreme Personality of Godhead. It is emphasized herein that only one who is outside devotional service would not engage in searching for the lotus feet of the Lord. Foolish people sometimes maintain that God may be attained in any way—either by *karma-yoga, jñāna-yoga, dhyāna-yoga,* etc.—but here it is clearly stated that it is impossible to obtain the mercy of the Lord by any means but *bhakti-yoga.* The word *durārādhya* is especially significant.

It is very difficult to attain the lotus feet of the Lord by any method other than *bhakti-yoga.*

TEXT 56

यत्र निर्विष्टमरणं कृतान्तो नाभिमन्यते ।
विश्वं विध्वंसयन् वीर्यशौर्यविस्फूर्जितभ्रुवा ॥५६॥

yatra nirviṣṭam araṇaṁ
kṛtānto nābhimanyate
viśvaṁ vidhvaṁsayan vīrya-
śaurya-visphūrjita-bhruvā

yatra—wherein; *nirviṣṭam araṇam*—completely surrendered soul; *kṛta-antaḥ*—invincible time; *na abhimanyate*—does not go to attack; *viśvam*—the entire universe; *vidhvaṁsayan*—by vanquishing; *vīrya*—prowess; *śaurya*—influence; *visphūrjita*—simply by expansion; *bhruvā*—of the eyebrows.

TRANSLATION

Simply by expansion of His eyebrows, invincible Time personified can immediately vanquish the entire universe. However, formidable Time does not approach the devotee who has taken complete shelter at Your lotus feet.

PURPORT

In *Bhagavad-gītā* it is said that the Lord in the shape and form of death destroys all a person's possessions. *Mṛtyuḥ sarva-haraś cāham:* "I am all-devouring death." (Bg. 10.34) The Lord in the shape of death takes away everything that is created by the conditioned soul. Everything in this material world is subject to perish in due course of time. However, all the strength of time cannot hamper the activities of a devotee because a devotee takes complete shelter under the lotus feet of the Lord. For this reason only is a devotee free from formidable time. All the activities of the *karmīs* and *jñānīs,* which have no touch of devotional service, are spoiled in due course of time. The material success of the *karmīs* is destined to be destroyed; similarly, the impersonal realization attained by the *jñānīs* is also destroyed in the course of time.

āruhya kṛcchreṇa paraṁ padaṁ tataḥ
patanty adho 'nādṛta-yuṣmad-aṅghrayaḥ (*Bhāg.* 10.2.32)

To say nothing of the *karmīs,* the *jñānīs* undergo severe austerities to attain the impersonal *brahmajyoti,* but because they do not find the lotus feet of the Lord, they fall down again into this material existence. Unless one is fully situated in unalloyed devotional service, there is no guarantee of liberation, even if one is elevated to the heavenly planets or to the impersonal Brahman effulgence. A devotee's achievement, however, is never lost by the influence of time. Even if a devotee cannot completely execute devotional service, in his next life he begins from the point where he left off. Such an opportunity is not given to the *karmīs* and *jñānīs,* whose achievements are destroyed. The *bhakta's* achievement is never destroyed, for it goes on perpetually, be it complete or incomplete. This is the verdict of all Vedic literatures.

śrī bhagavān uvāca
pārtha naiveha nāmutra
vināśas tasya vidyate
na hi kalyāṇa-kṛt kaścid
durgatiṁ tāta gacchati

prāpya puṇya-kṛtāṁ lokān
uṣitvā śāśvatīḥ samāḥ
śucīnāṁ śrīmatāṁ gehe
yoga-bhraṣṭo 'bhijāyate

"The Blessed Lord said: Son of Pṛthā, a transcendentalist engaged in auspicious activities does not meet with destruction either in this world or in the spiritual world; one who does good, My friend, is never overcome by evil. The unsuccessful *yogī,* after many, many years of enjoyment on the planets of the pious living entities, is born into a family of righteous people, or into a family of rich aristocracy." (Bg. 6.40-41)

Thus if one is unable to complete the process of *bhakti-yoga,* he is given a chance in his next life to take birth in a pure family of devotees or in a rich family. In such families a person can have a good opportunity to further progress in devotional service.

When Yamarāja, the superintendent of death, was instructing his assistants, he told them not to approach the devotees. "The devotees should be offered respect," he said, "but do not go near them." Thus the devotees of the Lord are not under the jurisdiction of Yamarāja. Yamarāja is a representative of the Supreme Personality of Godhead, and he controls the death of every living entity. Yet he has nothing to do with the devotees. Simply by blinking his eyes, Time personified can destroy the entire cosmic manifestation, but he has nothing to do with the devotee. In other words, devotional service which is rendered by the devotee in this lifetime can never be destroyed by time. Such spiritual assets remain unchanged, being beyond the influence of time.

TEXT 57

क्षणार्धेनापि तुलये न स्वर्गं नापुनर्भवम् ।
भगवत्सङ्गिसङ्गस्य मर्त्यानां किमुताशिषः ॥५७॥

kṣaṇārdhenāpi tulaye
na svargaṁ nāpunarbhavam
bhagavat-saṅgi-saṅgasya
martyānāṁ kimutāśiṣaḥ

kṣaṇa-ardhena—by half of a moment; *api*—even; *tulaye*—compare; *na*—never; *svargam*—heavenly planets; *na*—neither; *apunarbhavam*—merging into the Supreme; *bhagavat*—the Supreme Personality of Godhead; *saṅgi*—associate; *saṅgasya*—one who takes advantage of associating; *martyānām*—of the conditioned soul; *kimuta*—what is there; *āśiṣaḥ*—blessings.

TRANSLATION

If one by chance associates with a devotee, even for a fraction of a moment, he no longer is subject to attraction by the results of karma or jñāna. What interest then can he have in the benedictions of the demigods, who are subject to the laws of birth and death?

PURPORT

Out of three kinds of men—the *karmīs, jñānīs,* and *bhaktas*—the *bhakta* is described herein as the most exalted. Śrīla Prabodhānanda Sarasvatī has sung: *kaivalyaṁ narakāyate tridaśapūr ākāśa-puṣpāyate* (*Caitanya-candrāmṛta,* 5). The word *kaivalya* means to merge into the effulgence of the Supreme Personality of Godhead, and the word *tridaśa-pūr* refers to the heavenly planets where the demigods live. Thus for a devotee, *kaivalya-sukha,* or merging into the existence of the Lord, is hellish because the *bhakta* considers it suicidal to lose his individuality and merge into the effulgence of Brahman. A *bhakta* always wants to retain his individuality in order to render service to the Lord. Indeed, he considers promotion to the upper planetary systems to be no better than a will-o'-the-wisp. Temporary material happiness holds no value for a devotee. The devotee is in such an exalted position that he is not interested in the actions of *karma* or *jñāna.* The resultant actions of *karma* and *jñāna* are so insignificant to a devotee situated on the transcendental platform that he is not in the least interested in them. *Bhakti-yoga* is sufficient to give the *bhakta* all happiness. As stated in *Śrīmad-Bhāgavatam: yayātmā suprasīdati* (*Bhāg.* 1.2.6). One can be fully satisfied simply by devotional service, and that is the result of association with a devotee. Without being blessed by a pure devotee, no one can be fully satisfied, nor can anyone understand the transcendental position of the Supreme Personality of Godhead.

TEXT 58

अथानघाङ्घ्रेस्तव कीर्तितीर्थयो-
रन्तर्बहिःस्नानविधूतपाप्मनाम् ।
भूतेष्वनुक्रोशसुसत्त्वशीलिनां
स्यात्सङ्गमोऽनुग्रह एष नस्तव ॥५८॥

athānaghāṅghres tava kīrti-tīrthayor
antar-bahiḥ-snāna-vidhūta-pāpmanām
bhūteṣv anukrośa-susattva-śīlināṁ
syāt saṅgamo 'nugraha eṣa nas tava

atha—therefore; *anagha-aṅghreḥ*—of my Lord, whose lotus feet destroy all inauspiciousness; *tava*—Your; *kīrti*—glorification; *tīrthayoḥ*—the holy Ganges water; *antaḥ*—within; *bahiḥ*—and outside; *snāna*—taking bath; *vidhūta*—washed; *pāpmanām*—contaminated state of mind; *bhūteṣu*—unto the ordinary living beings; *anukrośa*—benediction or mercy; *su-sattva*—completely in goodness; *śīlinām*—of those who possess such characteristics; *syāt*—let there be; *saṅgamaḥ*—association; *anugrahaḥ*—mercy; *eṣaḥ*—this; *naḥ*—unto us; *tava*—Your.

TRANSLATION

My dear Lord, Your lotus feet are the cause of all auspicious things and the destroyer ofall the contamination of sin. I therefore beg Your Lordship to benedict me by the association of Your devotees, who are completely purified by worshiping Your lotus feet and who are so merciful upon the conditioned souls. I think that Your real benediction will be to allow me to associate with such devotees.

PURPORT

The Ganges water is celebrated as being able to eradicate all kinds of sinful reactions. In other words, when a person takes his bath in the Ganges, he becomes freed from all life's contaminations. The Ganges water is celebrated in this way because it emanates from the lotus feet of the Supreme Personality of Godhead. Similarly, those who are directly in touch with the lotus feet of the Supreme Personality of Godhead and who are absorbed in the chanting of His glories are freed from all material contamination. Such unalloyed devotees are able to show mercy to the common conditioned soul. Śrīla Vṛndāvana dāsa Ṭhākura has sung that the devotees of Lord Caitanya are so powerful that each one of them can deliver a universe. In other words, it is the business of devotees to preach the glories of the Lord and deliver all conditioned souls to the platform of *śuddha-sattva,* pure goodness. Here the word *su-sattva* means *śuddha-sattva,* the transcendental stage beyond material goodness. By his exemplary prayers, Lord Śiva teaches us that our best course is to take shelter of Lord Viṣṇu and His Vaiṣṇava devotees.

TEXT 59

न यस्य चित्तं बहिरर्थविभ्रमं
तमोगुहायां च विशुद्धमाविशत् ।
यद्भक्तियोगानुगृहीतमञ्जसा
मुनिर्विचष्टे ननु तत्र ते गतिम् ॥५९॥

na yasya cittaṁ bahir-artha-vibhramaṁ
tamo-guhāyāṁ ca viśuddham āviśat
yad-bhaktiyogānugṛhītam añjasā
munir vicaṣṭe nanu tatra te gatim

na—never; *yasya*—whose; *cittam*—heart; *bahiḥ*—external; *artha*—interest; *vibhramam*—bewildered; *tamaḥ*—darkness; *guhāyām*—in the hole; *ca*—also; *viśuddham*—purified; *āviśat*—entered; *yat*—that; *bhakti-yoga*—devotional service; *anugṛhītam*—being favored by; *añjasā*—happily; *muniḥ*—the thoughtful; *vicaṣṭe*—sees; *nanu*—however; *tatra*—there; *te*—Your; *gatim*—activities.

TRANSLATION

The devotee whose heart has been completely cleansed by the process of devotional service and who is favored by the Bhaktidevī does not become bewildered by the external energy, which is just like a dark well. Being completely cleansed of all material contamination in this way, a devotee is able to understand very happily Your name, fame, form, activities, etc.

PURPORT

As stated in *Śrīmad-Bhāgavatam:*

satāṁ prasaṅgān mama vīrya-saṁvido
bhavanti hṛt-karṇa-rasāyanāḥ kathāḥ
taj-joṣaṇād āśv apavarga-vartmani
śraddhā ratir bhaktir anukramiṣyati
(*Bhāg.* 3.25.25)

Simply by the association of pure devotees one can understand the transcendental name, fame, quality and activities of the Supreme Personality of Godhead. Śrī Caitanya Mahāprabhu has repeatedly said:

'sādhu-saṅga', 'sādhu-saṅga'—sarva-śāstre kaya
lavamātra sādhu-saṅge sarva-siddhi haya (Cc. *Madhya* 22.54)

Simply by associating with a pure devotee, one becomes wonderfully advanced in Kṛṣṇa consciousness. *Sādhu-saṅga,* or association with a devotee, means always engaging in Kṛṣṇa consciousness by chanting the Hare Kṛṣṇa *mantra* and by acting for Kṛṣṇa. Specifically, chanting the Hare Kṛṣṇa *mantra* purifies one, and this chanting is therefore recommended by Śrī Caitanya Mahāprabhu. *Ceto-darpaṇa-mārjanam:* by chanting the names of Kṛṣṇa, the mirror of the heart is cleansed and the devotee loses interest in everything external. When one is influenced by the external energy of the Lord, his heart is impure. When one's heart is not pure, he cannot see how things are related to the Supreme Personality of Godhead. *Idaṁ hi viśvaṁ bhagavān ivetaro* (*Bhāg.* 1.5.20). He whose heart is purified can see that the whole cosmic manifestation is but the Supreme Personality of Godhead, but he whose heart is contaminated sees things differently. Therefore by *sat-saṅga,* or association with devotees, one becomes perfectly pure in heart.

One who is pure in heart is never attracted by the external energy, which urges the individual soul to try to dominate material nature. The pure heart of a devotee is never disturbed when he executes devotional service in the form of hearing, chanting, remembering, etc. In all, there are nine processes one can follow in the execution of devotional service. In any case, a pure-hearted devotee is never disturbed. The *bhakti-yoga* process must be carried out by avoiding the ten offenses one can commit while chanting the *mahā-mantra* and the sixty-four offenses one can commit while worshiping the Deity. When a devotee strictly follows the rules and regulations, Bhaktidevī becomes very much satisfied with him, and at that time he is never disturbed by anything external. A devotee is also called a *muni.* The word *muni* means thoughtful. A devotee is as thoughtful as a nondevotee is speculative. The nondevotee's speculation is impure, but a devotee's thoughts are pure. Lord Kapila and Śukadeva Gosvāmī are also called *muni,* and Vyāsadeva is addressed as Mahāmuni. A devotee is addressed as *muni,* or thoughtful, when he purely understands the Supreme Personality of Godhead. The conclusion is that when one's heart is purified by the association of devotees and by the avoidance of the offenses committed when chanting and worshiping the Lord, the transcendental name, form and activities of the Lord are revealed by the Lord.

TEXT 60

यत्रेदं व्यज्यते विश्वं विश्वस्मिन्नवभाति यत् ।
तत् त्वं ब्रह्म परं ज्योतिराकाशमिव विस्तृतम् ॥६०॥

yatredaṁ vyajyate viśvaṁ
viśvasminn avabhāti yat
tat tvaṁ brahma paraṁ jyotir
ākāśam iva vistṛtam

yatra—where; *idam*—this; *vyajyate*—manifested; *viśvam*—the universe; *viśvasmin*—in the cosmic manifestation; *avabhāti*—is manifested; *yat*—that; *tat*—that; *tvam*—You; *brahma*—the impersonal Brahman; *param*—transcendental; *jyotiḥ*—effulgence; *ākāśam*—sky; *iva*—like; *vistṛtam*—spread.

TRANSLATION

My dear Lord, You are the impersonal Brahman which is spread everywhere, like the sunshine or the sky. And You are also the entire manifested universe. Indeed, You are spread all over the universe.

PURPORT

In Vedic literature it is said that everything is Brahman and nothing else. The whole cosmic manifestation rests on the Brahman effulgence. The impersonalists, however, cannot understand how such a huge cosmic manifestation can rest on a person. Thus this inconceivable power of the Supreme Personality of Godhead is not understood by the impersonalists; therefore they are puzzled and always denying that the Absolute Truth is a person. This wrong impression is cleared by Lord Śiva himself, who says that the impersonal Brahman which is spread all over the universe is nothing but the Supreme Lord Himself. Here it is clearly said that the Lord is spread everywhere, just like the sunshine, by virtue of His Brahman feature. This example is very easy to understand. All the planetary systems are resting upon the sunshine, yet the sunshine, as well as the source of sunshine, are aloof from the planetary manifestations. Similarly, the sky or air is spread everywhere; air is within a pot, but it also touches filthy places and sanctified places alike. In any case, the sky is uncontaminated. The sunshine also touches filthy places and sanctified places, and both are actually produced by the sun, but in any case the sun is aloof from all filthy things. Similarly, the Lord exists everywhere. There are pious things and impious things, but in the *śāstras* the pious things are described as the front of the Supreme Lord, whereas impious things are described as the backside of the Supreme Personality of Godhead. In *Bhagavad-gītā* the Lord clearly says:

mayā tatam idaṁ sarvaṁ
jagad avyakta-mūrtinā
mat-sthāni sarva-bhūtāni
na cāhaṁ teṣv avasthitaḥ

"By Me, in My unmanifested form, this entire universe is pervaded. All beings are in Me, but I am not in them." (Bg. 9.4)

This verse explains that the Lord is spread everywhere by virtue of His Brahman feature. Everything rests in Him, yet He is not there. The conclusion is that without *bhakti-yoga,* without rendering devotional service to the Lord, even an impersonalist cannot understand the *Brahma-tattva,* the Brahman feature. In the *Vedānta-sūtra* it is stated: *athāto brahma-jijñāsā.* This means that Brahman, Paramātmā, or Parabrahman should be understood. In *Śrīmad-Bhāgavatam* also the Absolute Truth is described as the one without a second, but He is realized in three features–impersonal Brahman, localized Paramātmā and the Supreme Personality of Godhead. The Supreme Personality of Godhead is the ultimate issue, and in this verse Lord Śiva confirms that ultimately the Absolute Truth is a person. He clearly says: *tat tvaṁ brahma paraṁ jyotir ākāśam iva vistṛtam.* Here is a common example: a successful businessman may have many factories and offices, and everything rests on his order. If someone says that the entire business rests on such and such a person, it does not mean that the person is bearing all the factories and offices on his head. Rather, it is understood that by his brain or his energetic expansion, the business is running without interruption. Similarly, it is the brain and energy of the Supreme Personality of Godhead that carry on the complete manifestation of the material and spiritual worlds. The philosophy of monism, explained here very clearly, adjusts itself to the fact that the supreme source of all energy is the Supreme Personality of Godhead, Kṛṣṇa. This is described very clearly. It is also stated how the impersonal feature of Kṛṣṇa can be understood:

raso 'ham apsu kaunteya
prabhāsmi śaśi-sūryayoḥ
praṇavaḥ sarva-vedeṣu
śabdaḥ khe pauruṣaṁ nṛṣu

"O son of Kuntī [Arjuna], I am the taste of water, the light of the sun and moon, the syllable *om* in the Vedic *mantras;* I am the sound in ether and ability in man." (Bg. 7.8)

In this way Kṛṣṇa can be understood as the mystic power in everything.

TEXT 61

यो माययेदं पुरुरूपयासृजद्
बिभर्ति भूयः क्षपयत्यविक्रियः ।
यद्भेदबुद्धिः सदिवात्मदुःस्थया
त्वमात्मतन्त्रं भगवन् प्रतीमहि ॥६१॥

yo māyayedaṁ puru-rūpayāsṛjad
bibharti bhūyaḥ kṣapayaty avikriyaḥ
yad-bheda-buddhiḥ sad ivātma-duḥsthayā
tvam ātma-tantraṁ bhagavan pratīmahi

yaḥ—one who; *māyayā*—by His energy; *idam*—this; *puru*—manifold; *rūpayā*—manifestation; *asṛjạt*—created; *bibharti*—maintains; *bhūyaḥ*—again; *kṣapayati*—annihilates; *avikriyaḥ*—without being altered; *yat*—that; *bheda-buddhiḥ*—sense of differentiation; *sat*—eternal; *iva*—like; *ātma-duḥsthayā*—giving trouble to oneself; *tvam*—unto You; *ātma-tantram*—fully self-independent; *bhagavan*—O Lord, Supreme Personality of Godhead; *pratīmahi*—I can understand.

TRANSLATION

My dear Lord, You have manifold energies, and these energies are manifested in manifold forms. With such energies You have also created this cosmic manifestation, and although You maintain it as if it were permanent, You ultimately annihilate it. Although You are never disturbed by such changes and alterations, the living entities are disturbed by them, and therefore they find the cosmic manifestation to be different or separated from You. My Lord, You are always independent, and I can clearly see this fact.

PURPORT

It is clearly explained that Lord Kṛṣṇa has multi-energies that can be grouped into three: namely the external energy, the internal energy, and the marginal energy. There are also different cosmic manifestations—namely, the spiritual world and the material world—as well as different types of living entities. Some living entities are conditioned, and others are eternally free. The eternally free living entities are called *nitya-mukta*, for they never come in contact with the material energy. However, some living entities are conditioned in this material world, and thus they think themselves separated from the Supreme Lord. Due to their contact with the material energy, their existence is always troublesome. Being always in distress, the conditioned soul considers the material energy to be very much disturbing. This fact is explained by a Vaiṣṇava *kavi,* or poet: *kṛṣṇa bhuli' sei jīva anādi-bahir-mukha/ ataeva māyā tāre deya saṁsāra-duḥkha.* When the living entity forgets the Supreme Lord and wants to enjoy himself independently, imitating the Supreme Lord, he is captured by the false notion that he is the enjoyer and is separated from the Supreme Lord. This material energy is therefore very much troublesome to the spiritual energy, the living entity, but the material energy is never troublesome to the Supreme Lord. Indeed, for the Supreme Lord, both material and spiritual energy are the same. In this verse Lord Śiva explains that the material energy is never troublesome to the Supreme Lord. The Supreme Lord is always independent, but because the living entities are not independent—due to their false idea of becoming independently happy—the material energy is troublesome. Consequently the material energy creates differentiation.

Because the Māyāvādī philosophers cannot understand this, they want to be relieved from the material energy. However, because a Vaiṣṇava philosopher is in full knowledge of the Supreme Personality of Godhead, he finds no disturbance even in the material energy. This is because he knows how to utilize the material energy for the service of the Lord. In the government, the criminal department and civil department may appear different in the eyes of the citizens, but in the eyes of the government both departments are one and the same. The criminal department is troublesome for the criminal but not for the obedient citizen. Similarly, this material energy is troublesome for the conditioned soul, but it has nothing to do with the liberated souls who are engaged in the service of the Lord. Through the *puruṣa-avatāra* Mahā-Viṣṇu, the Supreme Personality of Godhead created the whole cosmic manifestation. Simply by breathing out all the universes, the Lord creates and maintains the cosmic manifestation as Lord Viṣṇu. Then as Saṅkarṣaṇa, He annihilates the cosmic manifestation. Yet despite the creation, maintenance and destruction of the cosmos, the Lord is not affected. The various activities of the Lord must be very disturbing to the tiny living entities, but since the Lord is supremely great, He is never affected. Lord Śiva or any other pure devotee can see this clearly without being blinded by *bheda-buddhi,* or differentiation. For a devotee, the Lord is the Supreme Spirit Soul. Since He is supremely powerful, His various powers are also spiritual. For a devotee, there is nothing material, for material existence only means forgetfulness of the Supreme Personality of Godhead.

TEXT 62

क्रियाकलापैरिदमेव योगिनः
श्रद्धान्विताः साधु यजन्ति सिद्धये ।
भूतेन्द्रियान्तःकरणोपलक्षितं
वेदे च तन्त्रे च त एव कोविदाः ॥६२॥

kriyā-kalāpair idam eva yoginaḥ
śraddhānvitāḥ sādhu yajanti siddhaye
bhūtendriyāntaḥkaraṇopalakṣitam
vede ca tantre ca ta eva kovidāḥ

kriyā—activities; *kalāpaiḥ*—by processes; *idam*—this; *eva*—certainly; *yoginaḥ*—transcendentalists; *śraddhā-anvitāḥ*—with faith and conviction; *sādhu*—properly; *yajanti*—worship; *siddhaye*—for perfection; *bhūta*—the material energy; *indriya*—senses; *antaḥ-karaṇa*—heart; *upalakṣitam*—symptomized by; *vede*—in the *Vedas; ca*—also; *tantre*—in the corollaries of the *Vedas; ca*—also; *te*—Your Lordship; *eva*—certainly; *kovidāḥ*—those who are experts.

TRANSLATION

My dear Lord, Your universal form consists of all five elements—the senses, mind, intelligence, false ego (which is material) and the Paramātmā, Your partial expansion who is the director of everything. With the exception of the devotees, the other yogīs—namely the karma-yogī and jñāna-yogī—worship You by their respective actions in their respective positions. It is stated both in the Vedas and in the śāstras that are corollaries of the Vedas, and indeed everywhere, that it is only You who are to be worshiped. That is the expert version of all the Vedas.

PURPORT

In the previous verse Lord Śiva wanted to see the form of the Lord which the devotees are always interested in. There are other forms of the Lord manifest in the material world, including Brahmā and other demigods, and these are worshiped by materialistic persons. In *Śrīmad-Bhāgavatam* it is stated that those who desire material benefits are recommended to worship different types of demigods.

akāmaḥ sarva-kāmo vā mokṣa-kāma udāra-dhīḥ
tīvreṇa bhakti-yogena yajeta puruṣam param (*Bhāg.* 2.3.10)

The devotees, the *jñānīs,* who are known as *mokṣa-kāma,* and the *karmīs,* who are known as *sarva-kāma,* are all aspiring to worship the Supreme Personality of Godhead, Viṣṇu. Even when one performs *yajñas,* as stated here *(kriyā-kalāpaiḥ),* he should always remember that the demigods are but agents of the Supreme Lord. Actually the worshipful Lord is Viṣṇu, Yajñeśvara. Thus even when different demigods are worshiped in the Vedic and Tantric sacrifices, the actual goal of sacrifice is Lord Viṣṇu. Therefore in *Bhagavad-gītā* it is said:

ye 'py anya-devatā-bhaktā
yajante śraddhayānvitāḥ
te 'pi mām eva kaunteya
yajanty avidhi-pūrvakam

"Whatever a man may sacrifice to other gods, O son of Kuntī, is really meant for Me alone, but is offered without true understanding." (Bg. 9.23)

Thus the worshipers of various demigods also worship the Supreme Lord, but they do so against the regulative principles. The purpose of the regulative principles is to satisfy Lord Viṣṇu. In the *Viṣṇu Purāṇa* the very same thing is confirmed:

varṇāśramācāravatā puruṣeṇa paraḥ pumān
viṣṇur ārādhyate panthā nānyat tat-toṣa-kāraṇam (*Viṣṇu P.* 3.8.9)

Here it is clearly mentioned that the *karmī, jñānī* or *yogī*—in fact, everyone—worships Lord Viṣṇu if he is actually expert in knowledge of the *Vedas* and *Tantras.* The word *kovidāḥ* is very significant, for it indicates the devotees of the Lord. Only the devotees know perfectly that the Supreme Personality of Godhead, Viṣṇu, is all-pervading. Within the material energy, He is represented by the five material elements as well as the mind, intelligence and ego. He is also represented by another energy, and all these manifestations in the spiritual and material world combined are but representations of the different energies of the Lord. The conclusion is that the Lord is one and that He is expanded in everything. This is understood by the Vedic version: *sarvaṁ khalv idaṁ brahma.* One who knows this concentrates all his energy in worshiping Lord Viṣṇu.

TEXT 63

त्वमेक आद्यः पुरुषः सुप्तशक्ति-
स्तया रजःसत्त्वतमो विभिद्यते ।

महानहं खं मरुदग्निवार्धराः
सुरर्षयो भूतगणा इदं यतः ॥६३॥

tvam eka ādyaḥ puruṣaḥ supta-śaktis
tayā rajaḥ-sattva-tamo vibhidyate
mahān ahaṁ khaṁ marud agni-vār-dharāḥ
surarṣayo bhūta-gaṇā idaṁ yataḥ

tvam—Your Lordship; *ekaḥ*—one; *ādyaḥ*—the original; *puruṣaḥ*—person; *supta*—dormant; *śaktiḥ*—energy; *tayā*—by which; *rajaḥ*—the passion energy; *sattva*—goodness; *tamaḥ*—ignorance; *vibhidyate*—is diversified; *mahān*—the total material energy; *aham*—egotism; *kham*—the sky; *marut*—the air; *agni*—fire; *vāḥ*—water; *dharāḥ*—earth; *sura-ṛṣayaḥ*—the demigods and the great sages; *bhūta-gaṇāḥ*—the living entities; *idam*—all this; *yataḥ*—from whom.

TRANSLATION

My dear Lord, You are the only Supreme Person, the cause of all causes. Before the creation of this material world, Your material energy remains in a dormant condition. When Your material energy is agitated, the three qualities—namely, goodness, passion and ignorance—act, and as a result the total material energy—egotism, ether, air, fire, water, earth, and all the various demigods and saintly persons—becomes manifest. Thus the material world is created.

PURPORT

If the whole creation is one, that is, nothing but the Supreme Lord, or Viṣṇu, then why do the expert transcendentalists make such categories as are found in the above verse? Why do learned and expert scholars distinguish between matter and spirit? In answer to these questions, Lord Śiva says that spirit and matter are not creations of various philosophers, but are manifested by Lord Viṣṇu, as described in this verse: *tvam eka ādyaḥ puruṣaḥ*. Spiritual and material categories are made possible by the Supreme Personality of Godhead, but actually there are no such distinctions for the living entities who are eternally engaged in the service of the Lord. There is only a material world for those who want to imitate the Lord and become enjoyers. Indeed, the material world is nothing but forgetfulness of the original Supreme Personality of Godhead, the creator of everything. The distinction between matter and spirit is created by the sleeping energy of the Lord when the Lord wants to give some facility to those living entities who want to imitate the Lord in His enjoyment. It is only for them that this material world is created by the dormant energy of the Lord. For instance, sometimes children want to imitate their mother and cook in the kitchen, and at such a time the mother supplies them with some toys so that the children can imitate her cooking. Similarly, when some of the living entities want to imitate the activities of the Lord, this material cosmic manifestation is created for them by the Lord. The material creation is therefore caused by the Lord through His material energy. It is by the glance of the Lord that the material energy is activated. At that time the three material qualities are set into motion, and the material energy is manifested first in the form of the *mahat-tattva,* then egotism, then ether, then air, fire, water, and earth. After the creation, the living entities are impregnated in the cosmic manifestation, and they emerge as Lord Brahmā and the seven great *ṛṣis,* then as different demigods. From the demigods come human beings, animals, trees, birds, beasts and everything else. The original cause, however, is the Supreme Personality of Godhead, as verified herein—*tvam eka ādyaḥ puruṣaḥ.* This is also confirmed in *Brahma-saṁhitā:*

īśvaraḥ paramaḥ kṛṣṇaḥ sac-cid-ānanda-vigrahaḥ
anādir ādir govindaḥ sarva-kāraṇa-kāraṇam

Those who are covered by the material energy cannot understand that the origin of everything is the Supreme Personality of Godhead, Kṛṣṇa. This is summarized in the *Vedānta* aphorism, *janmādy asya yataḥ* (*Vedānta-sūtra* 1.1.2). Kṛṣṇa also confirms this in *Bhagavad-gītā:*

ahaṁ sarvasya prabhavo
mattaḥ sarvaṁ pravartate
iti matvā bhajante māṁ
budhā bhāva-samanvitāḥ

"I am the source of all spiritual and material worlds. Everything emanates from Me. The wise who know this perfectly engage in My devotional service and worship Me with all their hearts." (Bg. 10.8)

When Kṛṣṇa says that He is the origin of everything *(ahaṁ sarvasya prabhavo),* He means that He is even the source of Lord Brahmā, Lord Śiva, the *puruṣa-avatāras,* the material manifestation and all the living entities within the material world. Actually the word *prabhava* (creation) only refers to this material world, for since the spiritual world is eternally existing, there is no question of creation. In the *catuḥślokī* of *Śrīmad-Bhāgavatam,* the Lord says: *aham evāsam evāgre (Bhāg.* 2.9.33). "I was existing in the beginning before the creation." In the *Vedas* it is also said, *eko nārāyaṇa āsīt:* "Before the creation there was only Nārāyaṇa." This is also confirmed by Śaṅkarācārya: *nārāyaṇaḥ paro'vyaktāt (Gītā-bhāṣya).* "Nārāyaṇa is transcendental to the creation." Since all the activities of Nārāyaṇa are spiritual, when Nārāyaṇa said, "Let there be creation," that creation was all-spiritual. The "material" only exists for those who have forgotten that Nārāyaṇa is the original cause.

TEXT 64

सृष्टं स्वशक्त्येदमनुप्रविष्ट-
श्चतुर्विधं पुरमात्मांशकेन ।
अथो विदुस्तं पुरुषं सन्तमन्त-
र्भुङ्क्ते हृषीकैर्मधु सारघं यः ॥६४॥

sṛṣṭaṁ sva-śaktyedam anupraviṣṭaś
catur-vidhaṁ puram ātmāṁśakena
atho vidus taṁ puruṣaṁ santam antar
bhuṅkte hṛṣīkair madhu sāra-ghaṁ yaḥ

sṛṣṭam—in the creation; *sva-śaktyā*—by Your own potency; *idam*—this cosmic manifestation; *anupraviṣṭaḥ*—entering afterwards; *catuḥ-vidham*—four kinds of; *puram*—bodies; *ātma-aṁśakena*—by Your own part and parcel; *atho*—therefore; *viduḥ*—know; *tam*—him; *puruṣam*—the enjoyer; *santam*—existing; *antaḥ*—within; *bhuṅkte*—enjoys; *hṛṣīkaiḥ*—by the senses; *madhu*—sweetness; *sāra-gham*—honey; *yaḥ*—one who.

TRANSLATION

My dear Lord, after creating by Your own potencies, You enter within the creation in four kinds of forms. Being within the hearts of the living entities, You know them and know how they are enjoying their senses. The so-called happiness of this material creation is exactly like the bees' enjoyment of honey after it has been collected in the honeycomb.

PURPORT

The material cosmic manifestation is an exhibition of the external energy of the Supreme Personality of Godhead, but because dull matter cannot work independently, the Lord Himself enters within this material creation in the form of a partial expansion (Paramātmā), and He enters also by His separated parts and parcels (the living entities). In other words, both the living entities and the Supreme Personality of Godhead enter into the material creation just to make it active. As stated in *Bhagavad-gītā:*

apareyam itas tv anyaṁ
prakṛtiṁ viddhi me parām
jīva-bhūtāṁ mahā-bāho
yayedaṁ dhāryate jagat

"Besides this inferior nature, O mighty-armed Arjuna, there is a superior energy of Mine, which are all living entities who are struggling with material nature and are sustaining the universe." (Bg. 7.5)

Since the material world cannot work independently, the living entities enter into the material manifestation in four different types of bodies. The word *catur-vidham* is significant in this verse. There are four types of living entities born within this material world. Some are born by way of an embryo *(jarāyu-ja)*, by way of eggs *(aṇḍa-ja)*, perspiration *(sveda-ja)*, and, like the trees, by way of seeds *(udbhij-ja)*. Regardless of how these living entities appear, they are all busy in the pursuit of sense enjoyment.

The materialistic scientists' contention that living entities other than human beings have no soul is nullified herein. Whether they are born through an embryo, eggs, perspiration or seeds, all living entities in the 8,400,000 species of life are parts and parcels of the Supreme Personality of Godhead, and each therefore is an individual spiritual spark and soul. The Supreme Personality of Godhead also remains within the heart of the living entity, regardless of whether the living entity is a man, animal, tree, germ or microbe. The Lord resides in everyone's heart, and because all living entities who come to this material world do so in order to fulfill their desire for sense enjoyment, the Lord directs the living entities to enjoy their senses. Thus the Paramātmā, the Supreme Personality of Godhead, knows everyone's desires. As stated in *Bhagavad-gītā:*

sarvasya cāhaṁ hṛdi sanniviṣṭo
mattaḥ smṛtir jñānam apohanaṁ ca

"I am seated in everyone's heart, and from Me come remembrance, knowledge and forgetfulness." (Bg. 15.15)

Remaining within the hearts of all living entities, the Lord bestows remembrance by which the living entities can enjoy certain things. Thus the living entities create their enjoyable honeycombs and then enjoy them. The example of the bees is appropriate because when bees try to enjoy their honeycomb, they have to suffer the bites of other bees. Because bees bite one another when they enjoy honey, they are not exclusively enjoying the sweetness of the honey, for there is also suffering. In other words, the living entities are subjected to the pains and pleasures of material enjoyment, whereas the Supreme Personality of Godhead, knowing their plans for sense enjoyment, is aloof from them. In the *Upaniṣads* the example is given of two birds sitting on a tree. One bird (the *jīva,* or living entity) is enjoying the fruits of that tree, and the other bird (Paramātmā) is simply witnessing. In the *Bhagavad-gītā* the Supreme Personality of Godhead as Paramātmā is described as *upadraṣṭā* (the overseer) and *anumantā* (the permitter).

upadraṣṭānumantā ca
bhartā bhoktā maheśvaraḥ
paramātmeti cāpy ukto
dehe 'smin puruṣaḥ paraḥ

"Yet in this body there is another, a transcendental enjoyer, who is the Lord, the supreme proprietor, who exists as the overseer and permitter, and who is known as the Supersoul." (Bg. 13.23)

Thus the Lord simply witnesses and gives the living entity sanction for sense enjoyment. It is the Paramātmā also who gives the intelligence by which the bees can construct a hive, collect honey from various flowers, store it and enjoy it. Although the Paramātmā is aloof from the living entities, He knows their intentions, and He gives them facilities by which they can enjoy or suffer the results of their actions. Human society is exactly like a beehive, for everyone is engaged in collecting honey from various flowers, or collecting money from various sources and creating large empires for common enjoyment. However, after these empires are created, the bites of other nations have to be suffered. Sometimes nations declare war upon one another, and the human beehives become sources of misery. Although human beings are creating their beehives in order to enjoy the sweetness of their senses, they are at the same time suffering from the bites of other persons or nations. The Supreme Personality of Godhead as Paramātmā is simply witnessing all these activities. The conclusion is that both the Supreme Personality of Godhead and the *jīvas* enter into this material world. However, the Paramātmā, or Supreme Personality of Godhead, is worshipable because He has arranged for the happiness of the living entity in the material world. Because it is the material world, however, no one can enjoy any kind of happiness without inebriety. Material enjoyment means inebriety, whereas spiritual enjoyment means pure enjoyment under the protection of the Supreme Personality of Godhead.

TEXT 65

स एष लोकानतिचण्डवेगो
विकर्षसि त्वं खलु कालयानः ।
भूतानि भूतैरनुमेयतत्त्वो
घनावलीर्वायुरिवाविषह्यः ॥६५॥

sa eṣa lokān ati-caṇḍa-vego
vikarṣasi tvaṁ khalu kālayānaḥ
bhūtāni bhūtair anumeya-tattvo
ghanāvalīr vāyur ivāviṣahyaḥ

saḥ—that; *eṣaḥ*—this; *lokān*—all the planetary systems; *ati*—very much; *caṇḍa-vegaḥ*—the great force; *vikarṣasi*—destroys; *tvam*—Your Lordship; *khalu*—however; *kālayānaḥ*—in due course of time; *bhūtāni*—all living entities; *bhūtaiḥ*—by other living entities; *anumeya-tattvaḥ*—the Absolute Truth can be guessed; *ghana-āvalīḥ*—the clouds; *vāyuḥ*—air; *iva*—like; *aviṣahyaḥ*—unbearable.

TRANSLATION

My dear Lord, Your absolute authority cannot be directly experienced, but one can guess by seeing the activities of the world that everything is being destroyed in due course of time. The force of time is very strong, and everything is being destroyed by something else—just as one animal is being eaten by another animal. Time scatters everything, exactly as the wind scatters clouds in the sky.

PURPORT

The process of destruction is going on according to the law of nature. Nothing within this material world can be permanent, although scientists, philosophers, workers and everyone else are trying to make things permanent. One foolish scientist recently declared that eventually life will be made permanent through science. Some so-called scientists are also trying to manufacture living entities within the laboratory. Thus in one way or another everyone is busy denying the existence of the Supreme Personality of Godhead and rejecting the supreme authority of the Lord. However, the Lord is so powerful that He destroys everything in the form of death. As Kṛṣṇa says in *Bhagavad-gītā: mṛtyuḥ sarva-haraś cāham.* "I am all-devouring death." (Bg. 10.34) The Lord is just like death to the atheists, for He takes away everything they accumulate in the material world. Hiraṇyakaśipu, the father of Prahlāda, always denied the existence of the Lord, and he tried to kill his five-year-old boy due to the boy's unflinching faith in God. However, in due course of time the Lord appeared as Nṛsiṁhadeva and killed Hiraṇyakaśipu in the presence of his son. As stated in *Śrīmad-Bhāgavatam,* this killing process is natural. *Jīvo jīvasya jīvanam:* "One animal is food for another animal." (*Bhāg.* 1.13.47) A frog is eaten by a snake, a snake is eaten by a mongoose, and the mongoose is eaten by another animal. In this way the process of destruction goes on by the supreme will of the Lord. Although we do not see the hand of the Supreme Lord directly, we can feel the presence of that hand through the Lord's process of destruction. We can see the clouds scattered by the wind, although we cannot see how this is being done because it is not possible to see the wind. Similarly, although we do not directly see the Supreme Personality of Godhead, we can see that He controls the process of destruction. The destructive process is going on fiercely under the control of the Lord, but the atheists cannot see it.

TEXT 66

प्रमत्तमुच्चैरितिकृत्यचिन्तया
प्रवृद्धलोभं विषयेषु लालसम् ।
त्वमप्रमत्तः सहसाभिपद्यसे
क्षुल्लेलिहानोऽहिरिवाखुमन्तकः ॥६६॥

pramattam uccair iti kṛtya-cintayā
pravṛddha-lobhaṁ viṣayeṣu lālasam
tvam apramattaḥ sahasābhipadyase
kṣul-lelihāno 'hir ivākhum antakaḥ

pramattam—persons who are mad; *uccaiḥ*—loudly; *iti*—thus; *kṛtya*—to be done; *cintayā*—by such desire; *pravṛddha*—very much advanced; *lobham*—greediness; *viṣayeṣu*—in the matter of material enjoyment; *lālasam*—so desiring; *tvam*—Your Lordship; *apramattaḥ*—completely in transcendence; *sahasā*—all of a sudden; *abhipadyase*—seizes them; *kṣut*—hungry; *lelihānaḥ*—by the greedy tongue; *ahiḥ*—snake; *iva*—like; *ākhum*—mouse; *antakaḥ*—destroyer.

TRANSLATION

My dear Lord, all living entities within this material world are mad after planning for things, and they are always busy with a desire to do this or that. This is due to uncontrollable greed. The greed for material enjoyment

is always existing in the living entity, but Your Lordship is always alert, and in due course of time You strike him, just as a snake seizes a mouse and very easily swallows him.

PURPORT

Everyone is greedy, and everyone makes plans for material enjoyment. In his lust for material enjoyment, the living entity is described as a madman. As stated in *Bhagavad-gītā:*

prakṛteḥ kriyamāṇāni
guṇaiḥ karmāṇi sarvaśaḥ
ahaṅkāra-vimūḍhātmā
kartāham iti manyate

"The bewildered spirit soul, under the influence of the three modes of material nature, thinks himself to be the doer of activities, which are in actuality carried out by nature." (Bg. 3.27)

Everything is enacted by the laws of nature, and these laws are under the direction of the Supreme Personality of Godhead. The atheists, or unintelligent men, do not know this. They are busy making their own plans, and big nations are busy expanding their empire. And yet we know that in due course of time many empires have come into existence and been destroyed. Many aristocratic families were created by the people in their extreme madness, but we can see that in the course of time those families and empires have all been destroyed. But still the foolish atheists do not accept the supreme authority of the Lord. Such foolish people unnecessarily concoct their own duties without referring to the supreme authority of the Lord. The so-called political leaders are busy making plans to advance the material prosperity of their nation, but factually these political leaders only want an exalted position for themselves. Due to their greed for material position, they falsely present themselves as leaders before the people and collect their votes, although they are completely under the grip of the laws of material nature. These are some of the faults of modern civilization. Without taking to God consciousness and accepting the authority of the Lord, the living entities become ultimately confused and frustrated in their planmaking attempts. Due to their unauthorized plans for economic development, the price of commodities is rising daily all over the world, so much so that it has become difficult for the poorer classes, and they are suffering the consequences. And due to lack of Kṛṣṇa consciousness, people are being fooled by so-called leaders and planmakers.

Consequently, the sufferings of the people are increasing. According to the laws of nature, which are backed by the Lord, nothing can be permanent within this material world; therefore everyone should be allowed to take shelter of the Absolute in order to be saved. In this regard, Lord Kṛṣṇa says in *Bhagavad-gītā:*

bhoktāraṁ yajña-tapasāṁ
sarva-loka-maheśvaram
suhṛdaṁ sarva-bhūtānāṁ
jñātvā māṁ śāntim ṛcchati

"The sages, knowing Me as the ultimate purpose of all sacrifices and austerities, the Supreme Lord of all planets and demigods and the benefactor and well-wisher of all living entities, attain peace from the pangs of material miseries." (Bg. 5.29)

If one wants peace of mind and tranquility in society, he must accept the fact that the real enjoyer is the Supreme Personality of Godhead. The Lord is the proprietor of everything all over the universe, and He is the supreme friend of all living entities as well. By understanding this, people can become happy and peaceful individually and collectively.

TEXT 67

कस्त्वत्पदाब्जं विजहाति पण्डितो
यस्तेऽवमानव्ययमानकेतनः ।
विशङ्कयास्मद्गुरुरर्चति स्म यद्
विनोपपत्तिं मनवश्चतुर्दश ॥६७॥

kas tvat-padābjaṁ vijahāti paṇḍito
yas te 'vamāna-vyayamāna-ketanaḥ
viśaṅkayāsmad-gurur arcati sma yad
vinopapattiṁ manavaś caturdaśa

kaḥ—who; *tvat*—Your; *pada-abjam*—lotus feet; *vijahāti*—avoids; *paṇḍitaḥ*—learned; *yaḥ*—who; *te*—unto You; *avamāna*—deriding; *vyayamāna*—decreasing; *ketanaḥ*—this body; *viśaṅkayā*—without any doubt; *asmat*—our; *guruḥ*—spiritual master, father; *arcati*—worships; *sma*—in the past; *yat*—that; *vinā*—without; *upapattim*—agitation; *manavaḥ*—the Manus; *caturdaśa*—fourteen in number.

TRANSLATION

My dear Lord, any learned person knows that unless he worships You, his entire life is spoiled. Knowing this, how could he give up worshiping Your lotus feet? Even our father and spiritual master, Lord Brahmā, unhesitatingly worshiped You, and the fourteen Manus followed in his footsteps.

PURPORT

The word *paṇḍita* means "a wise man." Who is actually a wise man? The wise man is described in *Bhagavad-gītā* in this way:

bahūnāṁ janmanām ante
jñānavān māṁ prapadyate
vāsudevaḥ sarvam iti
sa mahātmā sudurlabhaḥ

"After many births and deaths, he who is actually in knowledge surrenders unto Me, knowing Me to be the cause of all causes and all that is. Such a great soul is very rare." (Bg. 7.19)

Thus when the wise man actually becomes wise after many births and whimsical attempts at self-realization, he surrenders unto the Supreme Personality of Godhead, Kṛṣṇa. Such a *mahātmā,* or learned person, knows that Kṛṣṇa, Vāsudeva, is everything (*vāsudevaḥ sarvam iti*). Learned persons always think that life is wasted unless they worship Lord Kṛṣṇa or become His devotee. Śrīla Rūpa Gosvāmī also says that when one becomes an advanced devotee he understands that he should be reserved and persevérent *(kṣāntiḥ)* and that he should engage in the service of the Lord and not waste time *(avyartha-kālatvam).* He should also be detached from all material attraction *(viraktiḥ),* and he should not long for any material respect in return for his activities *(māna-śūnyatā).* He should be certain that Kṛṣṇa will bestow His mercy upon him *(āśā-bandhaḥ),* and he should always be very eager to serve the Lord faithfully *(samutkaṇṭhā).* The wise man is always very eager to glorify the Lord by chanting and hearing *(nāma-gāne sadā ruciḥ)* and he is always eager to describe the transcendental qualities of the Lord (*āsaktis tad-guṇākhyāne*). He should also be attracted to those places where the Lord had His pastimes *(prītis tad-vasati-sthale).* These are symptoms of an advanced devotee.

An advanced devotee or a perfect human being who is actually wise and learned cannot give up his service at the lotus feet of the Lord. Although Lord Brahmā has a long life span (4,320,000,000 years constitute twelve hours in a day of Brahmā), Brahmā is nonetheless afraid of death and consequently engaged in the devotional service of the Lord. Similarly, all the Manus who appear and disappear during the day of Brahmā are also engaged in the Lord's devotional service. In Brahmā's one day, fourteen Manus appear and disappear. The first Manu is Svāyambhuva Manu. Each Manu lives for seventy-one *yugas,* each consisting of some 4,320,000 years. Although the Manus have such a long life span, they still prepare for the next life by engaging in the devotional service of the Lord. In this age human beings only live for sixty or eighty years, and even this small life span is gradually decreasing. Therefore it is even more imperative for human beings to take to the worship of the lotus feet of the Lord by constantly chanting the Hare Kṛṣṇa *mantra,* as recommended by Lord Caitanya Mahāprabhu.

tṛṇād api sunīcena taror iva sahiṣṇunā
amāninā mānadena kīrtanīyaḥ sadā hariḥ

When one is engaged in devotional service, he is often surrounded by envious people, and often many enemies come to try to defeat him or stop him. This is not new in this present age, for even in the days of yore Prahlāda Mahārāja, who was engaged in the devotional service of the Lord, was harassed by his demonic father, Hiraṇyakaśipu. The atheists are always prepared to harass a devotee; therefore Caitanya Mahāprabhu suggested that one be very tolerant of these people. Nonetheless, one has to continue chanting the Hare Kṛṣṇa *mantra* and preaching the chanting of this *mantra* because such preaching and chanting constitute the perfection of life. One should chant and preach about the urgency of making this life perfect in all respects. One should thus engage in the devotional service of the Lord and follow in the footsteps of previous *ācāryas,* beginning with Lord Brahmā and others.

TEXT 68

अथ त्वमसि नो ब्रह्मन् परमात्मन् विपश्चिताम् ।
विश्वं रुद्रभयध्वस्तमकुतश्चिद्भया गतिः ॥६८॥

atha tvam asi no brahman
paramātman vipaścitām
viśvaṁ rudra-bhaya-dhvastam
akutaścid-bhayā gatiḥ

atha—therefore; *tvam*—my Lord, Yourself; *asi*—are; *naḥ*—our; *brahman*—O Supreme Brahman; *paramātman*—O Supersoul; *vipaścitām*—for the learned wise men; *viśvam*—the whole universe; *rudra-bhaya*—being afraid of Rudra; *dhvastam*—annihilated; *akutaścit-bhayā*—undoubtedly fearless; *gatiḥ*—destination.

TRANSLATION

My dear Lord, all actually learned persons know You as the Supreme Brahman and the Supersoul. Although the entire universe is afraid of Lord Rudra, who ultimately annihilates everything, for the learned devotees You are the fearless destination of all.

PURPORT

For the purpose of creation, maintenance and annihilation of this cosmic manifestation, there are three lords—Brahmā, Viṣṇu and Śiva (Maheśvara). The material body is finished at the time of annihilation. Both the universal body and the small unit, the individual living entity's body, are susceptible to annihilation at the ultimate end. However, the devotees do not fear the annihilation of the body, for they are confident that they will go back home, back to Godhead, after the annihilation. As stated in *Bhagavad-gītā:*

janma karma ca me divyam
evaṁ yo vetti tattvataḥ
tyaktvā dehaṁ punar janma
naiti mām eti so 'rjuna

"One who knows the transcendental nature of My appearance and activities does not, upon leaving the body, take his birth again in this material world, but attains My eternal abode, O Arjuna." (Bg. 4.9)

If one strictly follows the process of devotional service, he has no fear of death, for he is predestined to go back home, back to Godhead. The nondevotees are fearful of death because they have no guarantee of where they are going or of the type of body they are going to get in their next life. The word *rudra-bhaya* is significant in this verse because Rudra himself, Lord Śiva, is speaking of "fear of Rudra." This indicates that there are many Rudras—eleven Rudras—and the Rudra (Lord Śiva) who was offering this prayer to the Supreme Personality of Godhead is different from the other Rudras, although he is as powerful as they are. The conclusion is that one Rudra is afraid of another Rudra because each and every one of them is engaged in the destruction of this cosmic manifestation. But for the devotee, everyone is afraid of Rudra, even Rudra himself. A devotee is never afraid of Rudra because he is always secure, being protected by the lotus feet of the Lord. As Śrī Kṛṣṇa says in *Bhagavad-gītā:*

kṣipraṁ bhavati dharmātmā
śaśvac-chāntiṁ nigacchati
kaunteya pratijānīhi
na me bhaktaḥ praṇaśyati

"He quickly becomes righteous and attains lasting peace. O son of Kuntī, declare it boldly that My devotee never perishes." (Bg. 9.31)

TEXT 69

इदं जपत भद्रं वो विशुद्धा नृपनन्दनाः ।
स्वधर्ममनुतिष्ठन्तो भगवत्यर्पिताशयाः ॥६९॥

idaṁ japata bhadraṁ vo
viśuddhā nṛpa-nandanāḥ
sva-dharmam anutiṣṭhanto
bhagavaty arpitāśayāḥ

idam—this; *japata*—while chanting; *bhadram*—all auspiciousness; *vaḥ*—all of you; *viśuddhāḥ*—purified; *nṛpa-nandanāḥ*—the sons of the king; *sva-dharmam*—one's occupational duties; *anutiṣṭhantaḥ*—executing; *bhagavati*—unto the Supreme Personality of Godhead; *arpita*—given up; *āśayāḥ*—possessing all kinds of faithfulness.

TRANSLATION

My dear sons of the King, just execute your occupational duty as kings with a pure heart. Just chant this prayer fixing your mind on the lotus feet of the Lord. That will bring you all good fortune, for the Lord will be very much pleased with you.

PURPORT

The prayers offered by Lord Śiva are very authoritative and significant. Simply by offering prayers to the Supreme Lord one can become perfect, even though engaged in his occupational duty. The real purpose of life is to become a devotee of the Lord. It does not matter where one is situated. Whether one is a *brāhmaṇa, kṣatriya, vaiśya, śūdra,* American, Englishman, Indian, etc., one can execute devotional service anywhere and everywhere in the material existence simply by offering prayers unto the Supreme Personality of Godhead. The Hare Kṛṣṇa *mahā-mantra* is also a prayer, for a prayer addresses the Supreme Personality of Godhead by His name and invokes good fortune by petitioning the Lord to allow one to engage in His devotional service. The Hare Kṛṣṇa *mahā-mantra* also says, "My dear Lord Kṛṣṇa, my dear Lord Rāma, O energy of the Lord, Hare, kindly engage me in Your service." Although one may be lowly situated, he can execute devotional service under any circumstance, as stated, *ahaituky apratihatā* (*Bhāg.* 1.2.6). "Devotional service cannot be checked by any material condition." Lord Caitanya Mahāprabhu also recommended this process:

jñāne prayāsam udapāsya namanta eva
jīvanti san-mukharitāṁ bhavadīya-vārtām
sthāne sthitāḥ śruti-gatāṁ tanu-vāṅ-manobhir
ye prāyaśo 'jita jito 'py asi tais tri-lokyām
(*Bhāg.* 10.14.3)

One may remain situated in his own place or in his own occupational duty and still lend his ear to receive the message of the Lord from realized souls. The Kṛṣṇa conscious movement is based on this principle, and we are opening centers all over the world to give everyone a chance to hear the message of Lord Kṛṣṇa in order to go back home, back to Godhead.

TEXT 70

तमेवात्मानमात्मस्थं सर्वभूतेष्ववस्थितम् ।
पूजयध्वं गृणन्तश्च ध्यायन्तश्चासकृद्धरिम् ॥७०॥

tam evātmānam ātma-sthaṁ
sarva-bhūteṣv avasthitam
pūjayadhvaṁ gṛṇantaś ca
dhyāyantaś cāsakṛd dharim

tam—unto Him; *eva*—certainly; *ātmānam*—the Supreme Soul; *ātma-stham*—within your hearts; *sarva*—all; *bhūteṣu*—in every living being; *avasthitam*—situated; *pūjayadhvam*—just worship Him; *gṛṇantaḥ ca*—always chanting; *dhyāyantaḥ ca*—always meditating upon; *asakṛt*—continually; *harim*—the Supreme Personality of Godhead.

TRANSLATION

Therefore, O sons of the king, the Supreme Personality of Godhead Hari is situated in everyone's heart. He is also within your hearts. Therefore chant the glories of the Lord and always meditate upon Him continually.

PURPORT

The word *asakṛt* is significant, for it means not just for a few minutes but continually. This is the instruction given by Lord Caitanya Mahāprabhu in His *Śikṣāṣṭaka*. *Kīrtanīyaḥ sadā hariḥ.* "The holy name of the Lord should be chanted twenty-four hours daily." Therefore in this Kṛṣṇa consciousness movement we request the devotees to chant at least sixteen rounds on their beads daily. Actually one has to chant twenty-four hours daily, just like Ṭhākura Haridāsa, who was chanting the Hare Kṛṣṇa *mantra* 300,000 times daily. Indeed, he had no other business. Some of the Gosvāmīs like Raghunātha dāsa Gosvāmī were also chanting very rigidly and also offering obeisances very rigidly. As stated in Śrīnivāsācārya's prayer to the six Gosvāmīs (*Ṣaḍ-gosvāmy-aṣṭaka*): *saṅkhyā-pūrvaka-nāma-gānanatibhiḥ kālāvasānīkṛtau.* The word *saṅkhyā-pūrvaka* means "maintaining a numerical strength." Not only was Raghunātha dāsa Gosvāmī chanting the holy name of the Lord, but he was also offering obeisances in the same prolific numbers.

Because the princes were ready to enter into some severe austerity in order to worship the Lord, Lord Śiva advised them to constantly chant and meditate upon the Supreme Personality of Godhead. It is significant that Lord Śiva personally offered his prayers to the Supreme Personality of Godhead just as he was taught by his father, Lord Brahmā. Similarly, he was also preaching to the princes according to the *paramparā* system. One should not only practice the instructions received from the spiritual master but should also distribute this knowledge to his disciples.

The words *ātmānam ātma-sthaṁ sarva-bhūteṣv avasthitam* are also significant. The Personality of Godhead is the origin of all living entities. Because the living entities are parts and parcels of the Lord, He is the father of all of them. One can search out the Supreme Lord very easily within his heart, for He is situated in every living entity's heart. In this verse the process of worshiping the Lord is considered to be very easy and complete, for anyone can sit down anywhere and in any condition of life and simply chant the holy names of the Lord. By chanting and hearing, one automatically engages in meditation.

TEXT 71

योगादेशमुपासाद्य धारयन्तो मुनिव्रताः ।
समाहितधियः सर्व एतदभ्यसतादृताः ॥७१॥

yogādeśam upāsādya
dhārayanto muni-vratāḥ
samāhita-dhiyaḥ sarva
etad abhyasatādṛtāḥ

yoga-ādeśam—this instruction of *bhakti-yoga; upāsādya*—constantly reading; *dhārayantaḥ*—and taking within the heart; *muni-vratāḥ*—just take the vow of the great sages, the vow of silence; *samāhita*—always fixed in the mind; *dhiyaḥ*—with intelligence; *sarve*—all of you; *etat*—this; *abhyasata*—practice; *ādṛtāḥ*—with great reverence.

TRANSLATION

My dear princes, in the form of a prayer I have delineated the yoga system of chanting the holy name. All of you should take this important stotra within your minds and promise to keep it in order to become great sages. By acting silently like a great sage and by giving attention and reverence, you should practice this method.

PURPORT

In the *haṭha-yoga* system one has to practice bodily exercises, *dhyāna, dhāraṇā, āsana,* meditation, etc. One also has to sit in one place in a particular posture and concentrate his gaze on the tip of the nose. There are so many rules and regulations for the *haṭha-yoga* system that it is practically impossible to perform it in this age. The alternative system of *bhakti-yoga* is very easy not only in this age but in others as well, for this *yoga* system was advocated long ago by Lord Śiva when he advised the princes, the sons of Mahārāja Prācīnabarhiṣat. The *bhakti-yoga* system is not newly introduced, for even five thousand years ago Lord Kṛṣṇa recommended this *bhakti-yoga* as the topmost *yoga.* As Kṛṣṇa tells Arjuna in *Bhagavad-gītā:*

yoginām api sarveṣāṁ
mad-gatenāntarātmanā
śraddhāvān bhajate yo māṁ
sa me yuktatamo mataḥ

"Of all *yogīs,* he who always abides in Me with great faith, worshiping Me in transcendental loving service, is most intimately united with Me in *yoga* and is the highest of all." (Bg. 6.47)

In other words, this system of *bhakti-yoga* has been existing from time immemorial and is now continuing in this Kṛṣṇa consciousness movement.

The word *muni-vratāḥ* is significant in this regard because those who are interested in advancing in spiritual life must be silent. Silence means talking only of *Kṛṣṇa-kathā.* This is the silence of Mahārāja Ambarīṣa:

sa vai manaḥ kṛṣṇa-padāravindayor
vacāṁsi vaikuṇṭha-guṇānuvarṇane

"King Ambarīṣa always fixed his mind on the lotus feet of the Lord and talked of Him only." (*Bhāg.* 9.4.18) We should also take this opportunity in life to become as good as a great saint simply by not talking unnecessarily with unwanted persons. We should either talk of Kṛṣṇa or chant Hare Kṛṣṇa undeviatingly. This is called *muni-vrata.* The intelligence *(samāhita-dhiyaḥ)* must be very sharp and should always be acting in Kṛṣṇa consciousness. The words *etad abhyasatādṛtāḥ* indicate that if one takes these instructions from a spiritual master with great reverence *(ādṛta)* and practices them accordingly, he will find this *bhakti-yoga* process to be very, very easy.

TEXT 72

इदमाह पुरास्माकं भगवान् विश्वसृक्पतिः ।
भृग्वादीनामात्मजानां सिसृक्षुः संसिसृक्षताम् ॥७२॥

idam āha purāsmākaṁ
bhagavān viśvasṛk-patiḥ
bhṛgv-ādīnām ātma-jānāṁ
sisṛkṣuḥ saṁsisṛkṣatām

idam—this; *āha*—said; *purā*—formerly; *asmākam*—unto us; *bhagavān*—the lord; *viśva-sṛk*—the creators of the universe; *patiḥ*—master; *bhṛgu-ādīnām*—of the great sages headed by Bhṛgu; *ātma-jānām*—of his sons; *sisṛkṣuḥ*—desirous to create; *saṁsisṛkṣatām*—who are in charge of creation.

TRANSLATION

This prayer was first spoken to us by Lord Brahmā, the master of all creators. The creators, headed by Bhṛgu, were instructed in these prayers because they wanted to create.

PURPORT

Lord Brahmā was created by Lord Viṣṇu; then Lord Brahmā created Lord Śiva and other great sages headed by Bhṛgu Muni. These great sages included Bhṛgu, Marīci, Ātreya, Vasiṣṭha and others. All these great sages were in charge of creating population. Since there were not very many living entities in the beginning, Viṣṇu entrusted Brahmā with the business of creation, and Brahmā in his turn created many hundreds and thousands of demigods and great sages to continue with the creation. At the same time, Lord Brahmā cautioned all his sons and disciples by reciting the prayers now recited by Lord Śiva. The material creation means material engagement, but material engagements can be counteracted if we always remember our relationship with the Lord as that relationship is described in these prayers recited by Lord Śiva. In this way we can remain constantly in touch with the Supreme Personality of Godhead. Thus despite our engagement in the creation, we cannot be deviated from the path of Kṛṣṇa consciousness. The Kṛṣṇa consciousness movement is especially meant for this purpose. In this material world everyone is engaged in some particular occupational duty which is prescribed in the *varṇāśrama-dharma. Brāhmaṇas, kṣatriyas, vaiśyas, śūdras* and everyone are engaged in their occupational duty, but if one remembers his first duty—keeping in constant contact with the Supreme Personality of Godhead—everything will be successful. If one simply executes the rules and regulations of the *varṇāśrama-dharma* in the role of a *brāhmaṇa, kṣatriya, vaiśya, śūdra,* and keeps busy and does not remember one's eternal relationship with the Lord, one's business and activities as well as occupational duties will simply be a waste of time. This is confirmed in the First Canto of *Śrīmad-Bhāgavatam:*

dharmaḥ svanuṣṭhitaḥ puṁsāṁ viṣvaksena-kathāsu yaḥ
notpādayed yadi ratiṁ śrama eva hi kevalam (*Bhāg.* 1.2.8)

The conclusion is that even if one is busy executing his occupational duty, his business in Kṛṣṇa consciousness need not be hampered. He has simply to execute the devotional service of *śravaṇaṁ kīrtanam*—hearing, chanting, and remembering. One need not abandon his occupational duty. As stated in *Bhagavad-gītā:*

yataḥ pravṛttir bhūtānāṁ
yena sarvam idaṁ tatam
sva-karmaṇā tam abhyarcya
siddhiṁ vindati mānavaḥ

"By worship of the Lord—who is the source of all beings and who is all-pervading—man can, in the performance of his own duty, attain perfection." (Bg. 18.46)

Thus one can continue with his occupational duty, but if he worships the Supreme Personality of Godhead as Lord Śiva herein prescribes, he attains his perfection of life. *Svanuṣṭhitasya dharmasya saṁsiddhir hari-toṣaṇam* (*Bhāg.* 1.2.13). We should continue executing our occupational duties, but if we try to satisfy the Supreme Personality of Godhead by our duties, then our lives will be perfected.

TEXT 73

ते वयं नोदिताः सर्वे प्रजासर्गे प्रजेश्वराः ।
अनेन ध्वस्ततमसः सिसृक्ष्मो विविधाः प्रजाः ॥७३॥

te vayaṁ noditāḥ sarve
prajā-sarge prajeśvarāḥ
anena dhvasta-tamasaḥ
sisṛkṣmo vividhāḥ prajāḥ

te—by him; *vayam*—all of us; *noditāḥ*—ordered; *sarve*—all; *prajā-sarge*—at the time of creating population; *prajā-īśvarāḥ*—the controllers of all living entities; *anena*—by this; *dhvasta-tamasaḥ*—being freed from all kinds of ignorance; *sisṛkṣmaḥ*—we created; *vividhāḥ*—various kinds of; *prajāḥ*—living entities.

TRANSLATION

When all Prajāpatis were ordered to create by Lord Brahmā, we chanted these prayers in praise of the Supreme Personality of Godhead and became completely free from all ignorance. Thus we were able to create different types of living entities.

PURPORT

In this verse we can understand that the various types of living entities were created simultaneously at the very beginning of the creation. The nonsensical Darwinian theory of evolution is not applicable here. It is not that intelligent human beings did not exist millions of years ago. On the contrary, it is understood that the most intelligent creature, Lord Brahmā, was first created. Then Lord Brahmā created other saintly sages like Marīci, Bhṛgu, Ātreya, Vasiṣṭha, Lord Śiva and others. They in their turn created different types of bodies according to *karma.* In *Śrīmad-Bhāgavatam* Lord Kapiladeva told His mother that the living entity gets a particular type of body in accordance to his work and that this body is decided upon by higher authorities. The higher authorities, as appointed by the Supreme Personality of Godhead, are Lord Brahmā and all other Prajāpatis and Manus. Thus from the beginning of creation it can be seen that the first creature is the most intelligent. It is not that so-called modern intelligence has developed by the gradual process of evolution. As stated in *Brahma-vaivarta Purāṇa,* there is a gradual evolutionary process, but it is not the body that is evolving. All the bodily forms are already there. It is the spiritual entity or spiritual spark within the body that is being promoted by the laws of nature under the supervision of superior authority. We can understand from this verse that from the very beginning of creation different varieties of living entities were existing. It is not that some of them have become extinct. Everything is there; it is due to our lack of knowledge that we cannot see things in their proper perspective.

In this verse the word *dhvasta-tamasaḥ* is very important, for without being free of ignorance one cannot control the creation of different types of living entities. As stated in *Śrīmad-Bhāgavatam, daiva-netreṇa*—bodies are awarded under the supervision of superior powers. How can these superior powers control the evolutionary process of the living entity if they are not free from all imperfection? The followers of the Vedic instructions cannot accept the Darwinian theory of evolution, for it is marred by imperfect knowledge.

TEXT 74

अथेदं नित्यदा युक्तो जपन्नवहितः पुमान् ।
अचिराच्छ्रेय आप्नोति वासुदेवपरायणः ॥७४॥

athedaṁ nityadā yukto
japann avahitaḥ pumān
acirāc chreya āpnoti
vāsudeva-parāyaṇaḥ

atha—thus; *idam*—this; *nityadā*—regularly; *yuktaḥ*—with great attention; *japan*—by murmuring; *avahitaḥ*—fully attentive; *pumān*—a person; *acirāt*—without delay; *śreyaḥ*—auspiciousness; *āpnoti*—achieves; *vāsudeva-parāyaṇaḥ*—one who is a devotee of Lord Kṛṣṇa.

TRANSLATION

A devotee of Lord Kṛṣṇa whose mind is always absorbed in Him, who with great attention and reverence chants this stotra [prayer], will achieve the greatest perfection of life without delay.

PURPORT

Perfection means becoming a devotee of Lord Kṛṣṇa. As stated in the First Canto of *Śrīmad-Bhāgavatam: vāsudeva-parā vedā vāsudeva-parā makhāḥ* (*Bhāg.* 1.2.28). The ultimate goal of life is Vāsudeva, or Kṛṣṇa. Any devotee of Lord Kṛṣṇa can attain all perfection, material gains and liberation simply by offering prayers to Him. There are many varieties of prayers to Lord Kṛṣṇa chanted by great sages and great personalities such as Lord Brahmā and Lord Śiva. Lord Kṛṣṇa is known as *śiva-viriñci-nutam* (*Bhāg.* 11.5.33). *Śiva* means Lord Śiva, and *viriñci* means Lord Brahmā. Both of these demigods are engaged in offering prayers to Lord Vāsudeva, Kṛṣṇa. If we follow in the footsteps of such great personalities and become devotees of Lord Kṛṣṇa, our lives become successful. Unfortunately people do not know this secret. *Na te viduḥ svārtha-gatiṁ hi viṣṇum* (*Bhāg.* 7.5.31). "They do not know that the real interest and the highest perfection of life is to worship Lord Viṣṇu [Kṛṣṇa]." It is impossible to become satisfied by trying to adjust the external energy. Without being a devotee of Lord Kṛṣṇa, one can only be baffled and confused. To save living entities from such a calamity, Lord Kṛṣṇa points out in *Bhagavad-gītā:*

bahūnāṁ janmanām ante
jñānavān māṁ prapadyate
vāsudevaḥ sarvam iti
sa mahātmā sudurlabhaḥ

"After many births and deaths, he who is actually in knowledge surrenders unto Me, knowing Me to be the cause of all causes and all that is. Such a great soul is very rare." (Bg. 7.19)

We can achieve whatever benediction we want simply by becoming devotees of Vāsudeva.

TEXT 75

श्रेयसामिह सर्वेषां ज्ञानं निःश्रेयसं परम् ।
सुखं तरति दुष्पारं ज्ञाननौर्व्यसनार्णवम् ॥७५॥

śreyasām iha sarveṣāṁ
jñānaṁ niḥśreyasaṁ param
sukhaṁ tarati duṣpāraṁ
jñāna-naur vyasanārṇavam

śreyasām—of all benedictions; *iha*—in this world; *sarveṣām*—of every person; *jñānam*—knowledge; *niḥśreyasam*—the supreme benefit; *param*—transcendental; *sukham*—happiness; *tarati*—crosses over; *duṣpāram*—insurmountable; *jñāna*—knowledge; *nauḥ*—boat; *vyasana*—danger; *arṇavam*—the ocean.

TRANSLATION

In this material world there are different types of achievement, but of all of them the achievement of knowledge is considered to be the highest because one can cross the ocean of nescience only on the boat of knowledge. Otherwise the ocean is impassable.

PURPORT

Actually everyone is suffering within this material world due to ignorance. Every day we see that a person without knowledge commits some criminal act and is later arrested and punished, despite the fact that he actually may not have been conscious of his sinful activity. Such ignorance prevails throughout the world. People do not consider how they are risking their lives in an attempt to have illicit sex life, kill animals to satisfy their tongue, enjoy intoxication and gamble. It is very regrettable that the leaders of the world do not know of the effects of these sinful activities. They are instead taking things very easily and are succeeding in making the ocean of nescience wider and wider.

Opposed to such ignorance, full knowledge is the greatest achievement within this material world. We can practically see that one who has sufficient knowledge is saved from many dangerous pitfalls in life. As stated in *Bhagavad-gītā:*

bahūnāṁ janmanām ante
jñānavān māṁ prapadyate
vāsudevaḥ sarvam iti
sa mahātmā sudurlabhaḥ

"After many births and deaths, he who is actually in knowledge surrenders unto Me, knowing Me to be the cause of all causes and all that is. Such a great soul is very rare." (Bg. 7.19)

This Kṛṣṇa consciousness movement is determined to open wide the eyes of the so-called leaders who are full of ignorance and thus save them from the many pitfalls and dangerous conditions of life. The greatest danger is the danger of getting a body lower than a human being. It was with great difficulty that we attained this human form of life just to take advantage of this body and reestablish our relationship with the Supreme Personality of Godhead, Govinda. Lord Śiva advises, however, that those who take advantage of his prayers will very soon become devotees of Lord Vāsudeva and thus will be able to cross the ocean of nescience and make life perfect.

TEXT 76

य इमं श्रद्धया युक्तो मद्गीतं भगवत्स्तवम् ।
अधीयानो दुराराध्यं हरिमाराधयत्यसौ ॥७६॥

ya imaṁ śraddhayā yukto
mad-gītaṁ bhagavat-stavam
adhīyāno durārādhyaṁ
harim ārādhayaty asau

yaḥ—anyone; *imam*—this; *śraddhayā*—with great faith; *yuktaḥ*—devoutly attached; *mat-gītam*—the song composed by me or sung by me; *bhagavat-stavam*—a prayer offered to the Supreme Personality of Godhead; *adhīyānaḥ*—by regular study; *durārādhyam*—very difficult to worship;

harim—the Supreme Personality of Godhead; *ārādhayati*—he can, however, worship Him; *asau*—such a person.

TRANSLATION

Although rendering devotional service to the Supreme Personality of Godhead and worshiping Him are very difficult, if one vibrates or simply reads this stotra [prayer] composed and sung by me, he will very easily be able to invoke the mercy of the Supreme Personality of Godhead.

PURPORT

It is especially significant that Lord Śiva is a pure devotee of Lord Vāsudeva. *Vaiṣṇavānāṁ yathā śambhuḥ:* "Amongst all Vaiṣṇavas, Lord Śiva is the topmost." Consequently Lord Śiva has a *sampradāya,* a Vaiṣṇava disciplic succession, called Rudra-sampradāya. At the present moment those who belong to the Viṣṇusvāmi-sampradāya of Vaiṣṇavas come from Rudra, Lord Śiva. To become a devotee of Lord Kṛṣṇa, Vāsudeva, is very, very difficult. The word especially used in this connection is *durārādhyam.* The worship of the demigods is not very difficult, but becoming a devotee of Lord Vāsudeva, Kṛṣṇa, is not so easy. However, if one adheres to the principles and follows in the footsteps of the higher authorities, as advised by Lord Śiva, he can easily become a devotee of Lord Vāsudeva. This is also confirmed by Prahlāda Mahārāja. Devotional service cannot be practiced by a mental speculator. Devotional service is a special attainment which can be acquired only by a person who has surrendered unto a pure devotee. As confirmed by Prahlāda Mahārāja, *mahīyasāṁ pāda-rajo 'bhiṣekaṁ niṣkiñcanānāṁ na vṛṇita yāvat:* "Unless one accepts the dust of the lotus feet of a pure devotee, who is free from all material contamination, one cannot enter into the devotional service of the Lord." (*Bhāg.* 7.5.32)

TEXT 77

विन्दते पुरुषोऽमुष्माद्यद्यदिच्छत्यसत्वरम् ।
मद्गीतगीतात्सुप्रीताच्छ्रेयसामेकवल्लभात् ॥७७॥

vindate puruṣo 'muṣmād
yad yad icchaty asatvaram
mad-gīta-gītāt su-prītāc
chreyasām eka vallabhāt

vindate—achieves; *puruṣaḥ*—a devotee; *amuṣmāt*—from the Personality of Godhead; *yat yat*—that which; *icchati*—desires; *asatvaram*—being fixed;

mat-gīta—sung by me; *gītāt*—by the song; *su-prītāt*—from the Lord who is very pleased; *śreyasām*—of all benediction; *eka*—one; *vallabhāt*—from the dearmost.

TRANSLATION

The Supreme Personality of Godhead is the dearmost objective of all auspicious benedictions. A human being who sings this song sung by me can please the Supreme Personality of Godhead. Such a devotee, being fixed in the Lord's devotional service, can acquire whatever he wants from the Supreme Lord.

PURPORT

As stated in *Bhagavad-gītā, yaṁ labdhvā cāparaṁ lābhaṁ manyate nādhikaṁ tataḥ:* "Established thus, one never departs from the truth, and upon gaining it he thinks there is no greater gain." (Bg. 6.22) If one can attain the favor of the Supreme Personality of Godhead, he has nothing to aspire for, nor does he desire any other gain. When Dhruva Mahārāja became perfect by austerity and saw the Supreme Personality of Godhead eye to eye, he was offered any kind of benediction he wanted. However, Dhruva replied that he did not want anything, for he was perfectly satisfied with the benediction of seeing the Lord. Except for the service of the Supreme Lord, whatever we want is called illusion, *māyā.* Śrī Caitanya Mahāprabhu said: *jīvera 'svarūpa' haya—kṛṣṇera 'nitya-dāsa'* (Cc. *Madhya* 20.108). Every living entity is an eternal servant of the Lord; therefore when one engages in the service of the Lord, he realizes the highest perfection of life. A faithful servant can fulfill any desire by the grace of the master, and one who engages in the transcendental loving service of the Lord has nothing to aspire for separately. All his desires are fulfilled simply by engaging constantly in the Lord's loving service. Lord Śiva shows us that any devotee can be successful simply by chanting the prayers which he has recited.

TEXT 78

इदं यः कल्य उत्थाय प्राञ्जलिः श्रद्धयान्वितः ।
शृणुयाच्छ्रावयेन्मर्त्यो मुच्यते कर्मबन्धनैः ॥७८॥

idaṁ yaḥ kalya utthāya
prāñjaliḥ śraddhayānvitaḥ
śṛṇuyāc chrāvayen martyo
mucyate karma-bandhanaiḥ

idam—this prayer; *yaḥ*—a devotee who; *kalye*—early in the morning; *utthāya*—after getting up from bed; *prāñjaliḥ*—with folded hands; *śraddhayā*—with faith and devotion; *anvitaḥ*—thus being absorbed; *śṛṇuyāt*—personally chants and hears; *śrāvayet*—and gets others to hear; *martyaḥ*—such a human being; *mucyate*—becomes freed; *karma-bandhanaiḥ*—from all kinds of actions resulting from fruitive activities.

TRANSLATION

A devotee who rises early in the morning and with folded hands chants these prayers sung by Lord Śiva and gives facility to others to hear them certainly becomes free from all bondage to fruitive activities.

PURPORT

Mukti or liberation means becoming free from the results of fruitive activities. As stated in *Śrīmad-Bhāgavatam: muktir hitvānyathā rūpam. Mukti* means giving up all other activities, and *svarūpeṇa vyavasthitiḥ* means being situated in one's constitutional position. (*Bhāg.* 2.10.6) In this conditional state we are entangled by one fruitive activity after another. *Karma-bandhana* means the bonds of fruitive activity. As long as one's mind is absorbed in fruitive activities, he has to manufacture plans for happiness. The *bhakti-yoga* process is different, for *bhakti-yoga* means acting according to the order of the supreme authority. When we act under the direction of supreme authority, we do not become entangled by fruitive results. For instance, Arjuna fought because the Supreme Personality of Godhead wanted him to; therefore he was not responsible for the outcome of the fighting. As far as devotional service is concerned, even hearing and chanting is as good as acting with our body, mind and senses. Actually hearing and chanting are also activities of the senses. When the senses are utilized for one's own sense gratification, they entangle one in *karma*, but when they are used for the satisfaction of the Lord, they establish one in *bhakti*.

TEXT 79

गीतं मयेदं नरदेवनन्दनाः
परस्य पुंसः परमात्मनः स्तवम् ।
जपन्त एकाग्रधियस्तपो महत्-
चरध्वमन्ते तत आप्स्यथेप्सितम् ॥७९॥

gītaṁ mayedaṁ naradeva-nandanāḥ
parasya puṁsaḥ paramātmanaḥ stavam
japanta ekāgra-dhiyas tapo mahat-
caradhvam ante tata āpsyathepsitam

gītam—sung; *mayā*—by me; *idam*—this; *naradeva-nandanāḥ*—O sons of the king; *parasya*—of the Supreme; *puṁsaḥ*—Personality of Godhead; *paramātmanaḥ*—the Supersoul of everyone; *stavam*—prayer; *japantaḥ*—chanting; *ekāgra*—perfect attention; *dhiyaḥ*—intelligence; *tapaḥ*—austerities; *mahat*—great; *caradhvam*—you practice; *ante*—at the end; *tataḥ*—thereafter; *āpsyatha*—will achieve; *īpsitam*—the desired result.

TRANSLATION

My dear sons of the King, the prayers which I have recited to you are meant for pleasing the Supreme Personality of Godhead, the Supersoul. I advise you to recite these prayers, which are as effective as great austerities. In this way, when you are mature, your life will be successful, and you will certainly achieve all your desired objectives without fail.

PURPORT

If we persistently engage in devotional service, certainly all of our desires will be fulfilled in due course of time.

Thus end the Bhaktivedanta purports of the Fourth Canto, Twenty-fourth Chapter, of the Śrīmad-Bhāgavatam, *entitled "Chanting the Song Sung by Lord Śiva."*

ALL GLORY TO ŚRĪ GURU AND GAURĀṄGA

ŚRĪMAD BHĀGAVATAM

of

KṚṢṆA-DVAIPĀYANA VYĀSA

मुक्तानामपि सिद्धानां नारायणपरायणः ।
सुदुर्लभः प्रशान्तात्मा कोटिष्वपि महामुने ॥ ५ ॥

muktānām api siddhānāṁ
nārāyaṇa-parāyaṇaḥ
sudurlabhaḥ praśāntātmā
koṭiṣv api mahā-mune (p. 5)

BOOKS by
His Divine Grace A. C. Bhaktivedanta Swami Prabhupāda

Bhagavad-gītā As It Is
Śrīmad-Bhāgavatam, Cantos 1-6 (18 Vols.)
Śrī Caitanya-caritāmṛta (17 Vols.)
Teachings of Lord Caitanya
The Nectar of Devotion
The Nectar of Instruction
Śrī Īśopaniṣad
Easy Journey to Other Planets
Kṛṣṇa Consciousness: The Topmost Yoga System
Kṛṣṇa, the Supreme Personality of Godhead (3 Vols.)
Perfect Questions, Perfect Answers
Transcendental Teachings of Prahlad Mahārāja
Kṛṣṇa, the Reservoir of Pleasure
Life Comes from Life
The Perfection of Yoga
Beyond Birth and Death
On the Way to Kṛṣṇa
Rāja-vidyā: The King of Knowledge
Elevation to Kṛṣṇa Consciousness
Kṛṣṇa Consciousness: The Matchless Gift
Back to Godhead Magazine (Founder)

A complete catalogue is available upon request

The Bhaktivedanta Book Trust
3764 Watseka Avenue
Los Angeles, California 90034